Alexander Pope

THE POETRY OF
ALLUSION

Oxford University Press, Amen House, London E.C.4

GLASGOW   NEW YORK   TORONTO   MELBOURNE   WELLINGTON
BOMBAY   CALCUTTA   MADRAS   KARACHI   LAHORE   DACCA
CAPE TOWN   SALISBURY   NAIROBI   IBADAN   ACCRA
KUALA LUMPUR   HONG KONG

FIRST PUBLISHED 1959
REPRINTED LITHOGRAPHICALLY
AT THE UNIVERSITY PRESS, OXFORD
FROM CORRECTED SHEETS OF THE FIRST EDITION
1963

Alexander Pope

THE POETRY OF
ALLUSION

BY

REUBEN ARTHUR BROWER

OXFORD
AT THE CLARENDON PRESS

PRINTED IN GREAT BRITAIN

PARENTIBUS BENE MERENTIBUS
FILIUS FECIT

It would, to a few perhaps, have been sufficient to have pointed out particular beauties by inverted commas, or other marks of distinction; and the writer is aware of the ostentation of citing fine passages with *general applauses*, and empty *exclamations*, at the ends of them. But he recollected that slight intimations do not always strike precipitate readers. Besides, it is scarce possible sometimes, when we are smitten with a fine passage, to suppress those involuntary bursts of applause—*Euge! atque belle!* though, in truth, they are but empty exclamations.

Whenever such may have escaped from his pen, he trusts that the candid reader will ascribe them to a solicitude, which made him rather earnest to do justice to the poet's merit, than to raise an admiration of his own judgment.

(OWEN RUFFHEAD, *The Life of Alexander Pope, Esq.*)

PREFACE

WHEN planning this book twenty years ago, I thought of dedicating it 'To the Readers of Pope'. The irony, perhaps not timely then, is certainly out of date now. Thanks to a revolution in taste and to the efforts of critics and scholars, Pope has more readers at present, it seems safe to say, than at any time since the eighteenth century. Whatever the size of his audience, it presumably includes most of the older generation who experienced the revolution and many younger readers who accept and enjoy poetry of wit, whether of the seventeenth and eighteenth or the twentieth centuries. A writer on Pope can count on a body of readers familiar with his poetry and ready to give it the attention they give to poetry written in quite different traditions. Or perhaps it is better to say that they easily take for granted Pope's place among the English poets.

In the chapters that follow, my first and last concern is with the poems, with their poetic character and design. Pope's interest in 'Design' in poetry, painting, and architecture needs no demonstration to anyone who has read the poetry and the letters. It seems reasonable and charitable to look for unity in his poems, if we remember to look for *poetic* design, for the order created through using the full resources of language. Hence the necessity of beginning not from Pope's or Warburton's statements, but from the uses of words that characterize each poem.

But if Pope now has his readers, his poetry still offers difficulties even to the partisans of wit. The main stumbling-block is the obvious one: our lack of lively knowledge of the poetic traditions with which Pope and his eighteenth-century readers were easily familiar. Everyone knows from footnotes or special studies that Pope's satires were 'based on Horace' or that they are in some sense 'Horatian', or that *Eloisa to Abelard* is 'indebted' to Ovid's *Heroides*, or that Pope's *Iliad* was at least in intention a version of Homer's. But the knowledge remains inert and enters very little into our active experience of the poetry. What we want is to feel the *presence* of

the poets and the poetry of Greece and Rome in something like
the way in which Pope and his contemporaries felt it. I have
tried to make these poets present to the modern reader by
free translation and genial interpretation of particular passages, hoping to give him a concrete sense of the poetic voices
that Pope heard as he wrote. Very nearly the first half of
every chapter or section of the book is given over to Virgil or
Homer or Horace, or some other ancient poet and the main
tradition associated with his work. Conveniently enough for
my purposes, Pope moved forward quite steadily from one
tradition to another, from pastoral and georgic to the heroic
and the Horatian.

While there is a value in recognizing the conventions Pope
used and some pleasure in hearing echoes of earlier poets in
his verse, it is more important to see how he used the poetry
of the past for his own expressive purposes. For Dryden and
for Pope allusion, especially in ironic contexts, is a resource
equivalent to symbolic metaphor and elaborate imagery in
other poets. Through allusion, often in combination with
subdued metaphors and exquisite images, Pope gets his purchase on larger meanings and evokes the finer resonances by
which poetry (in Johnson's phrase) 'penetrates the recesses
of the mind'. Viewing Pope's work as a whole, we might describe his poems as translations of various ancient poetic
modes, or 'imitations', to use the term he would himself have
used. If 'imitation' had not lost its charm—the charm now
attached to 'mimesis'—this book might have been called a
study in imitation.

But some readers may be feeling apprehensive that Pope
is about to be considered as an example of classical influences.
They will say, and understandably, 'What of the influence of
other poets and other traditions?' 'What of Donne and the
Metaphysicals?' Others may ask what is to be said about the
French, the Italian, and the Spanish traditions? Both groups
of inquiring readers will find, I believe, that sufficient allowance has been made for native and later continental traditions
where their effect is especially prominent. But the major
emphasis remains on Homer and the Roman poets, because
they were central in Pope's mind and because they still are
central in our reading of his poetry. If apology is in order, it

might be said that to include everything is often to say little, that my object is to show how allusion works in Pope, not as an end in itself, but in order to bring the reader to a richer and livelier reading of the poetry.

It remains for me to acknowledge various kinds of assistance given me in the course of writing this book and preparing it for the press. The introductory essay (except for minor additions) was read at the 1950 meeting of the Modern Language Association, in New York, and first printed in *A Journal of English Literary History*, xix. 38–48. It is reprinted here with the kind permission of the editors of that publication. Chapter I, *The Shepherd's Song*, was given as the Margaret Sherwood Memorial Lecture at Wellesley College in 1956, and repeated (in an Italian translation) at the American Academy in Rome. The essay on Ovid is a version of a paper read at the 1958 meeting of the Classical Association of New England.

Most of the book was written during 1956–7, while I was holding a fellowship granted by the Guggenheim Foundation. I wish to thank particularly Dean McGeorge Bundy of Harvard University for his kindness in arranging a year's absence from teaching and administrative duties. For many courtesies during my stay in Rome I am indebted to the director of the American Academy, Mr. Laurance E. Roberts, and to Mr. Mason Hammond, Professor in Charge of Classical Studies. I owe a special debt to Professor Mario Praz, who generously loaned me various books otherwise unobtainable in Rome. For further assistance in bibliographical matters I am greatly obliged to Dr. Salvatore Rosati and to Monsignor G. W. Tickle, Rector of the Venerable English College.

I want also to thank a number of persons who have read all or part of the manuscript and offered most helpful criticisms: Mr. Wendell V. Clausen of Amherst College, Mr. Thomas R. Edwards of Riverside College (University of California), and Mr. Cecil Day Lewis. I am especially indebted to Mr. Walter J. Bate of Harvard University for many acts of kindness during the years while I have been completing this book. I stand in debt also to the staff of the Clarendon Press for most valuable editorial advice. In checking manuscript and printer's proof I have been ably assisted by Mrs. Robert B. Marr and Mrs. Gordon V. Smith. For secretarial help that has lightened the writer's task on numerous occasions, I am most grateful to Mrs. Dallas L. Hext of Adams House.

The Latin of the dedication is taken from the inscription in Twickenham Church on the monument erected by Pope in honour of his parents.

Scribebam Cantabrigiae
Mense Sextili MDCCCCLVII.

NOTE ON THE TEXTS AND
FOOTNOTES

My indebtedness to recent critics of Pope, especially to Geoffrey Tillotson, F. R. Leavis, and George Sherburn, will be evident on many pages of this study. Although I have made extensive use of the notes and introductions in the Twickenham edition, I have limited references in the notes to points where the argument turned on some particular piece of interpretation or information.

The principal texts used throughout the book are:

(Abbreviations used in the footnotes are set in parentheses.)

The Twickenham Edition of the Poems of Alexander Pope, General Editor, John Butt, vols. ii–vi (London, 1939–54). (TE)

The Best of Pope, ed. George Sherburn (New York, 1940). (The text of all poems not yet published in the Twickenham Edition is taken from this volume.)

The Works of Alexander Pope, ed. W. Elwin and W. J. Courthope, 10 vols. (London, 1871–89). (EC)

The Correspondence of Alexander Pope, ed. George Sherburn, 5 vols. (Oxford, 1956). (Let.)

The Poetical Works of John Dryden, ed. G. R. Noyes (2nd ed. Boston, 1950).

Quotations from: *The Iliad of Homer*, translated by Richmond Lattimore (Chicago, 1951), reprinted with permission of the University of Chicago Press; Wallace Stevens, 'Botanist on Alp (No. 1)', *The Collected Poems* (New York, 1955), reprinted with permission of Alfred A. Knopf, Inc.; and Robert Frost, 'Provide, Provide', from *A Further Range*, Copyright, 1936, by Robert Frost, by permission of Henry Holt and Company, Inc.

CONTENTS

INTRODUCTION

AN ALLUSION TO EUROPE: DRYDEN AND POETIC TRADITION

> He professed to have learned his poetry from Dryden,
> whom, whenever an opportunity was presented, he praised
> through his whole life with unvaried liberality; and perhaps
> his character may receive some illustration if he be com-
> pared with his master.
>
> (Samuel Johnson, *Life of Pope*)

ANY talk of Pope's achievement as a poet or of his relation to poetic tradition must begin with the tradition of Dryden. Like Dryden he was catholic in his tastes, and he enjoyed an easy commerce with the poetry of the past and present. From his early reading and imitations and translations, it is clear that Pope had direct and lively contact with Homer and the greater Roman and English poets and with many lesser English and French poets of his own generation and of the century before him. Feeling no nineteenth-century compulsion to be merely original, he took pleasure in imitating the poets he read and admired, one and all. Speaking years later of his youthful epic *Alcander*, he remarked to Spence,

I endeavoured, [said he, smiling] in this poem, to collect all the beauties of the great epic writers into one piece: there was Milton's style in one part, and Cowley's in another: here the style of Spenser imitated, and there of Statius; here Homer and Virgil, and there Ovid and Claudian.

Although it is highly probable that without Dryden's example Pope would have discovered a voice of his own and a way of mastering this embarrassment of poetical riches, the fact remains that he 'learned his poetry' from Dryden and that as Johnson also says,

By perusing the works of Dryden, he discovered the most perfect fabric of English verse, and habituated himself to that only which he found the best . . .

From Dryden he learned how to imitate without loss of

originality, how to make use of the resources of other poets and other poetic modes and yet remain himself and the same. The poetic education he received was more than technical training in versification and practice in the ancient literary art of skilful borrowing. While searching 'the pages of Dryden for happy combinations of heroic diction' or more musical cadences, he was also finding his relation to the poetry of the European past and to the mind of Europe. By following Dryden and surpassing him, Pope became after Chaucer, Shakespeare, and Milton the most European of English poets. Reduced to its simplest terms, his problem was how to connect the old world of Homer and Virgil and Horace, or of Spenser and Milton, with the actual society of eighteenth-century London in which he and his readers were living. His success as a poet depended directly on Dryden's achievement in solving a similar problem for the very different society and literary public of the Restoration.

As literary histories of the neo-classical period remind us far too often, it is easier to bury Dryden than to praise him. So much depends on the tradition we choose to place him in and on the standards by which we measure poetic success. If we follow Dr. Johnson and set Dryden in the succession of Waller and Denham, we arrive at a pious tribute to the 'reformer of our numbers'. If we follow F. R. Leavis and trace 'the line of wit', we bring out Dryden's undeniable limitations as compared with Donne or Marvell. (Leavis' strategy was justified in relation to his aims and results: he has made us aware that 'serious wit' did not end with the Metaphysicals.) But if we are to make a positive estimate of Dryden's achievement, we should include in his ancestry English poets of the earlier and later Renaissance and their ancient predecessors, and we need to maintain a keen sense of what Dryden accomplished for his contemporaries. So viewed, Dryden marks the reaffirmation of 'Europe' in English poetry and culture after an experiment in insularity and at a time of artificial essays in continental 'Classicism'.

Again, it would be easy to arrive at a rather tepid estimate of Dryden's career—true enough, but hardly of much concern to readers with a live interest in either history or poetry. Dryden's reaffirmation matters—aesthetically and historically—

because it is a poet's affirmation, realized in the shaping of new modes of expression and in the writing of poetry which is imaginatively various and unified. His direct critical propaganda for French and Latin literary standards counts for relatively little in the continuing life of the Renaissance tradition. A more adaptable Arnold, like Pope,

He won his way by yielding to the tyde.

By 'indirection', by creating his unique satirical mode, Dryden reaffirmed important European values, while engaging the most lively concerns of his readers. It is to this poetic feat that I want to draw attention.

Dryden's accomplishment is more remarkable in view of the situation in which he wrote. Charles had been 'restored', and with him an audience that was alien to the most vigorous of the surviving older poets. Milton withdrew; Cowley retired without producing much of the 'wit' he prescribed. Marvell dived as a Metaphysical and came up as a satirist; but as a poet he belonged to another world. Although Dryden talked sentimentally of 'retiring', he was unequivocally the 'first' man of this

Laughing, quaffing, and unthinking time.

His success lay in his ability to draw on a wide range of English and European literary traditions while 'speaking home' to this audience of Court and City. A glance at his development as a dramatist will suggest how he attained a style which had this twofold effectiveness.

In the period between *Astraea Redux* and *Absalom and Achitophel*, while Dryden was mightily pleasing his auditors in the theatre, he struck out two more or less distinct styles which were blended in the successes of his maturity: one, the 'heroic'; and the other, the style of public address which he somewhat scornfully regarded as Horatian. Whatever we call them, both styles bear traces of their mixed European and English origin. In the process of making his outrageous experiments in drama, the Heroic Plays, Dryden invented a style that gave an impression of ancient epic grandeur; at times, in narratives of quite incredible exploits, the impression became almost convincing, thanks to the skill with which

Dryden combined Virgilian allusions with rather obvious echoes of Virgilian rhythm.

In the last and best of these plays, *Aureng-Zebe*, we first hear distinctly what Mark Van Doren calls Dryden's 'grouping' of couplets, an enlargement of rhythm which comes when he had been reading Shakespeare, and, more significantly, soon after his reworking of *Paradise Lost*. Milton's example, along with Sylvester's and Cowley's, helped fix the Old Testament-ecclesiastical strain in Dryden's mature heroic style, as it finally emerged in *Absalom and Achitophel*. In tone the style is unmistakably a 'translation out of the original tongues'.

While Dryden was cultivating a manner that had almost no appropriateness to his auditors—except by a law of literary contraries—he was learning to speak to them with directness and ease in his prologues and epilogues. Here he acquired his mastery of more varied tones; and here 'the great reform' of language and rhythm was most happily realized. The language is 'such words as men did use' (in an age less polished than our own); and the moulding of speech idiom to the patterns of the couplet is admirable. After the tepid velleities of Waller—the 'crooner' of the couplet—Dryden's prologues mark a partial recovery of the toughness and 'juice' of Jonsonian English. But though they are highly original, they are linked via Jonson with an earlier tradition. The prologue, as used by Jonson to give instruction in literary taste, is a theatrical form of the Roman epistle. Dryden's later blend of the prologue-satirical style with the heroic is anticipated in the insolent debates of the plays and in the prologues themselves. Given a very slight excuse, Dryden will sound off with an ancient literary parallel, or a debased parody of one. Part of the game of amusing his listeners consisted in deliberately talking over their heads.

The 'huddled notions' of Dryden's satiric mode lay in readiness when the Monmouth 'conspiracy' offered the occasion his genius had been waiting for. He could now compose heroic narrative and dialogue while talking to his familiar audience. What is remarkable is that in scoring a journalistic and political success he produced poetry of a high order. Here is a representative passage, the commemoration

of Titus Oates, the Presbyterian 'weaver's issue' who testi-
fied that the Jesuits were plotting to murder Charles II:

> Yet, Corah, thou shalt from oblivion pass:
> Erect thyself, thou monumental brass,
> High as the serpent of thy metal made,
> While nations stand secure beneath thy shade.
> What tho' his birth were base, yet comets rise
> From earthy vapours, ere they shine in skies.
> Prodigious actions may as well be done
> By weaver's issue, as by prince's son.
> This arch-attestor for the public good
> By that one deed ennobles all his blood.
> Who ever ask'd the witnesses' high race,
> Whose oath with martyrdom did Stephen grace?
> Ours was a Levite, and as times went then,
> His tribe were God Almighty's gentlemen.
> Sunk were his eyes, his voice was harsh and loud,
> Sure signs he neither choleric was nor proud:
> His long chin prov'd his wit; his saintlike grace
> A church vermilion, and a Moses' face.
> His memory, miraculously great,
> Could plots, exceeding man's belief, repeat;
> Which therefore cannot be accounted lies,
> For human wit could never such devise.
> Some future truths are mingled in his book;
> But where the witness fail'd, the prophet spoke:
> Some things like visionary flights appear;
> The spirit caught him up, the Lord knows where;
> And gave him his rabbinical degree,
> Unknown to foreign university.
>
> (632–59)

To see the imaginative unity of these lines is to see the
blending of Dryden's earlier styles and to feel the active
pressure of older literary traditions. As in most satirical
verse, the lines are held together in part by the broad illogic
of irony: Dryden makes a series of triumphant assertions
every one of them the opposite of the truth from the Court
point of view. But it is Dryden's 'intonation' that sets his
mark on the lines and gives them life and singleness of effect.
His note is clearly heard in 'arch-attestor', with its upper
level of churchly associations, and in 'prodigious', which

nicely combines Latin solemnity with the literal Latin meaning of 'monstrous'. Dryden has anticipated the high level
of this commemoration by suggesting that it belongs to a
Homeric catalogue; he then addresses Oates in a line so
nobly reminiscent of Virgil that it is hardly recognizable as
parody:

> Yet, Corah, thou shalt from oblivion pass . . .

The occasionally Latin flavour of the diction is also vaguely
suggestive of Virgilian epic, while at many points the language is more or less Biblical, ranging from near-quota-
tion to expressions with religious or churchly associations.
Working within a fairly narrow range of allusion Dryden
maintains a declamatory tone that is both Biblical-eccle-
siastical and Roman-heroic. But the 'venom' of the address
depends on the contrast of another tone which is unmistakably the voice of the prologues, insolently vulgar and know-
ingly unliterary:

> Ours was a Levite, and as times went then,
> His tribe were God Almighty's gentlemen.

The blend of manners is most subtle in the lines of greatest
imaginative variety:

> Yet, Corah, thou shalt from oblivion pass:
> Erect thyself, thou monumental brass,
> High as the serpent of thy metal made,
> While nations stand secure beneath thy shade.

The focus of the ironies is also the focus of opposing styles
and of the widest range of literary and religious associations,
the ironies arising mainly from the double references of
'monumental' and 'brass'. Taking 'monumental' on its high
Latinate side, in a Virgilian address, we feel that this beneficent hero is 'monumental' in greatness. Or we may read the
whole line as a preposterous parody of Horace's

> Exegi monumentum aere perennius . . .

But Biblical and ecclesiastical connotations of 'brass' and
'monuments' suggest that our hero is worthy of a 'monumental brass' in an English church, the rude command implying that this monument, contrary to decent custom and
the laws of gravity, will rise of its own power. Finally, 'brass'

in its vulgar sense reminds us that such effrontery is otherwise 'monumental'.

In these lines Dryden's satirical mode appears at its characteristic best. There are the black-and-white oppositions of
irony with rhetorical and metrical emphasis striking in unison. There is the smack of life and vulgarity in a word from
'Jonsonian' London, the word which imparts the ironic intention and gives force to Dryden's thrust. But the irony is
most concentrated in a word of classical origin which is rich
in literary and historical connotations and which suggests the
Roman oratorical tone.

These features appear in close combination in many of the
best lines in Dryden's satirical verse:

> A fiery soul, which, working out its way,
> Fretted the pigmy body to decay,
> And o'er-inform'd the tenement of clay.

(The reminiscences of Aristotle and Plato, Bishop Fuller, and
Carew have often been pointed out.) Or consider:

> Besides, his goodly fabric fills the eye
> And seems design'd for thoughtless majesty;
> Thoughtless as monarch oaks that shade the plain,
> And, spread in solemn state, supinely reign.
> Heywood and Shirley were but types of thee,
> Thou last great prophet of tautology.

or

> But gentle Simkin just reception finds
> Amidst this monument of vanish'd minds:

or

> Thou leap'st o'er all eternal truths in thy
>   Pindaric way!

Finally, a delicious blend of neo-Platonic fancy and shrewd
analysis in these lines on the Church of England:

> If, as our dreaming Platonists report,
> There could be spirits of a middle sort,
> Too black for heav'n, and yet too white for hell,
> Who just dropp'd halfway down, nor lower fell;
> So pois'd, so gently she descends from high,
> It seems a soft dismission from the sky.

From these examples and from our analysis, it is clear that

'allusive irony' is a more adequate term than 'mock-heroic' for Dryden's satirical mode, whether in *Absalom and Achitophel* and *Mac Flecknoe* or in passages of incidental satire in his argumentative verse. His mode is allusive in a wide variety of ways: in close imitation or parody of other writers, in less exact references to language, styles, and conventions of other literatures—Classical, Biblical, and French—in drawing on the large materials of philosophy and theology, in playing on popular parallels between contemporary religious and political situations and those of ancient history, sacred and secular. Through this mode Dryden makes his 'affirmation of Europe'.

A solemn claim and a preposterous one, if we think of the mode as devices for heightening style. The difference between allusive irony and the heroic trimmings added to the *Annus Mirabilis* lies in the imaginative union of tones and levels of meaning that I have been describing: 'thou monumental brass'! The vulgar thrust is inseparable from the reference to high literary styles and to heroic behaviour and ecclesiastical splendour.

That the union of styles was more than an academic trick is further shown by the success of the poem with contemporary readers. As compared with Restoration plays or lampoons and gazettes, *Absalom and Achitophel* spoke to more of the interests of the reading public in 1681, and, as Beljame observed, to *more* of the public. Although the Classical heroic was especially flattering to the aristocrats' view of themselves, Latin culture was the common possession of educated men, whatever their political and religious allegiances might be. Dryden, Milton, and Marvell have at least this in common. The Old Testament flavour, satirically amusing to the Court, was richly meaningful and insidiously attractive to Nonconformists. And the colloquial idiom brought the high talk down to the level where Court and City lived. By responding so naturally to the double claims of both his audience and his development as a poet, Dryden 'made himself heard' and created a fresh form of art in English poetry.

By this fact alone, he affirmed an important European value to his audience: that poetic craft matters. Dryden's admiration for what Boileau had done for French satire is a

sign of his belief that he had performed a similar service for
English satire. Boileau would have recognized as art of a
high order the poise and finish of Dryden's mode:

> At his right hand our young Ascanius sate,
> Rome's other hope, and pillar of the State.
> His brows thick fogs, instead of glories, grace,
> And lambent dulness play'd around his face.

The poise is evident in the balance between crude burlesque
in 'thick fogs' and the subtle gravity of 'lambent dulness';
the finish is felt in the melodious and resilient verse. But the
smoothness is not merely fashionable: it functions poetically
in the strategy of civilized irony. The reader is momentarily
beguiled into taking the lines as an exquisite compliment.
Dryden had a right to claim that like Boileau he was bringing into modern satire a Virgilian refinement of 'raillery'. In
the fine Latin wit of 'lambent dulness' or 'spread in solemn
state, *supinely* reign', Dryden is 'alluding' to a culture and
the fineness of response which it fostered.

It is no great compliment to describe Dryden's achievement as a triumph of neo-classicism, if we mean by neo-
classicism mechanical use of conventions borrowed from
Boileau or Rapin. Dryden's achievement is not one of 'meeting requirements'; the conventions 'at work', as in the lines
just quoted, are expressive of larger aesthetic and cultural
values. In writing verse which combined the normality and
vigour of good talk with a musical pattern that was the apt
accompaniment of ironic wit and in using language which
was equally alive in its reference to immediate interests and
to literary tradition, Dryden expressed a community in attitude and standards of art with European poets and critics.
Some of these attitudes and standards—the detachment, the
refinement of ironic censure, the insistence on design and
precise mastery of language—were particularly salutary for
readers too well pleased with *Hudibras* and for writers who
mistook ease for art. But Dryden did not sacrifice the vigour
of Butler to 'correctness'. The Augustan reform as initiated
by Dryden, unlike that of Addison, kept close contact with
a masculine audience. Dryden's allusive mode shows a positive strength in neo-classicism which the odious term and its
theories completely conceal.

Let us consider more particularly how this mode worked, how and why epic allusions offered Dryden a way of expressing important values. In ironic contexts, the more or less close imitations of epic introduced a standard of manners and actions by which the exploits of politicians and poetasters might be measured. Fomenters of Popish plots and rash rebellions and slipshod writers were exposed to ancient and Biblical ideals of prince and prophet, and their operations were socially and intellectually 'placed'. In contexts less purely ironic, as in parts of the Shaftesbury and Monmouth 'characters', the allusions to Classical and Biblical heroic had another effect. The magnificence imparted by the Miltonic flavour was not merely literary. For Shaftesbury had great abilities as a judge and diplomat; Monmouth had noble looks and manners, and Dryden himself confessed a 'respect' for 'his heroic virtues'. By granting their loftiness some degree of pride the satirist, too, attained a largeness of temper: 'Preposterous plottings, but rather splendid persons!' Nevertheless, as Dr. Johnson observed, there are limits in heroic allegory: 'Charles could not run continually parallel with David'. But though the David–Aeneas incarnation cannot be taken seriously, the tone adopted in addressing Charles and attributed to him and his courtiers did have a certain validity. The parallel between state manners and Roman aristocratic manners was justified, even in Restoration England. In public discourse, the English aristocracy, like the Roman, had a hereditary right to high oratory. And heroic poetry had been by a long tradition an aristocratic possession.

The grand yet lively eloquence that characterizes and satirizes Shaftesbury and Buckingham is thus quite different from the inflated and dully insistent rant of the Heroic Plays, for Dryden had found the one kind of situation in which a Restoration poet might adopt the heroic style. As spokesman for aristocracy, Established Church, and monarchy, he could rightly assume the Roman dignity of Renaissance epic. As the critic of the King's enemies, he could parody his own heroic style and so express still another true relationship between contemporary events and the heroic ideal. The discovery of relationships which were true for Dryden both as poet and citizen made it possible for him to use his accumulated literary skills with a new freedom. His satirical poetry exhibits a fluidity and force and a concentrated range of reference which his earlier verse had rarely shown.

Why may we reasonably describe this success as 'European'? Not simply because Dryden's satiric mode was widely and often precisely allusive to European writers and styles and to English writers who were most consciously European in their styles and critical standards. Nor simply because he satisfied a continental standard of literary craft, although this is significant. But rather because he brought the larger light of European literature and a European past into verse of local public debate. He invited his readers, including Nonconformists, to take a less parochial attitude toward the persons and events of contemporary history. We have only to compare *Absalom and Achitophel* or *The Medal* with Marvell's satires to appreciate the imaginative value of linking these smaller and greater worlds. The Marvell of the *Ode* on Cromwell had brought to political history a similar largeness of scene and a poise of values much finer than Dryden's. But breadth of vision and sureness of rhythm are missing in *Last Instructions to a Painter*, although the poem has some of the obvious ear-marks of epic satire. The spectacle is rather painful: the earlier Marvell could not address this world without sacrificing many of his virtues as a poet. Dryden could; with losses, too, if his poetry is measured by the standard of the Cromwellian *Ode*; but he managed to translate to his audience something of the larger historic vision, the noble manner, and the justness of style of the Renaissance tradition in which the younger Marvell wrote. He was a vigorous civilizer among the sons of Belial.

Dryden did something else for his generation that Marvell and Milton, much less Cowley, could not do: he reaffirmed the public role of the poet, the Graeco-Roman conception of the poet as the voice of a society. It is true that Dryden succeeded only too well in fixing the public tone as the Augustan norm; but the voice we hear is not solely that of the party or class or church. Thanks to Dryden the tone of Augustan poetry is less parochial than it might have been: it is resonant with echoes of other literary worlds, of larger manners and events. Minor Augustan poetry is dead for modern readers not because it was too 'general', but because it was too local.

In praising Dryden for reaffirming the European tradition in his satirical mode, it is well to recall the conditions of our praise. The eighteenth century is littered with epics, odes, and philosophical poems that are traditional in the academic sense; the 'forms' and the 'diction' are too often reminiscent of the best writers of Greece and Rome. Dr. Johnson's remark on Gray's *Odes* is the appropriate comment on such products: 'They are forced plants raised in a hot-bed; and they are poor plants; they are but cucumbers after all.' Dryden's achievement matters because the verse through which he draws on the European tradition satisfies us as other poetry does by offering concentrated and surprising richness of relationship: we feel that language is being 'worked' for all its worth. (The allusive mode is for Dryden what the symbolic metaphor was for the Metaphysicals.) But Dryden's use of tradition satisfies also a condition of another sort. In the act of writing poetry that was far from provincial in implication, Dryden engaged the most active political and intellectual interests of his immediate audience. The particular issues are of little concern for us at present; but we can recognize their importance in the late seventeenth century, and see that the general issues involved are of a sort that is central in any conceivable society. There are local successes in literature that are instructive to later generations: Dryden's is one of them.

But Pope and the poets who were contemporary with him were not prepared to take instruction from Dryden the con-troversialist, since they quite consciously removed them-selves from the field of public debate. Although political pamphleteering of a violent sort continued throughout the age of Anne, the typical watchwords of the new world of *belles lettres* were 'politeness' and 'retirement'. That Pope could inhabit this Addisonian world of well-bred ameni-ties and moderate enthusiasms and yet rise above it to a serious criticism of life, he owes in part to Dryden's force-ful example.

Dryden's most valuable gift to Pope was the creation of his generously allusive mode with all of its wider cultural implications. (I am not overlooking 'the couplet': the style is inseparable from its rhythmic form.) With his shrewd flair for craft, Pope realized the principle within the mode, and possessing a finer responsiveness to the poetry of the past, both Classical and English, he enriched his satire with more subtle and more various kinds of reference. His obvious imitations of epic in the *Rape of the Lock* and the *Dunciad* are of less importance than his blending of the heroic with other literary styles and non-literary idioms into the complex modes appropriate to his two very different 'mock-epics'. Although some single traditional style or genre is dominant in each of Pope's major works, from the *Pastorals* and the *Rape of the Lock* to the satirical epistles and the *Dunciad*, his poetry is freshly and variously allusive to poets of many traditions and many periods. At random one can think of allusions to Spenser, Ovid, Catullus, to Shakespeare, Milton, and Crashaw, to Rochester, Denham, and Addison. From Dryden Pope also learned the art of self-parody, which he exploited with amusing thrift. He alludes with overtones of wit to his own pastoral insipidities, to the landscape-painting of *Windsor Forest*, to the Ovidian theatrical rhetoric of *Eloisa to Abelard*, and of course to the heroics of his *Iliad*.

As in Dryden, the Roman heroic is always breaking in; and though the modulation of tone is infinitely various in the *Moral Essays* and the *Satires*, the tone of Roman cultivation— more refined and more truly Horatian, less downright and less pompous than in Dryden—still prevails. With the changes in state and society that had been taking place since the Glorious Revolution, the tone had acquired a validity which it could hardly have had in the Restoration. It might well be argued that the actual society in which Pope wrote was considerably nearer to the ideal of the original Augustan Age than that of Charles II. Burlington, Bolingbroke, and Bathurst, in public and private life were certainly less unlike their ideal literary selves than Charles and Rochester. But if the society was not more Augustan, Pope was: his work taken as a whole shows that he had mastered the intellectual and aesthetic ideals which for the Age of Anne were embodied in the Age of Augustus and Virgil and Horace. In Pope's verse, the cultivated tone and the oblique reference to Roman

grandeur and decorum symbolize an ideal of culture which
he is frequently expressing by other more explicit means.
The symbolic force of the allusive mode which he had first
learned from Dryden can be felt wonderfully in his address
to Burlington in the fourth *Moral Essay*:

> You show us, Rome was glorious, not profuse,
> And pompous buildings once were things of Use.
> Yet shall (my Lord) your just, your noble rules
> Fill half the land with Imitating Fools;
> Who random drawings from your sheets shall take,
> And of one beauty many blunders make;
> Load some vain Church with old Theatric state,
> Turn Arcs of triumph to a Garden-gate;
> Reverse your Ornaments, and hang them all
> On some patch'd dog-hole ek'd with ends of wall,
> Then clap four slices of Pilaster on't,
> That, lac'd with bits of rustic, makes a Front;
> Or call the winds thro' long Arcades to roar,
> Proud to catch cold at a Venetian door;
> Conscious they act a true Palladian part,
> And, if they starve, they starve by rules of art.
>
> (23–38)

After that, the tradition of Dryden needs no further justification; renewed and refined, it speaks for itself.

I

THE SHEPHERD'S SONG

I no longer look upon *Theocritus* as a romantic writer; he
has only given a plain image of the way of life amongst the
peasants of his country. . . I don't doubt, had he been
born a Briton, but his *Idylliums* had been filled with
descriptions of thrashing and churning, both which are
unknown here, the corn being all trod out by oxen; and
butter (I speak it with sorrow) unheard of.
            (Lady Mary Wortley Montagu to Pope,
              1 April 1717 (from Adrianople))

EVERYONE remembers how the heroine of the *Rape of
the Lock* is pictured as she journeys down the Thames
to Hampton Court for an afternoon of cards and tea:

Not with more Glories, in th' Etherial Plain,
The Sun first rises o'er the purpled Main,
Than issuing forth, the Rival of his Beams
Lanch'd on the Bosom of the Silver *Thames*.
Fair Nymphs, and well-drest Youths around her shone,
But ev'ry Eye was fix'd on her alone.

                                        (II. 1–6)

This Nymph, to the Destruction of Mankind,
Nourish'd two Locks, which graceful hung behind
In equal Curls, and well conspir'd to deck
With shining Ringlets the smooth Iv'ry Neck.

                                        (19–22)

But now secure the painted Vessel glides,
The Sun-beams trembling on the floating Tydes,
While melting Musick steals upon the Sky,
And soften'd Sounds along the Waters die.
Smooth flow the Waves, the Zephyrs gently play,
Belinda smil'd, and all the World was gay.

                                        (47–52)

Most readers will catch in the opening lines an allusion to
the grand similes and the morning scenes of Homer; we are

all prepared to hear echoes of heroic poetry in the *Rape of the Lock*, because we know—at least in some vague way—that it is a 'mock epic'. Pope's simile, like many in the *Iliad*, takes us outside the immediate scene and into the world of nature. Homer's similes take us frequently into a pastoral world, 'pastoral' in the literal sense of a place where shepherds watch their flocks. We may perhaps not recognize the echoes of that early world here, though we may have noted that Belinda is a 'Nymph' surrounded with other 'fair Nymphs'. We can hear a more distinct echo of the shepherd's song in

> Smooth flow the Waves, the Zephyrs gently play,

that is, we can hear it if we are familiar with Pope's pastoral style.

But we must go back well beyond Pope if we are to catch the deepest pastoral note in these lines, the note struck in

> *Belinda* smil'd, and all the World was gay.

To appreciate that, we must go back to Homer and to the shepherd songs of Theocritus. To talk of Belinda in such terms is to imply she is very grand indeed, or at least it suggests that the poet is having fun with a very grand idea. Let us see where such ideas and expressions came from, and what Pope did with them in seriousness and in fun.

The heroes of Homer were always shepherds as well as warriors, herdsmen in peace, 'shepherds of the people' in war. In both roles they illustrate Goethe's remark that 'he who is no warrior can be no shepherd', a saying that is equally true when reversed. In the *Iliad* great heroes tend flocks and are honoured for their valour by gifts of 'fat sheep'; in the *Odyssey* the shepherd Eumaeus is depicted with the noble character and speech of a hero, and the cyclops Polyphemus addresses his sheep with tender yet heroic epithets. The scene at Eumaeus' hut is a little picture (the Greek word is 'idyll', *eidullion*) that anticipates the *idylls* of Theocritus. Though hardly a shepherd himself, Theocritus seems to have known very well the country life and country songs of his native Sicily, but most of his poems were written for sophisticated literary and courtly audiences in the island of Cos, in Syracuse, and in Alexandria.

Let us consider a pure pastoral, perhaps the purest of all,

Theocritus' First *Idyll*, *Thyrsis*, on the death of Daphnis. Here is how the poem opens in the translation of R. C. Trevelyan:

Theocritus: *Idyll* I

THYRSIS. Sweet is the whispering music of yonder pine that sings
Over the water-brooks, and sweet the melody of your pipe,
Dear goatherd. After Pan, the second prize you'll bear away.
If he should take the hornèd goat, the she-goat shall you win:
But if he choose the she-goat for his meed, to you shall fall
The kid; and dainty is kid's flesh, till you begin to milk.

GOATHERD. Sweeter, O shepherd, is your song than the melodious fall
Of yonder stream that from on high gushes down the rock.
If it chance that the Muses take the young ewe for their gift,
Then your reward will be the stall-fed lamb; but should they choose
To take the lamb, then yours shall be the sheep for second prize.

(1–11)

What is this poetry like? A shepherd and a goatherd are singing responsively in a curiously sweet style, 'sweet' because of its echoes and repetitions and the all but monotonous rhythm:

Sweet is the whispering music of yonder pine that sings
Over the water-brooks, and sweet the melody of your pipe . . .

The pattern slips easily into pure song, a refrain that we barely attend to as sense. We have a genuine refrain later on in this idyll:

Lead, now, I pray, dear Muses, lead you the pastoral song.

Note in the exchanges of the song how easily scenes in art and in country life are combined:

GOATHERD. Come then, let's sit beneath yon elm, over against the statues,
Priapus and the fountain Nymphs, there by the shepherd's seat
And the oak-tree grove; and if you will but sing as once you sang
In rivalry with that Chromis who came from Libya,
I'll give you for three milkings a goat, mother of twins,
Who yields two pailfuls every time, for all she feeds two kids.
A deep bowl of carved wood I'll give you too, rubbed with sweet bees-wax,
Two-eared and newly wrought, still smacking of the graver's tool.
Around the upper edges the winding ivy runs,

Ivy besprent with helicryse, and therewith interwined,
Rejoicing in its golden berries, the proud tendril curls.
Within, a woman is designed, such as the Gods might fashion,
Clad in a robe, with snooded hair; and upon either side
Two men with fair long locks contending in alternate speech
One with the other; but her heart is touched by naught they say:
For now at one she glances with a smile, and now again
Flings to the other a light thought; while they, with heavy eyes
Long wearied out for love of her, are wasting toil in vain.
Beyond these there is carved an ancient fisherman, who stands
On a jagged rock, and busily the old man gathers in
His great net for a cast, like one who toils with might and main.
You'ld say that he was fishing with the whole strength of his limbs;
Such swelling sinews everywhere stand out around his neck;
For grey-haired though he be, his strength is worthy of youth still.

(21-44)

There is an exquisite blend of 'the graver's' art and botany
in the lines on the twining ivy, and much rugged life in the
description of the old man of the sea. But this too is a
pictured life.

Thyrsis' song imperceptibly turns into a play as he tells
how animals and gods gather when they hear that Daphnis
is dying. Much of the poem is a noble monologue, with the
shepherd singing his own dirge. The greatest of shepherds is
a hero, and like the heroes of Homer he associates with gods,
and his sufferings and death are the concern of friendly or
malicious powers. But he is much nearer to a deity than to
Hector or Achilles. He is almost a nature spirit, his death is
wept by animals and has wondrous effects on flora and
fauna, and—most surprising of all to anyone familiar with
Homer's heroes—he is mysteriously dying of love. The
poem offers another surprise for a reader who hears Milton's
lament for Lycidas in

Where were ye then, while Daphnis pined away, where were ye,
    Nymphs?

Milton's elegy has its asperities, but this high lament for a
hero-spirit's death includes a conversation with the mocking
goddess of love and with Priapus, the lusty god of gardens
and herds. The elegy comes to a close with a joke about he-
goats and she-goats, an ending thoroughly characteristic of

Theocritean pastoral, with its strangely charming blend of country life and art, of sweet and artful song, of heroic sorrow and fun.

Let me draw from this and other poems by Theocritus and his successors a picture of the ideal shepherd in Greek pastoral. The reader should be warned in advance that the figure when detached from the poems will seem more simply serious than the poems themselves. For example, in the First *Idyll* Daphnis the herdsman is not the only actor. Besides Priapus and Aphrodite, there are also foxes and the old fisherman, and in the background the poet-dramatist and his audience of learned littérateurs. By surrounding his shepherd with a variety of characters Theocritus brings his vision of the country world nearer to Homer's vision of the world of hero-country-men. Both writers illustrate Empson's perceptive remark: 'This is indeed one of the assumptions of pastoral, that you can say everything about complex people by a complete consideration of simple people.'[1]

The ideal shepherd, like Daphnis, is a man living in mysteriously close relation to physical nature (trees, flowers, animals, mountains, streams). Although men and deities treat him cruelly, he has a compensation in his power over nature: other creatures weep for him, living things die with him, and in his incarnation as Adonis, nature is renewed when he returns to life. What is later called the pathetic fallacy is here no fallacy, since the ideal shepherd has genuine religious power. Nature 'really' responds. Whatever Theocritus or other poets themselves believed, the literary convention enshrined a belief that had once been active, one still alive for some members of the poet's audience (see, for example, the lament for Adonis in the Fifteenth *Idyll* of Theocritus). Although Greek pastoral poems recall country beliefs, the shepherd is the hero of an urban society, and the poet's image is addressed to the city, with tenderness and nostalgia softening the outlines. The manners of these shepherds are charming; they combine a taste for cheese with an eye for exquisite works of art. The hero of a high literary culture is not a warrior, but a poet, and a great one. He and his fellow

[1] William Empson, *Some Versions of Pastoral* (London, 1950: first published, 1935). p. 137.

shepherds engage in musico-literary contests, and they are critics, too, both appreciative and sharp. They are handsome, indeed heroically beautiful, but their beauty is all for love, which they believe they can command or cure with a song. Unlike Keats's 'happy melodists' they do not enjoy a 'happy, happy love', and curious difficulties and even paradoxes appear. Daphnis, for example, resists love and yet somehow is dying of it. In the life of less august shepherds than Daphnis or Adonis or Pan, the simple shepherd's task has its place, although tending flocks and singing have a way of becoming identified: 'Labour is blossoming', art that has become the accompaniment of song, rather than the opposite. But occasionally the singer will glance at his flocks or stop to scold an unruly goat. If as in Theocritus' Tenth *Idyll* a countryman reaps, he does it in a kind of rustic song and dance.

From picturing the shepherd as poet it is only a step for the poet to regard himself as a shepherd, as Milton does in *Lycidas*. The pastoral becomes very easily an allegory of the poet's life and the lives of his friends. Although personal allegory can be found in the works of Theocritus, Bion, and Moschus, it has been traditionally associated more closely with Virgil. In the first of the *Eclogues*, the shepherd Tityrus, like Virgil himself, has been driven from his ancestral acres, and in the Fifth *Eclogue*, Daphnis' ascent to the stars apparently symbolizes the deification of Julius Caesar.

The shepherd become again a martial hero brings us back to epic, and to the link between the pastoral and Homer. The most famous of Virgil's *Eclogues*, the Fourth (which Pope imitated in his *Messiah*), opens with a farewell to the usual pastoral subjects. Thinking of the Augustan Peace, Virgil sings of the age now dawning,

> The world's great age begins anew . . .
>
> magnus ab integro saeclorum nascitur ordo . . .[1]

and hails the birth of a child who will 'live the life of a god, who will see gods mingling with heroes, and will himself be

[1] All quotations of Virgil are from *P. Vergili Maronis Opera*, ed. F. A. Hirtzel (Oxford, 1900).

seen by them, who will rule a world made peaceful by his
father's valour':

> ille deum vitam accipiet divisque videbit
> permixtos heroas et ipse videbitur illis,
> pacatumque reget patriis virtutibus orbem.
>
> (15–17)

The child will live in a nature uncorrupted even by the
shepherd's task,

> ipsae lacte domum referent distenta capellae
> ubera,
>
> (21–22)

a world that has recovered its original innocence, the Golden
Age when Saturn ruled, *Saturnia regna*. The growing boy will
read of heroes' praises and his father's deeds, he will come to
understand the old Roman *virtus*, while around him rises a
visionary scene where the glowing grape hangs on the briar
and the rough oak drips with dew-like honey:

> at simul heroum laudes et facta parentis
> iam legere et quae sit poteris cognoscere virtus,
> molli paulatim flavescet campus arista,
> incultisque rubens pendebit sentibus uva,
> et durae quercus sudabunt roscida mella.
>
> (26–30)

What strikes us about this vision, especially when we read
the entire passage, is its pictorial character; objects, colours,
and other sensuous qualities, and the words that name them
stand out in clear symmetrical design. Facts give way to
miracle, even to absurdity, as living rams and lambs cavort
in saffron and glowing purple. ('Purple' is one of Pope's
favourite colour-words, though the term and meaning derive
from *purpureus*, rather than the *rubenti murice* of *Eclogue* IV.)

In writing the *Pastorals* Pope had in mind not only Virgil
and Theocritus, but a long succession of poets from Spenser
to Milton, Dryden, Waller, and his own contemporaries. He
owed much also to the example and criticism of his friend
William Walsh,[1] who introduced him to the theories of

---

[1] EC i, fn. 1, 256. See also J. E. Congleton, *Theories of Pastoral Poetry in
England 1648–1798* (Gainesville, Fla., 1952), pp. 5–6, 79–82, 179–80; R. F. Jones,
'Eclogue Types in English Poetry of the Eighteenth Century', *Journal of English
and Germanic Philology*, xxiv. 33–60.

Rapin and Fontenelle, and his prefatory essay, *A Discourse on Pastoral Poetry*, is greatly influenced by Walsh and the two French critics. Pope's theory, like that of his masters, shows his debt to Virgil and the Virgilian pastoral tradition in three important features: in the stress on the Golden Age and 'tranquillity', in the emphasis on the 'best' side of the shepherd's life, and in the fondness for 'a designed scene' or 'prospect'.

We shall see better what Pope meant by these ideal standards, what they meant to him as a poet, if we turn to the *Pastorals* and see what happens to the Greek shepherd's song in his transcriptions. To be just to Pope, let us take him at his poetic best, at the high point of the *Pastorals*, in the familiar lines from *Summer*:

> See what delights in sylvan scenes appear!
> Descending Gods have found Elysium here.
> In woods bright Venus with Adonis strayed,
> And chaste Diana haunts the forest-shade.
> Come, lovely nymph, and bless the silent hours,
> When swains from shearing seek their nightly bowers
> When weary reapers quit the sultry field,
> And crowned with corn their thanks to Ceres yield.
> This harmless grove no lurking viper hides,
> But in my breast the serpent Love abides.
> Here bees from blossoms sip the rosy dew,
> But your Alexis knows no sweets but you.
> 71 Oh deign to visit our forsaken seats,
> 72 The mossy fountains, and the green retreats!
> 73 Where'er you walk, cool gales shall fan the glade;
> 74 Trees, where you sit, shall crowd into a shade;
> 75 Where'er you tread, the blushing flowers shall rise,
> 76 And all things flourish where you turn your eyes.
> Oh! how I long with you to pass my days,
> Invoke the Muses, and resound your praise!
> Your praise the birds shall chant in every grove,
> And winds shall waft it to the powers above,
> But would you sing, and rival Orpheus' strain,
> The wond'ring forests soon should dance again;
> The moving mountains hear the powerful call,
> And headlong streams hang listening in their fall!

(59–84)

What strikes us here is hardly the pain and wonder of love; what we respond to actively is exquisite poetry for the eye and ear. The keynotes are 'see' (the 'sylvan scene') and 'sing', the song that gave Handel his clue. We are looking at 'a designed scene'—or rather a merging sequence of scenes—of wooded and open landscapes ornamented with mythological figures. They are presented not photographically but in a painter's fashion, through selected visual impressions of light, shade, colour, and movement: '*bright* Venus', 'forest *shade*', '*green* retreats', '*mossy* fountains', '*blushing* flowers', and '*descending* gods', '*moving* mountains', '*headlong* streams *hang* listening'. Note in passing the romantic quality, the vague strangeness, in words of movement: 'strayed', 'haunts', 'lurking', 'moving', 'wond'ring'.

But though the lines are pictorially vivid, they come close to sheer delightfulness of sound for its own sake, an English equivalent for Theocritean sweetness. Pure sound very nearly holds the place of sense—which is one reason why we attend so little to what the lover is saying about the joys and sorrows of love. Like Theocritus Pope uses many of the traditional devices of song: refrain-like repetition, euphonious alliteration, as in 'winds waft' and 'moving mountains', and the blend of assonance and alliteration with faintly sensuous imagery, as in 'cool gales shall fan the glade'. There is also the immediate impression, continuously renewed, of musical intricacy. Consider the variations in rhythm of the five numbered lines: first (71), the unbroken flow of 'Oh deign to visit our forsaken seats'; then (72) the exact balance of 'The mossy fountains, and the green retreats!', and (73) the assymetrical balance of 'Where'er you walk, // cool gales shall fan the glade'; the broken music of the following line (74) with an architectural triad of units increasing in length, 'Trees, // where you sit, // shall crowd into a shade'; next (75), an almost exact renewal of 73 in 'Where'er you tread, // the blushing flowers shall rise'; and finally the line (76) that ends this 'stanza', which recalls the unbroken flow of the first (71) by the lack of any sharp pause, the many liquids, and the rich assonance: 'And all things flourish where you turn your eyes.'

These lines, and in general the best parts of the *Pastorals*, are the poetry of picturesque song that Pope later dismissed with an indulgent smile. But are they nothing more? Our reading of earlier pastorals suggests some relevant questions: what of the gods, and 'the air of piety' that Pope says 'should shine through the Poem'? And what of responsive Nature? If Greek pastoral is the norm, an answer that is just to Pope is again hard to give. For it is quite true that the lively, quarrelsome, and loving gods of Theocritus have been reduced almost to mere picture. What is most alive in this poetry is not the Greek *mythos* (in the sense of story or plot), not the gods as characters in action, but Pope's choreographic sense. We are reminded of the dance gestures and poses of nymphs and shepherds and deities in the twilight landscapes of Poussin or Zuccarelli. But though we feel hardly at all the ancient power of Venus and Adonis to influence the physical world, still 'something moves'. Behind the painter's eye and the choreographic eye is the mythological eye that sees life in trees and mountains and streams. This is not only a kind of seeing but a power of dramatizing,[1] of catching the dramatic aspect of events in the natural world. For all his sophistication, Pope leaps back to the naïve view of Nature that underlies all myths, and like Keats he does so when he is being least obviously Greek. To this consciousness, trees do 'crowd into a shade', forests 'wonder' and 'dance', and streams 'hang in their fall', and 'listen'.

The song from *Summer* shows very well what Pope can do as a pastoral poet: he can realize the scene with charming circumstance and write (as he puts it) in 'flowing numbers', and he can create a vision of the Virgilian Golden Age with its innocent tranquillity and a sweetly if absurdly compliant natural world. A brief survey of a complete poem will show more distinctly what happened to ancient pastoral when Pope was working with all the neo-classical conventions and explain also why the form offered irresistible opportunities for parody to a heartier poet like Gay and, later, to Pope himself.

In *Spring*, two swains sing of their loves, Delia and Sylvia, and exchange the prizes they have each offered. As

---

[1] On 'mythical perception', see Ernst Cassirer, *An Essay on Man* (New York, 1953), Anchor Books, pp. 102-3.

in *Summer* there are passages of precise picture and pure song:

> Sing then, and Damon shall attend the strain,
> While yon' slow oxen turn the furrowed Plain.
> Here the bright crocus and blue vi'let glow;
> Here western winds on breathing roses blow.
>
> (29–32)

We recall Virgil's saffron (*croceo*) and his glowing purple (*suave rubenti murice*), but there are few signs of the mythological eye, except possibly in the Miltonic '*breathing* roses'. We see now what Pope means by the 'simplicity' of shepherds in the Golden Age, and what he means by saying that they are not to be 'too polite nor too rustic'. Politeness clearly wins the day, for though we get nearer to the soil in 'slow oxen turn the furrowed Plain', the talk of love is all gallantry and coquetry: 'gentle Delia beckons'; we hear of 'a kind glance', 'the willing fair', and that 'Thames's shores the brightest beauties yield'. With 'beauties' and 'fair' and 'feigns a laugh', we are quite sure that the nymphs are urban belles in disguise. It is not 'amiss', Pope says, 'to give these shepherds some skill in astronomy', and (after Virgil) he rather cleverly imparts a tone of *naïveté* to a question about the Zodiac:

> And what is that, which binds the radiant sky,
> Where twelve fair Signs in beauteous order lie?
>
> (39–40)

The swains become simple in the unfortunate sense when they sing of their woes with solemn surprise:

> While a kind glance at her pursuer flies,
> How much at variance are her feet and eyes!
>
> (59–60)

The report on the beauties of spring offers some not unexpected observations:

> Now leaves the trees, and flowers adorn the ground . . .

The witty turns that mar even the song from *Summer* occur too often:

> She runs, but hopes she does not run unseen . . .
> No lambs or sheep for victims I'll impart,
> Thy victim, Love, shall be the shepherd's heart.
>
> (58, 51–52)

The antiphonal convention that began with Theocritus leads to verbal criss-cross of a terribly predictable kind: for the 'bull' there's a 'lamb'; a 'laugh' for a 'glance'; 'brightness' pairs with 'shade'; 'nature mourns' and 'Delia smiles'; 'nature laughs' and (surprisingly) 'Sylvia smiles' too. Such is the 'simplicity' of 'not too rustic' shepherds well trained in social compliment and the arts of antiphonal song. Although Pope addresses the poem to a friend, no individual note is heard, no voice of Tityrus weeping for his lost farmlands. If we recall the voice of the pastoral hero in Theocritus, the loss in dramatic power will seem fairly painful, since command over Nature has now been reduced to a verbal game. But what survives from the past and what we do believe in is the transformation of the landscape to the eye. The poet's power exceeds Nature's:

> Two Swains, whom Love kept wakeful, and the Muse,
> Poured o'er the whitening vale their fleecy care . . .
>
> (18–19)

But where is great Daphnis or Priapus and he-goats? Violence and rudeness have no place here, and song so fills the shepherd's life that like all poets he suffers from insomnia. Labour can no longer include Theocritus' old man fishing or his singing reapers.

But these early poems do not mark the end of the pastoral in Pope's poetry. Like Yeats Pope was continually remaking himself throughout his career, and the man whom Swift called 'paper-saving Pope' was also a line and phrase saver, who practised a kind of poetic economy that Virgil had practised before him and that Mr. Eliot seems to have pushed to the point of bankruptcy. Pope continued to exploit his early successes in pastoral song and scene, and, characteristically, he made something out of artifices that seem to us least convincing. He puts the conventions to work in a new way, and in the process some of the vitality of ancient pastoral is recovered.

Consider these lines from *Spring*:

> All nature laughs, the groves are fresh and fair,
> The Sun's mild lustre warms the vital air;

If Sylvia smiles, new glories gild the shore,
And vanquished nature seems to charm no more.
(73–76)

And read again the lines from the *Rape of the Lock* with which
we began:

> Not with more Glories, in th' Etherial Plain,
> The Sun first rises o'er the purpled Main,
> Than issuing forth, the Rival of his Beams
> Lanch'd on the Bosom of the Silver *Thames* . . .

> But now secure the painted Vessel glides,
> The Sun-beams trembling on the floating Tydes,
> While melting Musick steals upon the Sky,
> And soften'd Sounds along the Waters die.
> Smooth flow the Waves, the Zephyrs gently play,
> *Belinda* smil'd, and all the World was gay.

The revival of the familiar motif and the similarity in rhythmic pattern become obvious, as the smile of the sun-like
nymph that changes 'all nature' is described in sweetly
balanced lines,

> Smooth flow the Waves, the Zephyrs gently play,
> *Belinda* smil'd, and all the World was gay.

The 'zephyrs' are the 'western winds' of Pope's *Spring*,
which blow on 'breathing roses', the 'vernal airs' that
'through trembling osiers play'. The scene is the Thames of
the *Pastorals*, more exactly the 'silver' Thames of *Summer*.
The beaming Belinda is

> Lanch'd on the Bosom of the Silver *Thames*.

In *Spring* we were told that

> Blest Thames's shores the brightest beauties yield.

We may be amused to come on the pastoral miracle and
these allusions in the *Rape of the Lock*, in an atmosphere of
urban social diversions. But we are of course aware that Pope
is playing with the true pastoral, that he too is amused with
the notion of replacing Sylvia, the woodland nymph, by city
Belinda. He achieves his effects in part by pressing a little
hard on the ancient conventions: '*Belinda* smil'd, and *all* the
World was gay.' That is a bit too much! Pope also takes

advantage of the social tone of the shepherd-lovers in *Spring*
and in his other pastorals. What seemed slightly idiotic there
is perfectly in place here. We knew that those 'beauties'
were no 'yield', no natural growth of 'Thames's shores'. They
were too obviously out from town for a *fête-champêtre*. Talk
in the *Pastorals* of loves and breezes that pant and play makes
it easy enough now to transfer the pastoral setting to the
London world of belles and coquettes. But then something
surprising happens: the pastoral myth survives and 'works'.
The natural beauty of the scene and of the actors is more
than comic, and the power of the deity[1] is not quite cancelled
out in laughter. The nymph Belinda exerts some of Daphnis'
ancient power—which is one of the minor wonders of the
Rape of the Lock.

In this scene on the river Pope has as usual managed to do
several things at once. Taking advantage of the beauty and
the absurdity of his early pastoral style, he makes fun of the
too perfect beauty of Belinda and her world while ridiculing
her 'destructive' wiles and her conceit. At the same time he
makes us feel so strongly the charm to the eye and ear of the
nymph and the settings that we half-believe in her divinity.
The survival of the pastoral myth affects us without our
quite realizing it, and a haunting sense of a world where
waves and zephyrs and nymphs once lived in mysterious
harmony momentarily qualifies the picture of eighteenth-
century belles and beaux and their amusements. The image
of that other world quietly reminds us of how trivial this
present social world is.

In the years between the *Rape of the Lock* and the great
satirical poems of the 1730's comes the transformation of
Pope's poetry that he described in the *Epistle to Arbuthnot*,
asserting a bit solemnly

> That not in Fancy's Maze he wander'd long,
> But stoop'd to Truth, and moraliz'd his song . . .
>
> (340–1)

Like most biographers, Pope over-simplifies. He did not
leave fancy entirely behind, and the moralizing of song

---

[1] On the comparison of Belinda to the sun and to deities, see Cleanth Brooks, *The Well Wrought Urn* (New York, 1947), pp. 79–81, 91–92.

began while he was still 'wand'ring in her maze'. The lines
on Belinda's journey to Hampton Court show that Pope was
already cutting the sweets of pastoral with moral and social
criticism, that his allusive irony, like Dryden's, always implied some subtle evaluation of the persons and manners he
was ridiculing.

But the composition of *An Essay on Man*, beginning in
1729 or 1730,[1] marks most definitely Pope's arrival as an
ethical poet. If at times the moral freight seems too heavy
for song, there are also passages in Pope's mature satirical
manner that are at once richly allusive, sensuously alive, and
morally serious. A fine example of the style from early in the
first Epistle also indicates what has happened to the pastoral
song of the Golden Age:

> Ask for what end the heav'nly bodies shine,
> Earth for whose use? Pride answers, " 'Tis for mine:
> "For me kind Nature wakes her genial pow'r,
> "Suckles each herb, and spreads out ev'ry flow'r;
> "Annual for me, the grape, the rose renew
> "The juice nectareous, and the balmy dew;
> "For me, the mine a thousand treasures brings;
> "For me, health gushes from a thousand springs;
> "Seas roll to waft me, suns to light me rise;
> "My foot-stool earth, my canopy the skies."
>   (131–40)

We may be tempted to hear in these lines the voice of a happy
Keatsian child of nature revelling in a 'genial' world that
serves his every desire. But as the first couplet implies, that
is hardly the tone. It is Pride, proud man, the 'vile worm',
who speaks, the tone is harshly sarcastic, and innocent
pastoral song is being used to undercut any flattering illusions. There was a time, Pope says later in the *Essay* (Epistle
III, 147–60), when man lived in a happy State of Nature
and 'walk'd with beast, joint tenant of the shade'. But 'Pride
then was not'; man was still uncorrupted. In such passages
we have hints of what Pope will do in his satires, of how he
will allude to the pastoral vision in order to symbolize ancient
virtues and to etch more sharply contrasting modern vices.

---

[1] TE iii. (i), pp. xii–xiii.

In his last and perhaps greatest poem, the Fourth Book of the *Dunciad*, Pope returned to the mock-heroic and transformed it almost completely, creating a poetic mode that combines fantasy both exquisite and monstrous with the most serious moral criticism. Consider, for example, the lines on the education of a young man, a passage that brings us back to where we began, to the link between the heroic and pastoral. The young man is being presented to the Goddess of Dullness by the 'Governor' who has taken him on the Grand Tour:

When thus th' attendant Orator begun.
"Receive, great Empress! thy accomplish'd Son:
Thine from the birth, and sacred from the rod,
A dauntless infant! never scar'd with God.
The Sire saw, one by one, his Virtues wake:
The Mother begg'd the blessing of a Rake.
Thou gav'st that Ripeness, which so soon began,
And ceas'd so soon, he ne'er was Boy, nor Man.
Thro' School and College, thy kind cloud o'ercast,
Safe and unseen the young Æneas past:
Thence bursting glorious, all at once let down,
Stunn'd with his giddy Larum half the town.
Intrepid then, o'er seas and lands he flew:
Europe he saw, and Europe saw him too.
There all thy gifts and graces we display,
Thou, only thou, directing all our way!
To where the Seine, obsequious as she runs,
Pours at great Bourbon's feet her silken sons;
Or Tyber, now no longer Roman, rolls,
Vain of Italian Arts, Italian Souls:
To happy Convents, bosom'd deep in vines,
Where slumber Abbots, purple as their wines:
To Isles of fragrance, lilly-silver'd vales,
Diffusing languor in the panting gales:
To lands of singing, or of dancing slaves,
Love-whisp'ring woods, and lute-resounding waves.
But chief her shrine where naked Venus keeps,
And Cupids ride the Lyon of the Deeps;
Where, eas'd of Fleets, the Adriatic main
Wafts the smooth Eunuch and enamour'd swain.
Led by my hand, he saunter'd Europe round,
And gather'd ev'ry Vice on Christian ground;

Saw ev'ry Court, heard ev'ry King declare
His royal Sense, of Op'ra's or the Fair;
The Stews and Palace equally explor'd,
Intrigu'd with glory, and with spirit whor'd;
Try'd all *hors-d'oeuvres*, all *liqueurs* defin'd,
Judicious drank, and greatly-daring din'd;
Dropt the dull lumber of the Latin store,
Spoil'd his own language, and acquir'd no more;
All Classic learning lost on Classic ground;
And last turn'd *Air*, the Echo of a Sound!
See now, half-cur'd, and perfectly well-bred,
With nothing but a Solo in his head;
As much Estate, and Principle, and Wit,
As Jansen, Fleetwood, Cibber shall think fit;
Stol'n from a Duel, follow'd by a Nun,
And, if a Borough chuse him, not undone;
See, to my country happy I restore
This glorious Youth, and add one Venus more."
(IV. 281–330)

The quality of the poetry is set by 'dauntless infant' or 'glorious', or best of all 'glorious Youth':

See, to my country happy I restore
This glorious Youth, and add one Venus more.

In the opening lines as in the final couplet Pope expects us to remember how Aeneas emerges from the cloud in which Venus has brought him to the Carthaginian court. He also assumes familiarity with pastoral poetry and with a particular passage in the Fourth *Eclogue*. We might notice two points especially, where Pope parodies the heroic-pastoral manner to produce richly ironic effects while making serious evaluations. The fun is in fact inseparable from the seriousness, both qualities depending on Pope's artful allusion to heroic and pastoral styles.

The first appearance of the 'dauntless infant' recalls the heroic child of Virgil's prophecy who will be educated in his father's *virtus* and rule a world made peaceful *patriis virtutibus*:

The Sire saw, one by one, his Virtues wake . . .

and a little later,

> Intrepid then, o'er seas and lands he flew:
> Europe he saw, and Europe saw him too.

He saw Europe well enough, but he had an unfortunate gift for *being* seen. Because of his absurd escapades, the 'giddy Larum' of a show-off, he made a spectacle of himself. The neat inversion of words re-enforces the inversion of values: one goes to Europe to see and to learn, not to be seen and 'learnt about'. The order exactly parallels Virgil's in the line we noticed earlier:

> . . . divisque *videbit*
> permixtos heroas et ipse *videbitur* illis . . .

We may also be expected to hear the schoolboy tag, Caesar's *veni, vidi, vici*. These 'sources' are worth noting only because of what they 'do' and because of what Pope does with them. They sharpen the irony and deepen its import as we hear in echoing allusions the contrast of this so-called education with Roman heroism and with education in ancestral civic virtues. The picture of the youth's awkward folly is more than funny, since it brings out the perversion of an ideal descended from Rome to the Renaissance. The education of the hero, revived in the renaissance education of the prince,[1] has now come to this—a fool's progress through Europe.

The decadence is shared by Europe too, by France and Italy. The youth goes

> To where the Seine, obsequious as she runs,
> Pours at great Bourbon's feet her silken sons;
> Or Tyber, now no longer Roman, rolls,
> Vain of Italian Arts, Italian Souls:
> To happy Convents, bosom'd deep in vines,
> Where slumber Abbots, purple as their wines:
> To Isles of fragrance, lilly-silver'd vales,
> Diffusing languor in the panting gales:
> To lands of singing, or of dancing slaves,
> Love-whisp'ring woods, and lute-resounding waves.
> But chief her shrine where naked Venus keeps,
> And Cupids ride the Lyon of the Deeps;

---

[1] Cf. George B. Parks, 'Travel as Education', *The Seventeenth Century* (Stanford, 1951), pp. 264–90.

Where, eas'd of Fleets, the Adriatic main
Wafts the smooth Eunuch and enamour'd swain.
(297–310)

This marvellous child, like Virgil's, is being brought up in a
scene of exquisite natural beauty, a designed scene reminiscent of the Fourth *Eclogue*, but described in rhythm and
diction that recalls at many points Pope's early pastoral style.
Note, for example: 'Isles', 'silver', 'vales', and 'panting
gales', 'whisp'ring woods', and 'swain'; and think of the song
from *Summer*. In the *Pastorals* these words—so rich in their
amorous connotations—were used of an innocent love in
harmony with natural powers. Gales and lovers gently sighed
in unison. In ironic antithesis we now have the art of love
cultivated by this youngster in Venice, at the time a city of
dubious reputation, 'where naked Venus kept her shrine'.
But the Virgilian pastoral scene recalls an Italy once symbolic of perfection in nature, government, and manners,
where the Christian religion still has its central shrine:

Led by my hand, he saunter'd Europe round,
And gather'd ev'ry Vice on Christian ground . . .
(311–12)

We can now appreciate those *happy* convents, not happy
with spiritual content, but happy in more genial ways. There
is a larger irony in 'happy' that links Pope again with Virgil
and with values they both honoured. 'Happy' in the present
scene suggests the rich natural abundance of the Italian landscape,[1] of monasteries like Certosa del Galluzzo resting on
hills 'bosomed deep in vines'. But to eighteenth-century ears,
'happy' (when used in a scene of such 'Georgic' quality)
would recall Virgil's *laetus*, a word implying fruitfulness that
has been divinely bestowed. Hence the force of Pope's
'happy' in a landscape where the divine blessing is turned to
such uses.

So by a kind of parody of himself and other poets, Pope
weights his language with allusions to heroic, pastoral, and
georgic poetry. But he goes beyond and through allusion to
symbolize ideals of conduct and visions of Nature and society.
The allusions in this passage from the *Dunciad* point to an

[1] See Berkeley's idyllic descriptions of Italy, Let. I, pp. 222, 446.

ideal of humanist Christian culture which Pope sees so en-
trancingly corrupted. And it is to the charm that I want to
return, the song so lightly moralized that its seriousness cuts
into the deeper consciousness where the beautiful and the
good and the gay are inseparable and indistinguishable. The
simple shepherd's song has recovered some of its ancient
complexity.

II

THE WORLD'S GREAT AGE

magnus ab integro saeclorum nascitur ordo.
(Virgil, *Eclogue* iv)

THE vision of Virgil's Fourth *Eclogue*, though innocent and miraculous, is also of this world, for his Golden Age, the *Pax Augustana*, is to begin with the consulship of Pollio. If he sings of woods, the woods must honour a consul (*si canimus silvas, silvae sint consule dignae*). As the song strikes a higher note (*paulo maiora canamus!*), a strong voice,[1] less sweetly pastoral, emerges, especially in lines where Virgil sings of Roman heroic deeds and virtues. The tone of the eclogue is prophetically grand, marked by solemn addresses, by insistent alliteration and anaphora *te . . . te consule . . . te duce; alter erit tum Tiphys, et altera quae vehat Argo*, and by exclamatory commands: *adgredere o magnos . . . honores; aspice . . . aspice!* Dryden's version of the poem, though far from accurate, is true to this stronger tone:

> See, lab'ring Nature calls thee to sustain
> The nodding frame of heav'n, and earth, and main!
> See to their base restor'd, earth, seas, and air;
> And joyful ages, from behind, in crowding ranks appear.
>
> (60–63)

But since Virgil, unlike Dryden, enjoys some of Theocritus' freedom in reference and in tone, he can also speak with unaffected tenderness to the child now being born:

> Come, little one, greet your mother with a smile . . .
> Come, little one . . .
>
> incipe, parve puer, risu cognoscere matrem . . .
> incipe, parve puer . . .
>
> (60, 62)

Although Virgil's subject has its political aspect, his feeling for the child and the realm, *Saturnia regna*, is easily and

---

[1] I owe this phrase and the point to Mr. Charles Blyth.

simply religious. It is not strange that medieval readers of the poem heard the divine rather than the Roman note and that they saw in the eclogue a parallel to the prophecies of Isaiah.

It is not more strange that a youthful poet of the Roman persuasion, perhaps eager to assure his friends and family that he was more pious than they might suppose, should translate the *Pollio* in terms of Isaiah. At least that was his intention; the result often seems to illustrate the reverse process. The clue to Pope's characteristic modes in the *Messiah*—to disregard his models for a moment—is the 'iron harvest' of exclamation points that spring up as we run our eyes down the page. (There are some twenty of them in all; they are also added very freely in Pope's quotations from the King James version.) Apostrophes and grand imperatives set a tone of tireless and wearisome 'surprise':

> The swain in barren deserts with surprise
> Sees lilies spring, and sudden verdure rise . . .
> (67–68)

Unexpected combinations greet us everywhere:

> See lofty Lebanon his head advance,
> See nodding forests on the mountains dance . . .
> (25–26)

The mountains are not only 'exalted' and 'made low' as in *Isaiah*; they 'dance' and 'sink'. The rocks are commanded to be 'smooth' (not 'plain'); and an almost comic miracle is introduced from Ovid:

> And harmless serpents lick the pilgrim's feet.
> (80)

Descriptive epithets flourish, often with the effect of making startling contrasts still more startling. Many of the surprises are highly scenic:

> Waste sandy valleys, once perplexed with thorn,
> The spiry fir and shapely box adorn . . .
> (73–74)

The most splendid scene in the poem, the picture of the New

Jerusalem, gives a marvellous impression of secular pomp and circumstance:

> Rise, crowned with light, imperial Salem, rise!
> Exalt thy towery head, and lift thy eyes!
> See, a long race thy spacious courts adorn;
> See future sons, and daughters yet unborn,
> In crowding ranks on every side arise,
> Demanding life, impatient for the skies!
> See barb'rous nations at thy gates attend,
> Walk in thy light, and in thy temple bend;
> See thy bright altars thronged with prostrate kings,
> And heaped with products of Sabaean springs!
> For thee Idume's spicy forests blow,
> And seeds of gold in Ophir's mountains glow,
> See heaven its sparkling portals wide display,
> And break upon thee in a flood of day!
> No more the rising Sun shall gild the morn,
> Nor evening Cynthia fill her silver horn;
> But lost, dissolved in thy superior rays,
> One tide of glory, one unclouded blaze
> O'erflow thy courts: the light himself shall shine
> Revealed, and God's eternal day be thine!
>
> (85–104)

In Pope's remaking of Isaiah, the beginning of Christ's reign becomes a grand imperial triumph in a setting made glamorous with royal architecture, precious metals, and perfumes from exotic regions. The whole scene is bathed in dazzling light, and the reign is ushered in with cosmic and rhetorical fireworks after the manner of Dryden's *Song for St. Cecilia's Day*:

> The seas shall waste, the skies in smoke decay,
> Rocks fall to dust, and mountains melt away;
> But fixed his word, his saving power remains:
> Thy realm for ever lasts, thy own MESSIAH reigns!
>
> (105–8)

Throughout the passage, Isaiah is heard speaking in Virgil's prophetic Roman tone, and there are also echoes of the address to the Roman people and the hailing of *Marcellus* in *Aeneid* vi, lines that both Pope and Dryden imitated more than once:

tu regere imperio populos, Romane, memento . . .
'aspice, ut insignis spoliis Marcellus opimis
ingreditur . . .'

(851, 855–6)

The 'long race' to come, the 'barb'rous nations', the sacrifice
at 'bright altars' recall the Virgilian scenes and diction and
the whole atmosphere of a Roman celebration. Although the
passage is of course not simply secular, the Christianity it
portrays is of a most pompous Roman variety. It is the
Christianity expressed in the architectural and decorative
splendours of seventeenth-century 'Jesuit' churches with
their 'spacious courts', their bursts of golden light in altar
pieces and frescoes, their crowding and ascending figures
'impatient for the skies'.

If as Pope urges we compare his poem with Isaiah,[1] 'to
see how far the images and descriptions of the Prophet are
superior to those of the Poet [Virgil]' we see rather how
imitation of Virgil has transformed the religious attitudes of
the Prophet. Consider for comparison these verses from
Isaiah, chapter lx:

Arise, shine; for thy light is come, and the glory of the Lord is risen
upon thee . . .
And the Gentiles shall come to thy light, and kings to the brightness
of thy rising . . .
For brass I will bring gold, and for iron I will bring silver, and for
wood brass, and for stones iron: I will also make thy officers peace, and
thine exactors righteousness.
Violence shall no more be heard in thy land, wasting nor destruction
within thy borders; but thou shalt call thy walls Salvation, and thy
gates Praise.
The sun shall be no more thy light by day; neither for brightness

---

[1] The editors of the *Messiah*, TE i, point out in the notes to the poem some
nine or ten instances where Pope's phrasing is closer to the Douai Bible than to the
Authorized Version. For example they note his use of 'basilisk' in

The smiling infant in his hand shall take
The crested basilisk and speckled snake.

(81–82)

which may recall Isaiah xxx. 6 or Psalms xc. 13 in the Douai version. 'Often of
course the two versions are much alike, but Pope would appear to have searched
them both to find the word or phrase which would most "beautify his piece".' TE i.
102. Pope's quotations in his notes are, with slight variations, from the Authorized
Version.

shall the moon give light unto thee; but the Lord shall be unto thee an everlasting light, and thy God thy glory.

Thy sun shall no more go down; neither shall thy moon withdraw itself: for the Lord shall be thine everlasting light, and the days of thy mourning shall be ended.

(1, 3, 17–20)

The difference between Pope and Isaiah comes out most clearly in the way they talk of the divine light. Through most of Pope's description of the New Jerusalem the light that shines is the splendour of a brilliant city; only at the end is it clearly identified with deity. For Isaiah the light is at once and simply 'the glory of the Lord', and he does not need to insist with Pope that it is 'the Light *himself*'. For the prophet of Israel the victory over other peoples brings a solidly material glory,[1] the blessings of 'gold', 'silver', and 'iron'. Officers become 'peace', the 'exactors' 'righteousness', the 'walls' become 'Salvation', and the 'gates' 'Praise'. Isaiah— or at least his seventeenth-century translator—moves like the Metaphysical poets easily from material to spiritual and back again. A wall *is* Salvation; and the glory of the Lord *is* light. Only with something of an effort can we feel that the details of Pope's scene have spiritual meaning: it is all too startlingly beautiful. For Isaiah, 'The sun shall no more go down; neither shall thy moon withdraw itself; for the Lord shall be thine everlasting light. . .' For Pope:

> No more the rising Sun shall gild the morn,
> Nor evening Cynthia fill her silver horn;
> But lost, dissolved in thy superior rays,
> One tide of glory, one unclouded blaze
> O'erflow thy courts . . .

(99–103)

We are distracted from the divine power to scene and to wit. 'Lost, dissolved' heighten the wonder by suggesting a process much more challenging to the eye and the mind. 'Dissolved' is one of Dryden's words, and the 'Virgilian' style of the *Messiah* is Dryden's (and to a lesser degree, Milton's), the dazzling 'supernatural' manner of the odes honouring St. Cecilia and Anne Killigrew. Following Dryden, Pope can command Virgil's high public tone, but unlike Virgil he

[1] Compare the 'glory' of the hero in the *Iliad*, and see Ch. IV, pp. 91–92.

cannot make us feel a divine presence. There is no place in his poem for the tenderness of the Fourth *Eclogue* or of the ode *On the Morning of Christ's Nativity*. The child of the *Messiah* is more Roman than the Romans:

> Oh spring to light, auspicious Babe, be born!

For Virgil, like Isaiah, resting secure within a religious and poetic tradition in which there was a less complete division between personal and public, human and divine, secular and religious, it was possible to sing of these several worlds at once. But Pope is writing at a time when the kinds of experience like the 'kinds' of literature are being defined with increasing clarity. Having chosen (unconsciously, we must suppose) to celebrate the ceremonial grandeurs of ancient religion, pagan and Christian, he succeeds in expressing only that and little more. He puts on such a 'good show' that we begin to suspect that in composing this poem he had no profound or personal religious feeling to express.

Our uncomfortable feeling that in the *Messiah* the secular is being worked up as a substitute for the religious disappears when we turn to *Windsor Forest*, which Pope was revising during the year in which he wrote his Sacred Eclogue. He now transfers the New Jerusalem to the England of Queen Anne, with patriotic feeling replacing religious, but in doing so he is still imitating Virgil. For Virgil did not remain in the visionary world of the Fourth *Eclogue*, where 'earth does not feel the plow, nor the vine the pruning hook', but went on in the *Georgics* to write of farming in the old Italian way—of growing olives and grapes, of raising cattle, and tending bees. In effect, he domesticated the Golden Age in Augustan Italy. For Virgil, as for the poets of the eighteenth century, the step from pastoral to georgic was a short one.

Many years after *Windsor Forest*, Pope closed his ironic portrait of a tasteless gardener with a glimpse into the future where he saw 'laughing Ceres re-assume the land'. 'Laughing' recalls with a difference a word we have already noticed, one of the key words of the *Georgics*, *laetus*, 'happy' or 'joyous':

> Quid faciat laetas segetes, quo sidere terram
> vertere, Maecenas, ulmisque adiungere vitis

conveniat, quae cura boum, qui cultus habendo
sit pecori, apibus quanta experientia parcis,
hinc canere incipiam.

(1. 1–5)

Laetus as here, or as in *laetus ager* ('happy', cultivated land)
is used of land fruitful in its growth. (Dryden translates
'plenteous'.) But it also implies the lively happiness of land
animate with divine energy. A 'happy' land means, or should
mean, that a blessing rests on it. Hence the irony of Pope's
'laughing' in a context that reminds us of Timon's far from
godlike cultivation. This joyous growth of the land and of all
living creatures is inseparable for Virgil from work (*labor*),
tilling of the soil (*terram vertere*), careful tending of cattle
(*cura boum*), and looking after flocks (*cultus habendo pecori*).

Throughout the *Georgics* labour and joyous growth are
illumined by divine presences. In the invocation Virgil prays
to the sun and the moon, *vos, o clarissima mundi/lumina*, and
to Bacchus and kindly Ceres, *Liber et alma Ceres*, and to the
Fauns, deities who are vividly present to help the farmer,
agrestum praesentia numina. In a culture where heroes had
not quite lost their divinity, Virgil turns easily to address
Augustus as all but a god, the figure having some justification since Augustus had brought the farmers peace and was
now wisely encouraging their efforts to restore agriculture.
Virgil is expressing his gratitude for the peace of Augustus
and his hope for a renewal of the old country life of the period
before the civil wars.

In the *Georgics* the poetry of earth embraces religion and
love of country, politics, and history. Addison, introducing
Dryden's translation, writes admiringly of Virgil's skill in
combining these various themes, one arising 'insensibly' out
of the other. But as a correct Georgic poet Virgil does not
forget countrymen and their life: 'We should never quite
lose sight of the Country, though we are sometimes entertained with a distant prospect of it.' 'Sight' and 'prospect'
are very active words as Addison uses them here. The art of
making pictures is of the essence in 'this kind of Poetry': 'It
raises in our mind a pleasing variety of scenes and landscapes,
whilst it teaches us; and makes the dryest of its precepts
look like a description.'

The variety and beauty of the *Georgics* may be seen best in the great passage of Book II on the praise of Italy:

Sed neque Medorum silvae, ditissima terra,
nec pulcher Ganges atque auro turbidus Hermus
laudibus Italiae certent, non Bactra neque Indi
totaque turiferis Panchaia pinguis harenis.
haec loca non tauri spirantes naribus ignem
invertere satis immanis dentibus hydri,
nec galeis densisque virum seges horruit hastis;
sed gravidae fruges et Bacchi Massicus umor
implevere; tenent oleae armentaque laeta.
hinc bellator equus campo sese arduus infert,
hinc albi, Clitumne, greges et maxima taurus
victima, saepe tuo perfusi flumine sacro,
Romanos ad templa deum duxere triumphos.
hic ver adsiduum atque alienis mensibus aestas:
bis gravidae pecudes, bis pomis utilis arbos.
at rabidae tigres absunt et saeva leonum
semina, nec miseros fallunt aconita legentis,
nec rapit immensos orbis per humum neque tanto
squameus in spiram tractu se colligit anguis.
adde tot egregias urbes operumque laborem,
tot congesta manu praeruptis oppida saxis
fluminaque antiquos subterlabentia muros.
an mare quod supra memorem, quodque adluit infra?
anne lacus tantos? te, Lari maxime, teque,
fluctibus et fremitu adsurgens Benace marino?
an memorem portus Lucrinoque addita claustra
atque indignatum magnis stridoribus aequor,
Iulia qua ponto longe sonat unda refuso
Tyrrhenusque fretis immittitur aestus Avernis?
haec eadem argenti rivos aerisque metalla
ostendit venis atque auro plurima fluxit.
haec genus acre virum, Marsos pubemque Sabellam
adsuetumque malo Ligurem Volscosque verutos
extulit, haec Decios Marios magnosque Camillos,
Scipiadas duros bello et te, maxime Caesar,
qui nunc extremis Asiae iam victor in oris
imbellem avertis Romanis arcibus Indum.
salve, magna parens frugum, Saturnia tellus,
magna virum: tibi res antiquae laudis et artis
ingredior sanctos ausus recludere fontis,
Ascraeumque cano Romana per oppida carmen. (136–76)

Dryden's translation, though more 'descriptive', gives some impression of the splendour and *amor patriae* of the original:

> But neither Median woods (a plenteous land),
> Fair Ganges, Hermus rolling golden sand,
> Nor Bactria, nor the richer Indian fields,
> Nor all the gummy stores Arabia yields,
> Nor any foreign earth of greater name,
> Can with sweet Italy contend in fame. }
> No bulls whose nostrils breathe a living flame}
> Have turn'd our turf; no teeth of serpents here
> Were sown, an armed host and iron crop to bear.
> But fruitful vines, and the fat olive's freight,
> And harvests heavy with their fruitful weight,
> Adorn our fields; and on the cheerful green
> The grazing flocks and lowing herds are seen.
> The warrior horse, here bred, is taught to train;
> There flows Clitumnus thro' the flow'ry plain,
> Whose waves, for triumphs after prosp'rous war,
> The victim ox and snowy sheep prepare.
> Perpetual spring our happy climate sees:
> Twice breed the cattle, and twice bear the trees; }
> And summer suns recede by slow degrees.
>
> Our land is from the rage of tigers freed,
> Nor nourishes the lion's angry seed;
> Nor pois'nous aconite is here produc'd,
> Or grows unknown, or is, when known, refus'd;
> Nor in so vast a length our serpents glide,
> Or rais'd on such a spiry volume ride.
>
> Next add our cities of illustrious name,
> Their costly labor, and stupendous frame;
> Our forts on steepy hills, that far below
> See wanton streams in winding valleys flow;
> Our twofold seas, that, washing either side,
> A rich recruit of foreign stores provide;
> Our spacious lakes; thee, Larius, first; and next
> Benacus, with tempest'ous billows vex'd.
> Or shall I praise thy ports, or mention make
> Of the vast mound that binds the Lucrine lake?
> Or the disdainful sea, that, shut from thence,
> Roars round the structure, and invades the fence,
> There, where secure the Julian waters glide,
> Or where Avernus' jaws admit the Tyrrhene tide?

Our quarries, deep in earth, were fam'd of old
For veins of silver, and for ore of gold.
Th' inhabitants themselves their country grace:
Hence rose the Marsian and Sabellian race,
Strong-limb'd and stout, and to the wars inclin'd,
And hard Ligurians, a laborious kind,
And Volscians arm'd with iron-headed darts.
Besides, an offspring of undaunted hearts,
The Decii, Marii, great Camillus, came
From hence, and greater Scipio's double name;
And mighty Caesar, whose victorious arms
To farthest Asia carry fierce alarms,
Avert unwarlike Indians from his Rome,
Triumph abroad, secure our peace at home.
  Hail, sweet Saturnian soil! of fruitful grain
Great parent, greater of illustrious men!
For thee my tuneful accents will I raise,
And treat of arts disclos'd in ancient days;
Once more unlock for thee the sacred spring,
And old Ascraean verse in Roman cities sing.

(187–246)

Dryden rings nearly all the possible changes on Virgil's
laeta in

But *fruitful* vines, and the *fat* olive's *freight*,
And harvests *heavy* with their *fruitful weight*,
Adorn our fields; and on the *cheerful* green
The grazing flocks and lowing herds are seen.

That 'grave, succinct writer', as Dryden once called him,
had said *sed gravidae fruges et Bacchi Massicus umor | implevere;
tenent oleae armentaque laeta*. In the famous lines on the
Italian hill towns Dryden is picturesque, where Virgil is
visually accurate, making us feel the sharpness and height
of cliffs in contrast to the smooth-gliding embrace of the
rivers below.

As a whole the passage expresses most wonderfully
the magic richness and the historical depth of the Italian
landscape. Virgil's appreciation (as James might say) is
at once aesthetic and historic and religious, the force of the
impression being strengthened by the contrast with the rich

confusion of Oriental lands. In Italy all is tranquilly ordered, poetically as in fact by a scenic mode that stresses design through symmetry of rhythm and descriptive epithets. But Italy is also a country of vigorous and keen stock, *genus acre virum*, of men like the Scipios, hard fighters in battle, *duros bello*. To worship Italy is to honour such heroes, to see it as the land once ruled by Saturn, the primitive god of sowing and the god of the Golden Age,

> salve, magna parens frugum, Saturnia tellus,
> magna virum . . .

The exultant note of this address recurs in a later passage of the poem, where Virgil sings of the 'great spring' at the beginning of creation. The picture of the great spring has been carefully modulated to fit the facts of Italy's climate,

> hic ver adsiduum atque alienis mensibus aestas . . .
> Here it is always spring, and summer in months not its own.

The line takes us back to the earliest vision in European literature of an ideal nature, the gardens of Alcinous, as described in the incantatory verses of the *Odyssey*:

> There the tall trees grow luxuriantly,
> Pears and pomegranates and apples with gleaming fruit,
> And sweet figs and luxuriant olives;
> Of all these the fruit never spoils nor ceases
> Winter or summer, the whole year through . . .
> (VIII. 114–18)

From the lines on the old Corycian gardener in the *Georgics*, Book IV, it appears that Virgil had once thought of writing a poem on gardens. In telling over the names of flowers and fruits that the old man grew and in describing how he hurried on the spring and brought every blossom to fruition, Virgil imparts a magical quality to his gardener's art. The Corycian, who rivals kings in contentment, is the ideal pastoral figure in a new role: *regum aequabat opes animis*. With Pope he might say,

> Who sprung from kings shall know less joy than I.

Virgil sets the farmer above successful men of every sort,

senators and kings, soldiers and merchants, popular orators and dramatists:

> O fortunatos nimium, sua si bona norint,
> agricolas!

(II. 458–9)

With this apostrophe Virgil opens his grand praise of the countryman, a passage that closes with a picture of the farmer living in an idyllic scene of labour and fruitfulness and innocence. 'This was the life that Golden Saturn lived':

> aureus hanc vitam in terris Saturnus agebat . . .

(538)

Earlier Virgil had said,

> From hence Astraea took her flight; and here
> The prints of her departing steps appear.
>
> Dryden (671–2)

By recalling so exactly the prophecy of the *Pollio* Virgil was able to bring the Golden Age home to his Roman contemporaries. In the same passage Virgil links the countryman's life with the ideal life of the poet-intellectual, an ideal that embraced literature and music, science and philosophy, all the gifts of the Muses. It is almost impossible to convey in English the deep longing and religious feeling of Virgil's prayer:

> Me vero primum dulces ante omnia Musae,
> quarum sacra fero ingenti percussus amore,
> accipiant . . .

(475–7)

Milton catches the warmth of the desire in

> . . . Yet not the more
> Cease I to wander where the Muses haunt
> Clear Spring, or shadie Grove, or sunnie hill,
> Smit with the love of sacred Song . . .

Dryden does very well with the poet's 'just petition' to understand the movements of the stars; and praise of the 'Lucretian' philosopher comes naturally to him, but Virgil's longing for the country turns into a cosy 'petition for an absolute retreat':

> Give me the ways of wand'ring stars to know,
> The depths of heav'n above, and earth below:

Teach me the various labors of the moon,
And whence proceed th' eclipses of the sun;
Why flowing tides prevail upon the main,
And in what dark recess they shrink again;
What shakes the solid earth; what cause delays
The summer nights, and shortens winter days.
But, if my heavy blood restrain the flight ⎫
Of my free soul, aspiring to the height   ⎬
Of nature, and unclouded fields of light, ⎭
My next desire is, void of care and strife,
To lead a soft, secure, inglorious life—
A country cottage near a crystal flood,
A winding valley, and a lofty wood.
Some god conduct me to the sacred shades
Where Bacchanals are sung by Spartan maids,
Or lift me high to Haemus' hilly crown,
Or in the plains of Tempe lay me down,
Or lead me to some solitary place,
And cover my retreat from human race!
　Happy the man, who, studying nature's laws,
Thro' known effects can trace the secret cause;
His mind possessing in a quiet state,
Fearless of fortune, and resign'd to fate!

(677–701)

'With the simple and elemental passions, as they spring separate in the mind', Johnson observed in his *Life* of Dryden, 'he seems not much acquainted . . .' He characteristically passes over the important word in Virgil's lines, 'love', *ingenti percussus* amore . . . *flumina* amem *silvasque inglorius*. Virgil prays that if he cannot become a poet-scientist, he may at least love and celebrate the country in song. (*Amem* includes both meanings.) Virgil temperately limits his aim, but he is not merely temperate. For a moment, at least, he longs to escape from sequestered vales to scenes of bacchic frenzy or the frigid valleys of Thrace and the deep darkness of forests. But after praising the philosopher who can see into Nature's laws, *rerum causas*, and rise above the fear of death, he returns to more moderate satisfactions:

Happy too the man who knows the country gods,
Pan and old Sylvanus and the sister Nymphs.

fortunatus et ille deos qui novit agrestis
Panaque Silvanumque senem Nymphasque sorores.

(493–4)

Though the ideal poet of Nature is a man who combines
science with high philosophy, Virgil sees his own role as
more modest. He will sing of what he knows and loves and
reveres, he will be a poet of 'natural religion' in its least
sophisticated form.

Pope underlined the pastoral quality of *Windsor Forest* at
the start by using as an epigraph lines (somewhat altered)
from Virgil's Sixth *Eclogue*. He ended the poem, in the
earliest as in later versions, with an imitation of the closing
lines of the *Georgics*:

> My humble Muse, in unambitious strains,
> Paints the green forests and the flowery plains,
> Where Peace descending bids her olives spring,
> And scatters blessings from her dovelike wing.
> Even I more sweetly pass my careless days,
> Pleased in the silent shade with empty praise;
> Enough for me, that to the list'ning swains
> First in these fields I sung the sylvan strains.

(427–34)

The allusion—youthfully ostentatious—implies that *Windsor
Forest* is the poet's georgic phase, perhaps with the added
suggestion that an *Aeneid* is coming next. Without taking
either of these hints too seriously, an eighteenth-century
reader would rightly feel that the first was not quite preposterous. For Pope's public the reference to Virgil as a
model for a poetic career was almost instinctive, particularly
since Dryden had so recently renewed the Renaissance image
of Virgil by his criticism and translation. As a contemporary
Virgilian imitator might put it, he was a 'present deity' in the
realm of poetry. Moreover, the *Georgics* occupied a unique
position, as the perfect poem, the finest example of poetic
craftsmanship in ancient literature. Although Pope was fond
of praising Homer's 'fire', the temper of his own poetry,
especially in the earlier years, was more Virgilian than
Homeric. In *The Temple of Fame*,[1] he says nothing very

---

[1] See below, Ch. X, pp. 354–5.

precise about the poetry of Homer, while he characterizes Virgil with a fine sense of his style and feeling. Pope's comment on Virgil to Spence[1] is perfectly apt and one of the wisest comments ever made on poetic intention: '. . . so constant an effect could not be the effect of chance.' The remark would fit equally Pope's own works and habits of composition.[2]

Windsor Forest is certainly not a georgic in the strict sense of Addison's definition, '. . . some part of the science of husbandry put into a pleasing dress, and set off with all the Beauties and Embellishments of Poetry'. But the *Georgics* of Virgil was not so purely georgic. In addition to 'husbandry', the poem finds a place for history, astronomy, meteorology, and decorative mythical tales. In the eighteenth century it was possible to write within the georgic convention[3] on almost any subject from the culture of silkworms to navigation, to philosophy and divinity. The indispensable features of the genre seem to have been a country setting and instruction in some art, but a 'georgic' could in fact have one feature without the other: for example, Gay's *Trivia* and Thomson's *Seasons*. During the century, notably after 1750, the purer georgic tended to coalesce with poetry of local description and with didactive verse of every sort. *The Seasons*, which *Windsor Forest* anticipates in its miniature sketch of seasonal sports, is the classic example of the mélange that may be labelled as 'eighteenth-century georgic' or 'didactive-descriptive' poetry. Although *Cooper's Hill* is usually considered the model for *Windsor Forest*, and though Pope learned from Addison's *Campaign*, his poem has a character and uses motifs that ally it more closely with the Virgilian georgic than with the poetry of places and historical events. Passages most surely related to the Virgilian tradition existed in the original version, and if the Peace of Utrecht gave an excuse for enlarging and revising the poem, the occasion simply helped

[1] Joseph Spence, *Anecdotes* (London, 1820), p. 24. Quoted in Robert M. Schmitz, *Pope's 'Windsor Forest' 1712, A Study of the Washington University Holograph* (Saint Louis, 1952), p. 65.

[2] George Sherburn, 'Pope at Work', *Essays on the Eighteenth Century*, Presented to D. Nichol Smith (Oxford, 1945), pp. 49–64.

[3] For the variety of topics and types see M. L. Lilly, *The Georgic* (Baltimore, 1915), pp. 13–18, 24–50, and Dwight L. Durling, *The Georgic Tradition in English Poetry* (New York, 1935), pp. x, 59, 192–206.

Pope to focus on the subject implicit in the parts he had written earlier, the 'peace and plenty' of England.

The imaginative design of the poem (in contrast to any superficial conformity to an established genre) and the quality of the poetry are distinctly Pope's and represent a natural development from the *Pastorals*. After the brief invocation comes the description of Windsor, the purest of 'designed scenes' in Pope's verse, a garden-picture with lights, shadows, and colours in symmetrical 'composition' and with mythological figures that blend harmoniously into the background. The literary history implied by the scene, and Pope's connexion with it, is fairly complex. Back of Windsor's groves are the 'groves of Eden' sung by Milton, which Pope half hopes to equal; and the ancestry of Milton's sylvan scene includes among other paradises the gardens of Alcinous. In Eden, too,

> Blossoms and Fruits at once of gold'n hue
> Appeerd, with gay enameld colours mixt . . .

A little more than six months after *Windsor Forest* came out, Pope published his famous essay on the 'natural' style in gardens. He introduces his grand examples of the style with some remarks[1] that throw light on *Windsor Forest* and later poems:

The two most celebrated Wits of the World have each of them left us a particular Picture of a Garden; wherein those great Masters, being wholly unconfined, and Painting at Pleasure, may be thought to have given a full Idea of what they esteemed most excellent in this way. These (one may observe) consist intirely of the useful Part of Horticulture, Fruit Trees, Herbs, Water *etc.* The Pieces I am speaking of are *Virgil's* Account of the Garden of the old *Corycian*, and *Homer's* of that of *Alcinous*.

The stress on 'Painting' and on 'the useful Part of Horticulture' are especially worth noting. Following these remarks he presents the reader with his own translation of the passage from the Odyssey. The opening lines show how Pope paints in items taken from the original:

> Close to the Gates a spacious Garden lies,
> From Storms defended and inclement Skies:

---

[1] *Guardian*, no. 173, 29 September 1713. The text is reprinted from *The Prose Works of Alexander Pope*, ed. Norman Ault, vol. i (Oxford, 1936), pp. 146–7.

Four Acres was th' allotted Space of Ground,
Fenc'd with a green Enclosure all around.
Tall thriving Trees confest the fruitful Mold;
The red'ning Apple ripens here to Gold,
Here the blue Figg with luscious Juice o'erflows,
With deeper Red the full Pomegranate glows,
The Branch here bends beneath the weighty Pear,
And verdant Olives flourish round the Year.

The balmy Spirit of the Western Gale
Eternal breathes on Fruits untaught to fail:
Each dropping Pear a following Pear supplies,
On Apples Apples, Figs on Figs arise:
The same mild Season gives the Blooms to blow,
The Buds to harden, and the Fruits to grow.

Here order'd Vines in equal Ranks appear
With all th' United Labours of the Year,
Some to unload the fertile Branches run,
Some dry the black'ning Clusters in the Sun,
Others to tread the liquid Harvest join,
The groaning Presses foam with Floods of Wine.
Here are the Vines in early Flow'r descry'd,
Here Grapes discolour'd on the sunny Side,
And there in Autumn's richest Purple dy'd.
Beds of all various Herbs, for ever green,
In beauteous Order terminate the Scene.

The glowing, luscious quality of the picture is nearly all
Pope's; every one of the words for colour, all the suggested
'tactile values' are his, too. The visual and rhythmic symmetry comes from Homer, and the order that Pope stresses
belongs to the original scene, but characteristically Pope has
abstracted it and given it a generalized, almost Platonic expression:

Beds of all various Herbs, for ever green,
In beauteous Order terminate the Scene.

This strong feeling for order and the fondness for 'painting' had their influence on the design and the sensuous
qualities of *Windsor Forest*. But aesthetic preferences happily
coincided with interests of another kind. Like the *Georgics*,
Windsor Forest is the poem of a generation that had lively
memories of a revolutionary period and that after long if
glorious wars was becoming almost obsessively attached to

peace. The large design and the principal themes of *Windsor Forest* are anticipated in the *Georgics*. In both poems there are phases of peace and order set in contrast with ruin and disorder. Pope had less to say of the horrors of war, since he was even more removed from the actualities than Virgil; and as a historian, he is at times amusingly inaccurate and inconsistent, as in his account of William I and his successors.

Like Virgil, he is happiest in writing of peace, and much of the poem is a series of composed pictures on this theme. In comparison with the *Georgics* the sheer amount of description and the pictorial quality of the diction are notable. Although the 'designed scene' of the neo-classical pastoral had its sanction in the *Eclogues*, eighteenth-century poets and critics gave much more importance to this element in pastoral poetry. There are many lively pictures in the *Georgics*, but most of them, like the passing glimpse of the Italian hill-towns, are vignettes that come in the course of the poet's 'instruction', while he is explaining how to read the clouds, or how to plant crops or choose a home for the bees, or what trees to select and how to graft them. The parallel of poetry and painting, *ut pictura poesis*, made both Addison and Dryden see more description in Virgil than we can see. Writing under their influence, Pope shows in *Windsor Forest* the effect on English country poetry of this reading of Virgil. The scenes of the poem also show the effect of the ideal painter's landscape that Pope and his contemporaries especially admired. Claude, the chief inventor of the style, had arrived through attentive study of the Roman Campagna at a kind of 'ideally composed landscape', a type of view that became for poets and painters almost synonymous with 'paradise'.[1] The landscapes of Claude, Kenneth Clark has said, are themselves full of 'the Virgilian spirit':

. . . the Virgilian element in Claude is, above all, his sense of a Golden Age, of grazing flocks, unruffled waters and a calm, luminous sky, images of perfect harmony between man and nature, but touched, as he combines them, with a Mozartian wistfulness, as if he knew that this perfection could last no longer than the moment in which it takes possession of our minds.[2]

[1] Christopher Hussey, *The Picturesque: Studies in a Point of View* (London, 1927), p. 25.
[2] Kenneth Clark, *Landscape into Art*, Pelican Books (London, 1956), pp. 77–78.

Windsor Forest gives clear evidence of Pope's interest in painting at this period of his life. During the year in which the poem appeared he was living with his artist-friend Jervas, making his most serious attempt to become a painter.

However slight may have been the influence of particular artists or painting techniques, *Windsor Forest* is rich in scenes that are proof of the painter's eye, from the Claude-like prospect of the Windsor-Eden to the glowing Breughelesque embroidery of the dying pheasant and the 'watery landscape' seen in the nymph Lodona's 'glass':

> Oft in her glass the musing shepherd spies
> The headlong mountains and the downward skies,
> The watery landscape of the pendant woods,
> And absent trees that tremble in the floods;
> In the clear azure gleam the flocks are seen,
> And floating forests paint the waves with green,
> Through the fair scene roll slow the ling'ring streams,
> Then foaming pour along, and rush into the Thames.
>
> (211–18)

(The later picture of the Thames and other river-gods is reminiscent of baroque fountains in the style of Bernini.) 'Paint' is a characteristic word in these scenes, all of which are compositions in light and shade, or in points and patches of colour, the language being finely suggestive of harmonious effects, though not always exact in reference. Note, for example, the subdued gloom running through the images in the description of Windsor: 'russet plain', 'bluish hills', 'Purple dyes', 'sable waste'. (That they are drawn from poetic diction doesn't matter; the point is that Pope selected and combined these particular phrases.) The colours in the picture of the pheasant are not altogether accurate, as Elwin points out with characteristic generosity:

> In transferring the expression ['painted wings', from *Paradise Lost*], he [Pope] overlooked the fact that the wings are not the part of the pheasant to which the epithet 'painted' is especially applicable.

Pope was looking elsewhere, not at the bird, but at a picture, a picture in language consecrated to such descriptive uses through literary tradition, since 'painted' goes back via Milton and via Dryden's translation to the *pictae volucres* of the

Georgics. The pheasant viewed as a dying hero recalls the dying ox in the third book of the *Georgics* (515–25). 'Ah! what avail his glossy varying dyes' echoes Virgil's 'quid labor aut benefacta iuvant?' The revision of a single adjective in the enamelled beauties of the 'various race' of fish again makes it clear that Pope's eye was on artful colouring, not on zoology. In the 1712 text,[1] the eel was very eel-like:

> The silver Eel in slimy Volumes roll'd.

Happily for the reader, if not for the ichthyologist, Pope changed the line to

> The silver Eel in shining Volumes roll'd.

The change is not surprising in a poet who was something of a painter and whose view of nature and of poetry emphasized the 'great shew', the large design, rather than minute accuracy to fact.[2] For Pope and his contemporaries, 'design', whether referred to the stars or to gardens, was a painter-draughtsman's metaphor. While Pope saw the value for verbal 'painting' of 'small circumstances', he was interested in the idea represented by the image, in the larger truth implied by the particular. Or, to put it plainly, Pope is a poet: the image is intensely and precisely *seen*, but it is valued also for its implication of 'general truth'. Poetry in any complete sense of the word cannot be merely general, or merely descriptive of minute particulars. The initial prospect in *Windsor Forest* gives more than a hint of the great order, where

> . . . earth and waters seem to strive again;
> Not Chaos-like together crushed and bruised,
> But, as the world, harmoniously confused:
> Where order in variety we see,
> And where, though all things differ, all agree.
>
> (12–16)

Pope's ideal poet of nature—also the poetic ideal he comes closest to realizing at this point in his career—appears in a passage that is a happy transcription of Virgil:

> Happy the man whom this bright court approves,
> His Sovereign favours, and his Country loves:

[1] Schmitz, p. 58.
[2] George Sherburn, 'The Great Shew of Nature', *The Seventeenth Century* (Stanford, 1951), pp. 306–15.

Happy next him, who to these shades retires,
Whom Nature charms, and whom the Muse inspires:
Whom humbler joys of home-felt quiet please,
Successive study, exercise, and ease.
He gathers health from herbs the forest yields,
And of their fragrant physic spoils the fields:
With chymic art exalts the mineral powers,
And draws the aromatic souls of flowers:
Now marks the course of rolling orbs on high:
O'er figured worlds now travels with his eye;
Of ancient writ unlocks the learnèd store,
Consults the dead, and lives past ages o'er:
Or wand'ring thoughtful in the silent wood,
Attends the duties of the wise and good,
T' observe a mean, be to himself a friend,
To follow nature, and regard his end;
Or looks on heaven with more than mortal eyes,
Bids his free soul expatiate in the skies,
Amid her kindred stars familiar roam,
Survey the region, and confess her home!

(235–56)

Certain strains and modes of expression, such as the theme of 'inglorious' retreat and the exclamatory yet restrained forms of address, are taken over quite directly from Virgil. But Pope acclimatizes his borrowed themes by introducing parallels and variations that belong to contemporary classical and 'enlightened' culture. For an eighteenth-century poet, the *secura quies* of Virgil merges easily with the moderate vision of Horace's and Milton's meditating scholar-poet. The poet's 'philosophy', recalling also Lucan's *sequere Naturam*, is stoic and ethical, not Lucretian as in Virgil, since his soul is not eagerly inquiring into the nature of things but 'expatiating' in familiar territory.

The science, amusingly enough, is of the eighteenth-century virtuoso type that Pope ridicules in the *Dunciad*, though transformed here by wit reminiscent of the seventeenth century,

> With chymic art exalts the mineral powers,
> And draws the aromatic souls of flowers . . .

a couplet that Pope was later to make more truly Metaphysical.[1]

[1] Cf. Ch. VII. ii, p. 220.

The poet-meditator of *Windsor Forest* is a thoughtful wanderer *among* different sorts of knowledge and *among* natural things, and his flight into nature and toward the divine is an even more moderate ascent than that of the soul in Lady Winchilsea's *Petition for an Absolute Retreat*. The 'kindred stars' are quite ambiguous, perhaps little more than a metaphor for Heaven. Contrary to what we might expect, the ancient poet gives a keener sense than the modern of closeness to unspoiled nature, of a desire to live in loving though definitely not mystical intimacy with it. When Pope longs for 'sequestered scenes', 'bowery mazes', and 'surrounding greens', we see that nature had indeed become a garden in a sense unknown to the Greeks and Romans. This cultivated garden imagery introduces the most awkward moment in the poem, Pope's attempt (after Virgil) to introduce his poet friends into the pastoral scene. The English names obstinately resist his efforts, and the clumsiness of his allusion to the young Marcellus is a fairly good sign that the imitation is deliberate and forced.

But there are glimpses of violence in this other Eden, especially in the hunting scenes, passages of Virgilian sensibility that show the poet in a truly Virgilian dilemma. Pope can 'do up' a spirited picture of the chase, much as he can 'do up' ceremonies in temples and courts, but he betrays far too much tenderness for the victims:

> Oft, as in airy rings they skim the heath,
> The clam'rous lapwings feel the leaden death:
> Oft, as the mounting larks their notes prepare,
> They fall, and leave their little lives in air.
>
> (131–4)

It is one of the paradoxes of *Windsor Forest* and of English country life that one of the chief activities in peace is mimic war: but in Pope as in Virgil hunters and conquerors do not come off as well as they should. Sympathy, humour, and unforced love of natural things keep coming out in tiny mythological *aperçus*:

> And lonely woodcocks haunt the watery glade . . .
> And pikes, the tyrants of the watery plains . . .
> The Loddon slow, with verdant alders crowned . . .
> And sullen Mole, that hides his diving flood . . .

As in the *Pastorals* Pope shows a gift for naïve mythologizing of a kind rare in eighteenth-century imitators of Virgil. The myth-making of the average georgic poet of Pope's time is described by A. R. Humphreys with some exaggeration, but with live appreciation of Virgil's special quality:

> The anthropomorphism of the *Georgics* is in the genuine Latin manner—mature, unaffected, simply and dramatically descriptive: that of English imitations (and translations—Dryden's version of the Fourth, for example) is stilted, artificial, explicit, and melodramatic.[1]

But nothing can save the story of the river nymph Lodona from Dr. Johnson's dismissal: 'a new metamorphosis is a ready and puerile expedient.' As Johnson's comment implies, this Ovidian set piece was already old-fashioned, a survival from the age of Dryden's *Fables*, a type of wholly serious mythological tale that Pope never introduced into any of his later poems. There is also in *Windsor Forest* something of Virgil's spontaneous natural religion, although the Virgilian attitude is constantly in danger of being over-shadowed by Nature's mighty plan.

How does Pope's poem fare in relation to Virgil's deeply felt love of the nation, perhaps the most genuine of Roman religions? Here Pope comes off fairly well since the time and his own temper favoured expression of patriotic feeling that was vigorous and yet self-respecting. But the stress on the patriotic theme in the poem as revised to celebrate the Peace of Utrecht led Pope into a curious bit of eighteenth-century harmonizing of values. As the reader may have noticed, the passage on the fortunate poet-philosopher is introduced in a rather odd fashion:

> Happy the man whom this bright court approves,
> His Sovereign favours, and his Country loves:
> Happy next him, who to these shades retires,
> Whom Nature charms, and whom the Muse inspires . . .

Giving the second place to the poet was probably less jarring to the more robust citizen of eighteenth-century London

---

[1] 'A Classical Education and Eighteenth-Century Poetry', *Scrutiny*, viii. 205.

than to twentieth-century intellectuals, but the praise of retirement in the lines immediately following is so enthusiastic
that we distrust Pope's 'Happy *next* him'. The first of these
two couplets, we learn,[1] was added during the revision of the
poem, perhaps in deference to Pope's friends and advisers,
and the second was altered from a more naïve and certainly
less melodious version:

> Happy the Man who to the Shade retires,
> But doubly happy, if the Muse inspires!

But we feel no uneasiness or doubts in the address to
'Albion's golden days' with which the poem ends. The assurance and the splendour of this passage and of the earlier lines
on England's 'peace and Plenty' show how successfully Pope
renewed the Virgilian prophecy in the new Augustan Age.
We feel as in *Absalom and Achitophel* that the occasion for
which the poet had been waiting has come and with it a new
boldness of tone and an enlargement of rhythm not unlike
Dryden's 'long majestic march, and energy divine'. We
recognize the tone of public patriotic address inherited by
the Augustans from Dryden and Virgil, and in the 'hails' and
'beholds' we hear again the *salve*'s and *aspice*'s of the Second
Georgic and the *Pollio*. The imagery in its activity and
strength is very different from the sweetness and pictur-
esqueness of the earlier more pastoral scenes of the poem.
With the opening lines,

> Hail, sacred peace! hail, long-expected days,
> That Thames's glory to the stars shall raise!
> Though Tiber's streams immortal Rome behold,
> Though foaming Hermus swells with tides of gold . . .
>
> (355–8)

it is clear enough that both the tone and the quality of
imagery were suggested by Virgil. The salute to peace
begins like the praise of Italy in the *Georgics* with a picture of
the contrasting riches of other lands, and the line,

> Though foaming Hermus swells with tides of gold . . .

is a beautiful rendering of

> nec pulcher Ganges atque auro turbidus Hermus . . .

[1] Schmitz, pp. 6–10, 35 (notes ad loc.).

From this line to the end of the passage the salient images are of expansive growth and energy, of glowing gold and red, brightness and metallic glitter. We are reminded of Virgil's 'strong' images, of the 'grape glowing red', *rubens uva*, and the 'tough oaks sweating dew-like honey', *durae quercus sudabunt roscida mella*. At one point the effect is surprisingly close in theme and texture to a famous passage in Keats's *Isabella*:

> For me the balm shall bleed, and amber flow,
> The coral redden, and the ruby glow,
> The pearly shell its lucid globe infold,
> And Phoebus warm the ripening ore to gold.

'All this juice and all this joy', like Hopkins'

> A strain of the earth's sweet being in the beginning
> In Eden garden . . .

is not simply descriptive, but expressive of a noble vision that goes well beyond eighteenth-century Britain. There were in 1714 legitimate grounds for national pride in the victories of Marlborough, in England's replacing France as the first power of Europe, in her mercantile wealth, her sea power and her extensive possessions. But Pope (again he resembles Virgil) rose above the facts to a vision of all nations joined by the seas, of imagination enriched by the knowledge of remote peoples and places, of a world without slavery and subject peoples:

> The time shall come, when, free as seas or wind,
> Unbounded Thames shall flow for all mankind,
> Whole nations enter with each swelling tide,
> And seas but join the regions they divide;
> Earth's distant ends our glory shall behold,
> And the new world launch forth to seek the old.
> Then ships of uncouth form shall stem the tide,
> And feathered people crowd my wealthy side,
> And naked youths and painted chiefs admire
> Our speech, our colour, and our strange attire!
> O stretch thy reign, fair Peace! from shore to shore,
> Till Conquest cease, and Slavery be no more;
> Till the freed Indians in their native groves
> Reap their own fruits, and woo their sable loves,
> Peru once more a race of kings behold,
> And other Mexico's be roofed with gold.

Exiled by thee from earth to deepest hell,
In brazen bonds shall barb'rous Discord dwell;
Gigantic Pride, pale Terror, gloomy Care,
And mad Ambition, shall attend her there:
There purple Vengeance bathed in gore retires,
Her weapons blunted, and extinct her fires:
There hateful Envy her own snakes shall feel,
And Persecution mourn her broken wheel:
There Faction roar, Rebellion bite her chain,
And gasping Furies thirst for blood in vain.

(397–422)

The allegorical figures of the conclusion, which in some
details recall similar figures from the *Aeneid*, come to life like
Virgil's in dramatic gesture and symbolic image. Throughout the passage as in the better parts of the poem the mythological painter's eye is at work in the service of ideas. In
contrast with the *Pastorals*, there are some ideas worthy of
the name, and they matter to the poet and his audience. The
scenes of perfect tranquillity, of Saturn's golden reign, of the
garden paradise, and the new Jerusalem are symbolic of
triumphant England and a world at peace, but they are also
the visions of a young man and a poet. Like contemporary
'world-makers', such as William Whiston, who excited him
so much, Pope sweeps on easily from here and now to the
millennium.

Perhaps we are inclined to smile when we set Pope's
picture beside the grimmer realities of the Tory Peace—the
betrayal of the Dutch and the Catalans, the ugly rivalry of
Oxford and Bolingbroke, the secret bargaining with France
and the Jacobites. But it is equally easy to smile at the contrast between Virgil's *Pax Augustana* and the actualities
hinted at in Gibbon's portrait of Augustus. The Rome of
the late Republic was probably less remote from the ideal in
effective power than the England of Anne, and yet, as Trevelyan makes clear, England had in 1714 arrived at the
point where her history as a Great Power begins: 'The wars
of Marlborough and the Treaty of Utrecht had secured the
greatness of England . . .' And Bolingbroke plays the role
of Augustus in this smaller scene:

. . . he stands in history as the man who, by courses however devious and questionable, negotiated a Peace which proved in the working more satisfactory than any other that has ended a general European conflict in modern times.[1]

But as a poet-prophet Pope was justified by the event more certainly and sooner than most dreamers. The leadership of Pitt, one of Pope's 'patriot' friends in later years, and the victories of Wolfe made it clear that England was to arrive, and grandly, as an imperial power, and to give the world a Pax Britannica of which the Augustan dream was the tiny and amusing model. But that 'deed of gift was many deeds of war'. As prophecy, Pope's poem like Virgil's improved with age: the Roman empire came much closer to fulfilling Augustus' grandiose schemes than he had any right to expect. There had been dictators and Caesars before Augustus, but the Fortuna Romae seemed to have waited to bless this particular one. A fragmentary inscription in the ancient temple of Fortune at Praeneste, now Palestrina, symbolizes the connexion in two unforgettable words: PACI AUGUSTI.

Windsor Forest, partly because of its youthful exaggerations, renewed the myth of the Roman Augustan Age in the England of Anne. Like other myths, it owes its validity to having a toe-hold in fact, though of course it goes preposterously beyond fact. But also like other beliefs expressed in symbol, the Augustan myth enhanced and dignified a way of life. Probably few in England,[2] outside the polite circles of London, were conscious of the analogy, and even those—notably Pope and Swift—could smile ruefully at the contrast between the reality and the dream. The dream had its main influence in the next generation, on Wolfe and Burke, on Pope's friends Pitt and Murray, on Gibbon and Dr. Johnson, as one of the great ideas that shaped their complex sense of past and present and of their personal role in memorable scenes. We remember Wolfe, the general of Pitt's choice, going down the St. Lawrence and reciting Gray's *Elegy*, or Gibbon on the steps of Ara Coeli as gestures symbolic of a culture informed by a noble historical image.

For the study of Pope's poetry and of the Virgilian

[1] G. M. Trevelyan, *England Under Queen Anne*, vol. iii, *The Peace and the Protestant Succession* (London, 1934), pp. 229–30.
[2] W. L. MacDonald, *Pope and His Critics* (London, 1951), 'Augusta', pp. 3–12.

tradition of the Golden Age, the more successful passages of *Windsor Forest*, especially the scenes of garden beauty and peaceful activity, have a more strictly literary interest. Comparison with the *Messiah* shows clearly enough that reliance on a particular literary tradition may be more or less justified, and the differences that come out between the two poems are proofs also of Pope's growth as a poet. In *Windsor Forest*, the hailings and hyperboles, the exotic splendours of an earthly paradise, are sufficiently anchored in historical and geographic fact and have some appropriateness to the actual and the poetic occasion. We are not disturbed by the suspicion that the poet is expressing one sort of glory while protesting that he is interested in another. In *Windsor Forest* when religious feeling is asked for, we feel that the demand is fairly made. Peace is a mysterious and sacred thing to the eye that sees in England's landscape an order at once aesthetic and patriotic and philosophic. Pope was not to see Nature or England quite like this again, at least not without some qualifying irony. But the image of a peaceful golden age and of a georgic landscape retains its power as picture and as norm in much of Pope's later poetry. The *Essay on Man*, as Sherburn has said, did not end with the millennium we might have expected, but the *Dunciad* did—though with a difference.

III

HEROIC LOVE

> . . . and then, what's brave, what's noble,
> Let's do it after the high Roman fashion
> And make death proud to take us.
> *(Antony and Cleopatra)*

POPE's *Elegy to the Memory of an Unfortunate Lady* begins in a way that has puzzled many readers:

> What beck'ning ghost, along the moonlight shade
> Invites my step, and points to yonder glade?
> 'Tis she!—but why that bleeding bosom gor'd,
> Why dimly gleams the visionary sword?
> Oh ever beauteous, ever friendly! tell,
> Is it, in heav'n, a crime to love too well?
> To bear too tender, or too firm a heart,
> To act a Lover's or a *Roman's* part?
> Is there no bright reversion in the sky,
> For those who greatly think, or bravely die?

The 'facts' in this opening passage and in the rest of the poem are not clear and will probably always remain unclear. The central fact of the lady's suicide is hinted at only in an oblique allusion, and as Johnson says with pardonable irritation, '. . . the tale is not skilfully told; it is not easy to discover the character of either the Lady or her Guardian'. A more important puzzle arises from our uncertainty as to Pope's tone and how we are to take it at various points in the poem. The first clear clue lies in 'a *Roman's* part'. We are expected to be familiar with the kind of poetic address suggested by this and similar phrases ('the noblest Roman of them all', 'the high Roman fashion'). We probably should feel too some vague reference to the theatre in the questions and exclamations and the setting, and in the unlikely event that we have read the tragedies of Rowe, we can be sure that our instinct was right. But the fine surprise of 'no bright reversion in the sky' does not seem properly solemn for such

a tragedy. The clue to the tone is again in 'a Roman's part',
and in the word '*Elegy*', which Pope substituted in 1736 for
'Verses'. It might be said that critics have paid too little
attention to the first word of the title, and too much to the
last two. Whether like Johnson they have regarded the lady
as 'a raving girl', or like Warton, as truly pathetic, they have
thought more of the 'real' woman than the poetic one. Who
she was outside the poem (if she existed) will perhaps never
be known, but in the poem she is cast as a Roman lover, and
the accent of the poet in addressing her is Roman-elegiac.
The frequent rhetorical questions, the exclamations, and the
antithetical shock of 'bright reversion' suggest Ovid rather
than Tibullus or Propertius and Ovid's voice in the *Heroides*
or in the more elegiac passages of the *Metamorphoses*. It seems
likely that the *Elegy* was written in 1717, the year in which
Pope was completing his own heroic epistle, *Eloisa to
Abelard*. The years 1716 and 1717 were, for Pope, an
'Ovidian' time, faintly amorous and self-consciously melancholy. The forced, highly literary character of his moods can
be judged from his letters to Martha Blount and to Lady
Mary Wortley Montagu, two loves who might well have
inspired some rather wry sorrow.

It is undoubtedly true, as Dr. Leavis' reading of the
Elegy suggests, that the wit of the poem goes beyond Ovid
into something quite Metaphysical:

> As into air the purer spirits flow,
> And sep'rate from their kindred dregs below;
> So flew the soul to its congenial place,
> Nor left one virtue to redeem her Race . . .
>
> (25–28)

Ovidian wit, it may be said in passing, is often scarcely distinguishable from the 'conceited' Elizabethan style from
which Metaphysical wit in part derives. But the accent of the
Elegy, whether scornfully or tenderly questioning, lyrically
praising, satirically denunciatory, or gently persuasive, is far
from Metaphysical in diction and rhythm. The manner
through many variations remains basically classical. An echo
of Ben Jonson sets the tone of the first line, and the closing
lines, though highly acceptable to romantic taste, recall

Pope's pastoral laments and the style of ancient epitaphs. The blend of satire and pathos, which troubled readers of the later eighteenth and the nineteenth centuries, did not bother Dr. Johnson. Johnson was not offended by any *stylistic* indecorum in the poem, since he was aware, as the Augustans generally were, that the generous decorum of Roman elegy[1] easily embraced lyric sorrow and high declamation both laudatory and satirical and that it allowed too for pointed antitheses and balanced rhythms. The close relationship between the elegiac metre and the heroic couplet is well known.[2] In Marlowe's translations of the *Amores* and Drayton's *Heroicall Epistles*—to take two early examples of the influence—the effect of the Latin verse form on the English can be seen very clearly.

Whether we accept Pope's *Elegy* as a whole depends very largely on the literary context in which we read it. Any attempt to take it as a nineteenth-century lyric is sure to be disastrous: the poem falls apart into the pathetic and the satirical, and the more personal passages are likely to be pressed for a degree of intimacy that is not quite 'there'. A more appropriate context is the one already suggested, of Ovidian elegy and epistle, in particular, of Pope's own *Eloisa to Abelard*. There are similarities between these two 'love' poems in tone and rhetorical devices, in basic motifs, and notably in the vagueness of the narrative. As the *Heroides* show, a heroic epistle always assumes that the facts are well known to the reader. Heroic love in the Ovidian tradition is not a private affair, but a drama played on the stage of history. Ovid expects, for example, that we are familiar with the stories of Dido and Penelope as handed down through

---

[1] See Elizabeth H. Haight, *Romance in the Latin Elegiac Poets* (New York, 1932), pp. 9–10, 13–14, 20–22, *et passim*; W. Y. Sellar, *The Roman Poets of the Augustan Age, Horace and the Elegiac Poets* (Oxford, 1891), pp. 208–22 ('. . . it cannot be doubted that he [Ovid] is the master of all who in modern times have employed it [the elegiac metre] to utter their sentiment, or wit, or sorrow, or for the description of nature or the interchange of friendly feeling').

[2] 'The closed couplet originated as a naturalization of the Latin elegiac distich, the single largest influence being Ovid'. Ruth C. Wallerstein, 'The Development of the Rhetoric and Metre of the Heroic Couplet, Especially in 1625–1645', *PMLA*, l. 166. By contrast, Mario Praz, *La Poesia di Pope e le sue Origini* (Rome, 1948), pp. 67–69, stresses the importance of George Sandys in this adaptation of the English couplet to Ovidian rhetorical patterns.

written and oral tradition. Pope's difficulties in the *Elegy* may
have come from trying to write a heroic epistle about a
private affair, or perhaps about no affair whatever, a 'non-
existent plot'. He seems to allude to facts that everyone must
know—hence the irritation felt by all readers and especially
by contemporaries.

We can appreciate what Pope was doing in the *Elegy to the
Memory of an Unfortunate Lady* and *Eloisa to Abelard* and
evaluate the result only if we have some direct contact with
the poetry of heroic love in its purest form, in the *Heroides*
and the *Metamorphoses*. We may begin where Pope did, with
Ovid's *Sappho to Phaon*, the letter of Sappho to the common
ferryman who had abandoned her for other loves in Sicily.
As early as 1707, Pope says, he had made a version of the
epistle, certainly a good choice of subject for a young poet,
since he presumably might have some insight into the feelings of a literary heroine. Let us turn to the poem and see
what sort of a lover and what sort of poetic style Pope was
attempting to 'bring over' into English poetry.

The Sappho of Ovid's epistle is a woman in love who has
a high sense of her role and her fame,

> Iam canitur toto nomen in orbe meum . . .[1]
>
> (28)
>
> My name is now sung through all the world . . .

but like other Ovidian heroines she 'burns' (*uror*) with passion,

> As a flame blazes through a rich field at harvest-time . . .
>
> Fertilis accensis messibus ardet ager.
>
> (10)

The rhetoric, though familiar enough in Ovid, is apt, the
point of the metaphor being sharpened by a picturesque
adjective and by balanced phrasing with alliteration. From
this beginning Sappho's complaint moves in a series of remembered scenes and *tirades* reminiscent of French tragedy.
As often in Ovid past moments of love are vividly caught
and expressed:

> I would be singing, I remember—lovers remember things—
> And you would steal kisses from me as I sang.

[1] All quotations of Ovid's text are taken from: *P. Ovidi Nasonis Heroides*, ed.
Arthur Palmer (Oxford, 1898).

Cantabam, memini—meminerunt omnia amantes—
Oscula cantanti tu mihi rapta dabas . . .

(43–44)

She continues,

> You praised my kisses—in every way I pleased you,
> But then especially, when we made love.
> Then more than other times, my gaiety amused you
> And quick embraces and jokes in love;
> But when at last our pleasure was over—
> Deep, deep languor and weariness of flesh.

> Haec quoque laudabas, omnique a parte placebam,
>   Sed tunc praecipue, cum fit amoris opus.
> Tunc te plus solito lascivia nostra iuvabat
>   Crebraque mobilitas aptaque verba ioco,
> Et quod, ubi amborum fuerat confusa voluptas,
>   Plurimus in lasso corpore languor erat.

(45–50)

The reality so convincingly seen has been formed by Ovid's art into a design of matching units of sense and sound. There is a play on words with chiasmus (*memini: meminerunt*), the underlining of anaphora (*tunc praecipue . . . tunc*), the rhyme-like effect of repeated endings (*cantabam . . . dabas . . . laudabas . . . placebam . . . iuvabat*), and the inevitable symmetry of paired lines and half-lines. But the devices are more than tricks, since they serve the vivid recollection of scene and sense, aptly suggesting the poet-lover's song and amorous response, the rhythm of love. The song is skilfully broken so as to give the impression of intimate speech:

> Cantabam, memini—meminerunt omnia amantes . . .

A little later in the poem we find Ovid using similar devices to express Sappho's conviction that her character is her fate. Ovidian wit is again an index to dramatic thinking, and although Ovid rises to an aphorism—and a justly famous one, *abeunt studia in mores*—he shows that he might have been a master of the theatre:

> Always there's a reason why I should always love:
> Whether the sister fates set this law at my birth
> And the threads of my life were not quite strong,
> Or whether pursuits make character and Thalia my guide,
> Teacher of my art, made my nature soft . . .

Et semper causa est, cur ego semper amem.
Sive ita nascenti legem dixere Sorores,
    Nec data sunt vitae fila severa meae,
Sive abeunt studia in mores, artisque magistra
    Ingenium nobis molle Thalia facit.

                                    (80–84)

There is a beautiful casualness in the description of how
Sappho receives the news that her lover is going away:

When someone or other said, 'Your joys are leaving',
For a long time I could not cry, nor speak.
No tears came to my eyes, my tongue did not move . . .

Cum mihi nescioquis 'fugiunt tua gaudia' dixit,
    Nec me flere diu, nec potuisse loqui.
Et lacrimae deerant oculis et verba palato . . .

                                    (109–11)

Ovid, constantly reminiscent of other writers, is thinking of
the symptoms of love in Sappho's famous ode. Conventional
beating of the breast comes, of course, and contradictions of
feeling are as usual in Ovid very consciously expressed:

Non veniunt in idem pudor atque amor . . .

                                    (121)

After this climax of feeling and wit we have a passage that
must have attracted Pope especially, since he later worked it
into *Eloisa to Abelard*. The poetry has qualities characteristic
of both Pope and Ovid:

You are my love, Phaon, you come back in my dreams,
Dreams more shining than lovely day.
There I find you, though you are in another country;
But the delights of sleep do not last long.
Often it seems I rest my head in your arms,
Often I hold yours in mine,
I recognize your kisses, the touch on my tongue,
Close kisses you take and give.
I caress you sometimes, speak words half-aloud,
And my lips wake for my senses.
The rest I can hardly tell—say we love.

Tu mihi cura, Phaon! te somnia nostra reducunt,
    Somnia formoso candidiora die.
Illic te invenio, quamvis regionibus absis;
    Sed non longa satis gaudia somnus habet.

Saepe tuos nostra cervice onerare lacertos,
    Saepe tuae videor supposuisse meos;
Oscula cognosco, quae tu committere linguae
    Aptaque consueras accipere, apta dare.
Blandior interdum verisque simillima verba
    Eloquor, et vigilant sensibus ora meis.
Ulteriora pudet narrare, sed omnia fiunt . . .
                                            (123–33)

In the original—for which plain English is a poor substitute
—the lines are saved by Ovidian *politesse* from smart vulgarity
and lyric sentimentality. The *politesse* is in part created by
rhythmic pattern. Note, for example, the placing of noun,
adjective, and adjective, noun in

> Somnia formoso candidiora die . . .

an order[1] often imitated by Pope. Or note in the third couplet
the ripple of amusement in the verbal interweavings that
mirror the interweaving arms and heads of the lovers.

When Sappho's dreams vanish and morning comes, she
flies to 'woods and caves', a scene that recalls the longed-for
haunts of Euripidean heroines, and that anticipates the
'gloomy' retreats of eighteenth-century poetry.[2] Ovid in fact
played a role in the history of such poetic landscapes through
his influence on Claude and Poussin. Pope must have felt
quite at home when he read a passage of this sort, and he
translates Ovid's lines with ease and with truth to impression,
both visual and rhythmic:

> Then frantic rise, and like some fury rove
> Through lonely plains, and through the silent grove,
> As if the silent grove, and lonely plains,
> That knew my pleasures, could relieve my pains.
> I view the grotto, once the scene of love,
> The rocks around, the hanging roofs above,
> That charmed me more, with native moss o'ergrown,
> Than Phrygian marble, or the Parian stone;
> I find the shades that veiled our joys before;
> But, Phaon gone, those shades delight no more.
>   (159–68)

---

[1] L. P. Wilkinson, *Ovid Recalled* (Cambridge, 1955), p. 37.
[2] Tillotson points out that many poets besides Ovid helped create this mode, TE
ii. 286–8.

The 'grotto' has been brought in from the garden and ultimately from Italy, but the rocky 'horror' already exists in
Ovid's description,

> Antra vident oculi scabro pendentia tofo ... (141)

The chiastic dance of 'lonely plains' and 'silent grove' is a
perfect match for

> Antra nemusque peto, tamquam nemus antraque prosint ... (137)

In Pope as in Ovid sweet sorrow is qualified by the artifice
of wit.

The scene that follows this lament, more pastoral and
more gloomy, evokes a sense of personal desolation and religious awe:

> I find the grassy spot I knew so well,
> The blades still pressed from our lying there;
> I fall down and touch the place where you have been,
> And the grass once kind now drinks my tears.
> The branches above bend low as if weeping,
> And no birds sing sweetly warbling
> Save the unholy avenger, most sorrowful mother,
> The Daulian bird, who sings of Ismarian Itys;
> The bird sings 'Itys', Sappho sings 'love ever lost'—
> So much—the rest is midnight silence.
> Nearby, gleaming and clearer than any glass,
> A sacred font, the home of a god,
> And above, a watery lotus spreads its branches,
> Itself a grove; the tender grass is green.

> Cognovi pressas noti mihi caespitis herbas:
>   De nostro curvum pondere gramen erat;
> Incubui tetigique locum, qua parte fuisti:
>   Grata prius lacrimas conbibit herba meas.
> Quin etiam rami positis lugere videntur
>   Frondibus, et nullae dulce queruntur aves.
> Sola virum non ulta pie maestissima mater
>   Concinit Ismarium Daulias ales Ityn:
> Ales Ityn, Sappho desertos cantat amores;
>   Hactenus; ut media cetera nocte silent.
> Est nitidus vitroque magis perlucidus omni
>   Fons sacer—hunc multi numen habere putant,—
> Quem supra ramos expandit aquatica lotos,
>   Una nemus; tenero caespite terra viret.

> (147–60)

Pope's translation of the descriptive part of the passage is about perfect, although his 'sylvan genius' is much too mild for Ovid's mysterious *numen*:

> A spring there is, whose silver waters show,
> Clear as a glass, the shining sands below:
> A flow'ry lotos spreads its arms above,
> Shades all the banks, and seems itself a grove;
> Eternal greens the mossy margin grace,
> Watched by the sylvan genius of the place . . .

But Pope cannot handle directly and warmly the physical facts of love, though he has to hand a contemporary rhetoric of passion,[1] partly Ovidian in origin, which can carry him part of the way:

> A thousand tender words I hear and speak;
> A thousand melting kisses give, and take:

But Ovid surprises us by transcending his rhetoric, by recording the exact gestures and sensations of men and women in love. The embraces, wittily and poignantly remembered in Ovid, are coy and comic in Pope's version:

> Then round your neck in wanton wreaths I twine,
> Then you, methinks, as fondly circle mine . . .
>
> Here the pressed herbs with bending tops betray
> Where oft entwined in am'rous folds we lay;

Ovid does not embarrass, as Pope obviously does.

The epistle ends with a *coup de théâtre*: a nymph suddenly rises from the spring and urges Sappho to hurry to the Leucadian cliff and win back her love by leaping into the sea. Although Sappho is fairly violent in her final resolve, she is on the whole more tender than most of the women in the *Heroides*, since like Penelope and Cydippe she is more nearly a passive sufferer. But in her reproaches to Phaon and in her confessions of lost dignity there is a mild parallel to the fierce conflicts of feeling typical of other Ovidian heroines. More often than not they are *wicked*, either in a light and amusing way, like Helen, or grandly and terribly wicked, like Dido and Phaedra and Medea. '*Culpa*' and '*crimen*' and

---

[1] For sources of this rhetoric, in 'French Romances, letters, plays, and poems', and in 'Roman epics and translations', see TE ii. 278.

'*pudor*' are familiar words on their lips and they sound very much like the criminal heroines of Seneca.[1] They keep reminding us of the close bonds between conflicting feelings or states of mind, between love, sorrow, and innocence on the one hand, and hate, jealousy, guilt, and the will to die on the other. These women—and Ovid, we feel—delight equally in the closeness and the conflict. In Medea's epistle the nearness of love to death comes out in the memorable lines describing her first meeting with Jason:

> Tunc ego te vidi, tunc coepi scire, quid esses;
>   Illa fuit mentis prima ruina meae.
> Et vidi et perii!
>
> (31–33)
>
> It was then I saw you, then I began to know you,
> That was the beginning of my soul's downfall;
> I saw: I was lost!

Here is Ovidian wit at its best: the repetitions and the matching forms, the abrupt compactness of idiom force on us the sharpness of the conflict and the suddenness of the realization. And it *is* a realization. We feel Medea's mind in the act of 'surrounding' a moment of personal and historical significance. Characteristically, and with irony, Ovid puts in Medea's mouth words echoing one of Virgil's most innocent pastoral lovers:

> ut vidi, ut perii, ut me malus abstulit error!
>   (*Ecl.* VIII. 41)

At many other points in the poem Ovid emphasizes by antithesis and epigram the close relationship between opposing emotions:

> Hinc amor, hinc timor est; ipsum timor auget amorem.
>
> (61)

He uses all of his arts of rhythmic and logical pointing to bring out the ugly contrasts in Medea's history:

> Virginitas facta est peregrini praeda latronis . . .
>
> (111)

---

[1] Seneca's *Medea,* at one time attributed to Ovid, 'was probably much influenced' by him. Wilkinson, p. 116.

Numen ubi est? ubi di? meritas subeamus in alto,
Tu fraudis poenas, credulitatis ego.

(119–20)

His Dido—a much cruder Dido than Virgil's—regards
herself as both sinned against and sinning, and talks of
purity (*pudor*), guilt (*culpa*), and vengeance (*exige poenas*) in
the same breath. Her confusion comes out most vividly as
she recollects that fatal day (*illa dies*) when she entered the
cave with Aeneas. The scene has the dark terribleness of
many scenes of love and death in the *Metamorphoses*: Philo-
mel's torture in the ancient wood, Myrrha's incestuous
meetings with her father at night, or Scylla's flight to Minos
when she carries him the purple lock from Nisus' head.
Dido's memory of the past goes from apostrophes to an
epiphany (the two are very close in Ovid):

Exige, laese pudor, poenas violate Sychaei . . .

*　　*　　*

Ad quas, me miseram, plena pudoris eo.
Est mihi marmorea sacratus in aede Sychaeus:
Oppositae frondes velleraque alba tegunt:
Hinc ego me sensi noto quater ore citari;
Ipse sono tenui dixit 'Elissa, veni!'
Nulla mora est, venio; venio tibi debita coniunx;
Sum tamen admissi tarda pudore mei.
Da veniam culpae: decepit idoneus auctor:
Invidiam noxae detrahit ille meae.

(97–106)

Pope, we shall see, had read these lines attentively.

Dryden's translation of the passage gets its full melodramatic flavour and with amusing appropriateness adds a
'gloomy' grove not in the original:

O chastity and violated fame,
Exact your dues to my dead husband's name!
By death redeem my reputation lost,
And to his arms restore my guilty ghost!
Close by my palace, in a gloomy grove,
Is rais'd a chapel to my murder'd love;
There, wreath'd with boughs and wool, his statue stands,
The pious monument of artful hands.

> Last night, methought, he call'd me from the dome,
> And thrice, with hollow voice, cried: 'Dido, come!'
> She comes; thy wife thy lawful summons hears,
> But comes more slowly, clogg'd with conscious fears.
> Forgive the wrong I offer'd to thy bed;
> Strong were his charms, who my weak faith misled.
>
> (101–14)

Dryden's tone is characteristically less personal ('she comes', for 'I come', *venio, venio*), and the fullness of the complaint is truer to Ovid's spirit than to the letter of this particular passage. But Dryden's excess may serve as a reminder of Ovid's least amiable quality, his tendency to go on and on. The local texture of many Ovidian monologues of this sort is often surprisingly fine, the words function in an expressive way, and the writing cannot be dismissed as 'mere rhetoric' in the crude sense of verbiage. But Ovid's abilities, as he confessed (*ingenio perii*) were too much for him, and he was rarely able to resist making another variation on a favourite theme. He is indeed often 'rhetorical' in the specific sense of using language to persuade, as may be observed almost everywhere in the *Heroides*. Dido, for example, is constantly apologetic, whether on the defensive or on the attack, and she is wonderfully agile in finding reasons and in making points. But while Dido and other Ovidian heroines are busy pleading their cases, they are also bringing to light inconsistencies in their lovers and in themselves, drawing out of the past the emotions and considerations that make up their fate. But what emerges finally, as in all poetic drama, is the writer's angle of vision and his attitude. Through the individual case, we see Ovid's intellectual delight in the tangle of human motives and in the absurdity of opposing impulses. His wit is more than wit, since it is an instrument for the revelation of character and the expression of his sense of life.

Taken by itself, *Eloisa to Abelard* may be misread much as the *Elegy* has been and be regarded as alternating oddly between tender melancholy and cold declamation. The dominant quality is of course not quiet tenderness, but 'this tumult in a Vestal's veins', the storm-centre of an Ovidian emotional tangle. Underlying the ambiguous tumult is a strong sense of asserted will, the will to be free in love.

> Oh happy state! when souls each other draw,
> When love is liberty, and nature, law . . .
>
> (91–92)

Eloisa is thus essentially a Corneillian heroine, though she has Racinian moments, as we shall see. (It is worth noting that Racine studied Ovid very carefully and planned to write a tragedy on his life.)

Eloisa to Abelard moves along, very much like an Ovidian epistle, in a series of *tirades* and remembered scenes. The settings are characteristically 'darksome', 'rugged', and 'cavernous', of 'noon-day night', or 'all-conscious night'. Throughout, as many readers must have noticed, Ovidian imagery of darkness is associated with Eloisa's tumultuous state, while contrasting images of brightness are connected with purely religious realms 'dim and remote' from Eloisa and her passions.

As in Ovid the remembered scene is usually an occasion for a 'speech', either an outburst of injured feelings or a moving appeal. Let us see what Pope makes out of the Ovidian mode in three of these moments in *Eloisa to Abelard*, all three among the best passages in the poem. The first, when Eloisa like Dido and Sappho reminds her lover of a 'fatal' day in the past:

> Canst thou forget that sad, that solemn day,
> When victims at yon' altar's foot we lay?
> Canst thou forget what tears that moment fell,
> When, warm in youth, I bade the world farewell?
> As with cold lips I kiss'd the sacred veil,
> The shrines all trembled, and the lamps grew pale:
> Heav'n scarce believ'd the conquest it survey'd,
> And Saints with wonder heard the vows I made.
> Yet then, to those dread altars as I drew,
> Not on the Cross my eyes were fix'd, but you;
> Not grace, or zeal, love only was my call,
> And if I lose thy love, I lose my all.
> Come! with thy looks, thy words, relieve my woe;
> Those still at least are left thee to bestow.

> Still on that breast enamour'd let me lie,
> Still drink delicious poison from thy eye,
> Pant on thy lip, and to thy heart be prest;
> Give all thou canst—and let me dream the rest.
> Ah no! instruct me other joys to prize,
> With other beauties charm my partial eyes,
> Full in my view set all the bright abode,
> And make my soul quit *Abelard* for God.
>
> (107–28)

We recognize Dido's '*illa dies*' in 'that sad, that solemn day', the allusion and the tone suggesting the voice of a historic lover who points to an occasion known to all the world. The stage is history, and as much Roman as Christian. At the beginning of the poem Eloisa speaks of a 'Vestal's veins', and later (line 99) she addresses Abelard with Aeneas' words of Hector, 'Alas how chang'd!' (*quantum mutatus*). She renounces empires in a tone that might be Cleopatra's:

> Should at my feet the world's great master fall,
> Himself, his throne, his world, I'd scorn 'em all:
> Not *Caesar's* empress wou'd I deign to prove;
> No, make me mistress to the man I love . . .
>
> (85–88)

In the present passage the analogy with an Ovidian heroine is emphasized indirectly by the rhetorical questions, the repetitions, and the impassioned imperatives, especially that 'Come!' in

> Come! with thy looks, thy words, relieve my woe . . .

Patterns of Ovidian wit and rhythm are recalled in the sharply contrasted adjectives and nouns, the antithetical play on a single word, 'lose thy love'/'lose my all', and in the shock of oxymoron doubled by alliteration, 'drink delicious poison'. (Cleopatra's 'delicious poison' may be Ovidian in origin; since there are parallels between Ovid's Dido and Cleopatra.)[1]

In this talk of love Pope and Ovid are most alike and most unlike. The combination of daring situation and verbal daring is of course Ovidian enough; and Pope makes use of

---

[1] The original in Shakespeare, *Antony and Cleopatra*, I, v. 27, may be Ovidian in type. For Ovid's Dido and Cleopatra, see Wilkinson, pp. 413–4.

the rhetoric of gallantry ('enamour'd', 'pant on thy lip', 'charm my partial eyes') that is his equivalent for Ovid's rhetoric of passionate 'fire'. But as in the translation of *Sappho to Phaon*, Pope can find no adequate language for the acts of love. For all the talk of passion in *Eloisa to Abelard*, no lips touch, no hands meet, except in one fairly revolting and macabre moment,

> And round thy phantom glue my clasping arms.

Only Dryden with his resolutely public manner, which he adopted even in domestic scenes, could equal that! One sign of Pope's individuality is that he was able to master Dryden's Roman style without being confined by it, but he did not surely win his freedom before the *Rape of the Lock*.

In one beautiful and subtle passage of *Eloisa* Pope succeeded in combining the tone of high heroic love with sensuous intimacy, though not in Ovid's way of moving briskly from *sententiae* to sex. The Ovidian tradition blends here with another tradition, but it is Ovid who offers a bridge between them:

> Thou know'st how guiltless first I met thy flame,
> When Love approach'd me under Friendship's name;
> My fancy form'd thee of Angelick kind,
> Some emanation of th' all-beauteous Mind.
> Those smiling eyes, attemp'ring ev'ry ray,
> Shone sweetly lambent with celestial day:
> Guiltless I gaz'd; heav'n listen'd while you sung;
> And truths divine came mended from that tongue.
> From lips like those what precept fail'd to move?
> Too soon they taught me 'twas no sin to love.
> Back thro' the paths of pleasing sense I ran,
> Nor wish'd an Angel whom I lov'd a Man.
> Dim and remote the joys of saints I see,
> Nor envy them, that heav'n I lose for thee.
>
>   (59–72)

Eloisa's manner throughout the speech fits the historic and dramatic occasion perfectly. At the beginning there is dignity and detachment in the impersonal references to herself ('Love approach'd' and 'My fancy form'd thee'), and in the abstractness of 'Angelick kind' and 'emanation'. The tone is at the same time sufficiently heroic, as indicated by echoes of

Ovidian epistles or translations of Dryden, Prior, and Otway. 'Lambent', for example, through its use by Dryden and its origin in the *Aeneid*, is very nearly consecrated to the heroic style. Yet Pope can move to the direct simplicity of

> Too soon they taught me 'twas no sin to love . . .

and the subtle inwardness of

> Back thro' the paths of pleasing sense I ran,

a line that expresses exquisitely the lapse into sensuousness and error. We can feel Eloisa slipping into a dark tangle of feeling in which quite appropriately the bright purity of the 'Angelick kind' seems 'dim and remote'. As in Shakespeare the imagery has been nicely readjusted to fit the dramatic movement while also fitting perfectly into the overall symbolism of the poem. Ovid, we have seen, had a similar instinct for dramatic thinking, especially at a crisis in a drama of heroic love:

> Tunc ego te vidi, tunc coepi scire, quid esses.

The look of love brought darkness for Medea, too:

> Abstulerant oculi lumina nostra tui.

But the inwardness of Pope's lines implies an intellectual complexity that Ovid's quickness never embraced.

Eloisa's falling in love is a fall from grace, and her review of the past involves a redefinition of love. Her lover, like Donne's in *Aire and Angels*, came to her first in the form of 'some lovely glorious nothing', a type of definition that sounds Platonic rather than scholastic. But talk of the 'Angelick kind' has a scholastic ring, and the medieval doctrine to which Donne alluded in *Aire and Angels* is Neoplatonic in origin.[1] If Pope was not in fact recalling Donne's poem, he was remembering a poetry of love in which fine distinctions were expressed through fairly technical philosophic analogies. The woman's situation in Pope's lines is the complement of the man's in *Aire and Angels*, and in talking of her fall Eloisa uses 'sense' in Donne's meaning of 'sensation'

---

[1] See *The Poems of John Donne*, ed. H. J. C. Grierson (Oxford, 1912), vol. ii, note to *Aire and Angels*, ll. 23-24, pp. 21-22.

as the collective powers of sensation. She later uses the word with very nearly this meaning in a similar context:

> How shall I lose the sin, yet keep the sense,   (191)

The qualifying thoughtfulness in Eloisa's history of her love belongs, as F. R. Leavis would again remind us, to the seventeenth-century 'line of wit'. The contrasts with that tradition are instructive, too. Although Donne's lover like Eloisa reaches a conclusion (expressed also in antithetical style), *Aire and Angels* leaves us feeling that what concerns Donne as always is the fine 'disparity' and the closeness of states so subtly differentiated. Eloisa, at least in the most obviously eighteenth-century parts of the poem, comes out clearly for sense, and in this passage finishes off her definition with a resounding point:

> Nor wish'd an Angel whom I lov'd a Man.

The shift from the man's to the woman's point of view, from intellect to sense, from subtle distinction to obvious contrast, points to the larger shift from Metaphysical to Augustan sensibility.

But Pope surprises us by including within the Ovidian wit of sharp oppositions a wit of intellectual exploration, and he employs this wit dramatically, to give a finer sense of his heroine's state of mind and feeling. Yet Pope found his *point d'appui* in Ovid, seeing the 'metaphysical' in his poetry and bringing it to light. More than once in *Eloisa to Abelard* Pope moves from typically Ovidian oppositions of feeling and phrase into fine 'confusions' reminiscent of Metaphysical poetry. The line,

> How shall I lose the sin, yet keep the sense,

occurs in a passage where one attitude is continually being bounced off another in a series of antitheses exactly as in the *Satires*. Without any obvious change in rhetorical pattern Pope shifts into a passage on heavenly love, where, as Warton noted, the mystic 'strain' is very much like Crashaw's:

> But let heav'n seize it [such a soul], all at once 'tis fir'd,
> Not touch'd, but rapt; not waken'd, but inspir'd!
> Oh come! oh teach me nature to subdue,
> Renounce my love, my life, my self—and you.

Fill my fond heart with God alone, for he
Alone can rival, can succeed to thee.   (201–6)

The last two lines are almost a parody of Donne:

                                    . . . for I
Except you' enthrall mee, never shall be free,
Nor ever chast, except you ravish mee.

Pope's transformation is both appropriate and amusing.
Donne is addressing God as a lover, but the sexual metaphor
is clearly expressing a spiritual desire. The poet *must* talk in
these terms because his need of God is so great. Eloisa is
addressing a man, ostensibly in a spiritual appeal, but with
an odd result: God is reduced to man, to the all too human
lover, and spirit gets lost in flesh. This ambiguous outcome
is exactly right for Eloisa, whose prayers have a way of
turning into lover's vows.

But we do not feel here or elsewhere in the poem that
Eloisa (or Pope) knows much about the experience of a
Christian mystic. The passage that follows immediately, on
the 'blameless Vestal's lot', is in every sense simply charming,
but it gives us a view of the saintly life definitely from the
outside. The ancestry of the closing lines is significant: they
derive from the picturesque lyrical vein of the *Pastorals*:

For her th' unfading rose of *Eden* blooms,
And wings of Seraphs shed divine perfumes;
For her the Spouse prepares the bridal ring,
For her white virgins *Hymenaeals* sing . . .
                                    (217–20)

Compare:

For her, the feathered quires neglect their song;
For her, the limes their pleasing shades deny;
For her, the lilies hang their heads and die.
                                    (*Autumn*, 24–26)

The 'flight' of the soul is a modest one, a 'retreat' in an
eighteenth-century rather than a religious sense, and the
moderate quality of the ideal is well indicated by the Horatian origin of its most famous line,

The world forgetting, by the world forgot.

oblitusque meorum obliviscendus et illis.
                                    (*Epistles*, i. xi. 9)

The line quoted from Crashaw's *Description of a Religious House* is also one that in rhythm and sentiment accommodates itself easily to the mood of Augustan retirement,

'Obedient slumbers that can wake and weep'. . . .

One of the best examples of how sexual and divine love get confused in Eloisa's mind comes in perhaps the most Ovidian passage of the poem, the ghostly summons of the 'sainted maid':

> In each low wind methinks a Spirit calls,
> And more than Echoes talk along the walls.
> Here, as I watch'd the dying lamps around,
> From yonder shrine I heard a hollow sound.
> Come, sister come! (it said, or seem'd to say)
> Thy place is here, sad sister come away!
> Once like thy self, I trembled, wept, and pray'd,
> Love's victim then, tho' now a sainted maid:
> But all is calm in this eternal sleep;
> Here grief forgets to groan, and love to weep,
> Ev'n superstition loses ev'ry fear:
> For God, not man, absolves our frailties here.
>   I come, I come! prepare your roseate bow'rs,
> Celestial palms, and ever-blooming flow'rs.
> Thither, where sinners may have rest, I go,
> Where flames refin'd in breasts seraphic glow.
> Thou, *Abelard*! the last sad office pay,
> And smooth my passage to the realms of day:
> See my lips tremble, and my eye-balls roll,
> Suck my last breath, and catch my flying soul!
> Ah no—in sacred vestments may'st thou stand,
> The hallow'd taper trembling in thy hand,
> Present the Cross before my lifted eye,
> Teach me at once, and learn of me to die.
> Ah then, thy once-lov'd *Eloisa* see!
> It will be then no crime to gaze on me.
> See from my cheek the transient roses fly!
> See the last sparkle languish in my eye!
> Till ev'ry motion, pulse, and breath, be o'er;
> And ev'n my *Abelard* be lov'd no more.
> O death all-eloquent! you only prove
> What dust we doat on, when 'tis man we love.
>   (305–36)

The scene recalls quite closely Dido's summons by her dead husband, and the whole passage is studded with allusions to Dryden and Virgil, to Ovidian epistles and heroic drama. At the climax,

> Teach me at once, and learn of me to die . . .

we are brought to Crashaw once more and to a love poem by Thomas Rowe. The echo of Marlowe's

> Her lips suckes forth my soull . . .

is marvellously apt. Eloisa, like Faustus, is unconsciously damning herself by using the language of earthly love for heavenly.

Ovid too loved such ambiguities, especially the daring combination of the pious and the impious or the salacious. His heroines find a guilty joy in their sins, as does Eloisa:

> O curst, dear horrors of all-conscious night!
> How glowing guilt exalts the keen delight!
>   229–30

The lover's dream is patterned on the similar scene in *Sappho to Phaon*, but the 'unholy joy' is Pope's addition and reminiscent of Dido or Myrrha or Scylla, rather than Sappho. Eloisa's religious feeling like her love is highly ambiguous. Indeed her chief religious emotion is guilt, the pang of conscience, rather than positive love of God or any vivid experience of salvation. Her faith might be described as *religio* (in the ancient Roman ritualistic sense), not *salus* (in the Christian sense). The Catholicism of the poem is intensely Roman, a Christianity of grand public rites and 'scenes' that like the close of the *Messiah* suggest the 'streaming glories' of baroque churches. The Christian experience expressed in *Eloisa to Abelard* is curiously external, and curiously generalized. We hear of 'grace', 'virtue', 'hope', and 'faith', and of the 'saints', but never of Christ or the Son or the Virgin. I am scarcely implying that Roman Catholic Christianity excludes the vividly personal religious experience: the poetry of Crashaw is an obvious and relevant example to the contrary. Whatever the biographical reasons for Pope's vagueness, his inclination to depict the public pomp rather than the personal agony had in this poem a certain literary con-

venience, making it easier for him to adopt the conventions
of a poet whose religious allegiances are equally difficult to
define.

Of the many kinds of passion in Ovid's poetry most have
little place in Pope, but love as the violent assertion of will
has a special affinity with the loves of the *Heroides* and the
Metamorphoses. Although expression of physical intimacy lies
outside Pope's range, he can express intricate states of a
lover 'whose soule is sense', and like Racine he can at his
best maintain heroic decorum while expressing subtle states
of mind and feeling. These are the moments we remember and
treasure in *Eloisa to Abelard*. Pope, we feel, must have shared
Ovid's intellectual delight in the absurdities of passion, but
he easily surpasses him in refinement of perception.

Most of *Eloisa to Abelard* is not Metaphysical, but Ovidian poetry of sharp oppositions between values and logical
positions, between emotions, or characters, or scenes. The
rhetoric, as Tillotson neatly defines it, is 'geometric', and the
larger effects come from setting one scene or tirade against
another, Eloisa 'taking a ride' down one emotion only to
be betrayed into its opposite. We go from melancholy to
ecstatic remembrance, from innocent communion to guilty
love, from assertions of freedom to the horrors of imprison-
ment and damnation, from visions of pure faith to passionate
abandonment. One state of mind or feeling is thus always
being qualified ironically by its opposite. The oppositions,
like the contrasts of theatrical scenes and *coups*, are further
evidence that the essential poetic design of the poem is
Ovidian.

They are proof too that Pope very nearly succeeded in
doing the impossible, in naturalizing an alien literary tradition and form. But the success set its own limitations. The
adjectives that come to mind after reading *Eloisa to Abelard*, however sympathetically familiar we may be with the
Ovidian tradition, are 'remarkable' and 'fine', not 'how
moving' or 'how convincing'. And yet it is no mean achievement to have given English literature something it does not
have elsewhere, a kind of poetry that is characteristically
Latin in the broad sense. In *Eloisa to Abelard* English readers
may get more than a glimpse of the poetry of Racine, a

transcendent Ovid. For Pope's later career the special character of his art in *Eloisa to Abelard* is peculiarly significant. The playing off of states of feeling or loyalties against one another, the relatively aloof treatment of faith and love, the ambiguous tumult of a woman's heart are all but satirical. Passages of simpler feeling, of almost too simple piety, 'the blameless Vestal's lot' or Abelard's 'dead calm of fix'd repose' are often on the verge of irony. With only a slight shift of tone, the rhetoric and rhythm of other more complex passages could easily slide into the verses of a satire:

> I ought to grieve, but cannot what I ought;
> I mourn the lover, not lament the fault;
> I view my crime, but kindle at the view,
> Repent old pleasures, and sollicit new:
> Now turn'd to heav'n, I weep my past offence,
> Now think of thee, and curse my innocence.
>
> (183–8)

We half expect the comment,

> And yet believe me, good as well as ill,
> Woman's at best a Contradiction still.

But that is a confidential remark, made in a tone that derives from another Roman poet and another literary tradition.

IV

TRUE HEROIC POETRY

> ... I am confirmed in my former application to you, ...
> that you wou'd proceed in translating that incomparable
> Poet, to make him speak good *English*, to dress his admir-
> able characters in your proper, significant, and expressive
> conceptions, and to make his works as useful and instructive
> to this degenerate age, as he was to our friend *Horace*,
> when he read him at *Praeneste*. . . .
>
> (Sir William Trumbull to Pope, 9 April 1708)

I. TRADITIONAL ORAL EPIC

In the version of the *Rape of the Lock* printed in his *Works*
of 1717, Pope introduced for the first time the well-
known speech in which Clarissa urges Belinda to take a
more sensible view of her loss of the lock, the lines beginning,

> Say, why are Beauties prais'd and honour'd most,
> The wise man's Passion, and the vain Man's Toast . . .
>
> (v. 9–10)

A note describes the passage as 'a parody of the speech of
Sarpedon to Glaucus in Homer'. Pope's public career as a
translator of the *Iliad* began with his publishing a version of
this speech in 1709,[1] although he probably tried his hand at
Englishing Homer some years before, since he tells us that
Homer was 'the first author' that made him 'catch the itch of
poetry'. Sarpedon's speech may have been especially vivid to
him in 1717 because he had almost certainly been translating
the twelfth book of the *Iliad*, in which it occurs, during that
year.[2] Both the note and the parody imply that the reader
will certainly know the original or at least a translation, perhaps that of Denham, which Pope himself may have had in
mind. Not only the *Rape of the Lock*, but much of Pope's

---

[1] The *Episode of Sarpedon, Translated from the Twelfth and Sixteenth Books of
Homer's Iliads. Poetical Miscellanies: The Sixth Part* (London, 1709), pp. 301–23.
The speech in question is on pp. 304–5.

[2] Volume iii of the *Iliad*, Books IX–XII (Griffith, 78) was published 3 June 1717
(Let. i. 407). The *Works*, 1717, also came out in early June (Let. i. 410).

later poetry assumes that readers will have a precise knowledge of the Homeric mode as Pope and his contemporaries
understood it. In his translation Pope produced one of the
classic examples of the mode and gave the eighteenth century the 'Heroic Poem, truly such' of which Dryden and too
many poets dreamed, from Spenser to inglorious Blackmore,
who unexpectedly attained immortality in Pope's first *Imitation* of Horace:

> What? like Sir *Richard*, rumbling, rough and fierce,
> With ARMS, and GEORGE, and BRUNSWICK crowd the Verse?
> Rend with tremendous Sound your ears asunder,
> With Gun, Drum, Trumpet, Blunderbuss & Thunder?
>
> (23–26)

Pope's *Iliad* and the eighteenth-century heroic style can
hardly be appreciated apart from that dream, just as no
translation can be understood or properly evaluated apart
from the conditions of expression under which it was made.
Pope's version offers one of the most interesting specimens
of the process of translation, of what happens when a writer,
especially a poet, attempts to bring over a literary experience
from one language and culture to another. For the poet-
translator must do more than reproduce his private experience of the text, more than set down what he regards as the
'literal sense' of the words. He must also satisfy his readers
by giving them the experience of poetry. And poetry will
mean necessarily the poetry of the age in which the poet and
his audience are living. Readers will expect to find uses of
language and kinds of experience that they recognize as
poetic, however vaguely these expectations may be defined.
Since they look to poetry for experiences of special value,
they will quite unconsciously expect to find feelings or philosophic and moral attitudes that are regarded as precious in
their own civilization. It is unlikely that an epic of the Tro-
briand Islanders, based on the belief that the souls of the
dead inhabit sweet-potato patches, could be received as a
serious poem by Western European readers. (Arnold, it will
be remembered, found some difficulty in accepting the Greek
burial customs of the *Antigone*.) A given literary public also
assumes that a translation will meet certain standards of

excellence, and if its members form a fairly compact group and share similar educational and social experiences, as was notably true in the Restoration and the age of Queen Anne, then writer and reader may have quite definite and clearly communicable notions of what they mean by a lyric poem, or a tragedy, or an epic. Even at the present time, in spite of the increase in the number of readers and the uncertainty as to whether there is a community of *belles lettres*, there are some fairly widespread assumptions about the nature of Greek epic. Many people have a vague awareness that epic is a kind of 'folk poetry', that the world of Homer has some connexion with Mycenae or Crete, or at a minimum that the society pictured in a translation of Homer ought to be markedly different from our own, suitably 'primitive'.

We can fully appreciate what Pope made out of the *Iliad* only by becoming quite conscious of our assumptions concerning Greek heroic poetry and by comparing with Pope's poem our own best reading of Homer. What we need is not merely a generalized description, but a reading in which our assumptions are working in a lively way. If we have a fairly concrete sense of how we read 'our' *Iliad* we can see much better what Pope's is like. In making the comparison it will be convenient to focus on his favourite 'Episode of Sarpedon'.

There are two features of the *Iliad* that make it novel and beautiful: the hero and the art of the bard or singer. The features are inseparable, since, as Byron says, 'Heroes were but made for bards to sing', and since the Homeric bard in fact exists for us only as the singer of heroes. With the passage of time he has quite simply become his song. But like all heroes, the Homeric hero began in history, and for most Greeks, including more critical students of the past such as Aristotle and Thucydides, the heroic narratives of the *Iliad* were genuinely historical. For us too they are historical, though to a much more limited degree. We now know, for example, that in so far as they are based on fact, they refer to no single period, but to a mixture of two or more.[1] (Pope's notes show

---

[1] M. P. Nilsson, *Homer and Mycenae* (London, 1933); Rhys Carpenter, *Folk Tale, Fiction, and Saga in the Homeric Epics* (Berkeley, 1946); M. I. Finley, *The World of Odysseus*, rev. ed. (London, 1956). (This is the sanest and most readable account of the historical and literary evidence on Homeric society, though the emphasis is definitely on conditions contemporary with the *Odyssey*.) For a brief summary of the

some awareness of this situation.) In large part the *Iliad* mirrors conditions of the time in which Homer lived and sang, in the eighth or ninth century B.C.; in part it embodies traditions that go back two or three centuries earlier, to the period of Mycenaean civilization (1400–1200 B.C.). The Mycenaeans, we can now say, were almost certainly the Achaeans of whom Homer sings and a Greek-speaking people.[1] It must be emphasized here that the *Iliad* does not give an accurate picture of Mycenaean civilization as it is known from the archaeological evidence or the records on Mycenaean tablets. It embodies rather certain memories of that world handed down (and probably distorted) by story-tellers and bards. The Mycenaean era was 'the heroic age' of Greece, a time in which new peoples from the north were coming into the Mediterranean world and making occasional raids on Egypt and the coast of Asia Minor, one of which may have been the original 'war against Troy'. Among the peoples moving about in the eastern Mediterranean at this time were the Lycians, the people to whom Sarpedon belonged and whom he led to Troy.

Chadwick, in his classic description of the typical heroic age, assigns as its main cause

> . . . a long period of 'education,' in which a semi-civilised people has been profoundly affected from without by the influence of a civilised people. Then a time has come in which the semi-civilised people has attained to a dominant position and possessed itself, at least to some extent, of its neighbour's property. The phenomena which we have recognised as characteristic of the Heroic Age appear to be the effects produced upon the semi-civilised people by these conditions.[2]

Among the many phenomena noted by Chadwick, one or two are especially relevant here. An Heroic Age is one when strong individuals are emerging from the older tribal order in which family ties are of the first importance. The bond that is now beginning to count for more is that of 'lord' and

relation between the Homeric poems and historical tradition, see C. M. Bowra, *Heroic Poetry* (London, 1952), pp. 376–7.

[1] Michael Ventris and John Chadwick, 'Evidence for Greek Dialect in the Mycenaean Archives', *Journal of Hellenic Studies*, lxxiii. 84–103; Michael Ventris, 'King Nestor's Four-Handled Cups', *Archaeology*, vii. 15–21; Sterling Dow, 'Minoan Writing', *American Journal of Archaeology*, lviii. 77–129.

[2] H. Munro Chadwick, *The Heroic Age* (Cambridge, 1912), pp. 458–9.

'man'. 'The form of government truly characteristic of the Heroic Age . . . is an irresponsible type of kingship, resting not upon tribal or national law—which is of little account—but upon military prestige.'[1] However vague the basis in law may have been, it is clear from the *Iliad* that there was often a strong feeling of loyalty between chiefs or kings, and between chiefs and superchief. Heroic society thus resembles the loose 'national' organization of the American Indians as described by Parkman. An heroic people like the Achaeans or the Trojans or the various minor peoples included under these names, is not in any strict sense a nation, but in a transitional stage somewhere between tribe and nation. A further sign of the transitional character of the Heroic Age can be seen in the realm of religion. As readers of the *Iliad* know, the heavenly society of Homer closely mirrors the earthly one. We see many independent, often local divinities only half organized into the new Olympian pantheon, the centralized rule of Zeus being maintained with considerable difficulty. Gods are like men, and men are *like* gods, but not demi-gods, not yet the august heroes of the post-Homeric cults. The modern reader may feel that Dryden was not far from right in speaking of them as 'ungodly man-killers, whom we poets, when we flatter them, call heroes; a race of men who can never enjoy quiet in themselves, till they have taken it from all the world'.

But general definitions will not give us the living hero, will not reveal the stance he takes toward the world and himself. To understand his 'code', as we may call it, let us turn to the dramatic moment in the *Iliad* that Pope selected for his first published translation. During the attack on the Greek wall (in Book XII), Sarpedon urges his friend Glaucus to join him in the fight:

'Glaukos, why is it you and I are honoured before others
with pride of place, the choice meats and the filled wine cups
in Lykia, and all men look on us as if we were immortals,
and we are appointed a great piece of land by the banks of Xanthos,
good land, orchard and vineyard, and ploughland for the planting of
    wheat?
Therefore it is our duty in the forefront of the Lykians

[1] Ibid., pp. 390–1.

to take our stand, and bear our part of the blazing of battle,
so that a man of the close-armoured Lykians may say of us:
"Indeed, these are no ignoble men who are lords of Lykia,
these kings of ours, who feed upon the fat sheep appointed
and drink the exquisite sweet wine, since indeed there is strength
of valour in them, since they fight in the forefront of the Lykians."
Man, supposing you and I, escaping this battle,
would be able to live on forever, ageless, immortal,
so neither would I myself go on fighting in the foremost
nor would I urge you into the fighting where men win glory.
But now, seeing that the spirits of death stand close about us
in their thousands, no man can turn aside nor escape them,
let us go on and win glory for ourselves, or yield it to others.'[1]

No single speech in the *Iliad* sums up better the essence of
the heroic attitude. It focuses in the single Greek word
iomen, 'let us go on', 'let us go forward'. In this context 'to go
forward' means to face the inevitability and immediacy of
death, to see its ten thousand shapes standing over one, and
yet to fight bravely and show one's prowess, and so win glory.
'The heroic world', André Malraux wrote in his preface to
Days of Wrath, 'is always the ancient world; in it there are
only two actors, man and his sense of life (or fate).' Sarpedon
is acting here with a full sense of his 'lot' or *moira*, the span
of life and the moment of death that have been assigned to
him. Generalized, the Homeric Moira becomes that great
'lot' or order which limits all action human and divine. The
exact relation between this order and the gods is not altogether clear in Homer,[2] and at times 'gods' or 'Zeus' or
'Moira' seem to be interchangeable terms for the same
shadowy but unchanging reality. The Homeric hero lives
and dies with an ever-present sense of a connexion between
his acts and a mysterious supernatural order, 'that huge
scenic background of stars, fires, blue or black air', which as
E. M. Forster says is assumed by 'all heroic endeavour'. For
the man like Sarpedon who accepts his lot, only heroic action
and renown matter, and not merely for the hero himself. If he

---

[1] *The Iliad of Homer*, tr. Richmond Lattimore (Chicago, 1951), Book XII, 310–
28. Quotations of the *Iliad* are from this translation, except for expressions literally
translated to explain particular points.
[2] William Chase Greene, *Moira: Fate, Good, and Evil in Greek Thought* (Cambridge, Mass., 1944), pp. 13–15.

does not win glory, someone else will. So the heroic code will be kept up and the heroic world maintained in its ideal form:

let us go on and win glory for ourselves, or yield it to others.

ἴομεν, ἠέ τῳ εὖχος ὀρέξομεν, ἠέ τις ἡμῖν.

The Homeric warrior fights also out of a sense of self-respect, *aidós*, the sense of shame that keeps a hero from being either a coward or a brute. In his cry to Glaucus Sarpedon is appealing indirectly to his *aidós*, and he is also reminding his friend and himself of the position they enjoy and of the demands it makes on them. The motives of the hero are not those of a Spenserian knight who fights for an other-earthly ideal or for 'he knows not why'. As Ker once noted, the Homeric hero goes to war for very sensible reasons, typically, to get a piece of land or to get back cattle (or a wife) of which he has been robbed. Although he is motivated by a noble ideal of conduct, and though he has a passion for renown during this life and after, the glory he wins is a very substantial glory. To be glorious is to be honoured by the songs of bards, to eat 'fat sheep' and drink 'choice honey-sweet wine'. In the heroic world there is no clash between spiritual and worldly goods, a condition analysed admirably by Empson in discussing the pastoral paradox of 'complexity-in-simplicity':

One idea essential to a primitive epic style is that the good is not separable (anyway at first level judgments) from a life of straight-forward worldly success in which you keep certain rules; the plain satisfactions are good in themselves and make great the men who enjoy them. From this comes the 'sense of glory' and of controlling nature by delight in it. It is absurd to call this a 'pre-moralistic' view, since the rules may demand great sacrifices and it is shameful not to keep them; there is merely a naïve view of the nature of good. . . The naïve view is so often more true than the sophisticated ones that this comes in later ages to take on an air of massive grandeur; it gives a feeling of freedom from humbug which is undoubtedly noble, and the Homeric heroes support this by the far from savage trait of questioning the beliefs they still die for. Stock epithets about 'the good wine' or 'the well-built gates' imply 'so one always rightly feels'; such a thing essentially has virtue in it, *is* a piece of virtue; a later reader feels this to be symbolic, a process of packing all the sorts of goods into a simple one. Material things are taken as part of a moral admiration, and to a later reader (with less pride, for example, in the fact that his culture uses iron) this seems an inspiriting moral paradox like those of pastoral—'to one who knows how to live the ideal is easily reached.' It is assumed that Ajax is still enormously grand when he cooks his dinner; the later reader feels he must really be very grand not to lose his dignity, whereas at the time it was a thing of some splendour to have so much dinner to cook or such implements to do it with.[1]

In describing the hero's code, we have also been describing the art of the singer, since it is through the epic style that the typical heroic attitudes are expressed. Corresponding to the fixed characteristic of the Homeric hero is the fixed epithet: 'god-like Hector', 'glorious battle', 'shepherd of the people', 'mighty son of Menoitios'. The bard has his own 'code' in the traditional oral mode of composition, the technique of oral verse-making that we have come to understand only within the last twenty-five years, through the work of Milman Parry. In proving conclusively that the Homeric poems were orally composed and in demonstrating the true nature of their style, Parry made one of the major discoveries in the history of literary criticism. His work has decisively altered the way in which we read and interpret Homeric poetry.[2] (The growth in the eighteenth century of the belief that the *Iliad* was composed by popular bards is a crude anticipation of Parry's work.)

The Homeric mode of composition is 'traditional', because it was handed down by a succession of singers who had gradually created its diction and its conventions. It is 'oral' in a limited and peculiar sense, referring to the singer's way of composing verses without writing, of making them up as he went along. We must shake all notions of the writer who chooses each word for a special purpose and who constantly ‧modifies his phrasing for a particular occasion. We must also not confuse the Homeric singer with the eighteenth-century bard who spontaneously poured out his song at Nature's bidding. He is rather the master of a special poetic art or

---

[1] Empson, *Some Versions of Pastoral*, pp. 140–1.
[2] Milman Parry, *L'Epithète traditionelle dans Homère* (Paris, 1928); 'Studies in the Epic Technique of Oral Verse-Making' I. 'Homer and Homeric Style', *Harvard Studies in Classical Philology*, xli. 73–147; II. 'The Homeric Language as the Language of an Oral Poetry', ibid. xliii. 1–50.

techné, a 'maker' who commands a large repertoire of devices, linguistic and metrical, and who has an immense knowledge of saga and folklore. He has acquired his skills and knowledge by imitating other older and more expert singers, though the Muses have helped by teaching him 'the ways of song'. The main features of his art are traceable to the simple fact that he is composing aloud and for hearers, not readers.

The effect of this prime condition can be seen very clearly in the verse form, the dactyllic hexameter. An oral composer must have a metrical pattern that is relatively fixed; for example, it is very convenient for him to know that a line always starts with a long foot and that the caesura usually comes after the first short of the third. These conventions have similar advantages for the hearer, too, since they help him to catch the rhythm more easily and surely. Although there are many subtle variations—all governed by convention—in the hexameter, the hearer will seldom fail to perceive the 'shape' of it, at least if the verse is properly recited. It is almost impossible to miss the marked pause that divides the line and gives the resulting balance of rhythm. This large and steady movement, poised yet rapidly progressing, runs under and through everything that Homer is telling us.

If a poet is composing orally, his diction will differ markedly from that of written verse. In Homer, for example, we find all sorts of words from various dialects (Ionic, Aeolic, Doric, Arcado-Cypriote), archaic words and words peculiar to the epic style, *glosses* that may not have been understood by Greeks of the fifth century. The meanings of some of the words had probably been lost even by Homer's time, that is, the period when the poems were taking something like their present form. These rare words and glosses were simply 'the epic way of saying it', so that to hear them was to feel 'How Homeric, how heroic!' Many of the expressions belonged to a large repertoire of ready-made formulas like 'white-armed Hera', 'spoke wingèd words', 'aegis-bearing Zeus'. Such expressions are formulaic in a technical sense first clearly defined by Parry: a formula is 'a group of words which is regularly employed under the same metrical conditions to express a given essential idea'. For example, 'divine grey-eyèd Athena' is an epithet for the goddess ('an essential idea'), which exactly fits the second half of the verse after the most common pause:

$$// \cup / - -/ - \cup\cup / - -$$
$$\quad 3 \quad 4 \quad 5 \quad 6$$
divine grey-eyèd Athena

This formula for Athena is used over fifty times in Homer, and there are almost no equivalent expressions serving the same metrical function.

It is fairly certain that only an oral poet would cling so resolutely to such standard verbal patterns. If, for example, a poet is to sing of Zeus's part in the *Iliad* with proper dignity, he will need some honorific epithet for the god, and he must have at least one in the nominative case, since Zeus is so terribly active. If he is composing orally, he hasn't time to invent or select a new adjective every time the god is mentioned. But with a ready-made formula, he can serenely begin a line by stating some action of Zeus (which also may be described in a formula), while knowing that after the caesura he can slip in a phrase that fills out the rest of the verse pattern. So when the poet begins to tell of Sarpedon's meeting with Patroclus: (The line is barbarously translated in order to keep the same word-order and the same number of syllables as in the Greek.)

$$- \cup\cup \qquad / - -/ - \cup // \cup / - - \qquad / - \cup\cup \quad / - -$$
$$\text{I} \qquad\qquad 2 \quad 3 \qquad 4 \qquad 5 \qquad 6$$
Those when he saw he pitied // Cronos' child crooked of counsels

Since the singer has a large collection of formulaic phrases and lines, and also ready-made groups of lines, similes, and parts of similes, the fixed expressions, particularly adjectival ones, are to be understood quite differently from qualifying expressions in later written literature. The traditional epithet modifies not the immediate word or line or context, but the whole story, the whole heroic character. Zeus is not being particularly cunning in the line just quoted—on the contrary he is grieving—and so there is no local point in calling him 'Cronos' child crooked of counsels'. The epithet simply names one of his permanent characteristics. As countless other examples show, the Homeric formula is ornamental to a degree not equalled by similar expressions in later non-oral poetry.

The oral mode of composition accounts also for one of the more obvious features of Homeric poetry, the extensive use of repetition, from repetition of single epithets to whole narratives. It has been long evident that if the poems were recited, repetition of previous bits of narrative, especially of messages and commands, would be particularly helpful to listeners. But what began as a necessity for singer and audience developed into a poetic convention. Often in the *Iliad* a report of actions carrying out an order will repeat verbatim the words of the order, not because the listener can have forgotten the order or because he would not be satisfied with some more summary account, but because 'that is the heroic way of telling the story'. One of the most striking features of Homeric style, its symmetry, is directly connected with the convention of repetition and with the underlying necessities of oral verse-making. Balancing elements are found everywhere, from metrical elements to phrases, lines, and larger narrative units. But description will hardly give the English reader a sense of the ever-varying harmony of the *Iliad*, of how these curious and relatively fixed conventions favoured the creation of poetry that was formally beautiful, yet resilient and alive, capable of registering the widest range of feeling and action. In Homer we see how the highest poetic art grew out of the bare necessities of telling a story to a circle of listeners. The aesthetic puzzle of Homer, how he can be at once so seemingly simple and so richly various, struck Pope at the time he was making his first translation of the Sarpedon episode:

> The great Beauty of Homer's Language, as I take it, consists in that noble simplicity, which runs through all his works; (and yet his diction, contrary to what one would imagine consistent with simplicity, is at the same time very Copious.)
>
> (Letter to Ralph Bridges, 5 April 1708)

To appreciate this art in the story of Sarpedon and to see exactly how it was transformed in Pope's version, it would be desirable ideally to turn to the original. In a less ideal world, I shall attempt to point out the dramatic structure of the episode and indicate its larger meanings and then give some hints of how the traditional oral style enters into its composition. (The excellent translation of Richmond Latti-more is given as an Appendix to this chapter.)

The story of Sarpedon is a typical heroic tragedy of the Homeric variety, the *aristeia* of a hero—the display in action of his *areté*, his excellence—ending with his death. Like Achilles, Sarpedon knows from early in his career that he will die at Troy, and his great speech to Glaucus implies an awareness of his destiny. At the start of the episode, seeing his men run from Patroclus, he appeals to their *aidós*, 'Shame [*aidós*], you Lykians, where are you running to? You must be fierce now. . .' With the slightest of transitions, the poet reminds us that the other actor in the heroic world, the divine power, is not far off. As Zeus looks down in pity, we understand that Sarpedon's death is involved in the work-ing out of Zeus's promise to avenge Agamemnon's insult to Achilles. When Zeus wonders whether his son might escape his *moira*, Hera reminds him firmly that there is an order antecedent to his will: Sarpedon is 'one long since/doomed by his destiny'. By his subsequent acts Zeus acknowledges what he has earlier confessed, that

'. . . it is destined that the dearest of men, Sarpedon,
must go down under the hands of Menoitios' son Patroklos.'

Zeus, it seems, may postpone fate, but he cannot change it. (It is worth noting, however, that in the fluid theology of Homer's world the question can be raised.) In Hera's beauti-ful suggestion for Sarpedon's burial by Death and Sleep, we are assured that his death will bring him glory and the material signs of glory, a tomb and a stele. Sarpedon dies with a cry to battle and with an appeal to Glaucus to save his weapons and his body from the enemy.

Sarpedon's story so described is heroic tragedy in its simplest and purest form. But the divine drama, the debate between Zeus and Hera, at once tragic and comic, brings out a special poignancy and irony in the death of Sarpedon. This very mortal father, who wants to change the course of destiny, is the 'Supreme Being' of an Heroic Age, and the relations between divine powers are as little fixed as those between earthly princes. The extraordinary gesture by which Zeus expresses his grief makes him seem quite primitive and almost incomprehensible: the old sky god rains tears of blood. But because his impulses are so human, because like Achilles he has made a choice that ironically involves the loss of the person he loved most dearly, Zeus becomes in this scene a more fully tragic figure than Sarpedon. In Zeus's statements of his plan in the early books of the *Iliad* there is no mention of the death of his son. Not until Book XV, when he is arranging for Patroclus' entry into battle, does he casually include Sarpedon's death in the chain of events leading to the death of Hector. As a deity he had prophesied, but now as a father he understands what the prophecy meant. In much the same way Lear in his godlike denunciations calls his daughters 'monsters' long before he fully sees that they really are. Zeus's tragic recognition comes in a scene of domestic comedy, the usual wrangle between the god and his wife. To his wish that he might save his son Hera replies in the fixed formulas of heroic quarrelling in the *Iliad*: (I translate baldly, in order to suggest the tone. The formulaic language of the Greek nicely combines public dignity with vulgarity of spirit.)

> Do it! but all of us gods will not praise you.
> Another thing I tell you,—and let it sink into your mind—
> If you *do* . . .

The effect of this tone is to increase the irony of Zeus's helplessness and to bring out by contrast the beauty of Hera's plan for sending Death and Sleep. Such combinations of high sorrow and low comedy in Greek poetry—for example, in the *Alcestis* of Euripides—were more disturbing to nineteenth-century critics and scholarly interpreters than to us. We can accept the blend more easily and yet feel through the dialogue the beautiful consolations of Homeric myth. None of the essential facts are altered: Zeus's promise to Thetis is being carried out, and Moira is not to be changed; Sarpedon must die and Zeus must suffer. But the myth offers us a beautiful and intelligible account of how Sarpedon's end will come and of the relation between his death and the will of Zeus and overruling Moira.

The account of Sarpedon's death is followed by more than one hundred and fifty lines of calls to battle and scenes of violence, an elaborate dance of death with each loss on the Greek side matched by another on the Trojan side. The narrative is most Homeric (not least in its length!) and thoroughly typical of the oral epic in subject and in composition. The name of every hero who fights and dies is rich in association with places or persons famous in heroic history (e.g. Meriones with Crete; Aeneas with Anchises and Aphrodite), and the perfect matching of speeches and actions is characteristic of the almost obsessive symmetry manifest in nearly every aspect of Homer's art. The balancing of formulas and metrical units can only be hinted at in English, but in translating the similes some of the original pattern and effect can be retained. Again a literal version may be useful:

> As eagle-beaked crook-taloned vultures scream out in a fight,
> So they screamed out as they rushed together in battle . . .

This comparison, which marks the beginning of the duel between Patroclus and Sarpedon, is one of the many similes that imply a good deal about the heroic world. Civilization, we are made to feel, is precarious, the wilderness is just 'up there' in the mountains, not far from where men live and tend their herds. In the simile describing the fight over Sarpedon's body, the parallels are almost lost in the differences:

>   No longer
> could a man, even a knowing one, have made out the godlike
> Sarpedon, since he was piled from head to ends of feet under
> a mass of weapons, the blood and the dust, while others about him
> kept forever swarming over his dead body, as flies
> through a sheepfold thunder about the pails overspilling
> milk, in the season of spring when the milk splashes in the buckets.
> So they swarmed over the dead man . . .   (637–44)

Read this simile without some allowance for the context of oral poetry, and it becomes comic. (The effect may be unavoidable in any translation.) But if read properly, in relation to the poem rather than the passage, this simile like many others in Homer has the important and beautiful effect of removing us from the immediate scene of gore and battle to a world of peace, the pastoral world familiar to the singer and his listeners. We look out from 'tearful war' to a life of tending cattle and sheep, of woodcutting and building, to all sorts of activities of a peaceful and productive sort. So Homer assures us that he and his audience recognize values other than courage and glory.

The conclusion of the episode shows very well how traditional oral techniques—repetition, use of formulas, the balancing of verbal and rhythmic elements—can be used to express important kinds of meaning and to produce effects that are aesthetically satisfying. We need to recall first Hera's words to Zeus as the battle began:

'No, but if he is dear to you, and your heart mourns for him,
then let him be, and let him go down in the strong encounter
underneath the hands of Patroklos, the son of Menoitios;
but after the soul and the years of his life have left him, then send
Death to carry him away, and Sleep, who is painless,
until they come with him to the countryside of broad Lykia
where his brothers and countrymen shall give him due burial
with tomb and gravestone. Such is the privilege of those who have
    perished.'   (450–7)

At the end, after debating again what he should do, Zeus calls to Apollo:

'Go if you will, beloved Phoibos, and rescue Sarpedon
from under the weapons, wash the dark suffusion of blood from him,
then carry him far away and wash him in a running river,
anoint him in ambrosia, put ambrosial clothing upon him;
then give him into the charge of swift messengers to carry him,
of Sleep and Death, who are twin brothers, and these two shall lay him
down presently within the rich countryside of broad Lykia
where his brothers and countrymen shall give him due burial
with tomb and gravestone. Such is the privilege of those who have
    perished.'
He spoke so, and Apollo, not disregarding his father,
went down along the mountains of Ida, into the grim fight,
and lifting brilliant Sarpedon out from under the weapons
carried him far away, and washed him in a running river,
and anointed him in ambrosia, put ambrosial clothing upon him,
then gave him into the charge of swift messengers to carry him,
of Sleep and Death, who are twin brothers, and these two presently
laid him down within the rich countryside of broad Lykia.
        (667–83)

The larger symmetries and much of the balanced phrasing survive in this sensitive and accurate translation; but in the original the balancing to the ear of vowel and consonant sounds and metrical patterns is more striking and continuous, in part because of the similarities in endings and the variant forms of the same roots in nouns and verbs. (The effect is something like that of Hopkins' rich use of internal rhyme and assonance.) The language throughout is common enough in the epic style and much of it formulaic, though the exact arrangement in this passage is unique. But the type of arrangement, it is clear, came originally from the need for recalling facts or statements that a listener might have forgotten. From these lines it is easy to see how devices of oral poetry, in themselves quite simple, may have great expressive power, how the original necessities and conveniences of oral verse-making led the way to effects of the highest art.

The end of the Sarpedon episode shows also the close connexion between the traditional oral mode and the consolations of heroic myth. The myth of Death and Sleep expresses symbolically the glory due to a hero, and at the same time it gives a beautiful and meaningful account of the relation between his death and the divine order. But the consolation is effected also through traditional narrative and verse patterns and traditional imagery. There is the immediate musical satisfaction of hearing the correspondences between sets of instructions repeated exactly, down to the most minute details; there is the lulling swing of the rhythm which seems to say 'all is ordered as it should be'; there are the suggestions of sleep, the images of immortal brightness and fragrance, and the hints of a broad and fertile countryside —all of which compensate for the horror and waste. 'Glory'— which includes both war and peace—has now been properly expressed. The full meaning of Sarpedon's heroic action and death is thus inseparable from the traditional oral style of the singers. A reader who has the episode freshly in mind can look back and see too why Homeric poetry is so inclusive in effect in spite of a seeming narrowness of subject. In the episode, as in the poem, there is the large historical setting suggested by glimpses of a violent past; there is the hero, with his will to fight in the front ranks and his high sense of self-respect, with his love of both pure and earthly glory, and his awareness that his drama is played in the sight of the gods and within the mysterious order of Moira; there is the sense, conveyed mainly through similes, of a contrasting world of peaceful occupations and natural wonders and terrors; and finally—always present but rarely speaking out —there is the singer, who by his handling of the manifold conventions of verse and diction, decorative simile and illuminating myth, reminds us of the peace and order of art.

II. FROM HOMERIC TO HEROICK

The critical framework within which poets of the seventeenth and eighteenth centuries made their translations of Homer was largely determined by poets and critics of the Italian Renaissance who first evolved the theory of the heroic poem. The principal aim of Cinthio[1] and Tasso is apparent enough, if not quite consistent: they wanted to effect a compromise between the medieval romance and the classical epic. Because of the extreme and almost absurd admiration of Virgil in the Renaissance—Vida and Scaliger are representative and influential examples of the attitude—'epic' meant primarily the *Aeneid*. How to include the delightful variety of romance while preserving the greater clarity and concentration of Virgilian epic, that was the problem for theorists. In practice, as both Tasso and Spenser show, hobgoblin tended to run off with Apollo, but by the end of the seventeenth century Apollo had won back his rights with a vengeance. The Renaissance spirit of genial if inconsistent imitation of both ancient epic and romance was replaced by the legalism of Le Bossu's *Traité du poème épique* (1675) and the cut-and-dried rules which Pope satirized so effectively in *A Receit to make an Epick Poem*. French neo-classical critics, Rapin, for example, in his *Réflexions sur la poétique d'Aristote* (1674), worked out a formula for epic that paralleled as far

[1] On Cinthio and Tasso, their theories of heroic poetry, and their defence of Romance, see E. M. W. Tillyard, *The English Epic and its Background* (London, 1954), pp. 226–7, 230–3. For Tasso, see also W. P. Ker, *Epic and Romance* (London, 1897), pp. 34–35. On Tasso's aim of combining romantic or chivalrous themes with a Virgilian pattern, see C. M. Bowra, *From Virgil to Milton* (London, 1945), pp. 139–43, and for illustration from his practice, pp. 144–90.

as possible the Aristotelian 'rules' for tragedy. But though the rules for heroic poetry grew more explicitly Aristotelian, the basic theory remained fairly constant from Tasso to Pope and continued to show the influence of the Virgilian ideal.[1]

The Renaissance heroic poem is of course a literary epic like the *Aeneid*, not a traditional oral epic like the *Iliad*. Virgil was not a bard composing within the conventions of oral poetry, but a highly conscious artist using fragments of the traditional technique to suggest the heroic manner. The *Aeneid* is in effect a grand allusion to the Homeric poems and the archetype of all later imitations of Greek epic. But in imitating Homer Virgil made something new. Although like Homer he sings of a man and his deeds, his main concern and the reader's is elsewhere, on a further non-dramatic subject, the greatness and the mysterious destiny of the Roman people:

> tantae molis erat Romanam condere gentem.

The Renaissance critics, with a long tradition of allegorical interpretation behind them, insisted that the True Heroick Poem must have not only a subject in the Virgilian sense, but an explicit moral purpose. Later theorists, averting their eyes from Aeneas' entanglement with Dido, ruled that the true hero must represent 'a type of virtue in its perfection'. Aeneas, if not perfect, is in contrast with Achilles or Odysseus a very Roman hero, solemnly noble, a Stoic and a patriot devoted to his family and his gods, *pius Aeneas*. With an eye on Aristotle rather than the *Aeneid*, the critics declared that the heroic poem must have strict unity of action. They also ruled that the poet must introduce the 'marvellous' in the form of divine machinery, but in setting up this requirement they prepared a dilemma that was never easily resolved. For while they insisted on Christian 'colouring' and the necessity of the supernatural in epic, they excluded from proper subjects the central mysteries of the faith. (With clear insight into the problem and with characteristic boldness, Milton chose the prohibited subject and wrote the most successful heroic poem of the Renaissance.) The level of style

---

[1] On the influence of the Virgilian ideal in the Renaissance and later, see *Essays of John Dryden*, ed. W. P. Ker (London, 1926), vol. i, p. xvii, and Bowra, pp. 14–17.

regarded as proper for an epic was also Virgilian rather than Homeric, for though the Greek epic has dignity of style, it never seems, like the Latin epic, to be *on* its dignity. The high decorum in manners and speech required in the heroic poem is modelled on Virgil in his most senatorial Roman manner, as in the debates of the assembled gods, Pope's 'senate of the skies'.

All the well-known English versions of Homer in the seventeenth and eighteenth centuries show the effect of this 'receipt' for heroic poetry, and in spite of Byron's ridicule (or perhaps because of his tacit homage to the ideal), the influence of the theory does not wholly disappear from nineteenth-century editions and translations. The pious Biblical strain in Lang, Leaf, and Myers and in Samuel Butler (!) is probably traceable to critics like Mme Dacier, who eagerly searched out parallels between Homer and the Bible. Chapman's great translation, at the beginning of the seventeenth century, was made at a time when the Renaissance theories were already fairly well known in England, and although he was happily not exposed to the rigour of the neo-classical formulas, he had breathed the critical atmosphere in which Sidney and Spenser wrote. His version of Sarpedon's speech to Glaucus may serve here as a measure of the degree to which Pope's translation[1] was 'truly Heroic' and also as a touchstone for its quality as poetry:

So far'd divine *Sarpedons* mind, resolv'd to force his way
Through all the fore-fights, and the wall: yet since he did not see
Others as great as he, in name, as great in mind as he:
He spake to *Glaucus*: *Glaucus*, say, why are we honord more
Then other men of *Lycia*, in place? with greater store
Of meates and cups? with goodlier roofes? delightsome gardens? walks?
More lands, and better? so much wealth, that Court and countrie talks
Of vs, and our possessions; and euery way we go,
Gaze on vs as we were their Gods? this where we dwell, is so:
The shores of *Xanthus* ring of this; and shall not we exceed,
As much in merit, as in noise? Come, be we great in deed

----

[1] *The Iliads of Homer Prince of Poets* . . . , tr. George Chapman (London, 1611). For a rather different comparison of Chapman and Pope, see George deF. Lord, *Homeric Renaissance, The Odyssey of George Chapman* (London, 1956), pp. 189–215.

As well as looke; shine not in gold, but in the flames of fight;
That so our neat-arm'd-*Lycians*, may say; See, these are right
Our kings, our Rulers; these deserue, to eate, and drinke the best;
These gouerne not ingloriously: these, thus exceed the rest,
Do more then they command to do. O friend, if keeping backe
Would keep backe age from vs, and death; and that we might not
　　wracke
In this lifes humane sea at all: but that deferring now
We shund death euer; nor would I, halfe this vaine valour show,
Nor glorifie a folly so, to wish thee to aduance:
But since we must go, though not here; and that, besides the chance
Proposd now, there are infinite fates, of other sort in death,
Which (neither to be fled nor scap't) a man must sinke beneath:
Come, trie we, if this sort be ours: and either render thus,
Glorie to others, or make them, resigne the like to vs.[1]　　(308–32)

　　　While the Homeric hero is nobly conscious of his role and
its obligations, Chapman's hero comes very close to moral
and social snobbery: 'Yet since' (says Chapman in one of his
characteristic interpolations)

　　　　　　　　　　　　. . . he did not see
　　　Others as great as he, in name, as great in mind as he:
　　　He spake to *Glaucus* . . .

The Lycians are made to say:

　　　　　　　　　　　　. . . See, these are right
Our kings, our Rulers; these deserue, to eate, and drinke the best;
These gouerne not ingloriously . . .

Homer says only that 'their strength is good' and 'they fight
among the first', that is, they exhibit the most common
heroic virtues. But Chapman's heroes are men of state, 'rulers'
and 'governors'—in other words, Renaissance Princes. The
heroes have been given a new dignity of position and chivalric
motives that relate them to the proper heroes of Spenserian
epic. They belong to the court and live in scenes of leisurely
splendour ('delightsome gardens', 'walks') appropriate to a
Burghley or a Leicester. And yet Chapman like the Homeric
singer can move without embarrassment to talk of food and
drink; 'high' facts and 'low' facts are not so sharply opposed
as they are in the next century, and hence both are easily
acknowledged and expressed in poetry.

　　　　　　　　[1]　See note on p. 103.

But in one important respect Chapman's hero resembles the Roman rather than the Greek model. The Homeric hero accepts danger and goes straight ahead to meet it, and though he speaks frankly of the risks, his words show a readiness for action that is almost cheerful. But in the closing lines of Sarpedon's speech as translated by Chapman, we find a very different tone, one implying a considerable difference in attitude and philosophy. In this slowly moving meditation on death, with its explicit recognition of 'infinite fates', with the heavy underlining of inescapable destiny ('infinite fates, of other sort in death'), we have moved from manly acceptance to the grandly gloomy poses of Roman stoicism. The final appeal of the hero is not to action and glory but to sad trial and resignation, an attitude more reminiscent of Tennyson's Ulysses than Homer's Sarpedon:

> Come, trie we, if this sort be ours: and either render thus,
> Glorie to others, or make them, resigne the like to vs.

Throughout the passage there is a complexity of rhythm and sensuous impression that is very different from the Homeric complexity, which as I have suggested arises from the whole episode or poem rather than from the texture of the parts. The rhythm of Chapman's verse—magnificent and not cumbersome if read aloud slowly and with correct rhetorical emphasis—is richly involuted through the use of long periods with many qualifying phrases and through all sorts of tricks of echo and alliteration, devices made more effective by heavy 'pointing' in the Elizabethan manner. The imagery as always in Chapman is much more plentiful than in Homer and full of metaphorical surprises: 'shine not in gold, but in the flames of fight'. The language is constantly and incorrigibly metaphorical, to a degree that goes well beyond the highly figurative style of Virgil:

> O friend, if keeping backe
> Would keep backe age from vs, and death; and that we might not wracke
> In this lifes humane sea at all: but that deferring now
> We shund death euer; nor would I, halfe this vaine valour show,
> Nor glorifie a folly so, to wish thee to aduance:
> But since we must go, though not here; and that, besides the chance
> Proposd now, there are infinite fates, of other sort in death,
> Which (neither to be fled nor scap't) a man must sinke beneath . . .

The style implies a consciousness of paradox, an intellectual sophistication, and a mind given to analysing motives and subtly balancing loyalties that is alien to Homer and that allies Chapman's Sarpedon with late Elizabethan and Jacobean descendants of the Senecan tragic hero. An audience that was looking for poetry of this type would be satisfied only with a hero much closer to Hamlet than to Sarpedon.

A little over a century later, Pope's translation, created for—and almost by—a very different literary public, was nevertheless in the tradition of English heroic poetry as it had developed through Elizabethan narrative verse and drama. As Douglas Knight has shown in his excellent study[1] of Pope's *Iliad*, Pope realized that 'the essential poetic qualities of Homer' as he saw them were 'an inseparable part of the development of poetry between Homer's time and his own'. To see what Pope did and why, we must understand the way in which he met the demands both of his audience and of Homer. But the 'demands of an audience', we have said earlier, are more than literary in a narrow sense. When there is a vigorous commerce between the making of literature and the ordinary business of living and when literary life and social are closely related, as in the Augustan period, the wants of readers readily reflect the most ordinary and the most profound concerns of daily life. So Pope's readers expected his version of the *Iliad* to satisfy a certain standard of aristocratic manners. They knew very well—as we can hardly know—how a noble lord behaved, how he walked and how he talked on great occasions. A chief or a prince in council could not quarrel like a fishwife, as Achilles and Agamemnon seemed to in any literal translation of their speeches.

On other levels of experience, the moral and philosophic, the assumptions of eighteenth-century readers were defined with equal certainty. They could agree with Pope that Nature and Homer were the same, because they shared a belief in the unchanging characteristics of human beings and, underlying that, a conviction that there was a stable order in

[1] Douglas Knight, *Pope and the Heroic Tradition* (New Haven, 1951), p. 33. Although the terms of my argument are often very different, I have found Knight's monograph most helpful.

the nature of things, the Great Nature that included both man and the universe. For the eighteenth-century reader Homer was the grand example of fidelity to this higher truth of 'general nature'. 'His positions', says Johnson, 'are general and his representations natural, with very little dependence on local or temporary customs . . .' For Pope, as Norman Callan[1] has said, 'Homer's chief characteristic is that he does nothing "from want of choice but from an insight into Nature".'

But these larger moral and philosophic assumptions were closely connected with more narrowly literary expectations, for example, that a poem should exhibit 'those happy combinations of words which distinguish poetry from prose', or that an epic should meet the accepted standards for the heroic poem. In connexion with such expectations Pope's double allegiance to Homer and to his audience becomes more complex and more interesting. For Homer was not simply Homer's Greek, nor the poet and the poetry of a civilization totally unconnected with the eighteenth century. No earlier poetry that continues to be read in later periods is so simply in the past. The historical past lives for us mainly by virtue of analogies with the present, and we reach our understanding of its sameness and difference by a series of analogical approximations. We approach a limit, but we shall never be, as Mr. Eliot would say, 'there' since we have only our contemporary hints and guesses to work with.

Although a modern historical view of Homer was only beginning to emerge in the early decades of the eighteenth century, Pope is surprisingly aware of the historical problem he faced as a poet-translator. 'It is my employment', he writes in the first year of translating Homer, 'to revive the old of past ages to the present . . .'[2] He might in some sense 'revive the past', but he could not hope to reproduce Homeric civilization or directly convey the truths of human nature as they appeared to Homer. His task as a translator was to find meaningful analogies within his own culture, more particularly within the body of literature familiar to his readers. The process was made somewhat easier for Pope because so much

---

[1] 'Pope's *Iliad*: A New Document', *Review of English Studies*, iv (N.S.), 121.
[2] Let. i. 239.

that was Homeric (as conceived in the seventeenth and eighteenth centuries) had already received expression in earlier poets both Roman and English. Moreover, if he wanted to write a poem that his contemporaries would recognize as heroic, he must make use of the style and the conventions which they accepted as 'poetic' and 'heroic'. So he observes in his *Preface*:

Perhaps the Mixture of some *Graecisms* and old Words after the manner of *Milton*, if done without too much Affectation, might not have an ill Effect in a Version of this particular Work, which most of any other seems to require a venerable *Antique* Cast.[1]

It is not surprising that he borrows freely also from Dryden and from Virgil (especially in Dryden's translation), or that, as Johnson puts it, he 'had very frequent consultations with Chapman'. He made use too of the despised versions of Hobbes and Ogilby and the prose translation of Mme Dacier.[2] Probably because of her example, he observes that the translator may

...give into several of those general Phrases and Manners of Expression, which have attain'd a Veneration even in our Language from their use in the *Old Testament* ...[3]

But while defending a 'venerable' style, and excluding certain types of technical term, he makes it clear that the Translator must sometimes use the modern equivalent whether it is 'heroic' or not:

... certainly the use of *modern Terms* of *War* and *Government*, such as *Platoon, Campagne, Junto*, or the like (which some of his Translators have fallen into), cannot be allowable; those only excepted, without which it is impossible to treat the Subjects in any living Language.[4]

Let us now turn to the Sarpedon speech in Pope's version, keeping in mind the conditions under which it was made and recalling for comparison our 'twentieth-century' reading of the same passage:

> Resolv'd alike, divine *Sarpedon* glows
> With gen'rous Rage that drives him on the Foes.
> He views the Tow'rs, and meditates their Fall,
> To sure Destruction dooms th' aspiring Wall;

---

[1] *The Iliad of Homer*, Translated by Mr. Pope, 6 vols., quarto (London, 1715–20), (vol. i—1715, ii—1716, iii—1717, iv—1718, v and vi—1720), Preface, E4ʳ.
[2] Knight, pp. 24–30; 114–9.   [3] Preface, E3ᵛ.   [4] Preface, E4ʳ.

Then casting on his Friend an ardent Look,
Fir'd with the Thirst of Glory, thus he spoke.
     Why boast we, *Glaucus*! our extended Reign,
Where *Xanthus*' Streams enrich the *Lycian* Plain,
Our num'rous Herds that range the fruitful Field,
And Hills where Vines their purple Harvest yield,
Our foaming Bowls with purer Nectar crown'd,
Our Feasts enhanc'd with Music's sprightly Sound?
Why on those Shores are we with Joy survey'd,
Admir'd as Heroes, and as Gods obey'd?
Unless great Acts superior Merit prove,
And vindicate the bount'ous Pow'rs above.
'Tis ours, the Dignity they give, to grace;
The first in Valour, as the first in Place.
That when with wond'ring Eyes our martial Bands
Behold our Deeds transcending our Commands,
Such, they may cry, deserve the sov'reign State,
Whom those that envy, dare not imitate!
Could all our Care elude the gloomy Grave,
Which claims no less the fearful than the brave,
For Lust of Fame I should not vainly dare
In fighting Fields, nor urge thy Soul to War.
But since, alas! ignoble Age must come,
Disease, and Death's inexorable Doom;
The Life which others pay, let us bestow,
And give to Fame what we to Nature owe;
Brave tho' we fall, and honour'd if we live,
Or let us Glory gain, or Glory give!

                                        (365–96)

This is noble oratory, 'decent' in a fine eighteenth-century
sense: we can respond to the appeal without embarrassment.
The basic heroic attitudes of the *Iliad* come through strongly
—the hero's acceptance of death, the clear-eyed vigorous
choice of action, the fine sense of responsibility to be 'first in
Valour' if one is 'first in Place'. But how august, compared
with the level seriousness of the same speech in Homer!
Through the use of generalized and Latinate diction, the
tone has been stepped up to a Roman grandeur: '*meditates*
their Fall', 'our extended *Reign*', '*elude* the gloomy Grave',
'Death's *inexorable* Doom' (the last is Virgil's *inexorabile
fatum* as translated by Dryden). Sarpedon's question, which
in Homer is really *to* Glaucus, has become rhetorical, being

addressed now to a larger and vaguer audience. The solemn generalizing character of 'Death's inexorable Doom' contrasts sharply with the particularity of Homer's 'spirits of death standing close about us in their thousands'. As in Chapman, stoic philosophizing has taken the place of mythological seeing.

The fixed generic quality of the Homeric formula is suggested reasonably well by expressions such as 'divine Sarpedon', 'th' aspiring Wall', and 'the fruitful Field', a kind of phrase that had also some metrical convenience, particularly when used to end the verse and make a rhyme. But 'purple Harvest' and 'foaming Bowls' have a descriptive and pictorial quality much more Popeian than Homeric, an indication that for Pope as for Spence, 'Epithets . . . like Pictures in Miniature, are often entire descriptions in one Word.' There is a great increase in another sort of generalization very rare in Homer, the use of many abstract terms for motives and emotions, especially in rationalizing summaries and explanations such as 'gen'rous *Rage* that drives him on the Foes' or 'fir'd with the *Thirst of Glory*'. What is implicit is made terribly explicit:

> Unless great Acts superior Merit prove . . .

Homer has his moral commonplaces—they are part of the singer's traditional lore—but Sarpedon's reasoning is in the sententious Latin manner. The *sententia*, with its neat epigrammatic balance, is almost a product of Pope's rhythmic pattern, as Homer's balance of phrasing was in part a product of his metrical conventions. But in the couplet one opposition leads far too easily to another, as may be seen from the resounding conclusion of Sarpedon's speech:

> The Life which others pay, let us bestow,
> And give to Fame what we to Nature owe;
> Brave tho' we fall, and honour'd if we live,
> Or let us Glory gain, or Glory give!

The contrast in the last line is Homer's—'improved', to be sure—but rightly made emphatic, since it expresses the essential heroic gesture. But in the contrast of 'pay' and 'bestow' there is an upper-class insolence, a Restoration swagger almost, that seems vulgar by the Homeric standard.

The antithesis that follows shows very well Pope's skill in balancing the claims of Homer's world view and his own:

> And give to Fame what we to Nature owe . . .

An eighteenth-century reader—and a twentieth-century reader, too—can get from the line some sense of the relation between the hero's glorious act and an unchanging power. But 'Nature', instead of 'a daimon' or 'Moira' or 'Zeus' introduces the familiar eighteenth-century concept of the 'great Shew of nature'. A hero who talks so clearly and so abstractly of his 'middle state' displays a consciousness of his role and its meaning that would fit a contemporary reader of the *Essay on Man* better than a Homeric hero. Pope's Sarpedon, in his way of speaking and in his whole cast of mind, is much less finely meditating than Chapman's. The Stoic has come out of his study to make a public pronouncement of principle, and his mind is a clean well-lighted place.

But the Stoicism is combined with another faith. 'Why are we', Sarpedon asks,

> Admir'd as Heroes, and as Gods obey'd?
> Unless great Acts superior Merit prove,
> And vindicate the bount'ous Pow'rs above.

The echo of

> And justifie the wayes of God to men . . .

is inescapable, especially because of the parallel in the *Essay on Man*,

> But vindicate the ways of God to man.

It is hard not to feel an ambiguity in the 'grace' of the following line (though apparently the verb, not the noun):

> 'Tis ours, the Dignity they give, to grace . . .

Pope's hero is arguing—somewhat vaguely through Milton's voice—that the two heroes are admired only because their acts justify the blessings (of 'place') sent from above and that therefore they must act in a way commensurate with these heavenly gifts. But Homer's Sarpedon is talking quite clearly about gifts from the Lycians, not from 'above', very specific evidences of heroic glory: meat, drink, and seats of honour at table. 'Therefore', he says with much clearer expression and logic, 'we must fight in the front ranks'. The generous divinity vaguely defined as 'bount'ous Pow'rs', conveniently adjusted to Christian theology and morality, was more acceptable to Pope's audience, Deists included, than a Zeus who bestows both good and evil on man, whose rule over far from generous powers is precariously maintained. Gibbon, observing that 'A republic of gods of such opposite tempers and interests required . . . the moderating hand of a supreme magistrate . . .', adds in a note:

> The rights, power, and pretensions of the sovereign of Olympus are very clearly described in the xvth book of the Iliad: in the Greek original, I mean; for Mr. Pope, without perceiving it, has improved the theology of Homer.[1]

One final comparison with Chapman will show how another type of assumption unconsciously influenced Pope, with a result that proved useful to the later moral and satirical poet. Homer pauses at the beginning of the sixth book for one of those miniature lives of a hero that Pope especially admired, the 'epitaph' on Axylus. Chapman's version runs:

> *Tydides* slue *Teuthranides*, *Axilus*, that did dwell
> In faire Arisbas well-built towres, he had of wealth a Well,
> And yet was kind and bountifull: he would a traueller pray
> To be his guest; his friendly house, stood in the brode high way;
> In which, he all sorts nobly vsd: yet none of them would stand,
> Twixt him and death; but both himselfe, and he that had command
> Of his faire horse, *Calisius*, fell liuelesse on the ground.
>
> (vi. 13–19)

Except for the un-Homeric wit in the phrase, 'of wealth a Well', Chapman does a minimum of damage to the sense and feeling of the original. In his world examples of dignified yet simple country hospitality were not hard to find. When inns were few, it was the natural thing, as in Homeric times, for a man of means to entertain strangers who came by.

Pope's translation is an admirable expression of another world, one more consciously civilized, and if you will more consciously hospitable:

> Next *Teuthras'* Son distain'd the Sands with Blood,
> *Axylus*, hospitable, rich and good:

[1] *The History of the Decline and Fall of the Roman Empire*, ed. J. B. Bury (New York, 1914), i. 29.

In fair *Arisba*'s Walls (his native Place)
He held his Seat; a Friend to Human Race.
Fast by the Road, his ever-open Door
Oblig'd the Wealthy, and reliev'd the Poor.
To stern *Tydides* now he falls a Prey,
No Friend to guard him in the dreadful Day!
Breathless the good Man fell, and by his side
His faithful Servant, old *Calesius* dy'd.   (15–24)

Pope's hero is a country gentleman 'holding his Seat' on
ancestral acres. The antitheses of this tribute fit very neatly a
new social consciousness and a conscience that is neither
Chapman's nor Homer's: 'the Poor' *as a class* have now
surely appeared. The new Axylus 'oblig'd the Wealthy' (in
similar fashion Homer's Axylus gave what was due to his
equals), but with self-conscious charity he also 'reliev'd the
Poor'. The passage might serve as an epitaph—and a handsome one—on the death of Ralph Allen, one of Pope's
heroes in later life and the original of Squire Allworthy. The
image created by Pope on Homer's model had, like the
image of the Augustan Golden Age, historical and practical
significance for Pope and his contemporaries. The eighteenth-
century country gentleman saw himself with some justification as the reviver of an older heroic role. But the model was
more Roman than Greek, since the country house and the
villa and the kind of life they harboured had very real affinities. In life, as in literature, the heroic and the Roman conveniently blended with the Biblical. Pope writes of himself
in this 'historic' role with humour and pardonable satisfaction: '. . . my house is like the house of a Patriarch of old,
standing by the highway side and receiving all travellers...'[1]
He was happily spared the ultimate social and literary degeneration of the ideal in the next century:

> Let me live in a house by the side of the road
> And be a friend to man.

III. POPE'S HEROIC MODE

By comparing brief passages in Pope and Chapman with
each other and with Homer, we have seen some of the ways
in which Pope transformed Homer while trying to satisfy

---

[1] Pope to Bethel, Let. ii. 386.

contemporary standards of the 'heroic' and the 'poetic'. But as he would be the first to say, his translation must be evaluated finally in relation to the larger design and effect of episodes and of the whole *Iliad*. We saw in Homer how the meaning and effect of the Sarpedon episode depended directly on the traditional oral style, how our experience of heroic tragedy is controlled by the local texture of rhythm, epithet, and repetitive device. What Pope expresses in a large way is similarly shaped and limited by his heroic mode. His version of Sarpedon's *aristeia* as a whole gives the impression we might expect from his translation of the appeal to Glaucus: Pope expresses very well the hero's grand confrontation of destiny and death, and he gives the English reader some equivalent in sound and rhythm for the symmetry of Homer's poetic design. The overall rhythm of balancing speeches and narratives of violent action comes out more distinctly if anything than in the original, perhaps because of the 'rapidity' that Arnold admired, a rapidity of effect due almost wholly to the lightness of Pope's couplet rhythm. Homer's rapidity, by contrast, depends less on metric pattern alone, and more on the use of the simplest narrative devices. Pope's statement of what happens is often difficult syntactically, and fuzzy in outline, sometimes because of the abstractness of his diction, at other times because of the necessities of rhyme (for example, the too frequent 'alongs' and 'shores' that blur the account of an action or a scene). But the sheerly musical order of promptly recurring rhymes and balancing phrases keeps us moving ahead even though we may be a bit vague as to exactly where we are.

Pope is a painter of scenes rather than a storyteller, and his narrative 'painting' in the Iliad shows very interestingly how he adapted traditional devices to suit his own genius and contemporary taste in poetry. As a translator he might be classified as an impressionist: he gives us the felt impression of a whole scene or of the Homeric style rather than accurate reproduction of the original text. Take, for example, the simile of fighting vultures, which introduces the battle between Sarpedon and Patroclus:

> As when two Vulturs on the Mountain's Height
> Stoop with re-sounding Pinions to the Fight;

> They cuff, they tear, they raise a screaming Cry;
> The Desert echoes, and the Rocks reply:
> The Warriors thus oppos'd in Arms, engage
> With equal Clamours, and with equal Rage.
>
> (XVI. 522–7)

Pope's simile in its fullness of detail is more 'Homeric' than Homer's, but he has built up his more complete picture in a manner suggested by similes in other parts of the *Iliad*. The likeness in the original had been limited to 'screaming', the eagles *klazonte* and heroes *keklegontes*, both participles being formed from the same root. Pope omits Homer's epithets 'hook-clawed' and 'beak-bent' but adds many other details of scene and movement, and by heaping up all sorts of 'sounding' words he gives the English reader some sense of the echoing participles in Homer. In elaborating the sound effects he is also imitating what Homer does elsewhere, for example, at the close of this episode:

> As the tumult goes up from men who are cutting
> timber in the mountain valleys, and the sound is heard from far off,
> such was the dull crashing that rose from earth of the wide ways,
> from the bronze shields, the skins and the strong-covering ox-hides
> as the swords and leaf-headed spears stabbed against them.
>
> (XVI. 633–7)

The lines in Greek are made intensely resonant through the use of many repeated roots and endings. Pope, not enjoying the same resources in English, translates:

> Shields, Helmets rattle, as the Warriors close;
> And thick and heavy sounds the Storm of Blows.
> As thro' the shrilling Vale, or Mountain Ground,
> The Labours of the Woodman's Axe resound;
> Blows following Blows are heard re-echoing wide,
> While crackling Forests fall on ev'ry side.
> Thus echo'd all the Fields with loud Alarms,
> So fell the Warriors, and so rung their Arms.
>
> (765–72)

The manner is obviously Dryden's, and like Dryden Pope is attempting to write as Homer would if he were an eighteenth-century English poet. He outdoes Homer because he is following Dryden in the attempt to represent actual sounds:

> The Trumpet's loud clangor
> Excites us to arms,
> With shrill notes of anger,
> And mortal alarms.
> The double double double beat
> Of the thund'ring Drum . . .

But in Homer's comparison of the woodcutters and warriors rich suggestiveness of sound is combined with remarkable economy in observation. Every item adds a distinct fact, and sensations are not merely turned over in slightly varying verbal forms, as too often in Dryden. In less elaborate similes, Pope's eye for telling visual detail makes us see what Homer merely implies:

> Then, as the Mountain Oak, or Poplar tall,
> Or Pine (fit Mast for some great Admiral)
> Nods to the Axe, till with a groaning Sound
> It sinks, and spreads its Honours on the Ground;
> Thus fell the King . . .

(XVI. 591–5)

'Nods to the Axe' is an apt addition, while the governance of the rhythm gives just the right sense of suspended motion before a fall.

This noble simile describing Sarpedon's death is followed by one less noble, of a bull being killed by a lion. Pope is again quite free in making omissions and in supplying his own details. He passes over Homer's pastoral setting and drops the epithet for cows that has long troubled translators and etymologists—*eilipodessin*, 'with swinging gait'—and adds a liberal amount of 'foamy Jaws' and 'smoking Blood'. The barbarity, if not the rhetoric, can be matched in many other Homeric similes. Pope is often less polite in his descriptions of death and battle than many readers may suppose. He recognizes with Dr. Johnson that Homer's images are 'drawn from physiology', and in death scenes he is often as anatomically exact as Homer. At times he lays on the gore with such a heavy hand that like Seneca he seems positively cold-blooded. The frequent protests against Homer's 'cruelty' in the

Observations seem to give a truer impression of Pope's own temper.

The notes also indicate that Pope was sometimes troubled by language of another sort in the similes, 'low' talk of the 'humble Flie' and the reluctant ass. But again the translation is often less anaemically decorous than we might expect. We must admire Pope's art in managing to be both polite and heroic, as when he translates

> On ev'ry side the busy Combate grows;
> Thick, as beneath some Shepherd's thatch'd Abode,
> The Pails high-foaming with a milky Flood,
> The buzzing Flies, a persevering Train,
> Incessant swarm, and chas'd, return again.
>
> (778–82)

The risk of a comic contrast has been artfully avoided by skilful 'distancing': the flies are off there in the shepherd's cot, in a charming pastoral scene that emphasizes not only peacefulness, but a difference in social milieu. Pope does not say that like *flies* the *heroes* swarmed—which is exactly what Homer does say. Instead of Homer's sharpness of line, we have a soft focus: the milk is 'a milky Flood', and the insects like Virgil's bees have become a 'persevering Train' of attacking warriors. 'High-foaming' is sufficiently heroic by eighteenth-century standards, and 'incessant swarm' is appropriately Miltonic-Latinate.

Pope's use of epic repetition, like his use of similes, reveals his gift for learning from Homer while maintaining his own style. The passages on Death and Sleep that frame the Sarpedon narrative show his advantage over later translators in having a verse form that easily produces rhythmic and phrasal echoes:

> Give the bold Chief a glorious Fate in fight;
> And when th' ascending Soul has wing'd her flight,
> Let *Sleep* and *Death* convey, by thy Command,
> The breathless Body to his native Land.
> His Friends and People, to his future Praise,
> A marble Tomb and Pyramid shall raise,
> And lasting Honours to his Ashes give;
> His Fame ('tis all the Dead can have!) shall live.
>
> (549–56)

Then thus to *Phoebus*, in the Realms above,
Spoke from his Throne the Cloud-compelling *Jove*.
Descend, my *Phoebus*! on the *Phrygian* Plain,
And from the Fight convey *Sarpedon* slain;
Then bathe his Body in the crystal Flood,
With Dust dishonour'd, and deform'd with Blood:
O'er all his Limbs Ambrosial Odours shed,
And with celestial Robes adorn the Dead.
Those Rites discharg'd, his sacred Corpse bequeath
To the soft Arms of silent *Sleep* and *Death*;
They to his Friends the mournful Charge shall bear,
His Friends a Tomb and Pyramid shall rear;
What Honours Mortals after Death receive,
Those unavailing Honours we may give!
    Apollo bows, and from Mount *Ida*'s Height,
Swift to the Field precipitates his Flight;
Thence from the War the breathless Hero bore,
Veil'd in a Cloud, to silver *Simois*' Shore:
There bath'd his honourable Wounds, and drest
His manly Members in th' immortal Vest;
And with Perfumes of sweet Ambrosial Dews,
Restores his Freshness, and his Form renews.
Then *Sleep* and *Death*, two *Twins* of winged Race,
Of matchless Swiftness, but of silent Pace,
Receiv'd *Sarpedon*, at the God's Command,
And in a Moment reach'd the *Lycian* Land;
The Corpse amidst his weeping Friends they laid,
Where endless Honours wait the sacred Shade.

(809–36)

Few translations of any poet can have been better than this.
We feel as in Homer the grand fulfilment of Zeus's and
Hera's plan, the tenderness and the ceremonial grandeur of
the actions of Apollo and the '*Twins* of winged Race'. Pope's
tact in suggesting the responsions of the original without
exactly copying them, is exquisite. Although there are fine
variations in wording and rhythm in the Greek, two lines
are exactly repeated by Zeus from Juno's speech, and five
lines are repeated later from Zeus's command to Apollo (except for slight changes in verb endings). Having English
poetic conventions firmly in mind, and with his penchant for
varying epithet and rhythm and for creating fine effects in
imagery and imitative sound, Pope produces a series of

musical and sensuous variations on the Homeric themes. He is 'realizing' Homer in terms of his own art and temperament:

> His Friends and People, to his future Praise,
> A *marble* Tomb and Pyramid shall raise . . .
> His Friends a Tomb and Pyramid shall rear . . .
>
> O'er all his Limbs Ambrosial *Odours* shed . . .
> And with *Perfumes* of *sweet* Ambrosial *Dews* . . .
> To the *soft* Arms of *silent Sleep* and *Death* . . .
> Then *Sleep* and *Death*, two *Twins* of winged Race,
> Of *matchless* Swiftness, but of *silent* Pace . . .

This, we feel, is how Spenser might have translated Homer had he lived in England under Queen Anne. The decorum of the elegy is Latin-Augustan, as the vocabulary indicates: '*descend*', '*convey*', a '*Pyramid*' (not a 'mound'), '*precipitates* his Flight', 'the *sacred Shade*'. In diction, rhythm, and restraint of tone the lines are closely related to the *Elegy to the Memory of an Unfortunate Lady*. Pope's note on the passage shows that like Homer he understands the more tender uses of the myth of Sleep and Death:

But after all these refin'd Observations [of Eustathius and Philostratus], it is probable the Poet intended only to represent the Death of this favourite Son of *Jupiter*, and one of his most amiable Characters, in a gentle and agreeable View, without any Circumstances of Dread or Horror; intimating by this Fiction, that he was delivered out of all the Tumults and Miseries of Life by two imaginary Deities, *Sleep* and *Death*, who alone can give Mankind Ease and Exemption from their Misfortunes.   (XVI, n. XLV, v. 831)

The sterner implications of the myth in relation to Zeus's commands and his submission to fate are less apparent here and elsewhere in Pope's version. The remaking of Homer's deity, on which Gibbon commented so shrewdly, can be seen clearly in this episode, and its effect on the narrative as heroic tragedy is marked. The tragic sense of Sarpedon's death is expressed in Homer through the reactions of Zeus and arises from our seeing his helplessness before Moira and his very human desire to change it. The doubt as to the exact relation between Zeus and Moira is almost indispensable to the tragic effect. A Zeus who could change fate at his pleasure, or one simply identified with the working out of a fate[1] that he had himself foreseen, would hardly be tragic. But Pope's note leaves little room for such human uncertainty:

> It appears by this Passage, that *Homer* was of Opinion, that the Power of God could over-rule Fate or Destiny. It has puzzled many to distinguish exactly the Notion of the Heathens as to this Point. . . *Homer's* Opinion at least, as to the Dispensations of God to Man, has ever seem'd to me very clear, and distinctly agreeable to Truth. We shall find, if we examine his whole Works with an Eye to this Doctrine, that he assigns three Causes of all the Good and Evil that happens in this World, which he takes a particular Care to distinguish. First the *Will of God*, superior to all.

— Διὸς δ' ἐτελείετο βουλή.	(*Il.* i.)
— Θεὸς διὰ πάντα τελευτᾷ.	(*Il.* 19. v. 90)
Ζεὺς ἀγαθόν τε κακόν τε δίδοι, —	(&c.)

> Secondly *Destiny* or *Fate*, meaning the Laws and Order of Nature affecting the Constitutions of Men, and disposing them to Good or Evil, Prosperity or Misfortune; which the supreme Being, if it be his Pleasure, may over-rule (as he is inclin'd to do in this Place) but which he generally suffers to take effect. Thirdly, our own *Free-will*, which either by Prudence overcomes those natural Influences and Passions, or by Folly suffers us to fall under them. *Odyss.* 1. v. 32.

> Ὦ πόποι, οἷον δή νυ Θεοὺς βροτοὶ αἰτιόωνται.
> Ἐξ ἡμέων γάρ φασι κάκ' ἔμμεναι· οἱ δὲ καὶ αὐτοὶ
> Σφῇσιν ἀτασθαλίῃσιν ὑπὲρ μόρον ἄλγε' ἔχουσιν.

> *Why charge Mankind on Heav'n their own Offence,*
> *And call their Woes the Crime of Providence?*
> *Blind! who themselves their Miseries create,*
> *And perish, by their Folly, not their Fate.*

(XVI, n. XXXVII, v. 535)

Pope, or his aides, have worked out a neat plan that would be thoroughly acceptable to a liberal theologian of the early eighteenth century. But the disposition of the problem of evil, though sufficiently enlightened, is hardly Homeric. The Zeus of the twenty-fourth book dispenses directly both

---

[1] Greene, *Moira*, p. 15, commenting on the relation between Fate and the gods, notes that Eustathius identified 'the will of Zeus and destiny'. Eustathius' view may have as usual influenced Pope's note.

good and evil, a statement that Plato 'accused as an impiety', as Pope observes in his note to the passage. Pope attempts to dismiss the difficulty there by describing Homer's myth as 'borrow'd from the Eastern way of speaking' and by citing a parallel from Psalms lxxv. 8.[1] Zeus is thus 'translated' into the fearful deity of Israel. The curious may be entertained by studying the index on 'Theology', in which 'Jupiter, *or the* Supreme Being', is described in terms that with one or two exceptions ('other Deities', 'inferior Deities') fit perfectly the God of the Old Testament, if not of the New. The reader will find for example: 'His Will his Fate'; 'His sole Will the Cause of all humane Events'.

Although Pope's translation in Book XVI is less clear than his note, there are signs that he is trying to emphasize Jove's superiority to fate and his power to change it:

> What Passions in a Parent's Breast debate!
> Say, shall I snatch him from impending Fate?
>
> (534–5)

Homer's Zeus is less flamboyant and less direct in challenging destiny,

> The heart in my breast is balanced between two ways as I ponder whether I should snatch him out of the sorrowful battle . . .

and his first word is a lament that Sarpedon is in fact doomed:

> Ah me, that it is destined that the dearest of men, Sarpedon,
> must go down under the hands of Menoitios' son Patroklos.

Pope's Juno is heavily fatalistic in the Roman fashion, so much so that Jove's power to make any change in destiny seems even less likely than in Homer, which is awkward for Pope's theology.

> Then thus the Goddess with the radiant Eyes:
> What Words are these, O Sov'reign of the Skies?
> Short is the Date prescrib'd to mortal Man;
> Shall *Jove*, for one, extend the narrow Span,
> Whose Bounds were fix'd before his Race began?
>
> (540–4)

---

[1] 'For in the hand of the LORD there is a cup, and the wine is red: it is full of mixture; and he poureth out of the same: but the dregs thereof, all the wicked of the earth shall wring them out, and drink them.' See Pope's Observation, Book XXIV, n. XXXI, v. 663. Pope's quotation is not accurate, but closer to the Authorised Version than to the Douai.

But in poetry theology is often style, not argument, and the effective differences between the scene in Pope and in Homer depend largely on unobtrusive implications of tone and epithet. Zeus is tragic just because he is not every inch a king, but humanly baffled and potentially comic. So he addresses his 'wife and sister', not 'his Sister and his Queen'. Although Homer uses a formulaic line for Zeus's inner questioning, the idiom is personal, 'The heart in *my* breast' (*emoi*). But Pope's Jove has 'a Parent's Breast' (relatively unassailable like 'the Bosom' in *Little Dorrit*), and the 'I' of his rhetorical question is addressing the world instead of an inner self. Juno is mounted so high on her royal manner that she can hardly stoop to the tone of Hera's wifely 'Do it, then . . .', and any comic quality utterly disappears from the dialogue.

The underlying difference between this eighteenth-century Jove and Zeus comes out in Pope's handling of the first line of the episode ('When Zeus son of crooked-counselling Cronos saw them, he pitied them.'):

> *Jove* view'd the Combate, whose Event foreseen,
> He thus bespoke his Sister and his Queen.
>
> (528–9)

The commerce between god and deity in this heroic world is not so easy nor so casual as in Homer's. In the Greek the ease of the transition grammatically and the directness of statement—'he saw, he pitied'—express exactly the closeness of connexion between the two realms. Pope's omission of the fixed epithet for Zeus, justifiable since it might sound absurd in the English context, and his substitution of 'whose Event foreseen', gives an impression of an omniscient deity far grander than Homer's. In the lines that follow, the simple human fact of Zeus's pity, salient in Homer, is lost in a soliloquy on 'impending Fate'. Here is a good example of how Pope's remaking of the traditional style, necessary as it was, produced a very different kind of god and a very different dramatic effect.

Pope's attitude toward the fixed epithet, as it appears in the Preface and the notes, is altogether sensible from an English poet's point of view and in part quite adequate to the nature of Homeric style. He observes that many of the epithets are obscure, that they were 'used only in general' to express abstract qualities, and at times he comes near to recognizing their ornamental character (in Parry's sense). Literal translations used on every occurrence of epithets, like 'swift of Foot' or 'Horse-tamer', would be misleading and absurd in English, he says, and besides,

> . . . in Verse, every Reader knows such a Redoubling of Epithets would not be tolerable. A Poet has therefore only to chuse that, which most agrees with the Tenor and main Intent of the particular Passage, or with the Genius of Poetry itself. (VIII, n. LIII, v. 706)

Although the view expressed in the last sentence is most un-Homeric, Pope compensates for it by using certain epithets in a quite bardic fashion. Norman Callan points out that

> Where the more or less conventional attributes of gods and heroes are concerned he seems to keep a stock supply of lines and phrases which he uses with the arbitrariness of a Humpty Dumpty—or indeed of a Homer.[1]

When Zeus assents to Hera's plan for Sarpedon's burial, Pope translates:

> She said; the Cloud-compeller overcome,
> Assents to Fate, and ratifies the Doom.
> Then, touch'd with Grief, the weeping Heav'ns distill'd
> A Show'r of Blood o'er all the fatal Field. (557–60)

Pope rejects the epithet in the text, 'father of men and gods', for 'Cloud-compeller', perhaps arbitrarily, perhaps because this more Mosaic-sounding epithet fits better the solemn ratification of a god who is, in Pope's eyes, superior to fate. He may also have preferred the more impersonal expression in view of having substituted 'the weeping Heav'ns' for Homer's personal subject, 'he', Zeus. In either case, Pope's choice has eliminated an epithet that would be finely appropriate to a father-god sorrowing for his son. Comparison with Lattimore's version suggests that the preference for the more august epithet implied other commitments:

> She spoke, nor did the father of gods and men disobey her;
> yet he wept tears of blood that fell to the ground, for the sake
> of his beloved son. . . (458–60)

[1] 'Pope's *Iliad*: A New Document', *Review of English Studies*, iv (N.S.), 118.

This more complex—not really simpler—god, at once a father, a great ruler, and yet a sky-god who sends rain and thunder, can weep tears of blood. But such curious and mysterious behaviour will hardly do for Pope's more uniformly majestic and impersonal deity. The primitive concept of a father-god who sheds tears of blood is softened by having 'the Heav'ns' weep, an action described in a metaphor with a somewhat chemical flavour:

> Then, touch'd with Grief, the weeping Heav'ns distill'd
> A Show'r of Blood . . .

'Touch'd with Grief', loosely attached to the subject of the sentence, like so many participles in Pope's translation, leaves us with no vivid awareness that a father is weeping for his son's death. Pope's note indicates that science as well as theology had influenced his choice of idiom:

> As to Showers of a bloody Colour, many both ancient and modern Naturalists agree in asserting the Reality of such Appearances, tho' they account for 'em differently. You may see a very odd Solution of 'em in *Eustathius*, Note 7 on the 11*th* Iliad [the cause being condensation of blood shed on the battlefield!]. What seems the most probable, is that of *Fromondus* in his *Meteorology*, who observ'd, that a Shower of this kind, which gave great Cause of Wonder, was nothing but a Quantity of very small red Insects, beat down to the Earth by a heavy Shower, whereby the Ground was spotted in several Places, as with Drops of Blood. (XVI, n. xxxix, v. 560)

Perhaps the impulse to give a rational explanation for a miracle had something to do with Pope's preferring the more meteorological epithet!

The nature and genealogy of Pope's supreme deity is still clearer from Jove's last appearance in the episode:

> *Jove* view'd the Combate with a stern Survey,
> And Eyes that flash'd intolerable Day;
> Fix'd on the Field his Sight, his Breast debates
> The Vengeance due, and meditates the Fates . . .
> (783–6)

This is not Homer's god who 'never turned his shining eye from the battle', but a combination of Milton's 'Eternal King . . . that brightest Seraphim/Approach not, but with both wings veil their eyes' and the jealous God of the Old Testament who exacts 'Vengeance due'. The many parallels between Pope's Jove and Milton's deity are not surprising, since Pope like Milton was attempting to interpret a primitive myth in terms acceptable to a more 'advanced' religious and moral consciousness. Pope's notes, following Mme Dacier's lead, indicate numerous points of similarity between Homeric religion and the religion of the Old Testament. For example, he comments on Jove's 'lightnings':

> This Notion of *Jupiter*'s declaring against the *Greeks* by Thunder and Lightning, is drawn (says *Dacier*) from Truth itself. *Sam*. I. *Ch.* 7.
> (VIII, n. xi, v. 95)

'Truth' is of course revelation, and the text from Samuel tells how 'the Lord thunder'd with a great Thunder'. But the last paragraph of the Observation shows Pope's uneasiness about such parallels:

> I must confess, that in comparing Passages of the sacred Books with our Author, one ought to use a great deal of Caution and Respect. If there are some Places in Scripture that in Compliance to human Understanding represent the Deity as acting by Motives like those of Men; there are infinitely more that shew him as he is, all Perfection, Justice, and Beneficence; whereas in *Homer* the general Tenor of the Poem represents *Jupiter* as a Being subject to Passion, Inequality, and Imperfection. I think M. *Dacier* has carry'd these Comparisons too far, and is too zealous to defend him upon every occasion in the Points of Theology and Doctrine.

This view, Miltonic in the concession made to human intelligence, comes nearer to the beliefs of Homer than to the concept of a Judaeo-Christian deity often implicit in the language of Pope's translation and commentary. One might well wonder whether Pope wrote or read carefully the remark about 'the general Tenor of the Poem'. The cautious and rather clerical tone of the note resembles Parnell's in the *Essay on Homer* prefixed to the translation. After stating that Homer had attributed to Jove 'Wisdom, Justice, Knowledge, Power, &c., which are essentially inherent to the Idea of a God', Parnell regretfully confesses that

> . . . all this grand Appearance, wherein Poetry paid a deference to Reason, is dash'd and mingled with the Imperfection of our Nature;

not only with the applying our Passions to the supreme Being (for
Men have always been treated with this Complyance to their Notions)
but that he is not even exempted from our common Appetites and
Frailties . . .   (Vol. i, pp. 49, 50)

(The implied definitions of 'a God' and 'Reason' are worth
considering.)

Parnell finally defends Homer for having 'preserved the
grand Moral from being obscur'd', an opinion Pope would
certainly endorse, to judge from many of the notes and from
his treatment of Homer's Supreme Being in the translation.
The commentary insists wearisomely on the moral, or rather
morals of the *Iliad*. We are instructed in the usual Renaissance interpretation of the *Iliad* as a lesson in the dangers of
discontent, and we hear of other lessons such as the harmful
effect of various passions, the need for piety, and the failure
to accept divine assistance, but the favourite moral is the
obvious one—the triumph of the will of God ('and the will
of Zeus was accomplished'). Pope and his aides found support for these interpretations in the allegorical readings of
Eustathius and a long line of commentators on Homer.
(Chapman found similar support for his allegorizing of the
Odyssey.)[1]

The effect in the Sarpedon episode of the stress on moral
instruction and the remaking of Zeus into an all-knowing
and all-just deity is all too apparent. As the tone is given
suitable solemnity and impersonality and traditional epithets
are adjusted to express a greater majesty and fatefulness, the
human and comic elements are reduced in importance, and
the tragic effect diminished. The edges of conflicting loyalties are blurred, while the assertion of the divine will, whether
of Zeus or fate, tends to minimize the sense of a personal
recognition on which tragedy depends. I do not believe there
is a single moment of tragic recognition in Pope's translation
that quite satisfies us if we recall the original—not Hector's
heroic acceptance of defeat and death when he turns to face
Achilles for the last time, not Achilles' realization of what his
wrath had meant, when Thetis comes to console him after
Patroclus' death, not the greatest of all tragic moments in the

---

[1] Lord, *Homeric Renaissance*, pp. 34–38.

Iliad, Achilles' vision of the connexion between his acts and
the mysterious order that sends both good and evil. Thinking
of his own father, he says,

> There was not
> any generation of strong sons born to him in his great house
> but a single all-untimely child he had, and I give him
> no care as he grows old, since far from the land of my fathers
> I sit here in Troy, and bring nothing but sorrow to you and your
> children.
> And you, old sir, we are told you prospered once . . .
>   (XXIV. 538–43)

Although no translation can quite reproduce the heroic decorum of Homeric rhythm and epithet, the tone of Lattimore's version is right. It is gently personal, the voice of an
individual acknowledging the link between his fate and man's
fate. As translated by Pope, the speech has its nobility, but
Achilles' recognition seems to be viewed at a distance. The
rhetorical questions, the exclamations seem to say, 'Behold!'
—as if Pope were addressing a reader on the subject of this
famous moment without quite taking him *into* the moment.
I suspect that the effect and the success of Pope's *Iliad* in its
time depended very much on this kind of allusive demonstration. A public that either knew Greek, or that had been given
an idea of what Homer was like, could supply a kind of
emotion which the English text by itself does not quite
evoke. Like the *Aeneid* for the Romans, Pope's *Iliad* was for
the Augustans a grand allusion to Homer.

Pope's heroic mode and the character of the poem he
created through this medium can perhaps be best explained
in relation to the 'Virgilian' heroic poem of Renaissance
and neoclassical critics. Though Pope's poem is very much his
own and more than a mechanical exemplum, the accepted conventions favoured emphases that were congenial to his temperament and gifts as exhibited in original poems earlier and
later in his career. The heroic poet includes both the poet of
Description and of Sense, and in both roles the translator of
the *Iliad* was clearly influenced by the Virgilian conventions,
particularly as domesticated by Chapman, Dryden, and Milton. The most obvious effect of current theory and practice
can be seen in the effort to bring out a clear moral purpose in

the *Iliad*. The aim of the theorists to provide an acceptable formula for the 'marvellous' is reflected in Pope's attempt to Christianize Homer's Zeus, to harmonize Greek and Christian doctrines of destiny and free will, and to minimize the disorder in the Olympian hierarchy, an attempt in which Milton was almost inevitably Pope's principal guide. The grand fatality of Pope's poem is, however, distinctly Roman in feeling and expression, and when Pope's heroes face death and destiny, they often remind us of the Senecan stoical hero in their self-consciousness and magnificence. Achilles' boastful speech to the dying Hector recalls Seneca's Medea or perhaps the Duchess of Malfi: '*Achilles* absent, was *Achilles* still . . .'/ (*Medea superest*; 'I am Duchess of Malfi still'.).

The level of the style in its seriousness and aristocratic tone, and in its oratorical character, is manifestly nearer to Virgil than to Homer, and to Virgil in his more declamatory vein. We hear the public questionings and exclaimings, the telling points of the majestic Roman style adopted by Dryden in his heroic satires and his *Aeneis*. As in Dryden the Roman manner is often suggested by specific allusion to Virgil. When 'some ignobler' Greek gloats over Hector's body, he uses the words of Aeneas on Hector's ghost:

> "How chang'd that *Hector*! who like *Jove* of late
> "Sent Lightning on our Fleets, and scatter'd Fate?"

(XXII. 469–70)

Thanks also to Dryden, the heroic style was almost inconceivable apart from the couplet, which as we have seen favoured Latinization through the use of antitheses and *sententiae* in epigrammatic form. The view of the epic as clearly didactic gave further encouragement to sonorous moralizing, the notes reminding us frequently that in this respect as in others Homer and Virgil were the same. Homer has his *gnomai*, his general expressions of proverbial truths, but they are dramatically appropriate and usually less neat in effect than Virgil's.[1] In Pope's translation, moral sentiments are discovered and brought out when there is little basis for

[1] Greene, pp. 24, 25.

them in the Greek, as in 'Jupiter's *speech* to Hector' in Book
XVII:

> Ah wretched Man! unmindful of thy End!
> A Moment's Glory! and what Fates attend?
>
> (231–2)

The note comments:

> How beautiful is that Sentiment upon the miserable State of Man-
> kind, introduc'd here so artfully, and so strongly enforc'd, by being
> put into the Mouth of the supreme Being!
>
> (XVII, n. XVI, v. 231)

The art and the sentiment—and the theology—are Pope's,
not Homer's. Lattimore translates:

> 'Ah, poor wretch!
> There is no thought of death in your mind now, and yet death stands
> close beside you . . .'

'Sentiment' is closely connected for Pope and his contemporaries with description, a point emphasized more than
once in the notes. Speaking of the 'Image of an Inundation'
in the scene just before the meeting of Patroclus and Sarpedon, Pope says,

> This is one, among a thousand Instances, of *Homer*'s indirect and
> oblique manner of introducing moral Sentences and Instructions.
> These agreeably break in upon his Reader even in Descriptions and
> poetical Parts, where one naturally expects only Painting and Amuse-
> ment.

(Note the near equivalency of 'Descriptions' and 'poetical
Parts' as in Warton's criticism of Pope.) He adds that this
art is 'the very distinguishing Excellence of *Cooper's Hill*',[1]

> throughout which, the Descriptions of Places, and Images rais'd by
> the Poet, are still tending to some Hint, or leading into some Reflec-
> tion, upon moral Life or political Institution: Much in the same
> manner as the real Sight of such Scenes and Prospects is apt to give the
> Mind a compos'd Turn, and incline it to Thoughts and Contemplations
> that have a Relation to the Object.   (XVI, n. XXXIII, v. 466)

The simile in the original is moral, but active, not reflective,
an account of how Zeus sends the flood against men who

---

[1] Cf. the remarks on description in *Windsor Forest*, ch. II, pp. 50–54.

judge crookedly. (In this particular instance Pope's translation is less descriptive than the note might suggest.) It is
worth noting that as there was a *rapprochement* in the eighteenth century between the didactic and the descriptive styles,
so there was a tendency for both styles to blend with the
heroic.[1] Pope, like Addison, associates the descriptive style
especially with Virgil, but Homer of course tends to be seen
through the Virgilian glass. Pope illustrates these tendencies
very clearly in explaining his treatment of the Catalogue
of Ships:

> A meer heap of proper Names tho' but for a few Lines together,
> could afford little Entertainment to an *English* Reader, who probably
> could not be appriz'd either of the Necessity or Beauty of this Part of
> the Poem. There were but two things to be done to give it a chance to
> please him; to render the Versification very flowing and musical, and
> to make the whole appear as much a *Landscape* or *Piece of Painting*
> as possible. For both of these I had the Example of *Homer* in general;
> and *Virgil*, who found the Necessity in another Age to give more into
> Description, seem'd to authorise the latter in particular.
>
> (II, *Observations on the Catalogue*, Vol. i, p. 179)

After the belief in Homer's truth to General Nature, the
most important governing idea of Pope's translation is the
pictorial. The dominant impressions from reading his *Iliad*
as a whole are of representative, stable truthfulness to Nature
and pictorial splendour. For readers unfamiliar with the heroic
world as we find it in Homer and as the eighteenth century
conceived of it, the picturesque quality may seem to prevail.
Although Homer's poetry shows great accuracy in recording
sights and sounds and though it carries its weight of moral
and religious truth, the first and last impression is of men in
action, of unfolding tragic actions, with Achilles' wrath at the
centre. Pope makes the point succinctly in his *Preface* when
he speaks of Virgil's 'colder Invention, that interests us less
in the Action describ'd: *Homer* makes us Hearers, and *Virgil*
leaves us Readers'. The same point is implied in the *Essay on
Homer's Battels*, in a passage that betrays at the same time
Pope's love of pictorial effect and design:

It is worth taking Notice too, what Use *Homer* every where makes

---

[1] Cf. the blend of descriptive and heroic styles in *The Temple of Fame*, ch. X,
p. 357.

of each little Accident or Circumstance that can naturally happen in a Battel, therby to cast a Variety over his Action; as well as of every Turn of Mind or Emotion a Hero can possibly feel, such as Resentment, Revenge, Concern, Confusion, &c. The former of these makes his Work resemble a large History-Piece, where even the less important Figures and Actions have yet some convenient Place or Corner to be shewn in; and the latter gives it all the Advantages of Tragedy in those various Turns of Passion that animate the Speeches of his Heroes, and render his whole Poem the most *Dramatick* of any Epick whatsoever.   (Vol. ii, pp. 325–6)

Pope talks much of Homer's action, of the 'fire' which he so much admires, and in his translation, it is as if he had been dazzled by his own metaphor. Favourite words for action are 'burns', 'fired', 'flame'. Imagery of 'fire' and 'shining' is plentiful in Homer, but in Pope it is extravagantly so, as he who runs and reads may see. While it is clear from the *Essay on Battels* that 'paint' is used sometimes for 'express', for representing actions and speeches, as well as for 'making pictures', it is equally clear in much of the commentary and at countless points in the translation that Pope is constantly seeing Homer's action in terms of painted and sculptured scenes. This is the glory of his translation, but also the quality that most distinguishes it from Homer and the Homeric mode.

The Observations include many comparisons between Homer's scenes and paintings or sculptured figures.[1] More than once the 'history-piece' is referred to or implied, as above or in a comment on the duel of Paris and Menelaus ('an exact Piece of Painting'), or again in the elaborate analysis of a battle in Book VIII, where the whole picture is plotted out with the use of proper technical terms (the *Fracas*, the *Eloignement*). In the *Observations on the Shield of Achilles*, Pope affirms that Homer took this occasion to 'shew in its full Lustre, his Genius for Description'. One section of the essay considers 'this Piece as a complete *Idea* of *Painting*, and a Sketch for what one may call an *universal Picture*'. The scenes on the shield are first analysed in general terms of

---

[1] For Pope's interest in sculpture as 'explaining' literature, see Stephen A. Larrabee, *English Bards and Grecian Marbles* (New York, 1943), pp. 68–73. See also Praz, *Poesia di Pope*, pp. 210, 216–17.

pictorial art (again in appropriate technical language), then
each scene is described in detail with frequent references to
various types of painting and sculpture, and to particular
artists (Raphael, Rubens, Guido, Julio Romano). We are
finally informed that Sir Godfrey Kneller 'entirely agrees
with my Sentiments on this Subject'. 'Prospects' are often
found where we should expect them, as in the famous simile
of the moon and stars at the end of Book VIII, and where we
should not expect them, in the Doloneia, the barbarous raid
of Ulysses and Diomede on the Trojan camp. We are given
an enthusiastic appreciation of the episode, in which 'Circumstances the most Picturesque imaginable' are composed,
though not at all as in Homer, into a 'most natural Night-
Scene'. The narrative has been read almost as if it were an
eighteenth-century 'night piece'. How picture tends to eclipse
action can be seen from the final comment on the Doloneia:

And tho' it must be owned, that the Human Figures in this Piece
are excellent, and disposed in the properest Actions; I cannot but
confess my Opinion, that the chief Beauty of it is in the Prospect, a
finer than which was never drawn by any Pencil.   (X, n. LIV)

'Picturesque' and 'circumstances' are key-words in other
admiring comments. Commenting on the surprising simile,
'[Hector] went on his way like a snowy mountain', Pope
'opens it up' in sentences that show his own visual imagination if not Homer's:

I am not of Mad. *Dacier*'s Opinion, that the Lustre of *Hector*'s
Armour was that which furnish'd *Homer* with this Image; it seems
rather to allude to the Plume upon his Helmet, in the Action of
shaking which, this Hero is so frequently painted by our Author, and
from thence distinguish'd by the remarkable Epithet κορυθαίολος.
This is a very pleasing Image, and very much what the Painters call
Picturesque. I fancy it gave the Hint for a very fine one in *Spenser*,
where he represents the Person of *Contemplation* in the Figure of a
venerable old Man almost consum'd with Study.

(XIII, n. LV, v. 948)

The translation fits the note:

This said; the tow'ring Chief, prepar'd to go,
Shakes his white Plumes that to the Breezes flow,
And seems a moving Mountain topt with Snow.

The mention of Spenser might have been anticipated. Other picturesque passages are illustrated from *The Faerie Queene* and, as we should expect, from *Paradise Lost*. One example, which owes something to the Miltonic parallel in rhythm and in composition, is worth looking at more closely. Lattimore translates:

He [Patroclus] drove them from the ships and put out the fire that was
    blazing,
and that ship was left half-burnt as it was, as the Trojans scattered
in terror and unearthly noise, and the Danaans streamed back
along the hollow ships, and clamour incessant rose up.
And as when from the towering height of a great mountain Zeus
who gathers the thunderflash stirs the cloud dense upon it,
and all the high places of the hills are clear and the shoulders out-
    jutting
and the deep ravines, as endless bright air spills from the heavens,
so when the Danaans had beaten from their ships the ravening
fire, they got breath for a little, but there was no check in the
    fighting . . .   (XVI. 293–302)

The stress in the Greek is on the 'beating off' in comparison with the 'stirring', and on the resultant changes, the main
emphasis, however, being on the actions rather than on the
effects. Pope's version has a characteristic emphasis:

> *Patroclus'* Arm forbids the spreading Fires,
> And from the half-burn'd Ship proud *Troy* retires:
> Clear'd from the Smoke the joyful Navy lies;
> In Heaps on Heaps the Foe tumultuous flies,
> Triumphant *Greece* her rescu'd Decks ascends,
> And loud Acclaim the starry Region rends.
> So when thick Clouds inwrap the Mountain's Head,
> O'er Heav'ns Expanse like one black Cieling spread;
> Sudden, the Thund'rer, with a flashing Ray,
> Bursts thro' the Darkness, and lets down the Day:
> The Hills shine out, the Rocks in Prospect rise,
> And Streams, and Vales, and Forests strike the Eyes,
> The smiling Scene wide opens to the Sight,
> And all th' unmeasur'd *Æther* flames with Light.
>   (XVI. 348–61)

Pope's eye is again fixed on the 'prospect', which he builds
up with details in part Homeric, and in part of his own

invention. The style of verbal 'painting', by increasing the
'kinetic energy' of the scene (Pope supplies 'sudden', 'flashing', 'lets down', 'strike', 'opens'), and by adding many more
contrasts of light and shade ('black', 'darkness', 'day', 'smiling scene', 'flames', 'light' are all added), creates one of those
'Salvator Rosa's' of which Pope speaks admiringly elsewhere. Although in his note Pope rightly denies that the
epithet for Zeus, 'gatherer-of-the-thunderbolt', has a local
application, his translation is conveniently ambiguous. The
interpretation given is legitimate and shows good sense in
reading Homeric similes:

> The Simile therefore seems to be of *Jupiter* dispersing a black
> Cloud which had cover'd a high Mountain, whereby a beautiful
> Prospect, which was before hid in Darkness, suddenly appears. This is
> applicable to the present State of the *Greeks*, after *Patroclus* had
> extinguish'd the Flames, which began to spread Clouds of Smoak over
> the Fleet. It is *Homer*'s Design in his Comparisons to apply them to
> the most obvious and sensible Image of the thing to be illustrated;
> which his Commentators too frequently endeavour to hide by moral
> and allegorical Refinements; and thus injure the Poet more, by
> attributing to him what does not belong to him, than by refusing him
> what is really his own.   (XVI, n. xxix, v. 354)

But Pope did not always follow these excellent principles in
his translation or commentary, though he usually rejects the
more preposterous 'allegorical Refinements' of both ancients
and moderns. As every reader knows, Homer's similes vary
considerably from those with only one or two points of likeness to others having many close correspondences. In the
notes Pope seems to stress the second type, and in his translations he tends to fill in the Homeric outline with many detailed resemblances. He praises Homer often as the poet of
'small Circumstances . . . so artfully chosen, that every
Reader immediately feels the force of them, and represents
the whole in the utmost Liveliness to his Imagination'. (VI,
n. xlviii, v. 395.)

In 'giving more into Description' in translating the Catalogue of Ships, Pope cited Homer as his example 'in general',
and Virgil, 'in particular'. His main reason for the indul-
gence, he explains, was to please the English reader, a reason
that operated—and rightly—in so many ways throughout

the whole translation. Epithets are dropped or made more vivid, repetitions suppressed or made more palatable by variation, and—less often than is usually supposed—'low' expressions are passed over or given 'lustre' by being surrounded with more magnificent diction than in the original. Pope's comment on his success in copying one of Homer's finer metrical effects may serve as a statement of his larger aim as a translator:

It is not often that a Translator can do this Justice to *Homer*, but he must be content to imitate these Graces and Proprieties at more distance, by endeavouring at something parallel, tho' not the same.

(XIII, n. xxxix, v. 721)

If we read Pope's *Iliad* in the context of contemporary theory and of the heroic tradition as it was renewed in the liveliest of his predecessors from Virgil to Dryden, and if we compare the result with our own best reading of the original, we may accept Pope's phrase as a just estimate of his achievement: 'Something parallel, tho' not the same'.

APPENDIX TO CHAPTER IV

But Sarpedon, when he saw his free-girt companions going
down underneath the hands of Menoitios' son Patroklos,   420
called aloud in entreaty upon the godlike Lykians:
'Shame, you Lykians, where are you running to? You must be
      fierce now,
for I myself will encounter this man, so I may find out
who this is who has so much strength and has done so much evil
to the Trojans, since many and brave are those whose knees he   425
      has unstrung.'
He spoke, and sprang to the ground in all his arms from the chariot,
and on the other side Patroklos when he saw him leapt down
from his chariot. They as two hook-clawed beak-bent vultures
above a tall rock face, high-screaming, go for each other,
so now these two, crying aloud, encountered together.   430
And watching them the son of devious-devising Kronos
was pitiful, and spoke to Hera, his wife and his sister:
'Ah me, that it is destined that the dearest of men, Sarpedon,
must go down under the hands of Menoitios' son Patroklos.
The heart in my breast is balanced between two ways as I ponder, 435

whether I should snatch him out of the sorrowful battle
and set him down still alive in the rich country of Lykia,
or beat him under at the hands of the son of Menoitios.'
   In turn the lady Hera of the ox eyes answered him:
'Majesty, son of Kronos, what sort of thing have you spoken?   440
Do you wish to bring back a man who is mortal, one long since
doomed by his destiny, from ill-sounding death and release him?
Do it, then; but not all the rest of us gods shall approve you.
And put away in your thoughts this other thing I tell you;
if you bring Sarpedon back to his home, still living,   445
think how then some other one of the gods might also
wish to carry his own son out of the strong encounter;
since around the great city of Priam are fighting many
sons of the immortals. You will waken grim resentment among them.
No, but if he is dear to you, and your heart mourns for him,   450
then let him be, and let him go down in the strong encounter
underneath the hands of Patroklos, the son of Menoitios;
but after the soul and the years of his life have left him, then send
Death to carry him away, and Sleep, who is painless,
until they come with him to the countryside of broad Lykia   455
where his brothers and countrymen shall give him due burial
with tomb and gravestone. Such is the privilege of those who have
    perished.'
   She spoke, nor did the father of gods and men disobey her;
yet he wept tears of blood that fell to the ground, for the sake
of his beloved son, whom now Patroklos was presently   460
to kill, by generous Troy and far from the land of his fathers.
   Now as these two advancing had come close to each other
there Patroklos threw first at glorious Thrasymelos
who was the strong henchman of lord Sarpedon, and struck him
in the depth of the lower belly, and unstrung his limbs' strength.   465
Sarpedon with the second throw then missed with the shining
spear, but the spear fixed in the right shoulder of Pedasos
the horse, who screamed as he blew his life away, and went down
in shrill noise into the dust, and the life spirit flittered from him.
The other horses shied apart, the yoke creaked, the guide reins   470
were fouled together as the trace horse lay in the dust beside them;
but at this spear-famed Automedon saw what he must do
and wrenching out the long-edged sword from beside his big thigh
in a flashing stroke and without faltering cut loose the trace horse
and the other horses were straightened out, and pulled in the   475
    guide reins,
and the two heroes came together in the heart-perishing battle.

Once again Sarpedon threw wide with a cast of his shining
spear, so that the pointed head overshot the left shoulder
of Patroklos; and now Patroklos made the second cast with the brazen
spear, and the shaft escaping his hand was not flung vainly   480
but struck where the beating heart is closed in the arch of the muscles.
He fell, as when an oak goes down or a white poplar,
or like a towering pine tree which in the mountains the carpenters
have hewn down with their whetted axes to make a ship-timber.
So he lay there felled in front of his horses and chariots   485
roaring, and clawed with his hands at the bloody dust; or as
a blazing and haughty bull in a huddle of shambling cattle
when a lion has come among the herd and destroys him
dies bellowing under the hooked claws of the lion, so now
before Patroklos the lord of the shield-armoured Lykians   490
died raging, and called aloud to his beloved companion:
'Dear Glaukos, you are a fighter among men. Now the need comes
hardest upon you to be a spearman and a bold warrior.
Now, if you are brave, let bitter warfare be dear to you.
First you must go among all men who are lords of the Lykians   495
everywhere, and stir them up to fight for Sarpedon,
and then you yourself also must fight for me with the bronze spear.
For I shall be a thing of shame and a reproach said of you
afterwards, all your days forever, if the Achaians
strip my armour here where I fell by the ships assembled.   500
But hold strongly on and stir up all the rest of our people.'
He spoke, and as he spoke death's end closed over his nostrils
and eyes, and Patroklos stepping heel braced to chest dragged
the spear out of his body, and the midriff came away with it
so that he drew out with the spearhead the life of Sarpedon,   505
and the Myrmidons close by held in the hard-breathing horses
as they tried to bolt away, once free of their master's chariot.
But when he heard the voice a hard sorrow came upon Glaukos,
and the heart was stirred within him, and he could not defend Sarpedon.
He took his arm in his hand and squeezed it, since the wound hurt him
where Teukros had hit him with an arrow shot as he swept in   511
on the high wall, and fended destruction from his companions.
He spoke in prayer to him who strikes from afar, Apollo:
'Hear me, my lord. You are somewhere in the rich Lykian countryside
or here in Troy, and wherever you are you can listen   515
to a man in pain, as now this pain has descended upon me.
For see, I have this strong wound on me, and my arm on both sides
is driven with sharp pains about, my blood is not able
to dry and stop running, my shoulder is aching beneath it.

I cannot hold my spear up steady, I cannot go forward   520
to fight against the enemy. And the best of men has perished,
Sarpedon, son of Zeus; who will not stand by his children.
No, but you at least, my lord, make well this strong wound;
and put the pains to sleep, give me strength, so that I may call out
to my companions, the Lykians, and stir them to fight on,   525
and I myself do battle over the fallen body.'
So he spoke in prayer, and Phoibos Apollo heard him.
At once he made the pains stop, and dried away from the hard wound
the dark running of blood, and put strength into his spirit.
And Glaukos knew in his heart what was done, and was happy   530
that the great god had listened to his prayer. And first of all
he roused toward battle all the men who were lords of the Lykians,
going everywhere among them, to fight for Sarpedon;
afterwards he ranged in long strides among the Trojans,
by Poulydamas the son of Panthoös and brilliant Agenor,   535
and went to Aineias and to Hektor of the brazen helmet
and stood near them and addressed them in winged words: 'Hektor,
now you have utterly forgotten your armed companions
who for your sake, far from their friends and the land of their fathers,
are wearing their lives away, and you will do nothing to help them.   540
Sarpedon has fallen, the lord of the shield-armoured Lykians,
who defended Lykia in his strength and the right of his justice.
Now brazen Ares has struck him down by the spear of Patroklos.
Then, friends, stand beside me, let the thought be shame in your
          spirit
that they might strip away his arms, and dishonour his body,   545
these Myrmidons, in anger for all the Danaans perished,
those whom we Lykians have killed with the spear by the swift ships.'
He spoke, and the Trojans were taken head to heel with a sorrow
untakeable, not to be endured, since he was their city's
stay, always, though he was an outlander, and many people   550
came with him, but he was the best of them all in battle
always. They went straight for the Danaans, raging, and Hektor
led them, in anger for Sarpedon. Meanwhile the Achaians
roused to the savage heart of Patroklos, the son of Menoitios.
First he spoke to the Aiantes, who were burning for battle already: 555
'Aiantes, now your desire must be to defend yourselves, and be
such as you were among men before, or even more valiant.
The man is fallen who first scaled the wall of the Achaians,
Sarpedon. If only we could win and dishonour his body
and strip the armour from his shoulders, and kill with the pitiless   560
bronze some one of his companions who fight to defend him.'

He spoke, and they likewise grew furious in their defence,
and when they on either side had made massive their battalions,
Trojans and Lykians, and Myrmidons and Achaians,
they clashed together in battle over the perished body   565
howling terribly, with a high crash of the men in their armour,
while Zeus swept ghastly night far over the strong encounter
that over his dear son might be deadly work in the fighting.
First the Trojans shouldered back the glancing-eyed Achaians
when a man, and not the worst of the Myrmidons, was struck down,
son of high-hearted Agakles, Epeigeus the brilliant.   571
He was one who was lord before in strong-founded Boudeion,
but now, since he had happened to kill his high-born cousin,
had come suppliant to Peleus and to Thetis the silver-footed,
and these sent him to follow Achilleus, who broke men in battle, 575
to Ilion of the horses and the battle against the Trojans.
As he caught at a dead man glorious Hektor hit him
with a stone in the head, and all the head broke into two pieces
inside the heavy helmet, and he in the dust face downward
dropped, while death breaking the spirit drifted about him.   580
And the sorrow took hold of Patroklos for his fallen companion.
He steered his way through the ranks of the front fighters, like a
     flying
hawk who scatters into flight the daws and the starlings.
So straight for the Lykians, o lord of horses, Patroklos,
you swept, and for the Trojans, heart angered for your companion.
Now he struck Sthenelaos, beloved son of Ithaimenes,   586
in the neck with a stone, and broke the tendons loose from about it.
The champions of Troy gave back then, and glorious Hektor.
As far as goes the driving cast of a slender javelin
which a man throws making trial of his strength, either in a contest
or else in battle, under the heart-breaking hostilities,   591
so far the Trojans gave way with the Achaians pushing them.
But Glaukos was first, lord of the shield-armoured Lykians,
to turn again, and killed Bathykles the great-hearted, beloved
son of Chalkon, who had dwelled in his home in Hellas   595
conspicuous for wealth and success among all the Myrmidons.
It was he whom Glaukos stabbed in the middle of the chest, turning
suddenly back with his spear as he overtook him. He fell,
thunderously, and the closing sorrow came over the Achaians
as the great man went down, but the Trojans were gladdened greatly
and came and stood in a pack about him, nor did the Achaians   601
let go of their fighting strength, but steered their fury straight at them.
And there Meriones cut down a chief man of the Trojans,

Laogonos, bold son of Onetor, who was Idaian,   604
Zeus' priest, and who was honoured in his countryside as a god is.
Meriones struck him by jaw and ear, and at once the life spirit
fled from his limbs, and the hateful darkness closed in about him.
But Aineias threw his bronze spear at Meriones, hoping
to hit him as he came forward under his shield's covering,
but Meriones with his eyes straight on him avoided the bronze spear.
For he bent forward, and behind his back the long spearshaft   611
was driven into the ground so that the butt end was shaken
on the spear. Then and there Ares the huge took the force from it
[so that the vibrant shaft of Aineias was driven groundward
since it had been thrown in a vain cast from his big hand].   615
But Aineias was angered in his spirit, and called out to him:
'Meriones, though you are a dancer my spear might have stopped you
now and for all time, if only I could have hit you.'
    Then in turn Meriones the spear-famed answered him:
'Aineias, strong fighter though you are, it would be hard for you   620
to quench the strength of every man who might come against you
and defend himself, since you also are made as a mortal.
But if I could throw and hit you with the sharp bronze in the middle,
then strong as you are and confident in your hands' work, you might
give the glory to me, and your soul to Hades of the horses.'   625
    He spoke, but the fighting son of Menoitios reprimanded him:
'Meriones, when you are a brave fighter, why say such things?—
See, dear friend, the Trojans will not give back from the body
for hard words spoken. Sooner the ground will cover them.
    Warfare's
finality lies in the work of hands, that of words in counsel.   630
It is not for us now to pile up talk, but to fight in battle.'
    He spoke, and led the way, and the other followed, a mortal
like a god. As the tumult goes up from men who are cutting
timber in the mountain valleys, and the sound is heard from far off,
such was the dull crashing that rose from earth of the wide ways,   635
from the bronze shields, the skins and the strong-covering ox-hides
as the swords and leaf-headed spears stabbed against them. No longer
could a man, even a knowing one, have made out the godlike
Sarpedon, since he was piled from head to ends of feet under
a mass of weapons, the blood and the dust, while others about him   640
kept forever swarming over his dead body, as flies
through a sheepfold thunder about the pails overspilling
milk, in the season of spring when the milk splashes in the buckets.
So they swarmed over the dead man, nor did Zeus ever
turn the glaring of his eyes from the strong encounter,   645

but kept gazing forever upon them, in spirit reflective,
and pondered hard over many ways for the death of Patroklos;
whether this was now the time, in this strong encounter,
when there over godlike Sarpedon glorious Hektor
should kill him with the bronze, and strip the armour away from his
        shoulders,   650
or whether to increase the steep work of fighting for more men.
In the division of his heart this way seemed best to him,
for the strong henchman of Achilleus, the son of Peleus,
once again to push the Trojans and bronze-helmed Hektor
back on their city, and tear the life from many. In Hektor   655
first of all he put a temper that was without strength.
He climbed to his chariot and turned to flight, and called to the other
Trojans to run, for he saw the way of Zeus' sacred balance.
Nor did the powerful Lykians stand now, but were all scattered
to flight, when they had seen their king with a spear in his heart,
        lying   660
under the pile of dead men, since many others had fallen
above him, once Zeus had strained fast the powerful conflict.
But the Achaians took from Sarpedon's shoulders the armour
glaring and brazen, and this the warlike son of Menoitios
gave to his companions to carry back to the hollow ships.   665
And now Zeus who gathers the clouds spoke a word to Apollo:
'Go if you will, beloved Phoibos, and rescue Sarpedon
from under the weapons, wash the dark suffusion of blood from him,
then carry him far away and wash him in a running river,
anoint him in ambrosia, put ambrosial clothing upon him;   670
then give him into the charge of swift messengers to carry him,
of Sleep and Death, who are twin brothers, and these two shall lay him
down presently within the rich countryside of broad Lykia
where his brothers and countrymen shall give him due burial
with tomb and gravestone. Such is the privilege of those who have
        perished.'   675
    He spoke so, and Apollo, not disregarding his father,
went down along the mountains of Ida, into the grim fight,
and lifting brilliant Sarpedon out from under the weapons
carried him far away, and washed him in a running river,
and anointed him in ambrosia, put ambrosial clothing upon him,   680
then gave him into the charge of swift messengers to carry him,
of Sleep and Death, who are twin brothers, and these two presently
laid him down within the rich countryside of broad Lykia.

V

AM'ROUS CAUSES

What dire Offence from am'rous Causes springs,
What mighty Contests rise from trivial Things . . .

W<small>E</small> can imagine the amusement with which Pope and his fellow Scriblerians might overhear a discourse on the *Rape of the Lock* and heroic tradition. The *Key to the Lock* and the *Art of Sinking in Poetry* show what they might do with the theme—sufficient warning to any critic 'who delights to trace the mind from the rudeness of its first conceptions to the elegance of its last'. However much we may learn from such a study about the growth of the poem and the richness of its texture, we cannot, as Valéry reminds us, confuse the process of composition with poetic effect. For the critic, as for the common reader, the *Rape of the Lock* must be the final 'elegance', the 'easy art', the wit and good nature that Pope praised in Voiture:

> In these gay Thoughts the Loves and Graces shine,
> And all the Writer lives in ev'ry Line;
> His easie Art may happy Nature seem,
> Trifles themselves are Elegant in him.

The *Epistle to Miss Blount, With the Works of Voiture*, from which these lines come, and which is so close in tone and subject to the *Rape of the Lock*, was completed only a year or so before Pope wrote the first version of his 'Heroi-Comical Poem'.

Pope's poetry of wit in the *Rape of the Lock* is probably most perfect in the passage on the ceremony of afternoon coffee and the cutting of the lock:

> For lo! the Board with Cups and Spoons is crown'd,
> The Berries crackle, and the Mill turns round.
> On shining Altars of *Japan* they raise
> The silver Lamp; the fiery Spirits blaze.

From silver Spouts the grateful Liquors glide,
While *China*'s Earth receives the smoking Tyde.
At once they gratify their Scent and Taste,
And frequent Cups prolong the rich Repast.
Strait hover round the Fair her Airy Band;
Some, as she sip'd, the fuming Liquor fann'd,
Some o'er her Lap their careful Plumes display'd,
Trembling, and conscious of the rich Brocade.
Coffee, (which makes the Politician wise,
And see thro' all things with his half-shut Eyes)
Sent up in Vapours to the *Baron*'s Brain
New Stratagems, the radiant Lock to gain.
Ah cease rash Youth! desist ere 'tis too late,
Fear the just Gods, and think of *Scylla's* Fate!
Chang'd to a Bird, and sent to flit in Air,
She dearly pays for *Nisus*' injur'd Hair!
    But when to Mischief Mortals bend their Will,
How soon they find fit Instruments of Ill!
Just then, *Clarissa* drew with tempting Grace
A two-edg'd Weapon from her shining Case;
So Ladies in Romance assist their Knight,
Present the Spear, and arm him for the Fight.
He takes the Gift with rev'rence, and extends
The little Engine on his Fingers' Ends,
This just behind *Belinda*'s Neck he spread,
As o'er the fragrant Steams she bends her Head:
Swift to the Lock a thousand Sprights repair,
A thousand Wings, by turns, blow back the Hair,
And thrice they twitch'd the Diamond in her Ear,
Thrice she look'd back, and thrice the Foe drew near.
Just in that instant, anxious *Ariel* sought
The close Recesses of the Virgin's Thought;
As on the Nosegay in her Breast reclin'd,
He watch'd th' Ideas rising in her Mind,
Sudden he view'd, in spite of all her Art,
An Earthly Lover lurking at her Heart.
Amaz'd, confus'd, he found his Pow'r expir'd,
Resign'd to Fate, and with a Sigh retir'd.
    The Peer now spreads the glitt'ring *Forfex* wide,
T'inclose the Lock; now joins it, to divide.
Ev'n then, before the fatal Engine clos'd,
A wretched *Sylph* too fondly interpos'd;

> Fate urg'd the Sheers, and cut the *Sylph* in twain,
> (But Airy Substance soon unites again)
> The meeting Points the sacred Hair dissever
> From the fair Head, for ever and for ever!
>
> (III. 105–54)

It is easy enough to pick out the phrases that catch the essence of the poem: 'shining Altars', 'glitt'ring *Forfex*', 'fatal Engine', 'Airy Band'. All are characteristic of the whole, and yet perfect for the occasion. What do we mean by the 'poetry of wit' as illustrated by these expressions? 'Glitt'-ring *Forfex*', for example, sounds like an epic formula, the usual combination of epithet and noun with a flavour of mystery about its exact meaning. The use of a solemn Latin term for a familiar object, the word in which the point (!) focuses, is in Dryden's finest satirical-heroic style, but 'glitt'ring', a favourite adjective in the *Rape of the Lock* and other early poems, is pure Pope. It is the adjective that makes us feel the minuteness of the actual 'Forfex' and that diverts our attention to an irrelevant beauty. The Baron's heroic act seems very slight by the Homeric standard, yet exquisitely beautiful and touched somehow with the fire of that splendid world. The essence of Pope's wit in the *Rape of the Lock* lies in this beautiful diminution, where 'beautiful' implies the appeal of the surface and the appeal of a better world of noble manners and actions. Cutting the lock is absurd, but also much more than absurd.

Of the phrases we have chosen, 'fatal Engine' probably comes closest to the allusive irony of Dryden, with its echoes of Virgil and Milton. Dryden's *Aeneis* serves here for Virgil, the phrase being his translation of *fatalis machina*. For a moment Pope sustains the grander tone of *Absalom and Achitophel*,

> Ev'n then, before the fatal Engine clos'd . . .

but with the next line,

> A wretched *Sylph* too fondly interpos'd . . .

he restores the scale of the scene, and 'the fatal Engine' is reduced to

> The little Engine on his Fingers' Ends . . .

Both phrases give us in passing a sense of the precious slight-
ness of objects and actions. Presently, as in his *Iliad*, Pope
reinforces the heroic by borrowing from Milton:

> Fate urg'd the Sheers, and cut the *Sylph* in twain,
> (But Airy Substance soon unites again) . . .

Milton's '. . . but th' Ethereal substance clos'd' is adjusted to
fit Pope's more delicate myth and tone, where Dryden would
easily have taken 'ethereal'[1] in his stride. 'Airy', reminding us
of Pope's closeness to Donne, amuses by the contrast with
Milton and evokes the misty charm of Ariel and his 'lucid
Squadrons'. In 'shining Altars' there is the same witty diminution and sensuous appeal as in 'glitt'ring *Forfex*', but
here the visual detail fits into a scene of the heroic pictorial
type familiar in Pope's *Iliad*, a description that gives an
initial impression of being in Dryden's grandest epic manner.
Opening with Virgilian rhetorical pomp ('For lo!'), it rises to
a Latin gravity in 'frequent Cups prolong the rich Repast'.

But with 'hover round the Fair', we hear the familiar
accent of 'society', and with

> *Coffee*, (which makes the Politician wise,
> And see thro' all things with his half-shut Eyes)

we are in the coffeehouse where a worldly observer is speaking to us in an aside. 'Sent up in Vapours' is fashionable psy-
chology served up as a joke. In the *Rape of the Lock* the epic
grandeur is always being lightly qualified by this voice that
takes us into the poet's confidence. Compared to the delicate
game of innuendo that Pope plays with such consummate
skill, the usual mock-epic tricks of inflation seem almost
crude. Even at the climax of the action, the most heroic
moment in the poem, Pope manages to insinuate this confidential tone by the lightest of touches:

> But when to Mischief Mortals bend their Will,
> How soon they find fit Instruments of Ill!

The couplet, as the notes remind us, is indebted to *Henry VI*
and to *Absalom and Achitophel*. But,

> Just then, *Clarissa* drew with tempting Grace
> A two-edg'd Weapon from her shining Case . . .

[1] Cf. the use of 'th' ethereal plain' in the conclusion to the *Dunciad*, iv. 636,
where the Virgilian and Miltonic context makes the phrase perfectly appropriate.

'Just then' (the transition in a children's story), and a little later, 'just behind' (the feminine accent of 'just *there*, my dear'), incline the tone towards cosy intimacy. Dryden's manner is by comparison elephantine.

Yet Pope's '*Spectator*' tone, as Sherburn calls it, makes possible a personal moral seriousness rare in Dryden (to speak in these terms may be worse than elephantine). In the present passage the tone allows Pope to move out from 'coffee' to a sharp criticism of statesmanship. Although in recent years too much has been said too solemnly about Pope's serious concerns in the *Rape of the Lock*, it would be light-minded to disregard them. In the better 'case' implied by Pope's satire, marriage is not entered into lightly or unadvisedly, the ceremony of innocence is not drowned, and beauty in nature and in art are truly wonderful. But the chief moral, like all poetic 'morals', is inseparable from the poetry, from Pope's peculiar wit and tone:

> What then remains, but well our Pow'r to use,
> And keep good Humour still whate'er we lose?
> And trust me, Dear! good Humour can prevail,
> When Airs, and Flights, and Screams, and Scolding fail.
> Beauties in vain their pretty Eyes may roll;
> Charms strike the Sight, but Merit wins the Soul.
>
> (v. 29–34)

In a Dedication that is a perfect example of the virtue he recommends, Pope says to the original Belinda,

It will be in vain to deny that I have some Regard for this Piece, since I Dedicate it to You. Yet You may bear me Witness, it was intended only to divert a few young Ladies, who have good Sense and good Humour enough, to laugh not only at their Sex's little unguarded Follies, but at their own.

Through poetic laughter Pope is everywhere urging his readers to view these 'Follies' with the necessary distance, moral and aesthetic. He wins us over to mature 'Good Sense and good Humour' by the art of allusive irony that he had originally learned from Dryden and that he now adapts to suit his own aims and sensibility. He gets his purchase on his larger meanings by skilful handling of various literary traditions, Ovidian, pastoral, and heroic. Pope's keen responsiveness to the society about him is expressed through an equally keen responsiveness to literary modes that had imaged other societies, both human and divine.

While it is true that in its general conception the *Rape of the Lock* derives from the *Battle of the Frogs and Mice*, from Tassoni, and more immediately from Boileau and Garth, the actual style of the poem shows rather how much Pope owed to the tradition of Dryden and how much he still was learning from the first of the Augustans. In details of language, as nearly every page of the Twickenham Edition shows, Pope borrows more often from Dryden than from any other single poet. Even when he is not borrowing directly, he is indebted to the late seventeenth-century heroic style that Dryden had fixed as proper for epic and mock epic.

From early in his career we see Pope imitating Dryden, and yet imparting his own quality to his imitations. The two manners dominant in the older poet, the style of public address and the heroic, have left traces on Pope's earliest poems. Pope had seen Dryden once, and in his uneasy friendship with Wycherley he enjoyed a repeat performance of Restoration literary life in its less elegant form. His first attempt in satire, *To the Author of a Poem, intitled, Successio* (Settle),[1] has the hearty coarseness and the free-and-easy classical comparisons of Dryden's less finished prologues, while the lines *On Dulness* and other additions to Wycherley's poems resemble the heavier attacks on Shadwell in *Absalom and Achitophel*, Part II. The comparison of dullness with 'the Leaden Byass of a Bowl', patterned on the 'bias of the mind' simile in *Mac Flecknoe*, was to find a place in the *Dunciad*, the nearest to Dryden of all Pope's major works. But a lightness and grace of rhythm more characteristic of Pope can be felt in some of these fragments, especially in the '*Similitude*' on 'the Stream of Life'. Note that Pope's rhythm comes out more distinctly in the lines after the triplet (in itself characteristic of Dryden):

> The Stream of Life shou'd more securely flow
> In constant Motion, nor too swift nor slow,
> And neither swell too high, nor sink too low;

[1] Pope seems to have been imitating the style of the Earl of Dorset. See TE vi, fn., 16–17.

Not always glide thro' gloomy Vales, and rove
('Midst Flocks and Shepherds) in the silent Grove;
But more diffusive in its wand'ring Race;
Serve peopled Towns, and Stately Cities grace;
Around in sweet Meanders wildly range,
Kept fresh by Motion, and unchang'd by Change.
(18–26)

Though these are the lines of a town poet, there is a marked
similarity in idiom and descriptive style to the 'retirement'
passage in *Windsor Forest* (ll. 235–70). We have already
glanced at early experiments in the heroic style such as the
Episode of Sarpedon and the *Gardens of Alcinous*, which in
their choice pictorial details and smoother, more evenly
balanced couplets, show a sensibility quite different from
Dryden's.

The *Ode for Musick on St. Cecilia's Day*, though painfully
imitative of Dryden, has one passage that anticipates the
romantic mythological style of Collins and the early Keats:

By the Streams that ever flow,
By the fragrant Winds that blow
    O'er th' *Elysian* Flowers,
By those happy Souls who dwell
In Yellow Meads of *Asphodel*,
    Or *Amaranthine* Bowers:
By the Heroe's armed Shades,
Glitt'ring thro' the gloomy Glades,
By the Youths that dy'd for Love,
Wandring in the Myrtle Grove,
Restore, restore *Eurydice* to Life . . .
(71–81)

The blend of heroic reminiscence with delicate imagery, the
classical elegance of diction and movement, are what we
should expect from the future poet of the *Rape of the Lock*.
These qualities are combined with Pope's intimacy of address
(his *Spectator* tone) in the close of the *Epistle to Miss Blount,
With the Works of Voiture*, lines that might have been written
to Belinda:

Now crown'd with Myrtle, on th' *Elysian* Coast,
Amid those Lovers, joys his gentle Ghost,
Pleas'd while with Smiles his happy Lines you view,
And finds a fairer *Ramboüillet* in you.

The brightest Eyes of *France* inspir'd his Muse,
The brightest Eyes of *Britain* now peruse,
And dead as living, 'tis our Author's Pride,
Still to charm those who charm the World beside.

(73–80)

The epistle is a miniature exhibition of what Pope can do at
this point in his career and of what he will do in the *Rape of
the Lock* and in a number of his later satires. In the urbanity
of Voiture's art and personal life he sees an ideal for himself,
which he expresses with a lightness and sureness of rhythm
that beautifully symbolize an easy inner poise:

Thus wisely careless, innocently gay,
Chearful, he play'd the Trifle, Life, away,
'Till Fate scarce felt his gentle Breath supprest,
As smiling Infants sport themselves to Rest . . .

(11–14)

Pope offers the lady this image of freedom in contrast with
the formal restraint of custom and a 'successful' marriage.
Although he is charmed by feminine beauty, he sees through
the glitter with the eye of the later satirist and harshly brings
out the ugliness glimpsed 'thro' half-shut eyes' in the *Rape of
the Lock*. The lady is offered the same consolation and defence
in both poems:

Trust not too much your now resistless Charms,
Those, Age or Sickness, soon or late, disarms;
Good Humour only teaches Charms to last,
Still makes new Conquests, and maintains the past . . .

(59–62)

In the mastery of a personal attitude and of a corresponding
intimacy of tone and ease of rhythm, Pope sets himself apart
from Dryden while continuing to write within the mode of
Dryden's finest epistolary poems such as the prologue *To my
Dear Friend Mr. Congreve* or the epistle *To Sir Godfrey
Kneller*.

It was characteristic of Pope and of his integrity as a poet
that the traditional styles with which he had been experi-
menting should find a place in the work that most surely
marks his arrival at maturity. We have seen how he renewed
his early pastoral style in the scene of Belinda's journey down

the Thames, how he parodied the style without burlesquing
it, expressing in this way an awareness of a world where man
had once lived in significant and harmonious relationship
with Nature. It is not unexpected that his youthful experiments with Ovid also left a mark on the *Rape of the Lock*. In
making his versions of the *Metamorphoses* Pope had again
been imitating Dryden, and in particular the heroic style of
his translations from Ovid. As a result Pope's *Fables* are
closer to the heroic than to the implied tone of easy colloquial speech of the original, although his *Vertumnus and
Pomona* has a more Ovidian lightness of touch than his
Dryope. But whatever their failings as translations, they gave
Pope valuable experience in combining gallantry and heroics
in narratives of magical change. Partly owing to this early
practice the *Rape of the Lock* is epic 'Ovidianized'. There are
the specific borrowings such as the change of the lock into a
star, the allusion to Scilla's theft of Nisus' sacred lock, and
the comparison of Sir Fopling's death to 'th' expiring Swan'
of *Dido to Aeneas*. (All are discussed in Tillotson's excellent
introduction.) But more important proof of Ovid's influence
is the total effect of Ovidian transformation, of an imagined
region where belles become nymphs and goddesses, playing
cards become Homeric heroes, and where the whims and
concealed passions of lovers are turned into creatures of the
four elements. Significantly enough, Ariel comes from the
Tempest, the Shakespearean play that is most thoroughly
permeated by Ovidian metamorphosis. In its union of the
comedy of young love with classical myth and fairy lore, the
Rape of the Lock stands as Pope's *Midsummer Night's Dream*,
the last successful work in the Renaissance mythological
tradition that includes the tales of Marlowe, Lodge, and
Drayton, and the plays of Lyly. Pope's success in this mode,
like the Elizabethans', depends less on learning than on
a happy gift of mythological invention. As Tillotson finely
notes, Pope is being thoroughly Ovidian when he sees among
the wonders of the dressing table,

> The Tortoise here and Elephant unite,
> Transform'd to *Combs*, the speckled and the white.

(I. 135-6)

And where is there a better piece of mythological 'seeing'
than in the vision of the sylphs, in which the human and the
natural interchange with all the fluidity of metamorphosis?

> He summons strait his Denizens of Air;
> The lucid Squadrons round the Sails repair:
> Soft o'er the Shrouds Aerial Whispers breathe,
> That seem'd but *Zephyrs* to the Train beneath.
> Some to the Sun their Insect-Wings unfold,
> Waft on the Breeze, or sink in Clouds of Gold.
> Transparent Forms, too fine for mortal Sight,
> Their fluid Bodies half dissolv'd in Light.
> Loose to the Wind their airy Garments flew,
> Thin glitt'ring Textures of the filmy Dew;
> Dipt in the richest Tincture of the Skies,
> Where Light disports in ever-mingling Dies,
> While ev'ry Beam new transient Colours flings,
> Colours that change whene'er they wave their Wings.
>
> (II. 55–68)

The sylphs and the heroic actors of the *Rape of the Lock*
are Ovidian in still another way that links Pope's invention
with the *Metamorphoses*. In his epic of transformations Ovid
shocks and amuses by giving divine and heroic lovers the
manners and attitudes of contemporary Roman society.
Although Ovid knows what real passion is, the talk of love
among his heroes and divinities is full of coquetry and ex-
tremely 'wise'. In similar fashion Pope's spirits are 'Denizens
of Air' and of London society, unsubstantial, but very knowing in all the arts of love. Their view of beauty is reminiscent
of Ovid's *Ars Amatoria*:

> Our humbler Province is to tend the Fair,
> Not a less pleasing, tho' less glorious Care.
> To save the Powder from too rude a Gale,
> Nor let th' imprison'd Essences exhale,
> To draw fresh Colours from the vernal Flow'rs,
> To steal from Rainbows ere they drop in Show'rs
> A brighter Wash; to curl their waving Hairs,
> Assist their Blushes, and inspire their Airs;
> Nay oft, in Dreams, Invention we bestow,
> To change a *Flounce*, or add a *Furbelo*.
>
> (II. 91–100)

Belinda's charms are the product of magical cosmetic arts
over which the 'busy *Sylphs*' preside,

> And *Betty*'s prais'd for Labours not her own.
>   (I. 148)

Pope's refashioning of epic in Ovidian terms, making it more
splendid and more amusing, is one of the large ways in which
he adapted heroic poetry to his purposes in the *Rape of the
Lock*.

But Pope was thoroughly aware that he was writing in
an established genre practised by many poets before him.
Besides being familiar with well-known examples of mock-
heroic and burlesque poetry, he also must have read Dryden's
comments on the relations between satire and heroic poetry,
and he was certainly well acquainted with contemporary
theories of the epic. More important, he had first-hand knowledge of Homer, Virgil, and the English 'heroic' poets. The
1713 revision of the *Rape of the Lock*, in which the epic
machinery was added, was made at the time when Scriblerus
Club was in full swing,[1] in an atmosphere of mockery of
solemn learning and literature of all kinds. Earlier in the
same year Pope had published his ironic essay on pastoral
poetry and his prose burlesque, *A Receit to make an Epick
Poem*. The proposals for the *Iliad* had gone out in 1713, and
by May of 1714 he was surely at work on the translation. He
may have already started to translate before completing the
revision of the *Rape of the Lock* in December 1713. The resemblances between the poem and the translation of the *Iliad*
are at points very close, but as William Frost[2] has shown, it
is impossible to decide whether Pope is parodying his translation or anticipating it. In a broad sense, Pope had always
been a translator of Homer, from his early experiments in
epic and his translations of passages from the *Iliad* and the
Odyssey, to the *Rape of the Lock*, and the style of his *Iliad* is
hardly distinguishable from that of the considerably earlier

---

[1] For the chronology see *Memoirs of . . . Martinus Scriblerus*, ed. Charles Kerby-
Miller (New Haven, 1950), pp. 14–20, 26–28, 36–39; and also the *Art of Sinking in
Poetry*, ed. E. L. Steeves (New York, 1952), pp. xv–xvii. On the 'atmosphere' in
which the *Rape of the Lock* was revised, see Kerby-Miller, p. 28.

[2] William Frost, 'The *Rape of the Lock* and Pope's Homer', *Modern Language
Quarterly*, viii. 352–3.

Episode of Sarpedon and the *Gardens of Alcinous*. Whether or not he had completed any part of the translation before revising the *Rape of the Lock*, the poem is the inevitable example for comparing Pope's heroic and mock-heroic modes.

We have already seen how finely Pope transformed heroic poetry by the beautiful diminution of phrases like 'glitt'ring Forfex' and 'shining Altars'. In general he produces epic effects in the *Rape of the Lock* much as in his translation. Allusive imitation of Virgil or Dryden or Milton is the basis of his heroic style whether he is making a serious translation or writing a parody, and sharpening of visual details is as common in the epithets and scenes of the *Rape of the Lock* as of the *Iliad*. Pope's treatment of the fixed epithet in the *Rape of the Lock* makes clear what happened when he transferred the heroic style to a less serious subject. Exact translations of Homeric or Virgilian expressions are rare, though we do find 'seven-fold fence' for '*seven-fold* shield' and 'Garbs *succinct*' for Virgil's *succinctus*, and a fair number of phrases modelled closely on Virgil or Dryden, such as 'th' Etherial Plain', 'the Purpled Main', 'th' Aerial Kind', 'the wintry Main', and 'the kindly Rain'. By their generalized form and meaning, they give a passing if humorous glance at the great order of Nature 'out there', beyond the doings of Belinda and her friends. 'The gen'ral Fate', like similar phrases in Pope's *Iliad*, conceals the Homeric Moira under Roman solemnity and abstraction. Some of the combinations of epithet and noun—'th' Etherial Plain', 'th' Aerial Kind', 'the Finny Prey'—have a peculiar quality that makes them perfect for the *Rape of the Lock*. Like certain periphrases in Homer or in Virgil, especially as Englished by Dryden, they are tiny enigmas, some of them almost seventeenth-century scientific jokes, with an allusion to classification by genus and species. The definition of periphrase in the *Art of Sinking* fits precisely both the serious and the comic epic:

> *Periphrase* is another great Aid to *Prolixity*; being a diffus'd circum-locutory Manner of expressing a known Idea, which should be so misteriously couch'd, as to give the Reader the Pleasure of guessing what it is that the Author can possibly mean; and a Surprize when he finds it.

The wit latent in Virgil and apparent in Dryden (as in

volubile buxum, 'wooden engine', for a top)[1] works with a new
force in the context of the *Rape of the Lock,* since the slightly
enigmatic flavour and our 'Pleasure of guessing' and finding
what 'the Author can possibly mean' are now thoroughly in
place.

The use of heroic diction for ridicule might be described
simply as bad translation of the kind Pope refers to in the
Preface to the *Iliad.* Render literally an epithet like 'ox-eyed
Hera' and set it down mechanically in any context however
serious, and in English the result is absurd. (Literal translation of formulas will always seem comic to readers unfamiliar
with the conventions of oral epic.) Applying in reverse his
principle that the translator should use those phrases that
'agree with the tenor and main intent of the particular passage', Pope gets the desired effect in the *Rape of the Lock.*
Part of the fun comes from seeing Pope deliberately use
clichés of the type called 'diminishing Figures' in the *Art of
Sinking*:

THE EXPLETIVE,
admirably exemplified in the Epithets of many Authors.

> *Th' umbrageous Shadow, and the verdant Green,*
> *The running Current, and odorous Fragrance,*
> *Chear my lone Solitude with joyous Gladness.*

But the effect of even the most commonplace eighteenth-
century epithets is often more than comic. When used of the
card table at Hampton Court, 'verdant Field', 'velvet plain',
and 'level Green' have their sensuous value renewed, and unexpectedly fresh images come to mind. (The silken surface
becomes the smooth and shimmering expanse of an English
lawn. We may note again the fine imaginative extensions of
the technique in 'glitt'ring Forfex' and similar phrases.) In
these expressions and in many others the nice incongruity
and the slightly enigmatic quality of epic language blend
with lively sense impressions of scene, persons, and artifacts.

In the *Rape of the Lock,* as in the *Iliad* and the *Odyssey,*
there is much poetry of luxury and well-made things, of
'glitt'ring Spoil', 'rich Brocade' and 'silver Lamps', of 'rich

[1] See R. A. Brower, 'Dryden's Poetic Diction and Virgil', *Philological Quarterly,*
xviii. 211–17.

China Vessels' and 'gilded Chariots'. Through many descriptive devices Pope builds up little scenes of 'historic painting' that are the exact complement to the grander pictures of his *Iliad*. But the art and the artist in the epullion and the epic are the same, and positive effects of magnificence and pictorial beauty persist in the *Rape of the Lock* where they 'ought not to'. If we refer to the effects as 'exquisite', or 'charming' or 'Watteauesque', we also want to add something stronger. For through his use of epic style, at once traditional and highly individual, Pope realizes more serious meanings. If comparisons with battles, feasts, and sacrifices diminish the importance of the persons and events, they also express values of a world where greatness and ceremony were serious matters, where grace and beauty of manners were an index to civilization, a world alive in the 'historical present' of the mind of the poet and of readers who have a sense of the past.

Probably the largest single way in which Pope imparted qualities of splendour and wonder to his actors and action was through his brilliant adaptation of epic machinery. His success in producing the 'marvellous' needs little comment. Like Homer's gods, Pope's sylphs move easily in and out of the lower world, they surprise without offending our sense of the probable, and they give ordinary human impulses a sensuous form that makes us see them as they are, and yet as beautiful. What they 'really' stand for—feminine honour, flirtation, courtship, the necessary rivalry of man and woman —is seen in its essence, and a human impulse seen in its essence, as Keats observed of a street quarrel, is beautiful.

By inventing the sylphs Pope solved the almost impossible problem that the theorists set for the heroic poet. He is almost certainly the only modern poet to create a company of believable deities which are not simply the ancient classical divinities in modern dress, and which are not offensive to a Christian audience. As Warburton pronounced with his usual sententiousness:

. . . that sort of Machinery which his judgment taught him was only fit for his use, his admirable invention supplied. There was but one System in all nature which was to his purpose, the *Rosicrucian Philosophy*.

The tact with which Pope combined hints from *Rosicrucian Philosophy* with memories of Shakespeare, Milton, Lucretius, Ovid, and English country lore is finely described by Tillotson in his essay on the *Sylphs*. He brings out two main reasons for Pope's success in pleasing both epic theorists and the common reader: his choice of a mythology known well enough to count as 'established', and his

> ... grafting the whole heterogeneous system on 'all the Nurse and all the Priest have taught'... By this stroke he connects the machinery with the beliefs of his own country, a connection required of an epic poet.[1]

We may also add that it was Pope's familiarity with Ovid that helped him reach a unifying vision and metaphor (the sense of magical change), and that gave him hints for creating a style in which the marvellous, the socially sophisticated, and the heroic could be successfully combined.

Pope's achievement in introducing the marvellous into a modern poem carried him well beyond mere 'correctness', since he succeeded also in recovering something of Homer's vision of a human drama played in relation to a divine order. (To describe this feat without sinking in prose, we should need Pope's lightness of touch in poetry.) By deftly linking his invented deities with popular country beliefs and with the 'Heathen Mythology' of Fate and Jove, Pope makes us feel the presence of forces greater than Belinda and the Baron and their friends. The dwarfing of the persons, which everyone notices, is one sign that this is so. As unchanging Nature-Moira was implied in the diction and rhythm of Pope's *Iliad*, so in the *Rape of the Lock* a larger natural order is implied through setting or descriptive epithet and playful allusion. In the 'silver Thames' and the 'morning Sun', in 'the Rival of his Beams', and the 'Nymph' with her 'destructive' powers, we feel a link between social and natural worlds, and in the movement of stars and of time, we have an almost Homeric sense of the necessary end of Belinda's beauty and virtue:

> Then cease, bright Nymph! to mourn thy ravish'd Hair
> Which adds new Glory to the shining Sphere!
> Not all the Tresses that fair Head can boast
> Shall draw such Envy as the Lock you lost.

[1] TE ii. 358.

For, after all the Murders of your Eye,
When, after Millions slain, your self shall die;
When those fair Suns shall sett, as sett they must,
And all those Tresses shall be laid in Dust;
This Lock, the Muse shall consecrate to Fame,
And mid'st the Stars inscribe *Belinda*'s Name!
                                        (v. 141–50)

This is of course elegant spoofing, literary and social. We
are amused by the absurdity of the apotheosis and the analogies to Daphnis (Caesar) and to Achilles lying 'in the
Dust', and also by the allusion to the *Lock of Berenice*, which
was itself a spoof. (The effect is a kind of double parody.) We
are also reminded of the *Elegy to the Memory of an Unfortunate
Lady*:

How lov'd, how honour'd once, avails thee not,
To whom related, or by whom begot;
A heap of dust alone remains of thee;
'Tis all thou art, and all the proud shall be!
                                        (71–74)

But in the *Rape of the Lock* as in the *Elegy* the death of innocence and beauty are not laughing matters, and the apotheosis offers serious as well as playful consolation to Belinda
and Mrs. Arabella Fermor. With perfect deference to fact
and poetic fiction, Pope has found his equivalent for Homer's
Death and Sleep, and it is hard not to suppose that his sensibility and the internal form of his poem have been subtly
shaped by his familiarity with the Homeric use of myth. Not
only the mock apotheosis and the sylphs, but the whole drama
of the *Rape of the Lock* is a piece of wonderful myth-making.
'Mythos' as a fable or plot and 'mythos' as symbol are two
growths of the basic process of seeing and dramatizing that
we first observed in the *Pastorals*. Pope's growth as a poet may
be seen in his progress[1] from the pictorial mythologizing of
the *Pastorals* to the descriptive splendours and the fully
developed symbolism of *Windsor Forest*, to the 'fable' of
Belinda's lock. In the dramatic image of the *Rape of the Lock*
Pope created a native Augustan myth, as later readers have
instinctively and perhaps naïvely demonstrated, by taking the
poem for the stock symbol of the 'Age of Queen Anne'. A

[1] Cf. Ch. I, p. 24; Ch. II, pp. 50–54, 58–62.

not wholly adequate symbol, to be sure, if we think of the public grandeurs and the common miseries of London life in 1714. For the one, we need something like the Roman-Augustan myth of *Windsor Forest*; for the other, *The Harlot's Progress* or *Beer Street* and *Gin Lane*. But Pope gives at least a hint of the grandeur in

> Where *Thames* with Pride surveys his rising Tow'rs . . .
>
> (III. 2)

and of the misery in

> . . . Wretches hang that Jury-men may Dine . . .
>
> (III. 22)

Note that both references are made through epic allusion, that Pope has found in mock-epic a way like Homer's of 'looking out' on another world beyond the scene of his action. Pope uses allusion or parody to give us a glimpse of the great Homeric world, thus imitating Homer's technique while reversing the direction of our view. Similes compare Belinda with Aeneas,

> Not half so fixt the Trojan cou'd remain,
>
> (v. 5)

or the fracas over the lock with the quarrels on Olympus,

> So when bold *Homer* makes the Gods engage . . .
>
> (v. 45)

It was between these two heroic comparisons that Pope in 1717 set his '*parody*[1] *of the speech of Sarpedon to Glaucus*' in order to '*open more clearly the* MORAL *of the Poem*'.

> Then grave *Clarissa* graceful wav'd her Fan;
> Silence ensu'd, and thus the Nymph began.
>   Say, why are Beauties prais'd and honour'd most,
> The wise Man's Passion, and the vain Man's Toast?
> Why deck'd with all that Land and Sea afford,
> Why Angels call'd, and Angel-like ador'd?
> Why round our Coaches crowd the white-glov'd Beaus,
> Why bows the Side-box from its inmost Rows?
> How vain are all these Glories, all our Pains,
> Unless good Sense preserve what Beauty gains:

---

[1] Frost, 344, notes that Pope was not parodying Homer's Greek directly or only, but his own translation and possibly also a number of earlier versions.

That Men may say, when we the Front-box grace,
Behold the first in Virtue, as in Face!
Oh! if to dance all Night, and dress all Day,
Charm'd the Small-pox, or chas'd old Age away;
Who would not scorn what Huswife's Cares produce,
Or who would learn one earthly Thing of Use?
To patch, nay ogle, might become a Saint,
Nor could it sure be such a Sin to paint.
But since, alas! frail Beauty must decay,
Curl'd or uncurl'd, since Locks will turn to grey,
Since painted, or not painted, all shall. fade,
And she who scorns a man, must die a Maid;
What then remains, but well our Pow'r to use,
And keep good Humour still whate'er we lose?
And trust me, Dear! good Humour can prevail,
When Airs, and Flights, and Screams, and Scolding fail.
Beauties in vain their pretty Eyes may roll;
Charms strike the Sight, but Merit wins the Soul.
     So spoke the Dame, but no Applause ensu'd . . .
                    (v. 7–35)

Pope's treatment of the passage shows finally and clearly
where the mock-epic of the *Rape of the Lock* stands in relation
to Homer and the English heroic tradition. The main effect
of Clarissa's speech for readers not over-conscious of Homer
or Le Bossu comes from hearing the voice of common sense
in the midst of much ado about nothing. We feel too a fairly
hearty amusement in the obvious parallels to the *Iliad* and
a flicker of Walleresque sentiment,

     But since, alas! frail Beauty must decay . . .

An eighteenth-century reader would recognize that Pope
was now giving 'the moral' demanded by theorists and so
anticipating the objections of Dennis, who had found Pope's
purpose not sufficiently clear. Closer comparison with Homer
will show how skilful parody readjusted Homer's moral to
fit the values of Augustan society.
     The parody opens on Dryden's high-heroic level, with an
allusion to one of the most serious speeches in *Absalom and
Achitophel*, the 'temptation' of Monmouth:

     Say, why are Beauties prais'd and honour'd most,
     The wise Man's Passion, and the vain Man's Toast?

In the Homeric counterpart, Sarpedon cites as proofs of glory the simple goods of meat and drink, speaking of them with complete certainty as to their value. In Pope's version, as we noted in the last chapter, Sarpedon acknowledges these glories, but they have been raised to a nobler pitch, since they are signs of a divine blessing. The ultimate value is 'above', not here below. The translation in effect if not in fact anticipates Clarissa's attitude. In her appeal 'these Glories' of social success are in themselves 'vain', and the Homeric parallels underline the gap between true and false grandeur. But the superior virtue recommended by Clarissa, the combination of 'good Sense' and 'good Humour', is not quite transcendental and so altogether perfect for the occasion. It is a real virtue, but a 'smiling' one, and attainable within the limits of a worldly society more inclined to trust intelligence than enthusiasm. But it can accomplish some fairly wonderful things:

> Charms strike the Sight, but Merit wins the Soul.

As elsewhere in the poem, Pope attunes his moral sentiments to the mock-heroic by means of his tone,

> And trust me, Dear! good Humour can prevail,
> When Airs, and Flights, and Screams, and Scolding fail.

This is cosily feminine to the point of caricature: Clarissa moralizing is very much 'like a woman'.

But in adopting such a tone Pope is edging away from mock-heroic toward burlesque, and at some points in the passage he slips into the kind of 'jest', as Dryden would say, that 'gives us a boyish kind of pleasure'. In serious neo-classical parody ordinary persons and actions are presented in a style so nicely simulating the heroic as to barely break the epic decorum. (This is Dryden's manner at its best in his heroic satires.) In burlesque, by contrast, high-heroic persons are presented in a low style, a travesty of the heroic. We take 'a boyish kind of pleasure', in seeing the style debased, and we laugh less at the person than the language. By Canto V of the *Rape of the Lock* 'grave Clarissa', Belinda, and Thalestris have become surprisingly heroic, hence any descent seems more of a let-down. Set certain lines in the

passage beside Homer or beside Pope's translation, and they
become in an eighteenth-century sense 'vulgar':

> Oh! if to dance all Night, and dress all Day,
> Charm'd the Small-pox, or chas'd old Age away . . .
>
> To patch, nay ogle, might become a Saint . . .
>
> Curl'd or uncurl'd, since Locks will turn to grey,
> Since painted, or not painted, all shall fade . . .

The level of the diction comes perilously near to Swift's
Corinna or *The Progress of Beauty*. Dryden will go this far in
ridiculing the most despicable butts of his satire, but not
often, and his best parodies of Virgil have a Latin finesse rarely
equalled by Pope (probably because he was a better Latinist).
Pope shows a similar finesse in parodying English poets, including Dryden himself, but his occasional coarseness has
a value. By this mention of a horrid disease and the gross
deceptions of cosmetics, the ugly realities of the London
world are particularized and brought home to us. As a result
Pope comes closer to Homer's 'ten thousand shapes of
death' in this burlesque than in the bland abstractions of his
translation. The effect is like Gay's in *The Shepherd's Week*,
where Gay recovered some of the healthy charm of Theocritus by introducing exact if vulgar details. Pope's thrust
into realism in this speech and at other points in the *Rape of
the Lock* brings his trifle nearer to the 'naïve' realism and the
inclusiveness of vision of Homeric poetry.

That some coarsening of mockery appears in a passage
added in the 1717 edition is significant. Pope is no longer
quite the 'gayest valetudinaire alive' of his *Farewell to
London*, nor the would-be Voiture of his *Epistle to Miss
Blount*. He has been through his ugly experience with Curll,
and he has suffered more 'contamination' through various
Scriblerian projects and his collaboration with Gay in the
What D'Ye Call It, a burlesque of Addison's *Cato*. He is
nearer in mood to Swift now that Swift is no longer near at
hand. But he is not ready for a poem combining this vein of
harshness and tougher wit with the surface magnificence of
Dryden's heroic style; that is, he is not yet the poet of the
Dunciad.

For the *Rape of the Lock* and the world Pope is mocking in

the poem, consistent use of Dryden's tone would of course be absurd. It was justified in Dryden's own satires because his victims were elevated by the great public issues in which they were involved. But Pope at this point in his career has no scene or historic vision of similar scope. His social scene, in comparison with Dryden's, is private, and the vices ridiculed and the moral offered belong to private life. But the more intimate scene favoured Pope's use of the more personal tone denied to Dryden, and though Pope can allude to the high heroic manner for ridicule or serious placing of his action, he is not bound by it, as he was in translating the *Iliad*. In his translation Pope writes within the limits of proper heroic solemnity, and he cannot allow his Jove and Juno to come down to the comic level of Zeus and Hera. If he had done so, the 'true Heroick' artifice would have collapsed. But in the *Rape of the Lock*, starting from a premise of mockery, Pope is happily free to include ugly and serious implications in a literary and social *divertimento*. Pope, like Horace, can be convincingly serious only when it is certain that no one will take him quite seriously.

VI

THE IMAGE OF HORACE

I am now at my leisure hours reading Horace with some
diligence and find the world was just the same then, that
it continues to be now. . . .

(Thomas Burnet to George Duckett, 1 June 1716)

THE single fact that best expresses the difference between
Dryden and Pope is the active presence of Horace as a
writer and a symbolic figure in Pope's life and poetry.
In spite of his indebtedness to Horace in his prologues and
his essays in verse, Dryden confessed 'that the delight which
Horace gives me is but languishing', and he went so far as to
describe the style of the *Satires* and *Epistles* as 'generally
grovelling'. Horace and Pope might well reply with *de te
fabula narratur*. It was altogether natural for Dryden to rise
in satire to 'the majesty of the heroic', and though he adopts
the 'legislative style' of Horace in the *Religio Laici*, at his
most vigorous moments in the poem he writes in the heroic-
declamatory manner of *Absalom and Achitophel*. As we have
seen from the *Rape of the Lock*, there is in Pope an opposite
tendency to mask and modulate the heroic by talking to the
reader in a tone that is 'Spectator-Horatian'. The essayists of
the *Spectator* and the *Tatler* and similar periodicals were like
Pope writing with Horace over their shoulder. Their literary
style, their conception of their function as polite educators,
their picture of the good life in town and country, are further
signs of the effect of Horace's example. For the small yet
influential class that created what we call eighteenth-century
civilization, Horace was a kind of 'cultural hero', a description he would certainly find amusing, if we may judge from
his self-portrait:

> Quite small, grey before my time, made for the sun;
> Quick to anger, yet after all easily soothed.

> corporis exigui, praecanum, solibus aptum,
> irasci celerem, tamen ut placabilis essem.[1]

(Epp. I. xx. 24–25)

[1] All quotations from Horace are taken from *Q. Horati Flacci Opera*, ed.

Though Thomas Burnet was historically naïve in finding the world of Horace 'just the same' as the Age of Anne, he could easily have produced reasons to justify his impression. For example, he might have pointed out the broad historical parallels of the kind we have noted in speaking of *Windsor Forest*—between two societies in an era of concentration following an era of revolution, between nations just becoming aware of their imperial role, and between cultures enriched by increased leisure and easier contacts with 'earth's distant ends'. For the eighteenth-century gentleman enjoying the private benefits of these public improvements the world of Horace's *Satires* and *Epistles* offered striking parallels to his own. Like Horace, he could look about him and see some lives charmingly balanced between city and country, action and retirement, and other lives grossly submerged in political ambition or newly acquired wealth and conspicuous consumption. Whatever may have been the actualities of English life in the reign of Anne, it was quite easy for a citizen of that world to see himself and his fellows through Horace's eyes. We need to remember, of course, that Horace's world is not a documentary study of the Age of Augustus, but a poet's vision of reality. The fantasies of a Roman dinner party as pictured by Horace and the air of serenity that lingers about the Sabine farm are not Nature still, but Nature Horatianized. Nevertheless, Pope and his friends—writers, statesmen, artists, country gentlemen of many degrees of grandeur —often saw their own world through Horace's eyes and to a surprising degree tried to shape the actuality to fit the dream. The eighteenth-century villa, not too far from Town, stocked with the best authors and provided with a beautiful and useful garden, is 'translated' out of Horace. Pope's house at 'Twitnam' is the charming if amusing symbol of a life

Eduardus C. Wickham, 2nd ed., H. W. Garrod (Oxford, 1912). In interpreting and translating the text I am especially indebted to: *Quinti Horatii Flacci Opera*, ed. E. C. Wickham, vol. ii, *The Satires, Epistles, and De Arte Poetica* (Oxford, 1891); *Horace, Satires, Epistles, and Ars Poetica*, ed. and tr. H. Rushton Fairclough (London, 1929). I have made use also of W. Y. Sellar, *The Roman Poets of the Augustan Age, Horace and the Elegiac Poets* (Oxford, 1891); Elizabeth Hazleton Haight, *Horace and His Art of Enjoyment* (New York, 1925); A. Y. Campbell, *Horace, A New Interpretation* (London, 1924); *Horace, Satires*, ed. and tr. François Villeneuve, Coll. des Universités de France (Paris, 1932); Walter Wili Apel, *Horaz und die augusteische Kultur* (Basel, 1948).

and a literary career that became progressively an *Imitatio Horati*.

In the years following his translation of the *Iliad*—the work that provided the financial basis for that easy life of building, planting, and easy converse with the great—nearly everything that Pope wrote shows more or less distinctly the influence of Horatian poetic modes and themes. There were anticipations in the early epistles to Miss Blount, to Jervas, and to Addison, but with the noble *Epistle to Robert Earl of Oxford* (1721) Pope reached maturity as a poet of Horatian 'moral song', if he was not yet in Warton's unsympathetic phrase 'a moral, a satiric, and a didactic poet'. But 'the Horatian mode' and 'Horatian' are notoriously ambiguous terms as used in English literary criticism. At least four meanings need to be distinguished here. First, there is 'Horatian' as applied to poetry deriving from the *Odes*, the term being used to describe the fine poise of urbanity and feeling in poems on love and patriotic themes, the qualities so beautifully exemplified in Marvell's *Ode* on Cromwell or *To His Coy Mistress*. Next there is the 'Horatian' manner of Dryden and his contemporaries, the style of public address and instruction. This Restoration style was ultimately indebted to the true Horatian satirical-epistolary mode, to Horace's own style and 'manner of proceeding' in satire. Finally, there is Pope's own 'Horatian' mode, a variation on Dryden's style of public address and the manner of Horace himself.

Before attempting in the next chapter to describe the 'poetical character' of the *Essay on Criticism* and the *Essay on Man*, it will be useful to have some concrete definition of the true Horatian mode and some first-hand contact with the texture of Horace's poetry in the *Satires* and *Epistles*. It is also important to see as clearly as possible the total image of Horace that emerges from these poems, since it is constantly being reflected or refracted in Pope's moral and satirical poetry. But it is not easy to define the 'true Horatian mode' even if we are referring quite strictly to Horace's own poems. There is scarcely any poet who has revealed himself more fully as writer and person than Horace, and yet the result is to make us feel how elusive his or any personality is. We know Horace too well, just as we know a close friend too well, to sum him up in a convenient formula or two.

Moreover, Horace's work as a satirical-epistolary poet covers many years and a considerable development, from the crude lampooning attacks and farces of his early satires on clownish types and sexual adventurers, in the years when he was following Brutus and the Republicans, to the fine meditations on the good life and secure friendship, in the period of his intimacy with Maecenas and Augustus. Nor is it easy to know what term to use for Horace's discursive hexameter poems, since Horace himself is not too clear on the point. Although on occasion he uses *satura* in referring to poems in the two books of *Satires*, he uses *sermones*, 'conversations' or 'causeries', for both his *Satires* and *Epistles*.[1] The ancient Roman term *satura* is itself sufficiently obscure and ambiguous in meaning. As used of poems by the earliest Roman satirists, Ennius and Pacuvius, *satura* referred to a hodgepodge composition in various metres and on various subjects from violent personal abuse to earnest teaching of a philosophical doctrine. Lucilius, whom Horace regards as the real *inventor* of Roman satire, seems in Horace's view to depend on writers of Greek Old Comedy such as Cratinus and Aristophanes. Though Lucilius 'rubbed down the town' in harsh Aristophanic attacks on persons, and wrote philosophic sermons (in our sense of the word), he tended toward greater unity in subject and style than earlier Roman satirists. He also wrote dramatic and autobiographical sketches of the kind Horace imitated in the *Bore* and the *Journey to Brundisium*. But although all the features of earlier Roman satire, except the mixture of metres, turn up in Horace's *Satires*, Horace was himself a great inventor. The Horatian *sermo* as it developed in the later satires and in the *Epistles*, if not exactly an independent genre, is a unique kind of poetry. (It goes without saying that the common English meaning of satire as an attack, as a poem 'against' somebody or some-

---

[1] *Opera*, ed. Wickham, ii. 6–9. On the nature of *satura* and its relation to comedy see G. L. Hendrickson, 'Horace, *Serm*. i. 4. A Protest and a Programme', *American Journal of Philology*, xxi. 121–42: 'Satura—the Genesis of a Literary Form', *Classical Philology*, vi. 129–43; B. L. Ullman, 'Dramatic "Satura"', *Classical Philology*, ix. 1–23.

thing, will hardly apply to the bulk of Horace's conversational poetry.)

In one of the early satires[1] Horace further muddied the waters of criticism by raising the ugly and unnecessary question as to whether his poems were poetry. His object seems to have been tactical, a move to exclude his satires from attack by saying that they weren't really poems anyway. The kind of composition he describes in a later[2] defence seems sufficiently complex to be called poetic. After criticizing Lucilius for roughness in rhythm though praising him for his sharp satirical thrusts (*sale multo/urbem defricuit*), he adds that he cannot, however, regard such unfinished pieces as really beautiful poems (*pulchra poemata*). It is not enough, he says, to produce a horselaugh from the audience, though of course there is some virtue in doing that. No, there is a need for conciseness (*brevitas*) so that the thought moves along easily and clearly without boring the reader. There is need for a style that is sometimes serious, often gay, that adapts itself to various roles, the satirist playing now the orator and now the poet, now the man of the world (*urbanus*), who withholds his strength, sparing it with deliberate intent. Raillery (*ridiculum*) often cuts through a great issue more effectively than a bitter shaft of wit (*acri*):

> est brevitate opus, ut currat sententia, neu se
> impediat verbis lassas onerantibus auris;
> et sermone opus est modo tristi, saepe iocoso,
> defendente vicem modo rhetoris atque poetae,
> interdum urbani, parcentis viribus atque
> extenuantis eas consulto. ridiculum acri
> fortius et melius magnas plerumque secat res.
>
> (*Sat.* I. x. 9–15)

What Horace means exactly by the 'role of the poet' in this context is not quite clear. In the earlier satire where he rejects the title of poet for himself, he says that the true *poeta* possesses *ingenium*, genius, or natural talent rather than mere art, that he is gifted with divine—we might say, subconscious—powers of perception (*mens divinior*), and with eloquence capable of expressing high truths, *os/magna sonaturum*. From Horace's use of *ingenium* in other contexts (*Ars*

[1] *Sat.* I. iv. 39–62.   [2] *Sat.* I. x. 1–15.

Poetica, 323; *Odes*, ii. xviii. 9) and from the view of the poet-priest expressed in the *Odes*, it seems that 'the role of the poet' embraces the exercise of imagination in dramatic and lyric poetry. In using the expression, Horace is talking about the writer's power to go out of himself into other roles or into states of heightened feeling. Like Pope and like Dr. Johnson, he knows that the final aim of poetry is to move the reader. So he reminds us in the *Ars Poetica* that it is not enough for poems (dramas, in particular) to be beautifully and artfully made, they must also be affecting, *dulcia*. The reader will feel only if the writer has felt first:

> . . . si vis me flere, dolendum est
> primum ipsi tibi . . .
>
> (102–3)

A kind of literature that allows for writing at such levels of intensity and imaginative power and that also has a place for seriousness and fun, for irony and witty ridicule, seems to deserve the title of poetry. To adapt the question Johnson used of Pope, we may ask, 'If this be not poetry, where is poetry to be found?'

We may define this kind of poetry by considering a poem familiar to English readers in various forms, the Sixth Satire of the Second Book, *Hoc erat in votis*, 'The City Mouse and the Country Mouse'. The example is convenient since Pope and Swift joined in making a version of it, and since it is so little satirical in the harsh English sense of the term. The opening lines are a classic expression of perfect content and thankfulness that is religious without a trace of unction:

> This I prayed for; a piece of land not very large,
> With a garden and a spring of living water near the house,
> And a little wood beyond.—More and better
> The gods have given.—It's very good—I ask no more,
> O son of Maia, unless you'll make these gifts my own.

> Hoc erat in votis: modus agri non ita magnus,
> hortus ubi et tecto vicinus iugis aquae fons
> et paulum silvae super his foret. auctius atque
> di melius fecere. bene est. nil amplius oro,
> Maia nate, nisi ut propria haec mihi munera faxis.
>
> (1–5)

The tone and movement are remarkable and characteristic:
we come on the poet talking to himself, half-praying, in
language that varies little from familiar Latin prose in order
and vocabulary. Rhetorical emphasis and diction are kept at
the most moderate level of intensity, although *magnus* and
hortus and *fons* and *auctius* are thrown into sufficient relief to
suggest an inner warmth of feeling. Most wonderful is
the compromise between hexameter and prose rhythms, the
pauses that seem so natural coming at traditional points for
the caesura. The impression of the arrest and flow of casual
speech and thought are reminiscent of Robert Frost in his
most 'speaking' poems, and as in Frost part of our pleasure
comes from noting on the side that feeling, speech, and metre
are being so nicely managed.

As the poet prays, his voice ascends by subtle gradations
to something nearer oratory, the lines falling into a fairly
elaborate period and each clause starting with an 'if . . .'
si neque . . . si veneror . . . si quod . . . hac prece te oro. But the
prayer has been amusingly broken by a satirical echo of the
prayers of the discontented, and though Horace praises
himself, we are hardly aware of it,

> If I have not made my property greater by shady deals,
> If I do not mean to make it less by crime or wrong-doing . . .
>
> $$(6-7)$$

From such rural and moral satisfactions—the two are always
linked in Horace—the poet turns to address the god of urban
'busyness', Janus, god of mornings and beginnings. Though
there is no logical transition, there is a remarkable transition
in style:

> Matutine pater, seu 'Iane' libentius audis . . .
>
> $$(20)$$
>
> O Father Matutinal—or Janus hear'st thou rather?

The comically grand epithet can pass as prayerful, while the
rest of the line is dignified enough for Milton to work it into
Paradise Lost.

A passage follows next in which Horace tells how he
rushes about on his morning errands at Rome, while insults
and wry remarks are showered on him by people who get in
his way—lines of untranslatable art, one of those Horatian

conversational mosaics that sketch characters and satirize them at the same time. The final exchange may suggest the quality:

'*Do*, please, *do* have Maecenas seal these documents!'
(I say: 'I'll try'.) 'If you want to, you can!' he adds with a push.

'imprimat his, cura, Maecenas signa tabellis.'
dixeris, 'experiar': 'si vis, potes' addit et instat.

(38–39)

Without the slightest stir on the surface but with a calculated shock of contrast, Horace now slips into a tranquil narrative. Here is the point where we can feel the special excitement of Horace's conversational poetry, a kind of excitement which Eliot produces with equal skill:

> . . . he adds with a push.
> By now the seventh—almost the eighth—year has passed
> Since Maecenas began to consider me one of his own . . .

septimus octavo propior iam fugerit annus
ex quo Maecenas me coepit habere suorum
in numero . . .   (40–42)

The passage that follows is an answer to curious persons who imagine that Horace is in on state secrets, and it is also a fine defence of the decency and mutual self-respect of those who belonged to Maecenas' circle. Horace makes his case without a single priggish declaration, by exquisite innuendo, in another conversational mosaic. He says in effect, 'Yes, we're intimate enough for talk like this as we ride out on a winter morning':

'What time did you say?'—'Is the Thracian Chick* a match for
    Syrus?'—
'These morning frosts will nip people who aren't careful'.

* a gladiator

. . . 'hora quota est? Thraex est Gallina Syro par?
matutina parum cautos iam frigora mordent'. . .

(44–45)

Swift suggests admirably the intimacy of tone, though he has none of Horace's elegance of rhythm:

> 'Tis (let me see) three years and more,
> (October next it will be four)

Since HARLEY bid me first attend,
And chose me for an humble friend;
Wou'd take me in his Coach to chat,
And question me of this and that;
As, "What's o'clock?" And, "How's the Wind?"
"Who's Chariot's that we left behind?"
Or gravely try to read the lines
Writ underneath the Country Signs;
Or, "Have you nothing new to-day
"From Pope, from Parnel, or from Gay?"
Such tattle often entertains
My Lord and me as far as Stains,
As once a week we travel down
To Windsor, and again to Town,
Where all that passes, *inter nos*,
Might be proclaim'd at Charing-Cross.   (83–100)

In the original, after another onslaught of questions from busybodies, the poet reflects to himself,

And so my day is wasted, though not without prayers . . .
perditur haec inter misero lux non sine votis . . .   (59)

The line is a fine example of Horatian modulation in tone: it goes from the impersonal *perditur* to the discreetly personal 'ethical dative' in *misero*, to a phrase recalling the warmth and inwardness of *Hoc erat in votis*. Throughout the poem (as in many others) Horace is marvellously skilful in weaving his way from outer drama to inner desire, from personal to impersonal and back again. He has begun his conversation with 'I's' tactfully and unobtrusively introduced; then in the first passage of dialogue he slips in a reference to himself under the generalizing 'you', *dixeris* (an untranslatable refinement); he ends the interchange with Maecenas by calling himself *noster*, 'our friend Horace'; and finally there is a nice warming up of the tone as he comes back to 'me' after the second bout with the questioners.

'Prayers', *non sine votis*, is the signal for a return to the word in the first line of the poem:

o rus, quando ego te aspiciam? . . .
                (60)
O country, when shall I see you again?

For the first time in the satire we distinctly hear the voice of the *poeta*, and in the following lyric we have one of the purest expressions of the Horatian 'good life'. No commentary or translation can quite catch the attitude of laughing reverence for the country, for sweet idleness, good food, good friends, and 'heavenly philosophy'. I print the Latin first in the hope that the reader may have a first impression unclouded by the English 'crutch' that follows:

> . . . quandoque licebit
> nunc veterum libris, nunc somno et inertibus horis,
> ducere sollicitae iucunda oblivia vitae?
> o quando faba Pythagorae cognata simulque
> uncta satis pingui ponentur holuscula lardo?
> o noctes cenaeque deum! quibus ipse meique
> ante Larem proprium vescor vernasque procaces
> pasco libatis dapibus. prout cuique libido est
> siccat inaequalis calices conviva, solutus
> legibus insanis, seu quis capit acria fortis
> pocula seu modicis uvescit laetius. ergo
> sermo oritur, non de villis domibusve alienis,
> nec male necne Lepos saltet; sed quod magis ad nos
> pertinet et nescire malum est agitamus: utrumne
> divitiis homines an sint virtute beati;
> quidve ad amicitias, usus rectumne, trahat nos;
> et quae sit natura boni summumque quid eius.
>
> (60–76)

> Oh my Sabine farm, when shall I see you, when again
> With old authors, with sleep and lazy hours
> Can I find sweet forgetfulness of painful life?
> Oh when will the beans (Pythagoras' cousins!) lie close
> With the greens well oiled with fat bacon?
> Oh nights and feasts of the gods! when I and my friends
> Eat near my Hearth-god, and my cocky slaves
> Feed on our leavings! Every man in his humour
> Drains a cup large or small—no toasts by law:
> Health first is the rule, whether you go
> For potent potations, or for cheerfully moderate boosing.
> Now comes good talk, not of neighbours' houses and lands,
> Or how Lepos is dancing, but questions more to the point,
> More for our good, where ignorance is sin: we ask
> If money or virtue makes men happy;
> What draws us to friendship, goodness or self-interest,
> What's the meaning of 'good', and what's the *summum bonum*.

The elements that make up this ideal vision and the poetic navigation from one element to another are well worth noting. The country that Horace longs for so intensely is valued as an escape from city business, but more positively for the life it makes possible—reading, sleep, and idleness, and a return to the simple patriarchal society of the Italian farmer-proprietor. The sweetly pastoral, almost 'celestial' quality of the scene is humorously undercut by talk of Pythagoras' 'cousinship with the bean' (a reference to his belief in transmigration), by the too ecstatic exclamations and by the intrusion of a shrewd comment on the cocky manners of the servants. The crown of life, amusingly enough, is *sermo*, Horatian poetry at home. In a passage like this, where Horace is being least obviously philosophical, we can see best what 'philosophy' means in much of his poetry. Philosophy is a part of a mature and civilized life, not a system or a doctrine, but the act of asking the important questions. The *raison d'être* is Socratic: 'the unexamined life is not worth living'. Philosophizing has value, especially in an acquisitive society, if only because it saves us from comparing the prices of villas and the styles of different dancers. The first question Horace and his friends raise is apropos—'Whether money or virtue makes men happy'. (Our impulse to dismiss the question as naïve is, one suspects, a sign of corruption rather than sophistication.) The third question, *natura boni summumque*, is the counterpart of our attempts to define 'value'. The question about friendship (a theme so near to us that we shrink from acknowledging its importance) is put in good eighteenth-century terms, *usus rectumne*, 'self-interest' versus 'moral good'. The real justification of philosophic conversation, Horace implies, is not in finding the answers, but in the difference it makes to the life of the man who philosophizes, in his realizing at least partially his capacity as a reflective animal.

With perfect appropriateness to the occasion, one of the diners at this 'feast of the gods' tells a country fable. In the first line of the story, by the art of arranging adjectives which he uses with such effect in the *Odes*, Horace points the moral of the tale and of the poem and draws a witty contrast between two characters:

> . . .'olim
> rusticus urbanum murem mus paupere fertur
> accepisse cavo . . .'
>
> (79–81)

> 'Once
> A country mouse had a city mouse to dinner (they say)
> In his simple cave . . .'

The best 'translation' of this tale, of the cosiness, the miniature grandeurs, the pomposity of the *urbanus* and the naïve good sense of the *rusticus*, is *The Wind in the Willows*. The country mouse brings a dried raisin and half-eaten bits of bacon (his serving-tray is his mouth), then lies like a patriarch 'stretched out on fresh straw':

> . . . pater ipse domus palea porrectus in horna . . .
>
> (88)

We hear remarks that satirize the speaker and perhaps Horace, as the city mouse takes the part of one of the poet's friends,

> 'Why do you insist, my friend', says he,
> 'On living at the edge of this wooded cliff?'

> . . .'quid te iuvat' inquit, 'amice,
> praerupti nemoris patientem vivere dorso?'
>
> (90–91)

Or he parodies Horace in one of his favorite roles as lyric poet. Not *'Carpe diem!'* but *'Carpe viam!'* he cries, and launches into a brief ode on time, death, and happiness. When the pair go off to the city, the style rises to epic, with effects exactly like the epic mockery of the *Rape of the Lock*:

> . . . iamque tenebat
> nox medium caeli spatium, cum ponit uterque
> in locuplete domo vestigia, rubro ubi cocco
> tincta super lectos canderet vestis eburnos . . .
>
> (100–3)

> And now was Night
> Midway in her celestial course, when they set foot
> In that luxurious abode where deep-dyed purple
> Stuffs lay in shining splendour on ivory couches. . .

Seen through a mouse's eye these splendours are grand

enough, but they are at the same time reduced to absurdity, like the treasures of Belinda's dressing-table and the magnificence of Hampton Court. The story of high life among the mice ends with a *coup-de-théâtre*, as the great doors creak and the barking of Molossian hounds is heard through the house. The *rusticus* wisely concludes, as Horace would, that 'this life is not for me'.

But the moral is only glanced at, like other incidental morals of the poem such as the conviction that busyness is a waste of spirit or that a patron and his protegé may be intimate and yet keep a certain distance. One moral, that it is *malum* not to study virtue, though stated directly, is brought out unobtrusively through the little dramatic lyric on the country feast. Although on occasion Horace can be as direct in denunciation as Juvenal, indirection is one of his chief characteristics as a moralist and a poet. A number of other prominent features of the Horatian mode appear in this same satire. Probably the most characteristic is the air of 'graceful negligence', as Pope calls it, the free-wheeling of the ideal conversationalist who now speaks to his listener as friend-to-friend, who next talks to himself as he speculates or expresses some personal desire, who at times stands aside to let a piece of comic dialogue or narrative speak for itself, who can without embarrassment take the part of an orator or a lyric poet or philosopher. He also enjoys other freedoms of a more specialized literary sort, of parodying well-known styles (including his own), of using a wide variety of rhythmic effects from prose-talk in hexameter lengths to lyric symmetry (*nunc veterum libris, nunc somno et inertibus horis*), and spacious epic paragraphing. *Hoc erat in votis* has also a kind of metaphorical design in the constant association of morning with city hurry and confusion, and of night with the country and delights of friendship and feasting. Though in this satire Horace keeps close to a single theme, he allows himself some of his usual freedom of working in satirical observations on other subjects more or less apropos, for example, on common views of patronage or on the greed of small landowners or the manners of Roman servants. Although there is some fairly direct satire, most of the hits like the morals are made by implication through speech or narrative. One further characteristic cannot be over-stressed, the fine balance maintained between personal and impersonal. The conversation is throughout cunningly addressed both to the poet's self and to the world, and just when Horace seems to be getting too close to home facts, as in the account of Maecenas' household, he withdraws and talks about 'our Horace', or brings the reader into the situation by an ambiguous 'you'. He is never—at least in this poem— too far above his audience, although he is in fact often reading us a lesson. Dryden, though a begrudging admirer of Horace, speaks warmly of him as a teacher,

> His sentences are truly shining and instructive; but they are sprinkled here and there. Horace is teaching us in every line, and is perpetually moral: he had found out the skill of Virgil, to hide his sentences; to give you the virtue of them, without showing them in their full extent. . . .

But the most Horatian quality is the freedom, the ideal resourcefulness in art that Horace praises in his picture of the poet:

> He will seem to play, and yet be suffering, as a dancer
> Who moves now like a Satyr, now like a boorish Cyclops.

> ludentis speciem dabit et torquebitur, ut qui
> nunc Satyrum, nunc agrestem Cyclopa movetur.
>
> (*Epp.* II. ii. 124–5)

But Horace's value and significance for Pope and his contemporaries was more than purely literary. The Augustans saw in Horace's poetry a concentrated image of a life and a civilization to which they more or less consciously aspired, a fact that we shall see illustrated later in the poetry of Pope's 'second career', the period of the original satires and the *Imitations*.

Some of the larger values and attitudes that Horace represented have already been brought out in our reading of *Hoc erat in votis*; in delineating other facets of the Horatian image, we can fill in and refine our account of the genuine Horatian mode. *Hoc erat in votis* is the original of all those petitions for a not-quite-absolute retreat, from Pomfret's *Choice* (1700) to Cowper's *Task* (1785). But other poems by Horace, especially among the *Epistles*, convey more seriously and more subtly the meaning of country life and reveal keener responsiveness to the natural world. Although Horace did not have Wordsworth's insight or Tennyson's exquisite powers of observation, he sees and records broad effects of landscape with clarity and affection. He notices how the sun falls on the slopes of his Sabine valley, he has an eye for the play of light on grass and swiftly flowing streams; and he sees the gleam of hoarfrost on fields and the dazzling white of snow on distant mountains. Horace has the Roman passion for the sound of running water, and he tries, perhaps too often, to echo the liquid lapse of murmuring streams:

> ... per pronum trepidat cum murmure rivum ...
>
> (*Epp.* I. x. 21)

Although Horace loves country sights and sounds, he does not forget that water is salubrious and useful for irrigation, or that the oaks in his valley produce food for cattle and shade for the master. But Horace values the country most for the opportunity it gives him to enjoy the sweet society of *Hoc erat in votis* and to cultivate the private life of the soul. He often catches the quality of the inner life best in brief incidental phrases referring to his country retreats: *mihi me reddentis agelli*, 'my little farm that restores me to myself' or *vivo et regno*, 'I live and reign' (when once I leave the city). The best of Horace's 'thought' is his belief in the necessity to possess oneself, to discipline feeling and action through solitude. His finest expression of the ideal comes at the end of an epistle of prudent advice to a young man on how to handle a patron. With pleasant irony Horace says (in effect), 'While you are thinking of how to please, you might also consider':

> What lessens cares, what makes you a friend to yourself;
> What makes you surely calm,—honours or a tidy income,
> Or travelling obscurely along a hidden path of life.
> Whenever I find rest beside Digentia's icy stream
> (Which Mandela drinks, a village wrinkled with cold),
> What do you suppose are my feelings, what, my friend, are
>   my prayers?
> To have what I now have, or less, to live to myself
> For the rest of my days—if the gods give me more—,
> To have plenty of books, a good supply of food for the year,
> And not to ebb and flow with the tide of wavering hope.

But all I can ask of Jove (he gives and he takes away)
Is life and means; serenity of mind I myself must make.

quid minuat curas, quid te tibi reddat amicum;
quid pure tranquillet, honos an dulce lucellum,
an secretum iter et fallentis semita vitae.
me quotiens reficit gelidus Digentia rivus,
quem Mandela bibit, rugosus frigore pagus,
quid sentire putas? quid credis, amice, precari?
sit mihi quod nunc est, etiam minus, et mihi vivam
quod superest aevi, si quid superesse volunt di;
sit bona librorum et provisae frugis in annum
copia, neu fluitem dubiae spe pendulus horae.
sed satis est orare Iovem qui ponit et aufert,
det vitam, det opes: aequum mi animum ipse parabo.
(*Epp.* i. xviii. 101–12)

The passage is an Horatian anticipation of the close of
Juvenal's satire on the *Vanity of Human Wishes*. The difference in weight, in tragic fearsomeness (especially in
Dr. Johnson's version) is obvious, but Horace's prayer, so
prudent and so aware of *l'homme moyen sensuel*, belongs to
the same moral and poetic tradition. The important value is
independence and balance of mind, release from 'hope and
fear', which is not given but attained by meditation and
self-discipline. Horace's tone is less noble than Juvenal's,
his questions are not addressed to the cosmos but to a friend
who may laugh, he half-implies, that the *urbanus* should
spend his country hours in such speculations. But Horace
is writing an epistle, and his seriousness is exactly of the sort
we allow ourselves in a letter to a friend. In writing a personal letter we may expose our secret desires, but because
we are speaking to a friend we protect our seriousness by
joking about it.

After all this, it is surely superfluous to ask (as Johnson
might say) whether Horace was a Stoic or an Epicurean or a
philosopher of any particular type. The most direct answer
he gives, in the first *Epistle*, tells us more about the poet
than the philosopher. After telling Maecenas that he is too
old for lyric poetry and that his sole concern henceforth is to
learn 'what is true and right', he explains,

I'm no gladiator bound by oath to a master,
But where the storm drives me, I take shelter:

Now a man of action, I plunge into the waves of state,
A guardian of true virtue and her stern defender;
Now I slyly glide into the paths where Aristippus leads
And try to wrest the world to my will, not myself to the world.

nullius addictus iurare in verba magistri,
quo me cumque rapit tempestas, deferor hospes.
nunc agilis fio et mersor civilibus undis,
virtutis verae custos rigidusque satelles;
nunc in Aristippi furtim praecepta relabor,
et mihi res, non me rebus subiungere conor.

(Epp. i. i. 14–19)

The metaphors indicate fairly well Horace's 'position'.
While ridiculing Maecenas' talk of going back to school and
while picturing his own wayward course in life's stormy sea,
he is neatly expressing an appreciation of two ways in
philosophy. The terms he uses to describe his dolphin-like
plungings and cavortings are borrowed in part from the
Stoics and the Cyrenaics. With fine economy Horace gives
us first an impression of the life of an Aurelius: *agilis fio et
mersor·civilibus undis*. Then glancing at his own slyness with
amusement (*furtim*), he tells how he glides into the Cyrenaic
way, which he also describes from within and with full
justice. The 'gliding' of these lines—the shifting in style and
attitude—is characteristic of Horace's poetry and philosophy. He insists on enjoying the values of quite different
views of the world, but with good-humoured wisdom confesses his inconsistency. The true Horatian seriousness is
this fine residue of the self that 'sits in the centre and knows'.

In *Nil admirari* the position taken by Horace is nominally
Epicurean, the pose of *ataraxia*, the aloof calm of one who
views without amazement all forms of human endeavour—
striving after money, position, love, and even pursuing
virtue with excessive zeal. But the poetic mode is again the
best index to Horace's attitude. The poem is a piece of
ironic advice, at times of Juvenalian intensity:

Go now, gape at silver and old marbles, bronzes and bibelots,
Marvel at jewels and goods dyed with Tyrian purple . . .

i nunc, argentum et marmor vetus aeraque et artes
suspice, cum gemmis Tyrios mirare colores . . .

(Epp. i. vi. 17–18)

Horace is speaking as a satirist, not a philosopher, and he moves in a most Horatian way through ironic commands and hints to his correspondent, through heroic and proverbial allusions or examples lightly etched in by a piece of gossip or a tale. What we feel rather than Epicurean calm is a fine scepticism about all the activities by which we try to forget that

Nevertheless in the end we go where Numa and Ancus have gone . . .

ire tamen restat Numa quo devenit et Ancus.

(27)

Horace has little confidence in any good advice, including his own, and as a result the irony of *Nil admirari* is as puzzling to some readers as Robert Frost's in *Provide, Provide*:

> Die early and avoid the fate.
> Or if predestined to die late,
> Make up your mind to die in state.
>
> Make the whole stock exchange your own!
> If need be occupy a throne,
> Where nobody can call *you* crone.
>
> Some have relied on what they knew;
> Others on being simply true.
> What worked for them might work for you.

In an earlier piece, the Second Satire of Book II, 'Ofellus, or Plain Living', Horace is also working from an Epicurean basis, and again it is not doctrine that impresses, but tone and dramatic exemplum. Most of the poem—it is nearer a lecture than a conversation—is put in the lips of an old countryman whom Horace knew in his youth. The attack is often highly rhetorical, marked by sharp scornful questions and rude imperatives. But the final speech of Ofellus is wholly admirable, an indirect tribute to old-time country toughness and instinctive acceptance of Nature. Although Ofellus has lost his land to a new owner and become a tenant, he sees little difference in his actual state:

> 'For Nature makes neither him nor me, nor anyone,
> Lord of the land forever; he drove us out;

And either wickedness or ignorance of tricky laws
Or some long-lived heir will finally drive him too.
Now the farm goes by Ofellus' name, now by Umbrenus';
Unwilling to be owned by anyone long, it falls for use
Now to me and now to another.—So my sons, live bravely,
And bravely set your faces to meet trouble when it comes.'

> nam propriae telluris erum natura neque illum
> nec me nec quemquam statuit: nos expulit ille;
> illum aut nequities aut vafri inscitia iuris,
> postremum expellet certe vivacior heres.
> nunc ager Vmbreni sub nomine, nuper Ofelli
> dictus, erit nulli proprius, sed cedet in usum
> nunc mihi nunc alii. quocirca vivite fortes,
> · fortiaque adversis opponite pectora rebus.

$$(129\text{--}36)$$

Though Horace makes fun of the Stoicism of the schools, he treats this native country Stoicism without a trace of irony.

There are three or four other themes that Horace treats with equal seriousness—'busyness' of all sorts (whether in pursuit of money or position), friendship, and death. Country content with a sufficiency is regularly contrasted with the city passion for mere accumulation, and in the epistle in which Horace pictures his oscillation between Aristippus and the Stoics, he turns on his fellow Romans with surprising vehemence:

> 'Oh citizens, citizens, be sure to go for money first,
> Virtue last, pennies first!'

> 'o cives, cives, quaerenda pecunia primum est;
> virtus post nummos'. . .

$$(Epp.\ \text{i. i. } 53\text{--}54)$$

'Recreation' and 'going places' are the curse of his world as of ours,

> caelum non animum mutant qui trans mare currunt.
> strenua nos exercet inertia: navibus atque
> quadrigis petimus bene vivere. quod petis hic est . . .

$$(Epp.\ \text{i. xi. } 27\text{--}29)$$

> The sky not mind they change, who rush across the sea.
> Violent idleness wears us out; with ships and cars
> We try to find the way to live: what you seek is here . . .

The moral energy and the rhythmic urgency of these lines is

nearer to Donne than any other English poet, a fact too seldom emphasized. As Donne well knew, Horace is not always the blandly smiling poet of the Sabine farm.

If Horace reserves his most cutting sarcasm for the *amor habendi*, for those who are slaves of *regina Pecunia*, 'Queen Property', he writes some of his most whole-hearted and least ambiguous lines on friendship:

> nil ego contulerim iucundo sanus amico.   (*Sat.* i. v. 44)

Nothing—while I'm in my senses—can I compare to a good friend.

This exclamation, perhaps too simple to bear translating, comes from a poem of happy intimacy, 'The Journey to Brundisium'. Horace is the poet of friendship as we may know it in this world, and if he does not Platonize, he gives us more than one picture of very nearly ideal literary friendship. In the well-known epistle to Tibullus—one of the sources of Pope's lines on the happy poet-philosopher—Horace without a trace of envy praises a fellow writer for his art, his riches, and his goodness, closing his tribute with the comic sketch of himself as a 'sleek fat pig from Epicurus' flock'. His relations with his friends are by no means all in one key, and he exercises personal and stylistic tact in adapting his manner to all sorts of occasions and themes, from a good-natured invitation to ebriety, to irritation at his own defects and at a friend's over-cockiness, to a piece of worldly advice or a half-serious sermon on the good life.

The supreme exhibitions of Horatian tact come in the letters to Maecenas. Whatever the actuality may have been, the poems present a human relationship that is a model in its kind. Patron and protegé should be ever so! Though Horace honours Maecenas for his nobility and generosity, he never loses his own perfectly respectable position, he remains as loyal to his father and his origins as before he entered Maecenas' circle, and he talks to his patron with a flat directness or a joking insolence that ensures his own self-respect. We have already seen him evading Maecenas' invitation to take up lyric poetry again. Hear him now refusing to come to Rome when it suits his patron's mood (*Epp.* i. vii.): 'Maecenas, my sweet friend (*dulcis amice*), you will see me again with the spring breezes and the first swallow'. Horace takes the occasion to read the general a lesson: *parvum parva decent*, and he enforces the point with one of his best parables, the story of how patronage corrupted a simple citizen of Rome.

With Augustus Horace is certainly more distant and even coy. For despite the odes that lift Augustus to the gods and the tactful allusions to divinity in the *Epistle to Augustus*, Horace wrote no epic or historical poem commemorating the *res gestae Augusti*. In the *Epistle*, written apparently after the *Princeps* had complained because no letter had been addressed to him, Horace praises the Age rather than the Man, and in a rather curious way: he presents Augustus with a fairly complete history of Latin literature and a defence of the New Poetry against the Old, along with some sharp criticism of contemporary taste. Whatever Augustus may have thought of this performance, we can only admire. An age in which the leading poet could honour the chief of state with a piece of literary criticism seems to us fairly agreeable. Horace's world was one in which a writer could say without apology,

principibus placuisse viris non ultima laus est.   (*Epp*. i. xvii. 35)

To have pleased the first men of the age is not the lowest praise.

And where, the reader may ask, in this splendid image of Horace and his age, is the satirist, the master of Pope the poet? It is significant that the question should be asked, because the total impression of Horace's work, even in the *Satires*, is not of a man on the attack. We shall have a fairly just picture of Horace in his maturity if we think of him with Dryden as 'perpetually moral'. But to be 'perpetually moral', however even one's temper may be, is certainly to reflect on the rest of mankind. Horace strikes us as neither a prig nor a bore because he is so skilful in finding different ways of scoring his points against individuals and society. The many disguises he assumes as a critic of manners and morals fall under the two main roles of comic dramatist and conversationalist, both of which he refers to in his comments on the *Satires* and *Epistles*. He began his career in the tradition inherited from Lucilius, of the Aristophanic direct assault, of naming names and vices. But he found that this tactic did not please, and in a satire that Pope was to imitate he defended personal attacks from Lucilius' example. Names of individuals,[1] including contemporaries, never wholly disappear from Horace's satirical verse, but he tends after his early satires to use type names borrowed from Lucilius (some of them originally belonging to actual persons), or names of persons from an earlier generation, or symbolic names apparently of his own invention. Avidienus, for example, is certainly a Roman name, but in using it Horace plays on the obvious suggestions of *avarus*. Sometimes a name with biographical references, such as Tigellius, the singer, or the countryman, Ofellus, becomes symbolic simply because Horace creates a character that seems completely alive and exactly appropriate to the theme of the satire. Time, we must remember, has softened the personal quality of Horace's references and in many cases has made it impossible to decide whether he is writing of a type or of a historical figure.

From a critical point of view, Horace's humorous explanation of his use of personal references seems correct: they are like the examples his father pointed out to him in his youth as warnings or as models. Although Horace occasionally makes use of more direct attacks through serious (*triste*) invective or sarcastic addresses, he more often acts as the 'producer' of comic interludes reminiscent of Middle or New Greek Comedy. In two or three rare instances, a whole satire is cast in the form of a comic drama, as in 'Nasidienus, or Dining in the Worst Possible Taste', where he combines social gossip and parodies of philosophic speeches and religious ceremonies with downright farce. As Horace develops, the conversationalist gradually absorbs the dramatist. The urban observer and raconteur takes charge, moving with marvellous versatility through bits of comic dialogue and parenthetical reflections, retelling with economy and

---

[1] On Horace's use of names, see *Opera*, ii. 9–14; on personal attacks in his satires, see B. L. Ullman, 'Horace on the Nature of Satire', *Transactions of American Philological Association*, xlviii. 111–32, espec.: 'As a matter of fact, Horace's position on the matter of personal attack is that of an eclectic. He believes in a sparing use of the "direct method" of the Old Comedy together with the "enigmatic" method of the Middle Comedy and the generalizing method of the New Comedy' (p. 130).

freshness a popular tale, quietly ridiculing persons or pretensions by ironic innuendo and parody. He is easily the most
subtle ironist among Roman writers of satire, designedly
sparing his strength so that the blow is often felt only after
the conversation has moved on to another point. Much of
Horace's irony is of the high sort produced by indirect
reflection of the noble example and principle on the less
noble actuality, and though there is direct moral poetry, as
in Donne's satires, it is not inert platitude because Horace's
individual voice is always present and because statement is
carried on a tide of feeling. The truths, however familiar, are
freshly realized in particular dramatic contexts. So in the
advice to his friend Lollius, where he speaks with unforgettable *brevitas*:

> Why hurry
> To get rid of something that hurts your eyes, when if something
> Is eating your mind, you put off the cure for a year?
> 'Well begun is half-done', we say.—Dare to be wise:
> Begin! The man who puts off the hour for living well
> Is like the rustic who waits for the river to pass: but the river
> Flows on and will flow on, lapsing into time without end.

> . . . nam cur
> quae laedunt oculos festinas demere, si quid
> est animum, differs curandi tempus in annum?
> dimidium facti qui coepit habet: sapere aude:
> incipe. qui recte vivendi prorogat horam,
> rusticus exspectat dum defluat amnis: at ille
> labitur et labetur in omne volubilis aevum.

> (*Epp.* I. ii. 37–43)

The consideration of time and death is always in Horace's
ear; it is the present balance to everything he rejects in
himself and others: money-getting, seeking for place and
position, luxury for show not comfort, busyness and lack of
reflection. The 'mean', of which I have said very little, is in
Horace more than the platitude to which it has been reduced
by over-much quotation. It is the reward of attained wisdom,
though not often or easily attained. The Horatian *œuvre*, a
recent critic[1] has suggested, is directed toward a schooling

---

[1] Apel, *Horaz*, especially '*Correctio animi*', pp. 79–86, and '*Caelestis sapientia*',
pp. 291–308.

of the self, a *correctio animi*, the poet dramatizing his case so as to set before himself and others a model of the good life. But Horace has the happy faculty of including himself among his 'victims' and of regarding his most serious poses with amusement. The close of one of the later epistles shows how subtly Horace 'confused' his case with the imagined auditor's, so that even when he says 'you' (*tu*), he gives an impression of talking to an inner self in another role. After comparing happiness to the joys of school holidays 'snatched' in passing, and after saying that it makes little difference to him whether he travels in a big ship or a little one through the seas of life, he continues (now subtly using 'we' for 'I'):

> We travel . . .
> In health, talent, person, goodness, position, wealth,
> Last among the first, or if among the last, still well ahead.
> You do not love money, you say. Very well. But tell me, are other faults
> Gone with that? Is your heart free from empty .
> Ambition? Free from anger and the fear of death?
> Do you smile at dreams, terrors of magic, wonders and witches,
> Ghosts by night, Thessalian signs and omens?
> You count birthdays with pleasure? You forgive your friends?
> You are gentler and kinder with the coming of old age?
> But why be pleased because one thorn is plucked from many?
> If you do not understand the art of living, make way for better men;
> You have played enough, eaten and drunk enough;
> It's time to move on, or after one drink too many
> You'll be laughed from the feast by youths more charmingly gay.

> viribus, ingenio, specie, virtute, loco, re,
> extremi primorum, extremis usque priores.
> non es avarus: abi. quid? cetera iam simul isto
> cum vitio fugere? caret tibi pectus inani
> ambitione? caret mortis formidine et ira?
> somnia, terrores magicos, miracula, sagas,
> nocturnos lemures portentaque Thessala rides?
> natalis grate numeras? ignoscis amicis?
> lenior et melior fis accedente senecta?
> quid te exempta iuvat spinis de pluribus una?
> vivere si recte nescis, decede peritis.

lusisti satis, edisti satis atque bibisti:
tempus abire tibi est, ne potum largius aequo
rideat et pulset lasciva decentius aetas.

(Epp. II. ii. 203–16)

The 'even temper', *aequus animus*, it is clear from these lines, is a fairly rare state, one presupposing a considerable moral and emotional discipline, and the demands it makes when expressed in such haunting questions are not easily set aside. The content of the Horatian guest as he is dismissed from life's feast is not too complete, but sufficiently disturbed by an image of perfection.

VII

ESSAYS ON WIT AND NATURE

Nature to all things fixed the limits fit,
And wisely curbed proud man's pretending wit.
(Essay on Criticism, 52-53)

If I could flatter myself that this Essay has any merit, it is
in steering betwixt the extremes of doctrines seemingly
opposite. . . .
*(An Essay on Man, '*The Design'*)*

I. THE SCALE OF WIT

THE *Essay on Criticism* and the *Essay on Man* are classic
examples of the need for distinguishing between what a
poem *says* and what it *expresses*. Both say so much in the
form of statement or argument that many readers, including
some of Pope's contemporaries, have doubted or forgotten that
they were poems of any sort whatever. Writers who have
attacked or defended the *Essay on Man* have tended to treat
it either as a philosophical treatise dictated by Bolingbroke
or a defence of Deism or as a metaphysical and ethical discourse in the Neoplatonic-Christian tradition. Critics and
editors in the nineteenth century and the early part of this
century usually (with the notable exceptions of Hazlitt and
Courthope) regarded the *Essay on Criticism* as a versification
of commonplaces gleaned from Greek, Latin, and French
sources. Eighteenth-century readers were probably better
prepared to take both works as poetic expressions rather
than bodies of doctrine because they saw at once that both
were collections of

What oft was thought, but ne'er so well expressed. . .

Being thoroughly familiar with what was being said, they
could relax and enjoy Pope's marvellous 'feat of words' as he
led them through familiar intellectual scenes. Their preparation for reading the two poems 'with the same spirit that its
author writ' was not doctrinal, not a matter of knowing the

right things, but literary and poetic. They were soaked in the
essays in verse of Dryden, Buckingham, Rochester, Ros-
common, Mulgrave, and countless others; and above all
they knew Horace from studying and imitating him in school
and from reading numerous translations and imitations in
English and French. The allusion to Horace in the *Essay on
Criticism* would have been obvious, especially to readers
familiar with Boileau's *L'Art poétique*. Pope himself suggests
the appropriateness of reading the *Essay on Man* in an
Horatian context: 'The work', he writes to Swift when he
had first projected it, '. . . is a system of Ethics in the
Horatian way'.[1] A later comment, also in a letter to Swift,
indicates clearly enough that Pope thought of 'the work' as a
piece of good-natured fairly relaxed 'advice' such as Horace
was fond of giving to his friends:

Yet am I just now writing (or rather planning) a book, to make
mankind look upon this life with comfort and pleasure, and put
morality in good humour.

But it is possible to read both *Essays* and all of Pope's
satirical-epistolary works with too much as well as too little
familiarity with Horace. A word of explanation may calm
restive readers who fear that I am about to trace Pope's
'sources' in Horace or make systematic comparisons between
the two writers. Let me say at once that Horace's effect on
Pope's career is too deeply pervasive and too unpedantic to
make the attempt appropriate or profitable. But in order to
interpret and evaluate the works of Pope's later phase
(beginning about 1729, with his first experiments in 'Ethical'
poetry), we need to keep in mind the Horatian mode and
'image'. 'He told me', Fenton writes in that year, 'that for
the future he intended to write nothing but epistles in
Horace's manner. . .'[2] The remark, as Sherburn notes, was
'prophetic'. Up until the last great invention of the Fourth
Dunciad, Pope wrote almost no poem of any length that does
not fall within 'Horace's manner', and his growth during
these years may be regarded as a gradual evolution from a

---

[1] 'The work' refers quite likely to the '*Opus Magnum*' (which included the *Essay
on Man*), not only to the *Essay* itself. Let. iii. 81; for the second reference, see Let. iii.
117.   [2] Let. iii. 37.

style resembling the 'legislative' of Dryden to the 'graceful negligence' of Horace's *Epistles*.

But Pope's growth and the character of his mature poetry are too complex to be described in these terms alone. As we have seen from *Eloisa to Abelard* and the *Rape of the Lock*, Pope advanced 'simultaneously on all fronts', so that while he was ostensibly imitating some single genre, he subtly subdued to his main design and style echoes of several other styles. As he moved forward he was always reaching back into earlier successes and incorporating the old in the new, with the result that beginning with his earliest poems he is continually anticipating future reincarnations. The *Pastorals* anticipate the descriptive manner of *Windsor Forest*, while *Windsor Forest*—one of Pope's most prophetic poems— looks ahead to the courtly and material glories of the *Rape of the Lock*, to the heroic 'painting' of the *Iliad*, and the splendid patriotic addresses of the *Moral Essays* and the *Satires*. Pope's heroic manner is anticipated in numerous earlier poems, pastoral, descriptive, and epistolary, and both the serious heroics of the *Iliad* and the parodies or burlesques of the *Rape of the Lock* point toward the more acid and more grandiose mockery of the *Dunciad*. While keeping the Horatian mode in view as we read the poems of Pope's 'epistolary' period, we must be ready to see how other manners and traditions enter to create the rich compositions of Pope's maturity.

The *Essay on Criticism* is another clear example of anticipation among the early works, since it is Pope's first essay in 'Horace's manner' and a pre-view of Warton's 'moral, satiric, and didactic poet'. It is also an early expression of many ideas and themes important in the later poems: 'wit', 'nature', 'good sense', 'taste', the hatred of 'fools' and 'dullness', the praise of friends and friendship. By concentrating on such key terms or themes in the *Essay on Criticism* and the *Essay on Man*, much can be learned about major stresses and large thematic patterns of the two poems, and perhaps still more about Pope's intellectual history in relation to his own and earlier generations. But we shall hardly appreciate what the terms mean in any full or precise sense unless we observe them in the poetic medium and see how they are defined in the poetic 'act' through various modes of expression. What Pope meant as a poet by 'wit' or 'nature' is very different from the meanings he *referred to* and which we separate out in our definitions.

In exploring the more important modes of the *Essay on Criticism* occasional comparisons with Horace will be of use in defining its poetic quality and design. The poem announces itself as a conversation in the Horatian manner by a first line that closely resembles the opening of the *Epistle to Burlington*:

> 'Tis hard to say, if greater want of skill
> Appear in writing or in judging ill . . .
> 'Tis strange, the Miser should his Cares employ,
> To gain those Riches he can ne'er enjoy . . .

But though we get the Horatian effect of a conversation in progress, the idiom and the aloofness of the pronouncement are nearer Dryden, who begins a number of lines in *Religio Laici* in the same fashion, one of which Pope may have recalled,

> 'Tis hard for man to doom to endless pains . . .
>
> (215)

There are also traces at other points in the poem of the free and easy talk of Dryden's literary prologues and argumentative verse. In the sharp lines on 'half-learned witlings,' the hearty scorn with which a fool is called a fool and dismissed, the cheerfully vulgar comparisons and the heroic allusion are all very like Dryden:

> Some have at first for Wits, then Poets past,
> Turned Critics next, and proved plain fools at last.
> Some neither can for Wits nor Critics pass,
> As heavy mules are neither horse nor ass.
> Those half-learned witlings, num'rous in our isle,
> As half-formed insects on the banks of Nile;
> Unfinished things, one knows not what to call,
> Their generation's so equivocal:
> To tell 'em, would a hundred tongues require,
> Or one vain wit's, that might a hundred tire.
>
> (36–45)

Pope's tone here and throughout the *Essay* carries with it a distinct sense of a supporting group behind what he is saying, a tone reminiscent of Dryden and his strong alliances with party, court, and town. During the years when Pope was working on the *Essay on Criticism* he was in close touch with the Restoration community through such literary guides and associates as Wycherly, Walsh, and Cromwell. 'I' never occurs in the poem, and even in the lines on his friend Walsh (which are Horatian in type), we hear little of the individual voice so distinct in Horace and in Pope's later verse.

But Pope's 'we' comes from a group more familiar and more polite than Dryden's, and if the last age is praised and perhaps envied for restoring 'Wit's fundamental laws', the new age, Pope's tone more than once implies, is better bred:

> Without Good Breeding, truth is disapproved . . .
> (576)

Walsh's plea for 'correctness' has had its effect, and Pope has also felt the powerful influence of Boileau, the fact that best explains why his mode of teaching is neither Dryden's nor Horace's. His appreciation of Horace's lack of method is enthusiastic and just, but in the *Essay on Criticism* he does not yet

> . . . like a friend, familiarly convey
> The truest notions in the easiest way.
> (655-6)

We find as in Boileau a good deal of direct advice and laying down the law, but if we set Boileau's cool and often pedantically detailed directions beside Pope's pungent general truths, we more easily forgive lapses into provincial superiority:

> The rules a nation, born to serve, obeys;
> And Boileau still in right of Horace sways.
> (713-14)

But like Dryden Pope does not let the British rest easy in their lack of art:

> But we, brave Britons, foreign laws despised,
> And kept unconquered, and uncivilised . . .
> (715-16)

Compared with Boileau's correctness, this sort of tightrope walking may seem less consistent, but it comes much nearer to the true Horatian navigation between opposing positions, and it is more complexly responsible and certainly more amusing. The amusement makes all the difference and accounts for the strange fact that so special a piece of poetry has lived on in proverbial quotation and in the experience of readers sufficiently unacademic not to know that the *Essay on Criticism* is 'pure neo-classicism'. In verses and passages of critical and satirical wit the poem still lives brightly, above all in the many lines that the man in the street quotes and confidently assigns to Shakespeare:

> For Fools rush in where Angels fear to tread.
>   (625)

> A *little learning* is a dang'rous thing . . .
>   (215)

> To err is human, to forgive, divine.
>   (525)

Such verses are 'true', but more than true; for they surprise us by a 'fine excess', by presenting parallels that unexpectedly meet. Angels may intervene with a rushing of wings, though fools should not, but here they do, and their officious action is touched with swift angelic grace. 'Learning', knowledge, is surely one of the most safe-guarding of things, and 'little' usually implies harmless, but when combined in a neat alliterative packet, these mild elements seem quite explosive. In reading

> To err is human, to forgive, divine . . .

we enjoy the momentary deception of grammatical and rhythmic parallels happily contradicted by a word that reverses accents and values: human: divine. But though Horatian *brevitas* often finds an English equivalent in Pope (both are among the most quotable of poets), in the *Essay on Criticism* Pope's passion for point is a little too much in evidence. He cannot, like Horace in the *Ars Poetica*, subdue his wit to a large rhythmic flow of talk that mounts to a *sententia* and then recedes to contrasting moods and rhythms of the deepest seriousness. From a neat remark about the coining of new words, Horace can glide into a passage on the decay of language that is Homerically grand in imagery and movement:

As the woods change their leaves with the headlong flight of years . . .

ut silvae foliis pronos mutantur in annos . . .

(60)

He then imperceptibly shifts to death and *mortalia facta*, and with equal ease comes back to the renewal and decay of words. Pope's eagerness to be bright on all occasions cheapens the original metaphor and produces only a local hit:

Words are like leaves; and where they most abound,
Much fruit of sense beneath is rarely found . . .

(309–10)

But in more deeply satirical passages Pope is often more successful in adapting Horatian modes to his own compact couplet style. He can touch off a glancing satirical portrait in even shorter space than Horace, as in the couplet on dull poets,

Still humming on, their drowsy course they keep,
And lashed so long, like tops, are lashed asleep.

(600–1)

and in the observation on textual critics:

Some on the leaves of ancient authors prey,
Nor time nor moths e'er spoiled so much as they.

(112–13)

or the unfortunate allusion to Dennis, a portrait that looks to the uninitiate like one of Horace's symbolic Romans:

But Appius reddens at each word you speak,
And stares, tremendous, with a threat'ning eye,
Like some fierce Tyrant in old tapestry.

(585–7)

The critical 'fools' who 'rush in' are neatly sketched through the use of quoted remarks in a somewhat Horatian fashion, but Pope has yet to master the art of the conversational 'mosaic'. Like Horace, he is fond of opening up historical vistas to accentuate the bad taste or the superior civilization of other ages or of his own (his purpose varies with his mood). As in the couplet quoted earlier on 'brave Britons', the irony often takes Pope's favourite form of compliment or praise. The Middle Ages are commended as a time when

> Much was believed, but little understood,
> And to be dull was construed to be good . . .
>
> (689–90)

In King William's reign

> . . . unbelieving priests reformed the nation,
> And taught more pleasant methods of salvation . . .
>
> (546–7)

Several· of these examples show decisively that English poetry is not Latin, that Pope is not Horace, and that he writes as he will continue to write, in an incorrigibly metaphorical tradition. The textual 'moths' and the 'insect-witlings', for example, anticipate common metaphors of disgust in later satirical poems. The dull critics and poets of the *Essay* are more commonly associated with clouds and gross darkness, while wits and true wits shine brightly glorious. 'Light' is the salient image of the poem, and as in Pope's earlier poetry it is often linked with the metaphor of painting and design, Horace's *ut pictura poesis*. All of these images are combined in a pleasant passage that is very characteristic in its tone of assured observation and superior refinement touched with Dryden's majesty and forthrightness:

> Yet if we look more closely, we shall find
> Most have the seeds of judgment in their mind:
> Nature affords at least a glimm'ring light;
> The lines, though touched but faintly, are drawn right.
> But as the slightest sketch, if justly traced,
> Is by ill-colouring but the more disgraced,
> So by false learning is good sense defaced:
> Some are bewildered in the maze of schools,
> And some made coxcombs Nature meant but fools.
> In search of wit these lose their common sense,
> And then turn Critics in their own defence:
> Each burns alike, who can, or cannot write,
> Or with a Rival's, or an Eunuch's spite.
> All fools have still an itching to deride,
> And fain would be upon the laughing side.
> If Maevius scribble in Apollo's spite,
> There are who judge still worse than he can write.
>
> (19–35)

The passage also illustrates the 'Horatian' manner as Pope understood it at this time. Horace's casualness is not quite out of sight:

> Yet if we look more closely, we shall find
> Most have the seeds of judgment in their mind . . .

a comment that is up to the best of the deceptively easy, politely insinuating couplets of the *Moral Essays* and the *Satires*. The themes of learning (*studium*) and natural talent (*ingenium*) can be paralleled in Horace, though the immediate sources are probably Cicero and Quintilian. The thrust at poets who insist on writing with or without art,

> Each burns alike, who can, or cannot write,

comes close to Horace both in sense and in antithetical phrasing:

> scribimus indocti doctique poemata passim.
> (*Epp*. II. i. 117)

Pope rounds off his satirical paragraph as Horace might with a thumb-nail sketch of 'stinking' Maevius (*Ep*. x. 2).

But the stance taken by the satirist is much more characteristic of Pope. It is not *we* (as in Horace) who 'burn', whether we 'can, or cannot write', but 'some' others, 'some' being Pope's usual way of introducing witless critics and over-witty poets in the *Essay on Criticism*. They are 'all fools', fair game for the attack of a writer who scores a point by wit or argument or both in nearly every line. A passage that starts with apparently harmless talk ('Yet if we look more closely . . .') turns into a dance of wit as antitheses are matched by the musical echo of phrasing and by expected yet surprising identities of rhyme.[1] This poetry is not 'graceful negligence' nor art concealing art, but versatility happily exhibiting itself. The *Essay on Criticism* has the bounce and go of verse by a terribly bright young man who has recently acquired all the 'right ideas', which he gets off with dazzling verbal skill and cheerful superiority.

Most of the 'right ideas' for Pope and his mentors are

---

[1] See W. K. Wimsatt, Jr., 'Rhetoric and Poems: The Example of Pope', *English Institute Essays*, 1948 (New York, 1949), p. 200; 'One Relation of Rhyme to Reason: Alexander Pope', *Modern Language Quarterly*, v. 323–38.

touched on in this passage, but their meaning is constantly being qualified by the poetic modes we have been describing above. In his indispensable anatomy[1] of 'wit' in the *Essay on Criticism*, Empson stresses the importance of interpreting 'the poem in the light of its social tone', and he is almost certainly right in assuming that 'there is not a single use of the word [wit] in the whole poem in which the idea of a joke is quite out of sight'. Of nearly equal value for seeing what the poem is about is Lovejoy's anatomy of 'nature',[2] for if we are to understand Pope's attitude toward poetry and criticism, we should connect the theme of true and false wit with the basic theme of 'following Nature'. But the uncommon reader who is interested in the poetry will want to experience these themes in the poem,

> To cat h the meanings living as they rise . . .

As Empson finely notes, we must feel the 'drag towards the drawing-room' in the *Essay on Criticism* in order to appreciate Pope's uses of 'wit' and—it is worth adding—to get the effect of his appeals to 'nature', 'judgment', and 'good sense'. It is also important to feel vividly the dramatic context of Horatian satire and the qualifying medium of imagery and rhythm. The drawing-room in view is a very masculine affair, nearer to the coffee-house of Dryden than the tea and card tables of the *Spectator* and the *Rape of the Lock*. Tone and setting are grand enough to sustain a Miltonic allusion to Nature in the sense of *Natura creans*, the fruitful source of life:

> Yet if we look more closely, we shall find
> Most have the seeds of judgment in their mind:
> Nature affords at least a glimm'ring light . . .

> But now at last the sacred influence
> Of light appears, and from the walls of Heav'n
> Shoots farr into the bosom of dim Night
> A glimmering dawn; here Nature first begins
> Her fardest verge, and *Chaos* to retire . .
>   (*Paradise Lost*, II. 1034–8)

---

[1] William Empson, 'Wit in the *Essay on Criticism*', in *The Structure of Complex Words* (Norfolk, Conn., 1951), pp. 84–100.
[2] A. O. Lovejoy, ' " Nature" as Aesthetic Norm', *Modern Language Notes*, xlii. 444–50.

Pope's metaphor is apt: nature like the Deity is a source of light, of the inner light of intelligence that sees things as in truth they are and that therefore judges without distortion. The metaphor that follows ('The lines, though touched but faintly, are drawn right') brings in a concept of nature important in this poem and in much of Pope's later poetry, the view of nature as artist-designer. 'Nature the creator originally draws the lines right, though faintly in some of her works'. 'Her', because divinely personified as in 'First follow Nature, and your judgment frame/By her just standard . . .' The vaguely personal quality is felt again in 'some made coxcombs Nature meant but fools'.

Another meaning still more fundamental for Pope and his contemporaries, also implied in the language of design, is that of nature as order and ordering principle,

> Nature to all things fixed the limits fit,
> And wisely curbed proud man's pretending wit.
>
> (52–53)

'Nature' is the personification of the cosmological order, at once the nature of Newton and the natural philosophers and the nature of traditional Platonic cosmology, the scale of created beings in which 'all things' have their assigned rank and powers. Human nature, referred to later in the poem also as 'Nature', has its place within the grand scheme, and 'Nature', as the above couplet indicates, may refer to the order in man which is analogous to the all-embracing greater Order. Too much learning, 'the maze of schools', tempts man to go outside his assigned role, to disrupt the inner and outer orders, and so become a 'fool'. The 'maze' of pedantry, unlike that 'mighty maze! but not without a plan', is a source of disorder and dullness.

The imagery of these lines on the generation of critics is a guide to the felt value of the concepts, to the aesthetic awe with which the great order ('the light') is viewed and the fine scorn ('glimm'ring') with which the perverters of order are damned. With Horatian finesse Pope so modulates his Miltonic allusion that critics are damned with the faintest praise: they enjoy '*at least* a glimm'ring light'. (Here is very nearly the essence of Horace and the quintessence of Pope's

poetry in the *Essay on Criticism*.) Pope directs all his art
against bad critics and writers, bending his grand concepts
to serve his sure satirical aim, the tone with which the
conversationalist handles his terms working with the imagery
to give them striking-power. He begins with impersonal
Miltonic grandeur, 'Nature affords . . .', but as he goes along
it appears that he is very much at home with 'Nature', that
she is certainly on his side. Nature the ironist who makes
some men fools is in this way subtly identified with nature
the grand designer. The gain of the identification in efficacy
of wit is obvious, for it is great designing Nature herself who
puts these fellows in their place, and they would be well
advised if they stayed 'put'.

Pope cunningly plays with similar identities in his use of
'wit' for jester, critic, and poet, convenient ambiguities for
a writer who is using the language of polite conversation to
express a fairly complex sense of the relationship between the
poet, the critic, and the man of the world. The potential
ambiguities in the cant term are a happy resource particularly if the writer is an ironist, since the ironist is always
expressing identities between opposites of praise and blame,
seeming ignorance and true knowledge. Pope's artful play
with 'wit' and the connexions between 'wit' and 'nature' can
be seen in the passage before us:

> In search of wit these lose their common sense,
> And then turn Critics in their own defence . . .

'Wit' is being used with Pope's characteristic suppleness.
Since those 'in search of wit' later 'turn Critics', it seems that
they are writers or even poets. Therefore 'wit' in general
would seem to mean some sort of creative power. But since
these searchers 'lose their common sense' (the inborn good
sense common to all men), 'wit' means also in this context
'unnatural wit', the extravagant ingenuities of the wit-about-
town whom Pope later attacks with so much zest. And yet
the dominant meaning here probably is that of 'wit' as true
poetic power, for Pope is certainly saying that poetry should
be left alone by fools and coxcombs. In later passages of the
poem, along with this sense of 'wit' as poetic power or poetry,
we have 'wit' simply for a poet, whether good or bad.

These tergiversations—the despair of anyone who would impose a system on the poem—are proof of Pope's versatility as a satirical observer of the literary scene. He conveniently implies that there is 'true wit' elsewhere while beating the 'witlings' over the head with their own favourite appellation. But the shiftings and turnings do not produce mere confusion, because of the control with which Pope poises his contrasts of phrase and rhythmic stress. As in the dialogue of Jane Austen, the reader finds not a blur, but alternatives distinctly defined. 'Wit' is one thing versus 'common sense', another if contrasted with 'critics', and still another if referred back to 'Nature', the source of true poetic power. And if we are properly enjoying this poetry of 'wit'—which a master of wit is producing—we are exhilarated by the game itself. Although the art is so Popeian in its pungency and continuous brilliance, the lesson that it hammers home is very Horatian: let everyone, poet or ploughman, do what he is by nature best fitted to do.

The link between 'wit' and 'nature' makes it easier for Pope to express other attitudes—also closely connected with Horace—which are more than amusing. When the critic-wit (and the poet-wit) are told to 'Follow Nature', the imagery tells us how to take this over-simple piece of advice. They are to follow

> Unerring NATURE, still divinely bright,
> One clear, unchanged, and universal light,
> Life, force, and beauty, must to all impart,
> At once the source, and end, and test of Art.
> Art from that fund each just supply provides,
> Works without show, and without pomp presides:
> In some fair body thus th' informing soul
> With spirits feeds, with vigour fills the whole,
> Each motion guides, and every nerve sustains;
> Itself unseen, but in the effects, remains.
>
> (70–79)

The metaphors of 'divine unchanging brightness' and of the 'informing soul' (nearly equivalent to the metaphor of design) put the stress again on nature as order. The critic is to test his judgements by his knowledge of the unchanging order of things in the physical and the human universe (they are of course one universe in the great scale of being). He is to have a knowledge of universal truth in both spheres, especially the human, as we can see from the later remarks about Homer and the ancients. The work of art draws its material from nature, and is organized by a similar ordering principle. The poet, it is implied, will try to produce a work having an organic order analogous to great nature's plan, just as the critic in judging the work looks for signs that the order has been achieved. 'Wit' when used of this concept of poetry and poetic creation certainly comes close to Coleridgean 'imagination', as Empson[1] has suggested. But wit in this high sense, which requires an educated judgement, is not wholly separated from wit as the untrammelled fancy of the late Metaphysicals or wit as the 'sprightly' jesting of a *bel esprit*. Pope pushes the relation so far as to use 'wit' for both the higher and the lower forms and perhaps even for judgement—all within a single couplet:

> Some, to whom Heaven in wit has been profuse,
> Want as much more, to turn it to its use;
> For wit and judgment often are at strife,
> Though meant each other's aid, like man and wife.
>
> (80–83)

The way to reach a perfect marriage of powers is to form one's judgement by study of the ancients, the experts in 'order', the order of art and the order of nature as exhibited above all in human nature. But when Pope says the 'Rules'

> Are Nature still, but Nature methodised . . .
>
> (89)

or

> Nature and Homer were, he found, the same.
>
> (135)

he is not solemnly presenting critical equations but using exaggerated metaphors to persuade and amuse.

These exaggerations are pleasantly matched by deviations in the other direction:

> Thus Pegasus, a nearer way to take,
> May boldly deviate from the common track;

1 Empson, p. 86; compare also the account in E. N. Hooker, 'Pope on Wit—the *Essay on Criticism*', *The Seventeenth Century* (Stanford, 1951), pp. 225–46.

From vulgar bounds with brave disorder part,
And snatch a grace beyond the reach of art,
Which without passing through the judgment, gains
The heart, and all its end at once attains.
In prospects thus, some objects please our eyes,
Which out of nature's common order rise,
The shapeless rock, or hanging precipice.
Great wits sometimes may gloriously offend,
And rise to faults true Critics dare not mend.

(150–60)

With fine inconsistency Pope says that the genius, the man
of great imaginative powers, may defy 'Nature's common
order', may leap 'beyond' the narrow order of art, by-pass
judgement, and 'gain the heart'. The change in the nature-
painting metaphor is noteworthy, the picturesque in Salvator
Rosa's manner replacing the garden-paradise. Pope in this
way expands his definition of nature to include irregularities
outside the basic general order. The 'true Critic', the counterpart of the 'great wit', recognizes the right of genius to go
beyond art. If read in this genial context, Pope's famous
definition of 'true Wit' is less 'neo-classic' and less superficial than many, including Dr. Johnson, have supposed:

Some to *Conceit* alone their taste confine,
And glitt'ring thoughts struck out at every line;
Pleased with a work where nothing's just or fit;
One glaring Chaos and wild heap of wit.
Poets like painters, thus, unskilled to trace
The naked nature and the living grace,
With gold and jewels cover every part,
And hide with ornaments their want of art.
True Wit is Nature to advantage dressed,
What oft was thought, but ne'er so well expressed;
Something, whose truth convinced at sight we find,
That gives us back the image of our mind.

(289–300)

Pope is again talking in metaphors of natural and artistic
order, both being subtly linked by the common analogy of
light. To poets who insist on being brightly fanciful or
original, although the result is 'chaos', he says in effect, 'Look
for light elsewhere, see by the light of nature, and you will
see things as in truth they are'. Writers who cannot see and

cannot present the truth of things in their harmonious ordering, 'The naked nature and the living grace', try to cover
their weakness by rhetorical displays. So when Pope says,
'True Wit is Nature to advantage dressed', it is clear that he
means much more by Nature than commonplace knowledge.
To know nature is to know a good deal; 'to dress Nature to
advantage' means to bring out what is inherently beautiful
in things, to bring out the order and grace, the life and the
surprising irregularity that only true poets can see. When
Pope says that such poetry 'gives us back the image of our
mind', he is not saying that poetry gives us platitudes
pleasantly served up in fancy dress. He means very nearly
what Johnson meant in saying that Gray's *Elegy*

> . . . abounds with images which find a mirrour in every mind, and
> with sentiments to which every bosom returns an echo. The four
> stanzas beginning 'Yet even these bones' are to me original: I have
> never seen the notions in any other place: yet he that reads them here,
> persuades himself that he has always felt them.

The 'mirrour' and the 'echo', like Pope's 'image' are
metaphors of metaphor in literature. Literature does not
give us the absolutely 'original', but experiences that we
recognize as true because they are like those we have known
before. Hence we 'persuade ourselves that we have always
known them'. Quintilian expresses the point admirably in a
remark quoted by Pope as one of his sources: *id facillime
accipiunt animi quod agnoscunt.*[1]

Although Pope uses the ancient metaphor of dress for
style, it is quite inconsistent with the context and with his
view of poetry in the *Essay* to suppose that he regarded
diction or style as a superficial adornment of thought. In the
lines concluding with the definition of 'true Wit' Pope is on
the contrary stressing the necessarily close relation between
'words' and 'sense' and satirizing critics or writers who value
style apart from thought. He is similarly hard on 'verbal
critics' who are on the watch for 'slight faults':

> Survey the WHOLE, nor seek slight faults to find
> Where nature moves, and rapture warms the mind:
> Nor lose, for that malignant dull delight,
> The gen'rous pleasure to be charmed with Wit.   (235–8)

[1] EC ii. 51.

'Where Nature moves', there is order and life. The great thing for the critic is to respond to the 'joint force and full result of all', just as the great thing for the poet is to create 'natural' unity. 'Generous' response is what Pope most exalts in the *Essay*, generous in a sense that includes 'nobly-born' and 'brave'. (The last is an important adjective, used five times in the poem.) The critic's daring is matched by the poet's 'brave disorder', and both are enemies of 'dull delight'. ('Dull', 'dullness', or 'dully' together appear thirteen times in the poem.) The *Essay on Criticism* is Pope's first round in his war on dullness, particularly when it comes in the guise of 'correctness'. The poem that proclaims the need of art, the disciplining of judgement and wit by ancient example, is also a plea for generosity in criticism and writing. The *Essay on Criticism* is most Horatian in expressing this genial attitude of wise compromise between the claims of art and life, an attitude central in the poem and in much of Pope's later poetry. Throughout the poem Pope is continuously illustrating Horace's

> respicere exemplar vitae morumque iubebo
> doctum imitatorem et vivas hinc ducere voces.
>
> (*A.P.* 317–18)

'Art' for Horace and for Pope includes knowing the best that has been thought and written in the past and knowing life and human character at first hand. Neither poet felt the sentimental attraction of substituting 'real life' for 'art'. When Pope speaks of 'snatching a grace *beyond* the reach of art', he means exactly what he says: craft is assumed as the necessary preparation for taking the longer flights of imagination.

The image of Horace in his role of critic-friend thus stands clearly behind Pope's first 'Horatian' essay. The ideal illustrated in the *Ars Poetica* of combining practical advice with friendly conversation was presented at the end of that poem, as so often in Horace's satires, through contrasting portraits having satirical overtones. The friend who is kind enough to be an 'Aristarch' and speak the truth is pictured beside the mad poet whom no advice can keep from making verses. In Pope's corresponding pair of portraits the critic-friend is set beside the ironic 'poet's friend' who is a 'bookful blockhead', one of the 'Fools' who 'rush in where Angels fear to tread'. Both figures show very clearly Pope's relation to Horace and to the English Horatian tradition. The critic-friend is described in the nobly serious style of balanced epithets used by Pope in his elegiac verses on Craggs and Oxford:

> But where's the man, who counsel can bestow,
> Still pleased to teach, and yet not proud to know?
> Unbiased, or by favour, or by spite;
> Not dully prepossessed, nor blindly right;
> Though learned, well-bred; and though well-bred, sincere,
> Modestly bold, and humanly severe . . .
>
> (631–6)

The matching portrait in Horace starts off in this generalizing style (*vir bonus et prudens*), but goes on to describe the critic in the act of pointing out particular faults and ends with a characteristic bit of mocking speech. Though in many ways so different, Pope's portrait concludes by summing up Horace's point in lines that begin to approach his conversational pace:

> [But where's the man . . .]
> Who to a friend his faults can freely show,
> And gladly praise the merit of a foe?
> Blest with a taste exact, yet unconfined;
> A knowledge both of books and human kind:
> Gen'rous converse; a soul exempt from pride;
> And love to praise, with reason on his side?
>
> (637–42)

In his picture of the mad critic Pope adopts some of Horace's most familiar satiric modes: the intimacy of tone and reference, the neat mimicry, the farcical caricature of a type. While the art of the *Epistle to Dr. Arbuthnot* has not yet been reached, it is clearly in sight. As the passage moves along the irony becomes more obvious, the rhetorical snap increases, and the tone rises to a blast in Dryden's blend of high exaggeration with rough handling:

> But rattling nonsense in full volleys breaks. . .

The whole attack in its pointedness and resourcefulness may

remind us again that the *Essay on Criticism* is both entertaining and instructive:

> Such shameless Bards we have; and yet 'tis true,
> There are as mad abandoned Critics too.
> The bookful blockhead, ignorantly read,
> With loads of learnèd lumber in his head,
> With his own tongue still edifies his ears,
> And always list'ning to himself appears.
> All books he reads, and all he reads assails,
> From Dryden's Fables down to Durfey's Tales.
> With him, most authors steal their works, or buy;
> Garth did not write his own Dispensary.
> Name a new Play, and he's the Poet's friend,
> Nay showed his faults—but when would Poets mend?
> No place so sacred from such fops is barred,
> Nor is Paul's church more safe than Paul's churchyard:
> Nay, fly to Altars; there they'll talk you dead:
> For Fools rush in where Angels fear to tread.
> Distrustful sense with modest caution speaks,
> It still looks home, and short excursions makes;
> But rattling nonsense in full volleys breaks,
> And never shocked, and never turned aside,
> Bursts out, resistless, with a thund'ring tide.

(610–30)

With those lines in our ears, we can hardly fail to take the 'doctrine' of this Essay on wit and nature with the necessary grain of salt, *merum sal,* at that, as Addison remarked of the *Rape of the Lock.*

II. THE SCALE OF WONDER

In the bravura address to Bolingbroke at the close of the *Essay on Man,* Pope declares

> That urg'd by thee, I turn'd the tuneful art
> From sounds to things, from fancy to the heart;
> For Wit's false mirror held up Nature's light . . .

In the language of the *Essay on Criticism,* Pope is saying that he has put behind him the 'wit' of fancy that distorts and decorates, and that he has now written a piece of 'true Wit'. In other words, he has seen and expressed the true nature

of things, especially the truth of human nature ('the heart').
But true wit does not exclude 'sprightliness', and so the
Essay on Man like the *Essay on Criticism* is a poem of 'nature'
and 'wit', of 'Nature to advantage dressed'. If it is easy in
reading the earlier essay to forget that 'the heart' is there,
it is still easier for readers of the *Essay on Man* to become
very solemn indeed and treat the poem as a Lucretian *De
Rerum Natura* rather than as an Horatian essay. At times
Pope may have fancied that he was actually writing in
Lucretius' manner. In a letter to Swift written a few months
after the publication of the fourth epistle (1734), he raises
the question, though not too seriously, as shown by the
context. He is speaking of his amusement at not being
recognized as the author when the epistles were published
earlier without his name:

The design of concealing myself was good, and had its full effect; I
was thought a divine, a philosopher, and what not? and my doctrine
had a sanction I could not have given to it. Whether I can proceed
in the same grave march like Lucretius, or must descend to the
gayeties of Horace, I know not, or whether I can do either?[1]

Although he had earlier written to Swift of the *Essay on Man*
and Bolingbroke's parallel prose work as 'aspiring to philosophy', he had followed this remark with a quotation from
Horace that again indicates a certain lightness of tone. He
says in effect, 'Let us forget about politics and like Horace
"spend our Time in the Search and Enquiry after Truth and
Decency".'[2]
  Whether Horace or Lucretius won the day in the completed poem can be best answered not by a philosopher
or a literary critic, but by the 'common reader'. He will
know, for example, how seriously to take the last couplet of
Pope's opening address to Bolingbroke:

> Laugh where we must, be candid where we can;
> But vindicate the ways of God to Man.

(I. 15–16)

The mere reader of poetry will note the chummy, clubby
'we's', the comfortable and worldly invitation to 'laugh' or
view with generosity (eighteenth-century 'candour') 'this

1 Let. iii. 433.   2 Let. iii. 249–50.

scene of man'. He will observe too the shift from Milton's
'justifie' to 'vindicate'. Milton's grammatical form is pur-
posive or optative, a clause of purpose used in a prayer:
'that . . . I may assert Eternal Providence,/And [may]
justifie. . .' To 'justifie' in Milton's context is to demonstrate
largely the divine order and justice; but such meanings taken
with Milton's prayerful tone have a very different effect from
Pope's 'vindicate'. Though 'vindicate' refers to similar kinds
of justification, the word reeks with the atmosphere of
debate and points scored. As qualified by Pope's tone the
meaning becomes positively hearty and jaunty, an assertion
of divine justice in the voice of a man ready to take on all
comers. Justification seems to come in almost as an after-
thought to other concerns: 'Laugh where we must, be
candid. . ./*But* vindicate. . .' The study of nature is all but
subdued to the purposes of wit, the happy hunting of the
poet and friend in their rural retirement:

> Together let us beat this ample field,
> Try what the open, what the covert yield;
> The latent tracts, the giddy heights explore
> Of all who blindly creep, or sightless soar;
> Eye Nature's walks, shoot Folly as it flies;
> And catch the Manners living as they rise . . .
>
> (9–14)

More often than not in the liveliest passages of the *Essay* the
grand exploration of nature's plan is closely linked with
'shooting folly' and 'catching the manners', with critical
observation and witty dramatization of human nature as we
generally know it. For the student of Pope's development,
the *Essay on Man* marks his arrival at maturity as a poet who
combined moral seriousness with satiric wit. In the *Essay on
Man*, as in occasional passages of the *Dunciad* of 1728 and
1729, we see how brilliantly Pope can exploit various
literary traditions and earlier 'imitations' in the pursuit of
his critical and satirical aims.

But we can hardly say what kind of a poem the *Essay on
Man* is, or where and when it is poetry, or whether it has
imaginative unity, unless we attend to what Pope says, to his
'argument'. He certainly does not have an argument in the
Miltonic and heroic sense of a myth that dramatizes impor-

tant values and beliefs. But it is clear enough that he has an argument in the persuasive sense of the word, and it is equally apparent that he claims to have an argument in the sense of a discourse with an ordered series of inferences that follow from certain first principles or assumptions. Few readers who have looked for this kind of logic in the poem, from Dr. Johnson to recent students of philosophy in literature, have been very happy with what they have found. Pope's language has the look of argument, his 'then's' and 'hences' indicate logical sequence, and some logical connexion can usually be discovered between the stages of his discourse. But as in most defective arguments, we are troubled less by what is present than by what is absent. If, for example, we look for full proof of Pope's most important principles either by example or by deduction, we shall not find it. Pope constantly *refers* to historic arguments about man and the universe without ever presenting them adequately in the poem. One illustration—from a passage that troubled Dr. Johnson—is worth looking at, since it summarizes some of the main principles that Pope assumes:

> Of Systems possible, if 'tis confest
> That Wisdom infinite must form the best,
> Where all must full or not coherent be,
> And all that rises, rise in due degree;
> Then, in the scale of reas'ning life, 'tis plain
> There must be, somewhere, such a rank as Man;
> And all the question (wrangle e'er so long)
> Is only this, if God has plac'd him wrong?
>   (1. 43–50)

Most readers will recognize the 'system' of nature, the great scale or Chain of Being, to which we referred in discussing the *Essay on Criticism*.[1] Thanks to Lovejoy's study and to the writings of numerous followers, this view of the universe has become almost as much of a commonplace for us as for Pope's contemporaries. One happy result of its return to the realm of the familiar is that like eighteenth-century readers we can attend to the poetry without being surprised or confused by the doctrine.

[1] Cf. Ch. VII. i, pp. 197–8; see A. O. Lovejoy, *The Great Chain of Being* (Cambridge, Mass., 1953). (First printing, 1936.)

The main features of this traditional view appear in Pope's summary. 'Wisdom infinite', the Platonic 'Good' that later became identified with God, must create 'the best' of universes. The 'best' is a 'full' universe, one in which all possible forms of being are created, and it is also a 'coherent' universe, one in which there is an unbroken continuity of created beings arranged hierarchically from the lowest to the highest forms. 'Then', says Pope, if we grant these principles, 'there must be, somewhere', in the scale of beings who have reason, the 'rank' of man. In the immediate context 'then' is logically exact, but if we reconsider the principles to which we are assenting we may feel decidedly uncomfortable. Pope does not present here or elsewhere the reasoning by which the Neoplatonists explained why God must create 'the best' universe and why the 'full' one is the best. He flatly states the principle, just as he lightly assumes the necessity of coherence and hierarchical order. Coherence is a most troublesome principle, as anyone can see who considers whether every conceivable form of being between fish and birds or monkeys and man has in fact been created. Or if we ask with Johnson what 'somewhere'[1] means, doubts arise as to what exactly Pope is concluding from his principles. The local exactness of 'then' diminishes in importance when we discover how little support Pope offers for his dogmas. It is then too much to be told that 'all the question' is only whether God has placed man in the wrong place, since—as Johnson saw—there could be no question of a wrong place in a universe created by 'Supreme Wisdom'. The thought occurs that Pope had not attended very closely to his own argument. The aside, 'wrangle e'er so long', which is surprisingly low in tone, is probably a sign of his impatience with the refinements of logical discourse. We are reminded of Dryden's brusque way of squelching arguments in the *Religio Laici*:

> For points obscure are of small use to learn;
> But common quiet is mankind's concern.
>
> (449–50)

But though not closely built as an argument, the poem

---

[1] 'Pope', *Lives of the English Poets*, ed. G. B. Hill (Oxford, 1905), iii. 243.

illustrates in a large way Pope's first principles and a number of related philosophical doctrines and ideas fashionable in the eighteenth century. For example, much of the poem centres on the typical optimist proposition that 'Whatever is, is Right', a statement, it must be emphasized, not expressive of naïve cheerfulness. When Pope and his contemporaries speak of this as the best of possible worlds, their emphasis is on *possible*. Of worlds possible, given the nature of God and the necessity of impartial and unchanging laws of nature, ours is the best that can be conceived. The creation is not designed for the individual, but for the whole, and of the whole man is not an adequate judge. Evil, though real and inevitable, is explained in terms of the ancient and Renaissance doctrines of the harmony of opposites:

> All Discord, Harmony, not understood;
> All partial Evil, universal Good . . .
>
> (I. 291–2)

After setting forth these general views of Nature's order in the first epistle, Pope goes on to illustrate them, first with respect to man as an individual (Epistle II), and next with respect to man as a member of society (Epistle III). He defends the rightness of the overall plan by showing how reason and self-love (in the various 'modes' of the passions) are harmonized within the individual. Reason, the guiding, restraining power, is given a fairly negative role in this process as compared with the 'ruling Passion', which in some inexplicable way strengthens our 'best principle' and provides the motive power of virtue. In society 'self-love', the drive to self-fulfilment in man, happily works for the good of the whole. Pope thus finds support for another favourite eighteenth-century conviction that 'Self-love and Social are the same'. It might seem that 'Happiness' (the theme of Epistle IV), in the sense of 'Good, Pleasure, Ease, Content!' could hardly be 'our being's end and aim' under a plan that necessarily involves evil and suffering and even complete disaster for many individual persons. Pope avoids the inconsistency by redefining happiness as virtue, a Stoic-Christian virtue which is not dependent on externals but an achievement of the inner life. The conclusion to the four epistles, that 'all our Knowledge is OURSELVES TO KNOW', is not unexpected since a dominant theme of the earlier epistles is the ancient Greek and Socratic doctrine that the 'proper study of Mankind is Man'. This humanist conviction, adjusted to the Christian doctrine that the greatest of the virtues is love, is probably not quite consistent with the emphasis put on the study of nature's plan in the physical universe.

But with all its minor and major inconsistencies the *Essay on Man* has a structure of ideas that are historically important[1] and that were regarded by many of Pope's readers as valuable and true. It need hardly be said here that a structure of ideas, however consistently worked out, does not of itself make a poem. One could almost certainly dig out a set of propositions of considerable if not equal importance and involving no more contradictions, in Prior's *Solomon*, Akenside's *Pleasures of Imagination*, or the *Night Thoughts* of Young. While granting that all three are better poems for having included some important ideas in some sort of order, we shall hardly be tempted to regard any of these awesome 'philosophic' pieces as poetry of a high quality. It is a happy thought that we should not think of putting the *Essay on Man* among these monuments of vanished minds. The dulling effects of the eighteenth-century grand subject on the brightest of minds have never been more perfectly illustrated than in Prior's colossal bore. A poet of urbane wit, who wrote at least one poem of finely serious reflection, the lines *Written in the Beginning of Mezeray's History of France*, he became a plodding, relentlessly elevated teacher when he addressed himself to *Solomon on the Vanity of the World*. Pope was not untouched by the same blight, but he comes off remarkably well when compared with his contemporaries. Unlike any other long 'philosophic' poem of the century, the *Essay on Man* is continuously readable, and at its best it is poetry of a high order. To put it baldly, Pope succeeded because he did not write the poem he seems to have thought he was writing, at least in moments when he was discussing his grandiose project with Bolingbroke or Spence. It is worth

---

[1] On the background of Pope's argument, see Maynard Mack's introductory essay, TE iii (i), especially xxxii–xl.

noting that he did not take an august tone in writing of the poem to Swift, who had a way of bringing out Pope's most human, least polite, or pretentious qualities. It is also quite certain that Pope did not write the kind of philosophic essay Bolingbroke would have written in prose, as it is equally clear that he did not systematically versify Bolingbroke's philosophy.[1]

To see how Pope escaped into poetry, how he made his own kind of poetry out of ideas that he had gathered from many sources besides his talks with Bolingbroke, we must consider the texture of his verse and the modes of expression that give the *Essay on Man* its special character. We may then be able to describe its poetic structure or design and see what emphases appear and where—if unconsciously— Pope was putting his weight and revealing his concerns. For Pope, almost invariably, a mode of expression includes a mode of imitation or allusion, a remark true even of the *Essay on Man*, probably the least obviously allusive of Pope's longer works. Although imagery plays a fairly important part in the *Essay*, allusion, as so often in Pope and Dryden, works as an equivalent for metaphor.[2]

To anyone who examines the poem without presuppositions, the most characteristic uses of language are almost always modes of address, ways of indicating tone and shifts of tone. The essence of Pope's 'drama' in the *Essay*, as in later satirical epistles, lies in the play of tone, the tone he takes to the fictive characters he is addressing, whether they are a set of readers, a friend, or a victim, any one of the many dramatic impersonations of the poet's other selves. The common reader who is surprised by the jauntiness and social heartiness with which Pope announces his 'high argument' is noticing something important if obvious, that the *Essay on Man* is written within the dramatic framework of an eighteenth-century Horatian epistle. But as Pope is speaking

---

[1] See Bolingbroke's letter to Swift, in which he outlines the argument of the *Essay on Man*, Let. III. 213, 214; and TE iii (i). xxix–xxxi (an excellent analysis of the problem). On Pope's indebtedness to Bolingbroke see John Laird, 'Pope's *Essay on Man*', *Review of English Studies*, xx. 286–98.

[2] Cf. Maynard Mack, ' "Wit and Poetry and Pope": Some Observations on his Imagery', *Pope and his Contemporaries, Essays presented to George Sherburn* (Oxford, 1949), pp. 23–28.

to a noble lord on a pompous theme, he has brought his tone nearer to the grand address of Dryden than to the casualness of Horace. The *Essay on Man* is on the whole closer to the more vigorous and less intimate passages of the *Essay on Criticism* than to the *Epistle to Dr. Arbuthnot*. Or to take examples from Horace—it is closer to the aloof nobility of *Nil admirari* than the inwardness and friendliness of *Hoc erat in votis*. As in the *Essay on Criticism* 'good breeding' is much—at times a little too much—in evidence:

> Awake, my ST. JOHN! leave all meaner things
> To low ambition, and the pride of Kings.

Throughout the four epistles Pope keeps up the illusion of well-bred good talk, injecting the conversational note by devices of many kinds: parenthetic asides to the reader, sensible observations often marked by an introductory ''tis', persuasive 'know's' and 'think's', more casual 'say's' (to introduce another point of view or a stronger argument), and rather too insistent questions as if to keep the reader's attention from wandering.

The two most frequent modes of address that give this conversation-lesson its peculiar quality go well beyond the usual conventions of intimacy and politeness. In the midst of his exhortation to Bolingbroke Pope steps aside for a moment to marvel at the universe,

> A mighty maze! but not without a plan . . .
>   (1. 6)

Some thirty lines later he interrupts his argument to marvel in another way to another auditor,

> Presumptuous Man! the reason wouldst thou find,
> Why form'd so weak, so little, and so blind!
>   (1. 35–36)

In the course of the *Essay* Pope keeps running up and down this scale of marvelling, from the grandly solemn to the rudely ironic. A rhetorical fever chart of such exclamations would reveal the interesting fact that as they increase in intensity and number, the poetic life of the verse increases in vigour and variety and also in fun or in profundity, whether 'the Muse now stoops, or now ascends'. The 'marvelling' expressions take almost every conceivable form, although a number of types keep recurring. In contexts of both the higher and lower attitudes, we find many lines or passages beginning with 'Lo!' 'Behold!' 'Mark!' 'Look!' 'See!' and 'Go!', salutes to abstractions ('Oh Happiness!' 'Vast chain of being!'), and wondering questions (often hard to distinguish from exclamations in Pope's punctuation). In purely ironic contexts, such expressions (especially 'Go!' and 'See!') appear in even greater numbers as the whole repertory of marvelling devices is turned on the unwilling pupil, that 'Vile worm!', man. Though an occasional 'my lord' or 'friend', or 'you', or a polite exhortation to 'know' or 'learn' remind us that the well-bred auditor is not forgotten, Pope's most striking addresses are in the vein of scornful wonder. 'Thou fool!' and 'fool!' or equivalent compliments are showered down on the 'wond'rous creature!' (Some samples: 'Go, wiser thou!', 'Oh blind to truth!', 'Oh sons of earth!', 'foolish man!'). Another type of expression also equating man and fool—though with an accent of wonder—is the aloof imperative, 'let fools', 'let graceless zealots', 'let subtle schoolmen'. But the two types of marvelling are always merging, and the nature of Pope's art and his central attitudes are clearest in addresses poised neatly between the extremes like 'great standing miracle!' or 'Painful preeminence!'

To see the kind of glissade Pope executes in passing from one attitude to its opposite, and the poetry of ideas he is creating, consider what happens between 'A mighty maze!' and 'Presumptuous Man!' the two examples with which we began. After urging St. John to join him in 'vindicating the ways of God to Man', the poet continues with another Miltonic echo,

> Say first, of God above, or Man below,
> What can we reason, but from what we know?
> Of Man what see we, but his station here,
> From which to reason, or to which refer?
> Thro' worlds unnumber'd tho' the God be known,
> 'Tis ours to trace him only in our own.
> He, who thro' vast immensity can pierce,
> See worlds on worlds compose one universe,

Observe how system into system runs,
What other planets circle other suns,
What vary'd being peoples ev'ry star,
May tell why Heav'n has made us as we are.
But of this frame the bearings, and the ties,
The strong connections, nice dependencies,
Gradations just, has thy pervading soul
Look'd thro'? or can a part contain the whole?
Is the great chain, that draws all to agree,
And drawn supports, upheld by God, or thee?
Presumptuous Man, the reason wouldst thou find,
Why form'd so weak, so little, and so blind!

(i. 17–36)

The rich adjustment of ideas and style through learned
reference and literary allusion is astonishing. The epic command of the first line becomes in the next the question of
men who argue by analogy from the known order to the
unknown, the change in style making way for the contrasting
picture of a mind that embraces the whole universe and its
plan. This wondrous mind is described in language recalling
Lucretius' high praise of Epicurus and also Virgil's lines on
the Lucretian philosopher, the passage of the *Georgics* echoed
in *Windsor Forest*. The philosopher's comprehensive view is
artfully presented in terms appropriate partly to a contemporary astronomer and partly to poets and theologians in the
Platonic-Christian tradition of the Great Chain of Being. The
final question, which calls for assent to the argument that
we can reason only from 'what we know', alludes to the
golden chain of Milton and Homer. Thus the reader is
prepared for the thrust of the next line, 'Presumptuous
Man!', which sounds on the surface like an heroic epithet
and is of course cuttingly sarcastic.

The modulation of tone to this level from the awe of
'mighty maze' is truly marvellous and shows how Pope felt
his way through his philosophic 'materials' to an attitude and
a kind of poetry peculiarly his own. As we noted above, the
'Say first' that he starts with does not remain Miltonic for
long. Milton was addressing the Holy Spirit (half-merged
with the 'Heavenly Muse'), but Pope, it soon appears, is
much nearer earth,

> Say first, of God above, or Man below,
> What can we reason, but from what we know?

The heroic 'say' is inclining toward the later argumentative 'say's', and 'we' is very much 'men like you and me', or 'man' addressed as 'thee' at the end of the passage. The high Lucretian praise of the all-seeing philosopher seems close in effect to wondering at the 'mighty maze', but unlike the ancient poets and the Pope of *Windsor Forest*, the poet of the *Essay* is ironic. He speaks in the voice of a man finely withdrawn from pretensions to 'Wisdom infinite'. The naïve listener who has been taken in by the encomium is gently knifed as the moral is brought home,

> . . . has thy pervading soul
> Look'd thro'? or can a part contain the whole?

'Thee' in the next couplet is cruelly *ad hominem*: 'Is the great chain . . . upheld by God, or *thee*?' 'Presumptuous Man!' is the final blow to aspiring 'wit' and the battery of unanswerable questions that follows reduces man to his finite 'foolish' status.

What has happened to the 'argument' and the 'structure of ideas' in Pope's poetic transformation? Certainly very little has been proved, either by deduction, or by citing evidence, and yet a great deal of 'doctrine' has been implied and, in spite of the irony, it has been made impressive and dramatically convincing. We get a sense of the great order of nature according to both the Newtonian and Platonic views, we have also a vivid impression of the fine ordering of parts within the whole, and we are left with a grand Homeric image of the lively dependency of the whole order on God. Here is wonder with some substance to it, wonder that is more than a rhetorical gesture. But the poetic drift is always towards irony, a tendency that has a marked effect on the philosophic 'content' and that gives us a clear indication of Pope's deepest concerns. What moves him, the feeling that shapes his style and governs the way in which he combines allusions and the tone with which he expresses them, is his strong antipathy to man's presumption, to pride, especially of mind or 'wit' (in the older sense of intelligence):

> In Pride, in reas'ning Pride, our error lies . . . (I. 123)

Absurd trust in human reason is as usual for Pope inseparable
from dullness:

> When the proud steed shall know why Man restrains
> His fiery course, or drives him o'er the plains;
> When the dull Ox, why now he breaks the clod,
> Is now a victim, and now Ægypt's God:
> Then shall Man's pride and dulness comprehend
> His actions', passions', being's, use and end . . .
>
> (I. 61–66)

Behind Pope's attitude is the enlightened distrust of
scholastic logic that can be traced in Bacon, Hobbes, and
Locke:

> Let subtle schoolmen teach these friends [Reason, Self-love] to fight,
> More studious to divide than to unite,
> And Grace and Virtue, Sense and Reason split,
> With all the rash dexterity of Wit:
> Wits, just like fools, at war about a Name,
> Have full as oft no meaning, or the same.
>
> (II. 81–86)

Such 'Wits' in philosophy, like merely clever 'wits' in
literature are little better than fools. In Pope this attitude
toward overconfidence in reason is identified with Socratic
confession of 'ignorance', which is accompanied as always by
the belief that the most valuable knowledge is to 'know
thyself'.

In the movement from wonder at the mighty maze to
scorn of presumptuous man and in the way Pope presses
traditional views and styles in the service of his irony lies the
essence of his poetry in the *Essay on Man*. To feel the link
between these modes of 'marvelling' is to grasp the key to its
imaginative design, to see how it is composed as a poem and
what it mainly expresses. We may now ask whether the
design is continuous and where and why the *Essay* succeeds
or fails as poetry. Our answers will also give us further
insight into the relation between Pope's achievement as a
moral and satirical poet and his earlier successes in quite
different poetic modes.

The First Epistle of the *Essay on Man*, on 'Man, with
respect to the Universe', is commonly regarded as the best

of the four. It includes more of the passages that are generally known and remembered, nearly all of the famous purple patches, except for the lines on man's 'middle state' in the Second Epistle. There are also relatively fewer moments in reading it when we are disturbed by doubts as to whether we are surely reading a *poem* (even of the conversational variety). The poetic design is clearest and most continuous in this first epistle since the polarity of man and the universe almost inevitably issues in a polarity of attitudes and rhetorical modes. As soon as Pope begins to expatiate on the blessings that accompany man's state—his ignorance of the future, his eternal hopefulness—irony intrudes:

> Oh blindness to the future! kindly giv'n,
> That each may fill the circle mark'd by Heav'n . . .
> (85–86)

Like the lamb that 'licks the hand just rais'd to shed his blood', man fortunately does not know the time and the manner of his end. The Advice to 'Hope humbly then' is brought home in the first passage of serious marvelling, the picture of the 'poor Indian' content with a simple hope, his soul uncorrupted by 'proud Science'. Pope's noble savage is a reincarnation of the shepherd-hero of the *Pastorals* and the *Iliad*, a dweller in the visionary America of *Windsor Forest*, where

> . . . the freed Indians in their native groves
> Reap their own fruits, and woo their sable loves . . .
> (409–10)

The diction has touches of the heroic-descriptive manner of *Windsor Forest* and the *Iliad*: 'the solar walk' (originally from Dryden's *Annus Mirabilis*), the 'cloud-topt hill', and 'the watry waste'. There is some civilized amusement in this picture of the Indian's simple desires, but in the first line that follows, the irony is turned on proud 'enlightened' man:

> Go, wiser thou! and in thy scale of sense
> Weigh thy Opinion against Providence . . .
> (113–14)

a couplet in the idiom and tone of Horace's advice in *Nil admirari*,

> i nunc, argentum et marmor vetus aeraque et artes
> suspice . . .
>
> <div align="right">(<i>Epp</i>. i. vi. 17–18)</div>

(A similar contrast between low and high stations is made by Horace in the satirical diatribe of slave to master, *Satires* ii. 7. 95–101.) Pope clinches the lesson in a piece of antithetical wit recalling a well-known couplet in the *Essay on Criticism*:

> In Pride, in reas'ning Pride, our error lies;
> All quit their sphere, and rush into the skies.
>
> (123–4)

But Pope could hardly fail to observe that primitive man can also be a victim of pride, and in the 'Keatsian' lines[1] on the happy child of nature ('For me kind Nature . . .'), he writes an ironic pastoral rhapsody. The pastoral dream-world of 'eternal springs and cloudless skies', referred to here in mocking accents, is contrasted with the true course of Nature, which works through unchanging laws that produce 'plagues' and 'earthquakes' as a part of 'Heav'n's design'.

Mock admiration for 'Man . . . whom rational we call' gives way to the most effective deflation of our desire to 'act or think beyond mankind':

> Why has not Man a microscopic eye?
> For this plain reason, Man is not a Fly.
> Say what the use, were finer optics giv'n,
> T' inspect a mite, not comprehend the heav'n?
> Or touch, if tremblingly alive all o'er,
> To smart and agonize at ev'ry pore?
> Or quick effluvia darting thro' the brain,
> Die of a rose in aromatic pain?
>
> (193–200)

The final couplet is one of the few in the poem where we are tempted to compare Pope's poetry of ideas with Donne's. In its exquisite accuracy and wit the image is inseparable from the subject of the metaphor, the disturbance that must follow if man were given powers not belonging to his place

---

[1] Cf. Ch. I, p. 29.

in the order of being. Though the bond of feeling and
thought is less close and the economy of style is less metaphysical in the lines that continue the argument, they are
almost the best passage of serious marvelling in the whole
poem:

> Far as Creation's ample range extends,
> The scale of sensual, mental pow'rs ascends:
> Mark how it mounts, to Man's imperial race,
> From the green myriads in the peopled grass:
> What modes of sight betwixt each wide extreme,
> The mole's dim curtain, and the lynx's beam:
> Of smell, the headlong lioness between,
> And hound sagacious on the tainted green:
> Of hearing, from the life that fills the flood,
> To that which warbles thro' the vernal wood:
> The spider's touch, how exquisitely fine!
> Feels at each thread, and lives along the line:
> In the nice bee, what sense so subtly true
> From pois'nous herbs extracts the healing dew:
> How Instinct varies in the grov'ling swine,
> Compar'd, half-reas'ning elephant, with thine:
> 'Twixt that, and Reason, what a nice barrier;
> For ever sep'rate, yet for ever near!
> Remembrance and Reflection how ally'd;
> What thin partitions Sense from Thought divide:
> And Middle natures, how they long to join,
> Yet never pass th' insuperable line!

> (207–28)

The language brings sharply to our senses what the scale
means in extensiveness and variety, in the distance between
the extremes, and in the thin partitions dividing successive
classes of being. The attitude of wonder and the 'ideas' of
order are expressed through minute particulars of visual and
tactile imagery: 'the green myriads in the peopled grass',
'the mole's dim curtain', and (a couplet that Tennyson
especially admired)

> The spider's touch, how exquisitely fine!
> Feels at each thread, and lives along the line . . .

The art of the lines is (like Tennyson's) Virgilian in delicacy
and exactness of epithet, a quality pointed out by Joseph
Warton. The diction has touches of Pope's georgic-pastoral

style, and the descriptions of animals, especially of smaller creatures, is very close to the semi-human and playfully heroic descriptions of the *Georgics*. But Pope's eye is so much on the detail and the image that relevance to the idea is not always kept clearly in mind: the 'spider's touch' and the bee's 'sense so subtly true' ought according to the argument to be matched by balancing extremes, but they are not. We are reminded of a similar fuzziness in the more philosophic lyrics of *In Memoriam*.

But in spite of some blurring of this sort, the large sequence of thought and feeling is clear and dynamic from here to the end of the epistle. We move naturally from wonder at fine details to the grand view of

> See, thro' this air, this ocean, and this earth,
> All matter quick, and bursting into birth.
> Above, how high progressive life may go!
> Around, how wide! how deep extend below!
>
> (233–6)

But Pope's generalized *O altitudo*'s are a little vacuous, and we are relieved when he returns to the more concrete 'beast, bird, fish', and 'insect'. The chaos that would follow any break in the chain of being leads to a fine passage of marvelling in the style of an Homeric oath:

> Let Earth unbalanc'd from her orbit fly,
> Planets and Suns run lawless thro' the sky,
> Let ruling Angels from their spheres be hurl'd,
> Being on being wreck'd, and world on world,
> Heav'n's whole foundations to their centre nod,
> And Nature tremble to the throne of God . . .
>
> (251–6)

This Newtonian-Biblical (and Miltonic) apocalypse has a destination we have been anticipating since the fairly complimentary question addressed to man,

> The pow'rs of all subdu'd by thee alone,
> Is not thy Reason all these pow'rs in one?
>
> (231–2)

The scene of chaos ends rudely with

> All this dread ORDER break—for whom? for thee?
> Vile worm!—oh Madness, Pride, Impiety!   (257–8)

The awe has been too extreme, the rhetorical exclaiming too
obvious to hold, and the heroic oath has a quality of mocking
magnificence that easily turns to sarcasm. We know from
the *Rape of the Lock* how easy it is to pass from imprecation
to bathos:

> Sooner let Earth, Air, Sea, to *Chaos* fall,
> Men, Monkies, Lap-dogs, Parrots, perish all!
> (IV. 119–20)

But ridicule of man's 'ruling Mind' bounces us back to its
opposite (the swing is almost inevitable in Pope), 'the great
directing MIND OF ALL', and prepares us for the lines that
express best the sense of wonder at the great life glowing
within each part. By combining images from astronomy,
gardening, and organic form in art, Pope alludes deftly to
other expressions of harmony and order at other points in
the epistle and the poem:

> All are but parts of one stupendous whole,
> Whose body Nature is, and God the soul;
> That, chang'd thro' all, and yet in all the same,
> Great in the earth, as in th' aethereal frame,
> Warms in the sun, refreshes in the breeze,
> Glows in the stars, and blossoms in the trees,
> Lives thro' all life, extends thro' all extent,
> Spreads undivided, operates unspent,
> Breathes in our soul, informs our mortal part,
> As full, as perfect, in a hair as heart;
> As full, as perfect, in vile Man that mourns,
> As the rapt Seraph that adores and burns;
> To him no high, no low, no great, no small;
> He fills, he bounds, connects, and equals all.
> (267–80)

The oscillation from the great to the small prepares us for
the final sharp injunction to proud man's 'erring reason',

> Cease then, nor ORDER Imperfection name . . .
> (281)

Though Pope may not have written the parts of this epistle
in their present sequence, he has composed them into poetry
with an order of linked attitudes and modes of expression
that grow easily out of the 'structure of ideas'.

Beginning with Epistle II passages of simply-serious wonder become less common as Pope reveals more and more that his true subject—the one he brings to poetic life—is the ironist's delight in the consequences of his metaphysics. The great scheme is there, but more often as a point of departure for irony instead of rapture. (A sign that if we seriously believe that 'The proper study of Mankind is Man', we can hardly be much concerned with the universe.) In the famous lines on that 'being darkly wise, and rudely great', Pope's wonder is always entwined with mockery:

> Go, wond'rous creature! mount where Science guides . . .
>
> (19)

In expressing amusement at the pretensions of intellect, Pope turns his irony on natural scientists, and on the very philosophers who were the authors of the tradition in which he is writing—Plato and the Neoplatonists. But with the section that immediately follows this lively and often comic picture of high-flying philosophers and scientists, Pope falls into a tone compounded of the didactic and the informative. The Horatian poetry of conversation—which is always dramatic, always changing its tone and its tactics—gives way to mere talk in verse. For the next 125 lines or more Pope and his readers nod, as the Muse stoops to describe the theory of the 'ruling passion' and the relation between instinct and the passions. But occasional shafts of irony remind us that men are 'fools' and help keep in view attitudes characteristic of the livelier parts of the *Essay*. The poetry revives when Pope leaves theory for ironic contradictions in human conduct and feeling, which he depicts not in general terms but (to borrow again Johnson's comment on Dryden), '. . . as they are complicated by the various relations of society and confused in the tumults and agitations of life'.

> The merchant's toil, the sage's indolence,
> The monk's humility, the hero's pride,
> All, all alike, find Reason on their side.
>
> (172–4)

The similarity of the last line to one of La Rochefoucauld's aphorisms is another sign that the view of both reason and the ruling passion is double-edged. Reason is certainly most

compliant. 'Th' Eternal Art educing good from ill', which
in some inexplicable way 'grafts' on the ruling passion 'our
best principle', produces a surprising harvest:

> What crops of wit and honesty appear
> From spleen, from obstinacy, hate, or fear!
> See anger, zeal and fortitude supply;
> Ev'n av'rice, prudence; sloth, philosophy;
> Lust, thro' some certain strainers well refin'd,
> Is gentle love, and charms all womankind:
> Envy, to which th' ignoble mind's a slave,
> Is emulation in the learn'd or brave:
> Nor Virtue, male or female, can we name,
> But what will grow on Pride, or grow on Shame.
>
> (185–94)

The consoling operations of 'th' Eternal Art' are much less
vividly expressed than the shrewd perception of the link
between our virtues and our vices. (The psychological insight and the rhetoric are Ovidian and hark back to *Eloisa
to Abelard*.) A similar vein of ironic wisdom and 'contrarious'
wit appears in another passage supporting the same general
argument, in which we are told that 'HEAV'N's great view'
(being 'One') provides all ranks with 'happy frailties'. The
irony of the adjective becomes clearer as we examine the
'frailties':

> That [heaven's great view] happy frailties to all ranks apply'd,
> Shame to the virgin, to the matron pride,
> Fear to the statesman, rashness to the chief,
> To kings presumption, and to crowds belief . . .
>
> (241–4)

As Pope reflects on the 'home-felt joys' we owe to human
weaknesses, he arrives at a state of smiling wisdom that
approaches Horace's 'equal mind':

> To these we owe true friendship, love sincere,
> Each home-felt joy that life inherits here:
> Yet from the same we learn, in its decline,
> Those joys, those loves, those int'rests to resign:
> Taught half by Reason, half by mere decay,
> To welcome death, and calmly pass away.
>
> (255–60)

But the less pleasant note of scorn for proud fools is heard with increasing frequency in the later sections of the epistle (IV, V, VI), and is struck with a new intensity in a passage anticipating the vision of a 'mad world' in *The Epilogue to the Satires*. The exclamatory rhetoric is familiar from the First Epistle:

> The learn'd is happy nature to explore,
> The fool is happy that he knows no more;
> The rich is happy in the plenty giv'n,
> The poor contents him with the care of Heav'n.
> See the blind beggar dance, the cripple sing,
> The sot a hero, lunatic a king;
> The starving chemist in his golden views
> Supremely blest, the poet in his muse.
>   See some strange comfort ev'ry state attend,
> And Pride bestow'd on all, a common friend. . .
>   (263–72)

'Strange comforts' indeed, if we note the mixture here of delusions with true satisfactions and the ironic light thrown on the second by being combined with the first: 'the starving chemist. . . Supremely blest' (in his folly), 'the poet in his muse' (likewise 'supremely blest in *his* folly'). In general, it may be said that Pope demonstrates the vanity of human wishes better than the comforting truth that 'not a vanity is giv'n in vain'. After his disturbing and vivid illustrations it is hard to accept the final piece of advice, especially since it is offered in a tone of flippancy if not irreverence:

> See! and confess, one comfort still must rise,
> 'Tis this, Tho' Man's a fool, yet GOD IS WISE.
>   (293–4)

Such are the consolations of the philosopher, which are quite different from the shrewd wisdom of the satirist. Nowhere in the poem is there a clearer sign of the contrast between Pope's professed subject and his expressed concern.

The Third Epistle is certainly the dullest of the four and proves—if it needs proving—that something more than logical-discursive order is necessary for poetry. There is, however, a fairly consistent irony, brought out through numerous contrasts, that connects the epistle with the richer poetic texture of the first two epistles and the last. Man's proud achievements in government and in the arts, his reasoning powers, and his love, are constantly being coupled with the activities of lower animals, with lower instincts in man, and with the impulse of self-love. The themes of folly and pride recur, particularly in the opening section, and there is the familiar oscillation between extremes of marvelling. The demonstration of how 'plastic Nature' works for 'the gen'ral Good' brings in some ugly associations:

> See dying vegetables life sustain,
> See life dissolving vegetate again . . .
> (15–16)

With his usual sarcasm the speaker turns on man in lines that deflate the pastoral illusion of a nature made to serve man's desires. The passage is a mocking inversion of pastoral songs in which the shepherd tells over the gifts which nature bestows on his beloved:

> Has God, thou fool! work'd solely for thy good,
> Thy joy, thy pastime, thy attire, thy food?
> Who for thy table feeds the wanton fawn,
> For·him as kindly spread the flow'ry lawn.
> Is it for thee the lark ascends and sings?
> Joy tunes his voice, joy elevates his wings:
> Is it for thee the linnet pours his throat?
> Loves of his own and raptures swell the note:
> The bounding steed you pompously bestride,
> Shares with his lord the pleasure and the pride:
> Is thine alone the seed that strews the plain?
> The birds of heav'n shall vindicate their grain:
> Thine the full harvest of the golden year?
> Part pays, and justly, the deserving steer . . .
> (27–40)

The wit with which high and low are brought together is delicious:

> Know, Nature's children all divide her care;
> The fur that warms a monarch, warm'd a bear.
> (43–44)

With the next couplet we are in the world of Gay's *Fables*:

> While Man exclaims, "See all things for my use!"
> "See man for mine!" replies a pamper'd goose. . .

But the pastoral illusion of civilized man is a corruption of nature through pride. In the *Essay on Man* the true pastoral world symbolizes for Pope as for Milton man's original innocence:

> Pride then was not; nor Arts, that Pride to aid;
> Man walk'd with beast, joint tenant of the shade;
> The same his table, and the same his bed;
> No murder cloath'd him, and no murder fed.
> In the same temple, the resounding wood,
> All vocal beings hymn'd their equal God . . .
>
> (151–6)

It is the period of uncorrupted reason ('To copy Instinct then was Reason's part'), a time when man learned the civilized arts from Nature herself. Nature's 'instructions' to man make us feel the charm of small beings, her words recalling the georgic vein of the passage on the mole and the spider in Epistle I. But the lines are also veiled in irony through the contrast with man's present refined stupidity. The state of nature was a state of 'true Wit':[1]

> Ere Wit oblique had broke that steddy light,
> Man, like his Maker, saw that all was right,
> To Virtue, in the paths of Pleasure, trod,
> And own'd a Father when he own'd a God.
>
> (231–4)

When man saw by the light of nature, he saw the divine plan, and without the aid of revelation, it seems, he conceived of God as a father, a god of love. In contrast with early natural religion, Pope satirizes a later age ruled by Superstition, the teacher of the tyrant and a sharer in his tyranny. The style of the attack is mock-heroic, a parody of Dryden's and Pope's august epic manner:

> She, 'midst the light'ning's blaze, and thunder's sound,
> When rock'd the mountains, and when groan'd the ground,
> She taught the weak to bend, the proud to pray,
> To Pow'r unseen, and mightier far than they:
> She, from the rending earth and bursting skies,
> Saw Gods descend, and fiends infernal rise . . .   (249–54)

The tone of the conclusion to the epistle, in its hard-boiled,

---

[1] Cf. the similar language of the *Essay on Criticism*, Ch. VII, i, p. 200.

commonsense English dismissal of the 'forms' for the 'fact', brings this discursive essay back to the epistolary and legislative style of the *Religio Laici*.

The Fourth Epistle marks a return to the rhetorical modes of the First. Exclamatory addresses to abstractions ('Oh Happiness!' 'O Virtue!'), and injunctions to 'See' and 'Behold' and 'Mark' are even more frequent. Soon after the initial salute to happiness, it becomes clear that wonder in this epistle will usually incline toward ridicule or sarcasm or some milder degree of irony. But Pope's tone was never more facilely solemn than in these first few lines:

> OH HAPPINESS! our being's end and aim!
> Good, Pleasure, Ease, Content! whate'er thy name:
> That something still which prompts th' eternal sigh,
> For which we bear to live, or dare to die,
> Which still so near us, yet beyond us lies,
> O'er-look'd, seen double, by the fool, and wise.

He is barely saved from his own solemnity by the deft strokes with which he parodies epic grandeur and august praise of courts and military conquests (note *propitious* and *iron harvests*):

> Say, in what mortal soil thou deign'st to grow?
> Fair op'ning to some Court's propitious shine,
> Or deep with di'monds in the flaming mine?
> Twin'd with the wreaths Parnassian lawrels yield,
> Or reap'd in iron harvests of the field?
>
> (8–12)

Still sharper thrusts lead to a reflection on a view of happiness that is less celestial, or rather nearer to the *caelestis sapientia* of Horace:

> Take Nature's path, and mad Opinion's leave,
> All states can reach it, and all heads conceive;
> Obvious her goods, in no extreme they dwell,
> There needs but thinking right, and meaning well;
> And mourn our various portions as we please,
> Equal is Common Sense, and Common Ease.
>
> (29–34)

If Pope's definition of happiness as virtue is Stoic in origin, it is Stoicism made obvious and attainable, as acclimatized by Horace, not the austere renunciation of a Marcus Aurelius:

> virtus est vitium fugere, et sapientia prima
> stultitia caruisse . . .
>
> (*Epp.* I. i. 41–42)

Pope's later translation of the lines might well have come from this part of the *Essay on Man*:

> 'Tis the first Virtue, Vices to abhor;
> And the first Wisdom, to be Fool no more.
>
> (65–66)

Horace, it is fair to say, appreciates better than Pope the difficulty of 'thinking right' (*recte sapere*), of schooling the mind and the emotions in order to reach 'our being's end and aim'.

With the first words that follow this cheerful view of happiness, 'Remember, Man . . .' Pope's teaching tone, like Horace's, brings him into a more familiar relation with his audience. Although he discourses on 'the Universal Cause' that 'Acts not by partial, but by gen'ral laws', and on the divine 'ORDER', he is never so august as in Epistle I, and his talk of virtue is sane and sensible:

> Reason's whole pleasure, all the joys of Sense,
> Lie in three words, Health, Peace, and Competence.
>
> (79–80)

There is less high argument and less low exposition in the epistle, and the whole poem is more dramatic in the Horatian way. We are more continuously aware that Pope is talking to a friend or a friendly enemy as he dexterously shifts his approach from the distinctly personal 'Tell (for you can)' (Bolingbroke, specifically), to editorial 'we's', to the publicly genial, 'I'll tell you, friend!' to the most sharply satirical addresses and imperatives: 'O fool!' 'Go, like the Indian'.

As dramatic setting and range of tone indicate, Epistle IV is an epistolary satire in Pope's later manner. The subject is not so much happiness, as man's misconceptions of happiness and virtue, a satirical view of human aspiration, whether it aims at wealth, fame, greatness of family, or superiority of intellect ('wit'). Pope prefaces his attack on types of false happiness by making fun of fools who imagine the good are unhappy because they suffer common physical ills. He neatly turns wonder to satirical advantage by hailing notable examples of good men who met tragic ends:

> See FALKLAND dies, the virtuous and the just!
> See god-like TURENNE prostrate on the dust!
> See SIDNEY bleeds amid the martial strife!
> Was this their Virtue, or Contempt of Life? (99–102)

Even when he uses a metaphysical argument, he seems in this epistle to be released from pomposity, and he writes vigorously in his favourite vein of ironic questioning and preposterous example:

> Think we, like some weak Prince, th' Eternal Cause,
> Prone for his fav'rites to reverse his laws?
>   Shall burning Ætna, if a sage requires,
> Forget to thunder, and recall her fires?
> On air or sea new motions be imprest,
> Oh blameless Bethel! to relieve thy breast?
> When the loose mountain trembles from on high,
> Shall gravitation cease, if you go by?
> Or some old temple, nodding to its fall,
> For Chartres' head reserve the hanging wall?
>   (121–30)

This passage, in its mixture of Italian-classical and contemporary personal, might easily belong to one of the *Moral Essays* or the *Imitations of Horace*. From here to the concluding section (VII) of the epistle Pope carries on a witty war against the pretensions of human wit, his athletic joy becoming at times unholy, as when he makes fun of men who want 'a kingdom of the Just' here and now:

> But still this world (so fitted for the knave)
> Contents us not. A better shall we have?
> A kingdom of the Just then let it be:
> But first consider how those Just agree.
> The good must merit God's peculiar care;
> But who, but God, can tell us who they are?
> One thinks on Calvin Heav'n's own spirit fell,
> Another deems him instrument of hell;
> If Calvin feel Heav'n's blessing, or its rod,
> This cries there is, and that, there is no God. (131–40)

In the grand demonstration against false conceptions of happiness, Pope comes near to the best of his satirical poetry 'in Horace's manner'. Though the tone of high admiration is uppermost, with each phase in the attack there are nice variations in satirical style and manner of address. In the first assault, on men who suppose that the 'trash' of wealth could be the reward of virtue, Pope combines his superior 'commanding' tone with burlesque of the noble savage theme of Epistle I:

> Go, like the Indian, in another life
> Expect thy dog, thy bottle, and thy wife . . .
> (177–8)

He darts aside from reflecting on rewards that 'would to Virtue bring/No joy', to drop in a snappy couplet of very worldly 'wonder':

> How oft by these at sixty are undone
> The virtues of a saint at twenty-one!
> (183–4)

The astonishingly bitter lines on pride of family start from Scriblerian vulgarity, rise in ironic *hauteur* to a fine appreciation of Roman nobility, and come to rest in the simplest of moral affirmations:

> Stuck o'er with titles and hung round with strings,
> That thou may'st be by kings, or whores of kings.
> Boast the pure blood of an illustrious race,
> In quiet flow from Lucrece to Lucrece;
> But by your father's worth if yours you rate,
> Count me those only who were good and great.
> (205–10)

The consideration of greatness begins more politely, 'Look next on Greatness . . .', but sours into Byronic casualness and disillusionment:

> Heroes are much the same, the point's agreed,
> From Macedonia's madman to the Swede;
> The whole strange purpose of their lives, to find
> Or make, an enemy of all mankind!
> (219–22)

The 'Politic and Wise' are polished off in a sketch that would
be perfect for a Talleyrand:

> No less alike the Politic and Wise,
> All sly slow things, with circumspective eyes:
> Men in their loose unguarded hours they take,
> Not that themselves are wise, but others weak.
>
> (225–8)

The next theme is launched with one of those brief rever-
berating questions of which Horace is especially fond:
'What's Fame?' (parallel to the question in Pope's imitation
of 'Ofellus', 'What's *Property*? Dear Swift!'). The examples,
mostly Roman, are grand enough, but the tone keeps close
to well-bred conversation,

> Just what you hear, you have, and what's unknown
> The same (my Lord) if Tully's or your own.
>
> (239–40)

The ironic queries that follow on 'Parts superior' have a
special application to Bolingbroke, but the ambiguous 'you's'
broaden the application, particularly in the couplet alluding
to Addison's *Cato*,

> Painful preheminence! yourself to view
> Above life's weakness, and its comforts too.
>
> (267–8)

Pope finishes off his 'strict accounting' of 'these blessings'
with two pieces of satirical annihilation, both in modes
adapted from Horace, and both characteristic of Pope's
mature style. In each the addresses to the reader and to the
victims are in the tone of cutting admiration typical of the
Essay on Man. In the first passage, Pope leads us through a
swiftly changing series of portrait-examples (symbolic Roman
or historical), rising to a climax of damnation. It is characteristic of Pope rather than Horace that each portrait
crystallizes in particulars of sense:

> Think, and if still the things thy envy call,
> Say, would'st thou be the Man to whom they fall?
> To sigh for ribbands if thou art so silly,
> Mark how they grace Lord Umbra, or Sir Billy:
> Is yellow dirt the passion of thy life?
> Look but on Gripus, or on Gripus' wife:

> If Parts allure thee, think how Bacon shin'd,
> The wisest, brightest, meanest of mankind:
> Or ravish'd with the whistling of a Name,
> See Cromwell, damn'd to everlasting fame!
>   (275–84)

The second passage is a grand example of Popeian character
painting, only little below the best characters of the *Moral
Essays* and the *Satires*. Though perhaps personal[1] in origin,
the portrait as it stands in the present context is purely
symbolic. In form it is half narrative and half moral analysis,
with splendid pictorial impressions of shadowy glory:

> In hearts of Kings, or arms of Queens who lay,
> How happy! those to ruin, these betray,
> Mark by what wretched steps their glory grows,
> From dirt and sea-weed as proud Venice rose;
> In each how guilt and greatness equal ran,
> And all that rais'd the Hero, sunk the Man.
> Now Europe's laurels on their brows behold,
> But stain'd with blood, or ill exchang'd for gold,
> Then see them broke with toils, or sunk in ease,
> Or infamous for plunder'd provinces.
> Oh wealth ill-fated! which no act of fame
> E'er taught to shine, or sanctify'd from shame!
> What greater bliss attends their close of life?
> Some greedy minion, or imperious wife,
> The trophy'd arches, story'd halls invade,
> And haunt their slumbers in the pompous shade.
> Alas! not dazzled with their noon-tide ray,
> Compute the morn and ev'ning to the day;
> The whole amount of that enormous fame,
> A Tale, that blends their glory with their shame!
>   (289–308)

In its magniloquence and seriousness the conclusion resembles Johnson's lines on Charles XII, who

> Left the Name at which the World grew pale,
> To point a Moral, or adorn a Tale.

It may well be that Pope had Juvenal as well as Horace in

---

[1] Pope later (probably 1735) revised and expanded the portrait as a satire on
Marlborough, a version not published in his lifetime. See EC iii. 87, 88, and Bate-
son's appendix on 'Atossa', TE. iii. 159.

mind when he was composing this whole section on vain forms of happiness, but it is worth remembering that Horace could be Juvenalian[1] when he wanted to be. In Horace's Stoic diatribes, such as 'Ofellus' or 'Damasippus', the irony is driven home almost as relentlessly and consistently as in this part of the Fourth Epistle. Ofellus presses his attack with harsh questions and insulting addresses, *insane, improbe*, and Damasippus puts his audience through a severe anatomy of similar follies—avarice, ambition, luxury, and superstition.

After exposing 'the false scale of Happiness complete', Pope returns in Stoic vein to the theme of virtue. But virtue has been redefined, Maynard Mack reminds us, as 'benevolence', the tender concern for the well-being of others so perfectly exemplified in Pope's and Fielding's friend, Ralph Allen. 'Benevolence', we are to understand, is 'self-love push'd to social, to divine', and this mellow conclusion to the poem and the argument is supported by a final appeal to 'that Chain which links th' immense design'. The 'good, untaught' arrive at the knowledge of God and his plan through no particular church but through enlightened natural religion:

> Slave to no sect, who takes no private road,
> But looks thro' Nature, up to Nature's God . . .
>
> (331–2)

Although faith, hope, and charity are brought in, the context (as Pope explained to his Catholic friend Caryll) did not make it appropriate 'to mention our Saviour directly'. While the *Essay on Man* does in a way 'magnify Christian doctrine', it is Christian without any clear reference to Christ or to revelation. The worldly audience implied, the quality and tone of the talk hardly made it possible for Pope to speak in terms that bring us close to the Gospels or the mysteries of Christian faith. One of the main lessons enforced by the poem, the danger of 'erring Pride', is certainly Judaeo-Christian, but it is not exclusively so nor so presented by Pope. He does not speak of pride as sin—it is worth noting that sin is never mentioned to the polite audience of the *Essay on Man*—but rather as an error of intelligence, of 'wit oblique'. This failure

---

[1] Cf. Ch. VI, pp. 179–80.

or error, *hamartia*, was perfectly familiar to the ancient world, and much of Socrates' teaching was aimed at correcting it not by revelation or conversion, but by self-exploration. Pope's conclusion to the *Essay on Man* is Socratic and Horatian, a doctrine for achieving happiness in this world, with no mention of the next:

> That VIRTUE only makes our Bliss below;
> And all our Knowledge is, OURSELVES TO KNOW.

Although in much of the poem Pope is expressing his wise understanding of how easily the human mind is led astray, he expresses with equal force his belief that only by a fuller exercise of intelligence can mind be saved from itself. What we need if we are to avoid the disease of pride is not less wit but more, a point Pope had already made in the *Essay on Criticism*:

> Of all the Causes which conspire to blind
> Man's erring judgment, and misguide the mind,
> What the weak head with strongest bias rules
> Is *Pride*, the never-failing vice of fools.
> Whatever nature has in worth denied,
> She gives in large recruits of needful pride;
> For as in bodies, thus in souls, we find
> What wants in blood and spirits, swelled with wind:
> Pride, where wit fails, steps in to our defence,
> And fills up all the mighty Void of sense.
> If once right reason drives that cloud away,
> Truth breaks upon us with resistless day.
>   (201–12)

Pope is thus the poet of intelligence, of 'reason' in the large sense of full self-knowledge, of inborn good sense that saves us from the deceptions of our reasoning. And Pope's belief in intelligence—qualified of course by a wise scepticism[1]— supplies the motive power of his poetry in the *Essay on Man*. This conviction is the source of the activating attitudes of wonder and scorn and of the correlative modes of expressing them. Although the Neoplatonic scheme of the universe and contemporary cosmological views excite Pope's awe, and though he is tempted to pierce 'thro' vast immensity', he

[1] Cf. Ch. X, p. 352.

does not rest in this attitude for long, but uses it rather as a
basis for ironic reflection on man's boasted reach of mind.
His mood of serious marvelling is rarely sustained for long
and is most convincing when it prefaces sharper views of the
human condition. When Pope is moved by his double sense
of the cosmic setting and human littleness and by other closely allied feelings—his exquisite sense of the beauty in micro-
cosms, his hatred of pretensions and dullness, his amusement at man's proneness to mistake the false goals for the
right one—his poetry has the richness of texture we have
found in much of the First and the Fourth Epistles and
intermittently in the Second and the Third. When argument
gets in the way and this complex vision fails, the poetry becomes painfully thin, expertly rhymed exposition of harmony and disturbance or of reason and passion, but little more.
Fortunately, irony is always breaking in to remind us that
there is a better Pope and better poetry elsewhere.

The signs of life in poetry as in the eighteenth-century
universe are activity and change in an orderly pattern, a truth
fully illustrated by Pope's doctrine and art in the *Essay on
Man*. We have seen sufficient evidence of poetic life and
design in the overall movement of idea and feeling in the
poem, through phases of order and disorder and of wonder
and ironic amusement. We have more particular and more
convincing proof in the pictures of 'creation's ample range'
with their glowing and precise imagery, in the idyllic description of primitive humility sharply contrasted with sophisticated pride 'rushing into the skies', in heroic and apocalyptic
scenes of disorder brought on by that 'vile worm', Man, and in
mocking injunctions to 'mount where Science guides' coupled
with homely advice to 'drop into thyself, and be a fool!' We
have seen other signs of the energy and controlling hand of
the poet in Pope's expression of the wonderful contradictions
and surprisingly close relationships between vices and virtues, in his fine display of the pleasures that pride supplies
for 'each vacuity of sense', and in his ridicule of the pastoral
illusion or in his charming pictures of the lower orders from
which human nature has learned some of its most important
lessons. But in the satire on man's mistaken view of happiness, Pope's use of persuasion and mockery, of literary and

historical example—and in general his mastery of literary tactics of every sort—show him near the height of his powers. The Fourth Epistle also begins to show the suppleness in varying the tone and adapting the rhythm to changes of thought and feeling that marks the best of Pope's later work from the *Epistle to Burlington* to the Fourth *Dunciad*. In the satire on happiness there is clearer proof than in the other epistles that Pope has mastered the art described in the final address to Bolingbroke:

> Form'd by thy converse, happily to steer
> From grave to gay, from lively to severe;
> Correct with spirit, eloquent with ease,
> Intent to reason, or polite to please.
> Oh! while along the stream of Time thy name
> Expanded flies, and gathers all its fame,
> Say, shall my little bark attendant sail,
> Pursue the triumph, and partake the gale?
>
> (379–86)

The metaphor of poetic navigation (which Pope used also in describing 'The Design' of the Essay)[1] and the ideal of style in poetic 'converse' are of course Horatian. Though the qualities mentioned are only in part those named by Horace, the aim of versatility in movement, feeling, and tone is basically the same for both poets. It has been the 'little bark' of the poet (the figure is used by Horace too) that has carried the larger vessel of the philosopher 'along the stream of Time', and Pope's tribute indicates that he learned more from Bolingbroke the master of conversation than from Bolingbroke the philosopher. Perhaps the most important by-product of their intimacy and the experiments with ethical poetry that it encouraged was Pope's discovery of his role and style as a mature poet. It was Bolingbroke who wrote, apropos of Pope's ease of 'execution' in the *Essay on Man*,

. . . this is eminently and peculiarly his, above all the Writers I know living or dead; I do not Except Horace.[2]

---

[1] See the quotation at the head of this chapter, p. 188.

[2] Bolingbroke's 'this' is somewhat ambiguous, as the full quotation shows:
Bid him talk to you of the Work he is about. I hope in good earnest; it is a fine one: it will be in his hands an Original. His sole complaint is, that he finds it too easy in the execution. This flatters his laziness, it flatters my Judgment, who always thought that, (universal as his Talents are) this is eminently and

It was Bolingbroke also who suggested to Pope (in 1733) that there was an analogy between 'his case' and Horace's, a hint that encouraged Pope to make his first *Imitation* of Horace. Viewed in relation to the poems that Pope was working on during the same period and others that were to follow immediately, the *Essay on Man* appears as a free and original variation on the Horatian diatribe-epistle. The sources of its life and of its limitations are alike Horatian. Pope had been tempted—perhaps by Bolingbroke—to write in Horace's manner a kind of systematic philosophic poem that is contrary to the genius of the style, and hence the sensation we have at times of hearing Sir Thomas Browne or Milton speaking in the accents of the coffee-house; hence, too, the solemn expositions and the least convincing passages of 'argument'. But perfect consistency in poetry as in life, we might observe, is either boredom or death. Pope's good sense told him that the unforgiveable sin in conversation and in friendship is boredom, and he won his way out of argument into a freedom which he exploited more happily and more seriously in poems where he felt less obliged to play the solemn philosopher.

peculiarly his, above all the Writers I know living or dead; I do not Except Horace.   (Let. iii. 71–72)

VIII

THE PROPER STUDY OF MANKIND

On human actions reason tho' you can,
It may be reason, but it is not man . . .
(*Epistle to Cobham*, 35–36)

T HE doubts that occur in reading even the best parts of
the *Essay on Man* disappear completely when we turn
to one of the great passages in the *Moral Essays*:

At Timon's Villa let us pass a day,
Where all cry out, "What sums are thrown away"
So proud, so grand, of that stupendous air,
Soft and Agreeable come never there.
Greatness, with Timon, dwells in such a draught
As brings all Brobdignag before your thought.
To compass this, his building is a Town,
His pond an Ocean, his parterre a Down:
Who but must laugh, the Master when he sees,
A puny insect, shiv'ring at a breeze!
(*Epistle to Burlington*, 99–108)

Here is the *élan* and rapture of genius, of a poet moving
freely and yet with perfect control, compressing into a few
lines a great variety of rhythmic and dramatic effect with
swift changes of irony and brilliant contrasts of image. The
passage goes easily from the grand narrative swing of the
first couplet to the resounding oratorical architecture of
preposterous praise, to the small-voiced thrust of the last
murderous line. The irony of exaggerated compliment, 'So
proud, so grand . . .' gives way first to the muted politeness
of 'Soft and Agreeable come never there', then rises to a
tremendous Swiftian parody of Milton,

As brings all Brobdignag before your thought.

The final reduction of 'Greatness' is cinematographic, the
eye shifting from Vanbrughian monstrosity to the mean
and almost charmingly microscopic. We are left with an

impression not of vindictiveness, but of fantastic agility creating a vision of the grossness and littleness of man's attempt to raise himself by conspicuous consumption.

The *Epistle to Burlington*, from which these lines come, shows much more certainly than the *Essay on Man* that Pope had now found his true subject and form as a mature poet. He is not the poet of systematic reason and reasoning, but of man and of the free play of intelligence over the human scene. The *Epistles to Several Persons*, as they were originally called, are much more important as poetry than the more ambitious poem that proclaims 'Man' as its subject, since in these more casual pieces Pope attained a variety and wholeness of expression equalled only in the two extremes of his art, the *Rape of the Lock* and the Fourth Book of the *Dunciad*. All four essays are rich compositions in irony, and two, *To Burlington* and *To a Lady*, are masterpieces. While there are signs in the other two of the strain between 'philosophy' and sensibility that mars the *Essay on Man*, both poems show Pope trying to express a complex if precarious vision of man and society.

Although Pope's speculations on morals and metaphysics and his experimentation with philosophic poetry undoubtedly contributed to his growth as a satiric poet, the *Essay on Man* is not in any simple sense the forerunner of the *Moral Essays*. From Pope's habits of work[1] and the order of composition of the *Essay on Man*, the *Moral Essays*, and the earlier *Imitations of Horace* we gain a picture of a poet working more or less simultaneously on a number of closely related epistolary poems. As Warburton pointed out in the so-called 'death-bed edition', the *Essay on Man* and the *Moral Essays* were originally planned as parts of a stupendous whole, the philosophical *Opus Magnum* that was to have treated almost every conceivable aspect of human life from man's relation to the universe, to learning and wit, 'Civil and Religious Society', and 'private Ethics or practical Morality'. The well-known memorandum of Spence[2] includes topics, phrases, and fragmentary verses later incorporated into the *Essay on Man* and the *Epistles to Several Persons*, a fair indication that Pope did

---

[1] Sherburn: 'Pope at Work'. See above, p. 49.
[2] Reprinted, TE iii (ii), pp. xxi–xxiii, from Sherburn, op. cit.

not think of these various poems as distinctly separate in style or genre. From Sherburn's picture of the way in which Pope moved passages from an earlier version of the *Essay on Man* to his satires, it is clear enough that he was composing all of his later epistolary and satirical poems in more or less the same 'Horatian way'. While it is true that distinctly personal satire (of the biographical sort) is eliminated from the final version of the *Essay on Man*, much that is satirical in quality remains; and it seems probable that the *Imitations of Horace* had their effect on the Fourth Epistle of the *Essay on Man*, just as '. . . the *Essay on Man* has cast its shadow over what are essentially four Horatian satires'.[1]

But if we are interested in understanding the *Moral Essays* as poems, as the completed compositions we now read, the term 'Horatian satire' will not carry us very far. To begin with, it will be best to forget terms and consider how the poems are put together—or more accurately, how they 'compose' in our reading. We may then describe their poetic design and determine the kind and degree of imaginative unity they possess. There is evidence enough that Pope himself was eager to make them wholes of some sort, and that although he may have written them first by couplets or paragraphs, he spent great care in working the parts into poems. Because we know of the separate existence of fragments, we are too much inclined to think of Pope's method of composing larger units as a scissors-and-paste affair or as exceedingly deliberate or 'logical and uninspired'. But the process by which Pope or Horace made his poetic connexions and transitions is not necessarily less mysterious than that of other writers, nor less a matter of art, as Pope makes clear in his remarks on the composition of the *Epistle to Bathurst*. Writing to Tonson about the lines on the Man of Ross, he refuses, perhaps for devious reasons, to let Tonson see the passage apart from the completed poem, because, he explains,

To send you any of the particular verses will be much to the prejudice of the whole; which if it has any beauty, derives it from the manner in which it is *placed*, and the *contrast* (as the painters call it)

---

[1] TE iii (ii), p. xxi. See also Robert Rogers, *The Major Satires of Pope* (Urbana, Ill., 1955), pp. 38–39, 66–67.

in which it stands, with the pompous figures of famous, or rich, or high-born men.[1]

As might have been anticipated, Pope's metaphor for composition is drawn from painting, and both his language and his aim, to create beauty with moral significance, would be equally congenial to Keats or to Shelley. He is describing an art of *contrast* at once picturesque and ironic. The union of qualities can be felt in the full Latin weight of 'pompous', an adjective recalling the portrait in Epistle IV of the *Essay on Man*, where the satiric point is borne in imagery of baroque splendour:

> What greater bliss attends their close of life?
> Some greedy minion, or imperious wife,
> The trophy'd arches, story'd halls invade,
> And haunt their slumbers in the pompous shade.
>
> (301–4)

If we put the question of unity to Pope's satires (just as we do to Keats's odes), we shall hardly be surprised to learn that though a more or less common principle of order can be traced in all of the poems, they are not built on a mechanically unvarying pattern, and they are not all equally well composed. But the failures are instructive and as often the best measure of the successes. Each is a 'composition in irony', a kind of poetry that is essentially an art of contrast, and each has its special design, realized with more or less completeness. But as in all poetry the felt, the experienced design is indescribable. It must be 'had', and it is not to be confused with our necessarily crude attempts to describe it. So obvious a point needs more emphasis in dealing with Pope than with a poet in the Elizabethan or the Romantic traditions, because it is easier to extract from his poems an argument or a formal arrangement of parts which may be 'there', but which is very different from the poetic connexions made by using the full resources of words.

The essential poetic design[2] of the *Essays* can be seen most clearly in the first in order of writing, the epistle

---

[1] Let. iii. 290.
[2] The following description of the design is a considerably revised and shortened version of my analysis in *The Fields of Light* (New York, 1951), pp. 138–63.

addressed to Burlington, the amateur architect and publicist for Palladian architecture and the new more 'natural' manner of gardening in which Pope had a special interest. The poem moves along conversationally through exempla of bad taste to reflections and hints on good taste, to the grand narrative-portrait of Timon and the brief epilogue in which Burlington is hailed as the author of 'Imperial Works, and worthy Kings'. In its broad outline and type the poem is Horatian, as can be seen from the briefly sketched portraits in the first half of the poem, the casual introduction of pieces of doctrine, and the concentration in the second half on a single bad case and its nobler opposite. But the poetic life and the more subtly Horatian quality of the epistle come out in the masterly variation of tones, with all the attendant ironies.

Speaking as one aristocratic amateur to another, Pope allows himself the lordly freedom of conversational intimacy ('you'd' and 'you'll') and also some upper-class vulgarity ('spew' and 'squirt'). But the voice heard throughout the conversation, which holds the poem together, is one of polite Roman cultivation. It is the tone inherent in the dramatic situation of the poem and in the cultural situation of Augustan England: Pope speaks as Horace to Burlington as Maecenas. (Burlington, we might note, gave Pope some stone for his villa and a good deal of advice, if not the villa itself.) The Roman character of the voice is brought out through casual reference to the paraphernalia of ancient culture—'hecatombs', 'quincunxes', and 'Tritons', through pompous exclamations and commands associated with Roman satirical and prophetic styles, and finally by parody of various classical styles, heroic, pastoral-descriptive, and elegiac. Similar tones, most of them touched with the Roman accent, keep recurring and with them go recurrent ironies. Two or three examples will give some sense of the rich variety of devices and ironic effects. Here, for instance, is a satiric comment on Timon's manners, which is created by simultaneous parody of Pope and Milton:

> My Lord advances with majestic mien,
> Smit with the mighty pleasure, to be seen . . .
>   (127–8)

Compare *Paradise Lost*,

> Smit with the love of sacred Song . . .

and Pope's *Iliad*,

> And smit with Love of Honourable Deeds.

The sound of 'smit'—ugly because of the morpheme and its associations—makes the literary echo sound like a vulgar wisecrack, an effect underlined by the crude bathos of 'to be seen'. In a later passage, a neat allusion to Greek myth is wittily compressed into a single word of exotic flavour, a device similar to Dryden's use of resounding Greek and Latin cognates:

> In plenty starving, *tantaliz'd* in state . . .
>
> (163)

The scene of Timon's dinner opens with an heroic announcement and continues in language associated with ancient architecture and religious ceremonies, diction at once undercut by hints of modern grossness:

> But hark! the chiming Clocks to dinner call;
> A hundred footsteps scrape the marble Hall:
> The rich Buffet well-colour'd Serpents grace,
> And gaping Tritons spew to wash your face.
>
> (151–4)

A subtler irony is then created by high-flying rhetorical questions matched with seemingly more august 'classical' answers:

> Is this a dinner? this a Genial room?
> No, 'tis a Temple, and a Hecatomb.
> A solemn Sacrifice, perform'd in state,
> You drink by measure, and to minutes eat.
>
> (155–8)

The play of antithetical wit is particularly apt in a poem satirizing the clash between ideal and actual in the antics of these latter-day Romans. The attitude of ironic wonder, conveyed here through question and answer, is kept up through the poem by all sorts of devices and quiet pressures, from Pope's usual 'marvelling' exclamations to exaggerated praise and fine understatement, but underneath the irony there is

always a more or less direct allusion to the Roman achievement and an ideal civilization.

The irony in the dinner scene and in many other passages
is descriptive as well as allusive, and Pope gives fine pictorial
impressions of the buildings and gardens whose owners he is
satirizing, as in these lines reminiscent of *Windsor Forest*:

> Behold Villario's ten-years toil compleat;
> His Quincunx darkens, his Espaliers meet,
> The Wood supports the Plain, the parts unite,
> And strength of Shade contends with strength of Light;
> A waving Glow his bloomy beds display,
> Blushing in bright diversities of day . . .   (79–84)

There is also a hint of self-parody in the last line, which is
lifted without change from Pope's imitation of Cowley,
perhaps his earliest garden-piece. The sensuous quality of
what is seen is active even when the language is ambiguously
'aesthetic'. The billowy splendours of baroque painting
survive the mockery of

> On painted Cielings you devoutly stare,
> Where sprawl the Saints of Verrio or Laguerre,
> On gilded clouds in fair expansion lie,
> And bring all Paradise before your eye . . .
>   (145–8)

where the painters' unconscious parody of a great style
(quite appropriate in this travesty of religion) is suggested
through the happy ambiguity of 'sprawl' and 'expansion'
and through parody of Milton,

> And bring all Heav'n before mine eyes.
>   (*Il Penseroso*, 166)

Timon's garden is a caricature of Pope's early descriptive
manner, 'a designed scene' with a vengeance, but in spite of
the mechanical absurdities, the picture has the romantic
charm of one of those eighteenth-century landscapes where
classical sculptures lie in a tangle of vines and flowers:

> Here Amphitrite sails thro' myrtle bowers;
> There Gladiators fight, or die, in flow'rs;
> Un-water'd see the drooping sea-horse mourn,
> And swallows roost in Nilus' dusty Urn.
>   (123–6)

By similar uses of pictorial imagery at many points in the poem Pope creates a vague continuity of metaphor: we feel that the visual beauties of nature are 'picturesque' in the simplest sense of the term, and beyond the particular images we feel quite distinctly the larger metaphor of Nature as 'Great Designer' or 'Designing Power'. Through this permeating analogy, and especially through recurrent patterns of tone and irony, Pope builds up a unity of style expressive of unity of vision.

The importance of rhythmic patterns recurring along with the same or similar patterns of image and irony can be easily seen by comparing different parts of the epistle. When ironic meanings become violently antithetical, Pope uses the same patterns of exact balance that accentuate the symmetries of art in more descriptive passages. In the account of the clock-like service at Timon's dinner, there is the same obnoxious symmetry of words and stresses as in the earlier picture of his gardens. The inversion of time is expressed by the rhetorical figure used to depict the inversion of nature:

> You drink by measure, and to minutes eat.
> (158)

> Trees cut to Statues, Statues thick as trees . . .
> (120)

With the return of the familiar ironic contrast we hear a swing and a pause, a grouping of accents and syllables already associated with that particular type of irony. In addition to such *reprises* of irony-with-metrical pattern, there is the larger compositional rhythm of separate verse paragraphs, which is especially clear in purely ironic contexts. The shorter portraits and the individual paragraphs of the Timon narrative tend to develop in much the same way. Ordinarily Pope opens at the top of his tonal scale, often with an exclamation or some semi-heroic note, and descends at the end to a semi-vulgar conversational level. Toward the middle of the verse-paragraph comes a pictorial phase with balanced beauties that so easily become balanced incongruities, but in the last couplet or two the ironic pretence

of beauty and consistency is given up, and nobility and
politeness of tone completely disappear:

> The thriving plants ignoble broomsticks made,
> Now sweep those Alleys they were born to shade.
>
> (97–98)

Some such development, with many fine variations in detail,
may be traced in nearly all of the more satirical passages of
the poem. Particularly when we read aloud—and Pope's
satires must be 'recited'—we begin to anticipate in each
phase of the attack a more or less regular gamut made up of
familiar elements, an expectation similar to that in reading
Corneille. (We should recall here the *tirades* of *Eloisa to
Abelard*.)[1]

The continuities I have been describing—far too sche-
matically—would be of little more than formal value if they
were not the living medium through which Pope expresses
a larger vision of art and society and an important criticism
of builders and cultivators of the arts. As in all serious irony
the force of local ironies depends on a vibrant reference to
what James calls 'the ideal other case', in the *Epistle to
Burlington*, to the cultural ideal implied in the dramatic texture of the poem, as in Pope's address to Burlington:

> You show us, Rome was glorious, not profuse,
> And pompous buildings once were things of Use.
>
> (23–24)

Here is the poem's imaginative germ, the nucleus of its felt
relationships. The ideal that ratifies the ironies and makes
them meaningful is the type of aesthetic and social behaviour
implicit in addressing Burlington as an aristocrat and re-
storer of Roman and Renaissance principles of architecture,
implicit too in the Latinate accent of 'profuse' and 'pompous',
in the balancing of values, and in the corresponding formality
of verbal pattern. As further expressed in the closing section
of the poem, the ideal is that of the responsible aristocrat
who builds and plants for socially useful ends, whose whole
style, in acting as a public benefactor and in designing and building, is Roman. Unlike 'Imitating Fools' he
considers the propriety of classical design to its modern

[1] Cf. Ch. III, pp. 66, 75.

use. His 'pompous buildings' owe their 'Splendour' to his 'Sense':

> 'Tis Use alone that sanctifies Expence,
> And Splendour borrows all her rays from Sense.
> (179–80)

'Good Sense,' the faculty indispensable for classical propriety, is equally necessary for the exercise of a larger propriety, for 'following Nature':

> Good Sense, which only is the gift of Heav'n,
> And tho' no science, fairly worth the seven:
> A Light, which in yourself you must perceive;
> Jones and Le Nôtre have it not to give.
> To build, to plant, whatever you intend,
> To rear the Column, or the Arch to bend,
> To swell the Terras, or to sink the Grot;
> In all, let Nature never be forgot.
> But treat the Goddess like a modest fair,
> Nor over-dress, nor leave her wholly bare;
> Let not each beauty ev'ry where be spy'd,
> Where half the skill is decently to hide.
> He gains all points, who pleasingly confounds,
> Surprizes, varies, and conceals the Bounds.
> Consult the Genius of the Place in all;
> That tells the Waters or to rise, or fall,
> Or helps th' ambitious Hill the heav'ns to scale,
> Or scoops in circling theatres the Vale,
> Calls in the Country, catches opening glades,
> Joins willing woods, and varies shades from shades,
> Now breaks, or now directs, th' intending Lines;
> Paints as you plant, and, as you work, designs.
> (43–64)

The relevant meanings of 'Sense' and 'following Nature' can be gathered as in the *Essay on Criticism*[1] from metaphor and imagery as much as from the direct statements. It is worth noting that 'Sense' is an inner 'Light', and 'the gift of Heav'n', not acquired by learning, but an inborn power, essentially aristocratic. The true gardener is a poet of the landscape who in Horace's words, *omne tulit punctum* not by excessive ornament, but by bringing out the 'living grace'

[1] Cf. Ch. VII. i, pp. 198, 200–4.

of things, both their beauty and their 'pleasing confusion'. It is also significant that 'the Genius of the Place' is described in imagery borrowed from painting and drawing. To 'follow Nature' in gardening as in Wit is to work with the artistry of Nature the Designer. Vaguely enough for us, but in terms clear to readers of the *Essay on Man*, Pope is again alluding to nature as the principle of order in all things, an order that includes spontaneous variety. If the architect-gardener works according to Nature's order,

> Parts answ'ring parts shall slide into a whole,
> Spontaneous beauties all around advance . . .   (66–67)

This generous concept of propriety in design that imitates the grand artistry of nature and that includes 'surprise' is inseparable from the remembered image of ancient art and the Roman-aristocratic code with its stress on appropriateness of design to use. (We might note that for Horace the beautiful garden is a useful one.)

The connexion between Pope's modes of expression and the cultural ideal is not a relation between ideas, or between ideas and devices, but a connexion continually being renewed in the resonances of words, a peculiarly poetic experience of language. The finest examples of this active relationship come in the noble epitaph that closes the satire on Timon's monstrosities:

> Another age shall see the golden Ear
> Imbrown the Slope, and nod on the Parterre,
> Deep Harvests bury all his pride has plann'd,
> And laughing Ceres re-assume the land.   (173–6)

The impersonality and formality of tone with its Latinate 'laughing Ceres' and 're-assume the land' belong to the voice of the idealized aristocrat: it is not Pope himself who speaks. The pictorial imagery brings to mind the 'design' of Nature and the noble builder's aim of imitating its varied order in his creations. The future scene will be one of useful art, of fields that are picturesque in cultivation, not stupidly landscaped nor abandoned to 'wild disorder'. 'Gold', symbolic in Timon's villa of waste and impropriety, is in this setting a symbol of 'Splendour' that 'borrows all her rays from Sense'. 'Laughing Ceres' signifies among other things the Nature of cultivated fields smiling in mocking triumph over waste and the 'inversion' of nature. In using a phrase that echoes the *laeta seges* of the *Georgics*, Pope reminds us that his vision of nature and art and society has a great historical model.

In the next of the *Moral Essays*, the *Epistle to Bathurst*, Pope found more difficulty in connecting his satire with his 'philosophy', that is, in connecting it with the doctrines he was versifying in the *Essay on Man*. The epistle evidently caused him some anguish in writing, for he took over two years to get it into final shape and afterward told Swift that 'I never took more care in my life of any poem'. But though there is a disturbing—and interesting—gap between the ideas directly stated and concerns expressed more indirectly, the epistle has a unity of satiric manner and attitude in relation to these less obvious but deeper concerns.

The centre of the poem does not lie in the optimistic couplet Pope also used in the *Essay on Man*,

> "Extremes in Nature equal good produce,
> "Extremes in Man concur to gen'ral use."
>
> (163–4)

but in the tension between two attitudes expressed in less pontifical passages. There is first the ironic acceptance of 'the two sorts of men' voiced in the rather flippant lines near the beginning of the poem:

> But I, who think more highly of our kind,
> (And surely, Heav'n and I are of a mind)
> Opine, that Nature, as in duty bound,
> Deep hid the shining mischief under ground:
> But when by Man's audacious labour won,
> Flam'd forth this rival to, its Sire, the Sun,
> Then careful Heav'n supply'd two sorts of Men,
> To squander these, and those to hide agen.   (7–14)

Set against this worldly wisdom is the *aurea mediocritas* of the lines to Bathurst:

> O teach us, BATHURST! yet unspoil'd by wealth!
> That secret rare, between th' extremes to move
> Of mad Good-nature, and of mean Self-love.   (226–8)

The poem is in the main a pageant of contrasting 'extremes —of miserly Cotta and his spendthrift son, of prodigal

Villiers and bourgeois Sir Balaam—with Bathurst and the
Man of Ross holding the golden mean. But this crude
pattern is complicated by other concerns and impressions.
For Pope—almost inevitably in view of his taste in poetry
and in living—the extremes belong to court and city or to a
countryside put to ill uses, the mean to a rural world in-
habited by country gentlemen. (Pope is quite Jeffersonian.)
But the cases go far beyond easy classifications of country
versus city, or of 'mad Good-nature' and 'mean Self-love',
as Pope shows with increasing realism what wealth and
money-making mean in the City of London and in the
modern world generally. Pope's ideal is Horatian and patriarchal, and like Horace he is more deeply disturbed by the
auri sacra fames than by lapses in taste and manners.

Although the large pattern of the poem in many ways
resembles that of the *Epistle to Burlington*, there is a marked
difference in tone and attitude. If not so successful as a whole,
it shows an increased moral seriousness and a sombreness
of mood that look ahead to the *Epilogue to the Satires* and
the Fourth *Dunciad*. Like the epistle on taste, the *Epistle to
Bathurst* is a conversation essay, but much less polite, descending more often to gossip and vulgarity, sometimes of
the middle-class variety,

> . . . one Christmas-tide
> My good old Lady catch'd a cold, and dy'd.
> (383–4)

And though there are grand addresses and exclamations,
rhetorical questions and heroic parodies, the total effect is
certainly less nobly Roman. In writing of the epistle, Pope
referred to it with some appropriateness as one of his 'sermons', and to himself as 'the preacher'.[1] There are notes of
Old Testament lamentation and prophecy in the more exclamatory passages, and the high diction is as often Biblical as
heroic. A poem of the City brings Pope nearer to Dryden's
blend of tones in *Absalom and Achitophel*.

In the imagery there is a nastiness and gloominess and a
strain of ugly fantasy more characteristic of Pope's latest

---

[1] For an excellent analysis of Pope's opposition to Mandeville and of his con-
sequent difficulty in concluding this epistle, see Paul J. Alpers, 'Pope's *To Bathurst*
and the Mandevillian State', *English Literary History*, xxv. 23–42.

poetry. Images of darkness, foulness, sinking, and floods are associated with excesses springing from money, whether squandering or pennypinching. We hear how 'secret Gold saps on from knave to knave', and how

> In heaps, like Ambergrise, a stink it lies,
> But well-dispers'd, is Incense to the Skies.
>
> (235–6)

The demon who tempts Sir Balaam

> . . . makes his full descent,
> In one abundant show'r of Cent. per Cent.,
> Sinks deep within him, and possesses whole . . . (371–3)

More than once we have a blend of similar imagery with elements of fantasy, as in these lines illustrating the balance of financial extremes in nature's happy plan:

> Riches, like insects, when conceal'd they lie,
> Wait but for wings, and in their season, fly.
> Who sees pale Mammon pine amidst his store,
> Sees but a backward steward for the Poor;
> This year a Reservoir, to keep and spare,
> The next a Fountain, spouting thro' his Heir,
> In lavish streams to quench a Country's thirst,
> And men and dogs shall drink him 'till they burst.
>
> (171–8)

Here and in other passages of the *Epistle* riches are connected with mysterious flight and with insects, and though as elsewhere in Pope the insect imagery is ambiguously charming, the monstrous picture of the closing lines makes the beneficent effects of waste scarcely palatable. The most exquisitely ironic lines in the poem are an antithetical parody of the sunny flight of the sylphs in the *Rape of the Lock*:

> Blest paper-credit! last and best supply!
> That lends Corruption lighter wings to fly!
> Gold imp'd by thee, can compass hardest things,
> Can pocket States, can fetch or carry Kings;
> A single leaf shall waft an Army o'er,
> Or ship off Senates to a distant Shore;
> A leaf, like Sibyl's, scatter to and fro
> Our fates and fortunes, as the winds shall blow:
> Pregnant with thousands flits the Scrap unseen,
> And silent sells a King or buys a Queen. (69–78)

Characteristically, one kind of parody blends with another. This elegant lyric with its echo of a familiar seventeenth-century conceit ('gold imp'd by thee') and an allusion to the Biblical wind that 'bloweth whither it listeth' also has heroic and Roman accents. There is talk of senates, fates, and kings and queens, and in the 'flitting leaf' of the Sybil, a recollection of Dryden's *Aeneis*. It would be harder to find a more beautiful poise of tones and sensuous associations than in

> Pregnant with thousands flits the Scrap unseen,
> And silent sells a King or buys a Queen.

The ugly actualities—hints of royal bribery and South Sea Company finaglings, buying and selling of states or thrones, and cruel banishments—gain force by the surface elegance of the diction. Pope's most deeply felt reaction, his disgust with the machinations of high finance in court and city, comes out strongest in these least obviously doctrinaire lines—a fair proof, if wanted, of genuine moral sensibility. In another passage with dark and ugly imagery of floods and mists, Pope paints a kingdom of corruption to match the kingdom of Dullness in the *Dunciad*:

> Much injur'd Blunt! why bears he Britain's hate?
> A wizard told him in these words our fate:
> "At length Corruption, like a gen'ral flood,
> "(So long by watchful Ministers withstood)
> "Shall deluge all; and Av'rice creeping on,
> "Spread like a low-born mist, and blot the Sun;
> "Statesman and Patriot ply alike the stocks,
> "Peeress and Butler share alike the Box,
> "And Judges job, and Bishops bite the town,
> "And mighty Dukes pack cards for half a crown.
> "See Britain sunk in lucre's sordid charms,
> "And France revenged of ANNE's and EDWARD's arms!"
> 'Twas no Court-badge, great Scriv'ner! fir'd thy brain,
> Nor lordly Luxury, nor City Gain:
> No, 'twas thy righteous end, asham'd to see
> Senates degen'rate, Patriots disagree,
> And nobly wishing Party-rage to cease,
> To buy both sides, and give thy Country peace.
>
> (135–52)

The irony here is particularly tricky since Blunt is at once being praised for his vision and satirized for his hypocrisy. The elevated salute to this 'great Scriv'ner' and the neat mockery of his dissenting piety recall Dryden's treatment of similar City characters in *Absalom and Achitophel*.

In a passage of fairly obvious but comic fantasy, the picture of what might happen if bribes were made in kind, the diction draws on biblical-patriarchal, heroic, and pastoral styles (always closely related in Pope). Allusion to the 'good old country world' has a symbolic value here and in nearly all of the longer satirical 'characters' of the poem:

> Oh! that such bulky Bribes as all might see,
> Still, as of old, incumber'd Villainy! . . .
>
> His Grace will game: to White's a Bull be led,
> With spurning heels and with a butting head.
> To White's be carried, as to ancient games,
> Fair Coursers, Vases, and alluring Dames.
> Shall then Uxorio, if the stakes he sweep,
> Bear home six Whores, and make his Lady weep?
> Or soft Adonis, so perfum'd and fine,
> Drive to St. James's a whole herd of swine?
>
> (35–36, 55–62)

By this travesty of pastoral simplicity Pope expresses his scorn for the dubiously complex operations of city finance. At various points in the epistle parody of pastoral-heroic and other serious styles underlines the main moral of the satire, that the corruption of city finance is the degeneration of ancient rural virtue. But Pope is not an urban sentimentalist who has never seen his pastoral heroes on the home ground. With admirable honesty he describes the corruptions of rural virtue in their meanness and grossness as equally ugly extremes of wealth. 'Old Cotta', a miserly caricature of the noble host of medieval times, is presented in a style that might be called 'Spenserian-Gothick'.

> Like some lone Chartreux stands the good old Hall,
> Silence without, and Fasts within the wall;
> No rafter'd roofs with dance and tabor sound,
> No noontide-bell invites the country round;
> Tenants with sighs the smoakless tow'rs survey,
> And turn th' unwilling steeds another way:

> Benighted wanderers, the forest o'er,
> Curse the sav'd candle, and unop'ning door;
> While the gaunt mastiff growling at the gate,
> Affrights the beggar whom he longs to eat.
>
> (189–98)

An echo of *Absalom and Achitophel* and more significantly of Virgil's lines on the Old Corycian gardener,

> With soups unbought and sallads blest his board.
>
> (184)

fits easily into Pope's anti-pastoral ridicule of this most un-patriarchal Roman. His son, who 'mistook reverse of wrong for right', feasts heroically in the manner of a Roman Squire Weston:

> What slaughter'd hecatombs, what floods of wine,
> Fill the capacious Squire, and deep Divine!
>
> (203–4)

He leaves the sylvan scene in ruin and

> To town he comes, completes the nation's hope,
> And heads the bold Train-bands, and burns a Pope.
>
> (213–14)

The bankrupt shepherd of the people is being praised in words recalling 'Rome's other hope and pillar of the state', an expression Dryden used for another illustrious son, Shadwell-Mac Flecknoe. Both parodies go back to Virgil's description of young Ascanius, *magnae spes altera Romae*. The perversion of heroic nobility through wealth is illustrated most cruelly in the scene of Villiers' death, a piece of Hogarthian realism:

> In the worst inn's worst room, with mat half-hung,
> The floors of plaister, and the walls of dung,
> On once a flock-bed, but repair'd with straw,
> With tape-ty'd curtains, never meant to draw,
> The George and Garter dangling from that bed
> Where tawdry yellow strove with dirty red,
> Great Villiers lies—alas! how chang'd from him
> That life of pleasure, and that soul of whim! . . .
>
> (299–306)

The turn in the portrait, which brings out the contrast

between the tawdry scene and greatness, comes in the words
of Milton's line on Satan,

> ... But O how fall'n! how chang'd
> From him ...

an exact translation of Virgil's words on Hector,

> ei mihi, qualis erat, quantum mutatus ab illo
> Hectore ...

The most relentless piece of satire in the poem, the tale
of Sir Balaam, is the least heroic and the most biblical, an Old
Testament parable with many scriptural and pious overtones
and occasional touches of middle-class colloquialism. The
style is most appropriate for the history of a 'dull cit' bred up
in the heart of London, an area long associated with bourgeois
success and protestant piety. The connexion between getting
ahead and churchgoing has never been more perfectly dramatized, and the link between high profession and low motive
are beautifully matched in the poise of pious allusion and
common talk:

> The Dev'l was piqu'd such saintship to behold,
> And long'd to tempt him like good Job of old:
> But Satan now is wiser than of yore,
> And tempts by making rich, not making poor.
> Rouz'd by the Prince of Air, the whirlwinds sweep
> The surge, and plunge his Father in the deep;
> Then full against his Cornish lands they roar,
> And two rich ship-wrecks bless the lucky shore.
> Sir Balaam now, he lives like other folks,
> He takes his chirping pint, and cracks his jokes:
> "Live like yourself," was soon my Lady's word;
> And lo! two puddings smoak'd upon the board ...
>
> Behold Sir Balaam, now a man of spirit,
> Ascribes his gettings to his parts and merit,
> What late he call'd a Blessing, now was Wit,
> And God's good Providence, a lucky Hit ...
>
> (349–60, 375–8)

In 'contrast', wrote Pope, with the 'pompous figures of
famous, or rich or high-born' is 'placed' the Man of Ross,
who is indeed a shepherd of the people, who 'hung with
woods yon mountain's sultry brow' and Moses-like 'from

the dry-rock . . . bade the waters flow'. Nature in truly pastoral sympathy sings his praises,

> Pleas'd Vaga echoes thro' her winding bounds,
> And rapid Severn hoarse applause resounds.
>
> (251–2)

The waterworks promoted by the Man of Ross are contrasted with lavish if beautiful displays:

> Not to the skies in useless columns tost,
> Or in proud falls magnificently lost,
> But clear and artless, pouring thro' the plain
> Health to the sick, and solace to the swain.
>
> (255–8)

Use and expense are here seen in the happy harmony disrupted by Timon and his 'brother peers'. And yet, though the Man of Ross is distinctly not a lord, he plays the familiar role in Pope of the idealized country gentleman who is a landscaper-improver and a patron of the poor. With modest means he realizes the aims of the true aristocrat. (He bears some resemblance to the patriarch of Twickenham.)

The Goldsmithian tenderness of the portrait is at one point almost unbearable:

> Who taught that heav'n-directed spire to rise?
> The MAN of Ross, each lisping babe replies.
> Behold the Market-place with poor o'erspread!
> The MAN of Ross divides the weekly bread . . .
>
> (261–4)

The too idyllic quality of the scene gives it an air of being in another country, and Pope's admission that the Man of Ross achieves

> "What all so wish, but want the pow'r to do!"   (276)

makes us feel the precariousness of the achievement in the actual England Pope knew. The ineptness of 'the Market-place with poor *o'erspread*' may indicate that he was not quite at home in dealing with the deserving poor. The fine aim proposed,

> To balance Fortune by a just expence,
> Join with Œconomy, Magnificence;
> With splendour, charity; with plenty, health . . .
>
> (223–5)

is almost lost in the over-powering impression left by the squire-patriot, and Villiers, and finally Sir Balaam. Their histories and the poem as a whole hardly give convincing support to the thesis that

"Extremes in Man concur to gen'ral use."

There are in fact many signs in the epistle that Pope was unable to maintain the philosophic calm of the *Essay on Man*, that as he studied mankind more closely in his local habitation he became less certain that 'partial evils were universal good'. The guzzling of Cotta's son does not cancel out the evil of his father's parsimony, and his career is decidedly not a blessing to society. Pope feels too vividly the monstrousness of wealth 'spouting thro' an heir', and he depicts too well the moral horror of the lives of Balaam and Villiers. He can qualify his picture of Timon's wastefulness by reflecting that 'hence the Poor are cloath'd, the Hungry fed', but the triumphant Nature of the scene that follows really has no place for Timon and his abuses:

Deep Harvests bury all his pride has plann'd . . .

Though Pope may have been attracted by Mandeville's thesis, 'Private vices, public benefits', he was wise enough to feel the fallacy spotted by Dr. Johnson. The trouble with Mandeville's theory, Johnson saw, was his definition of vice. If we call every luxury however harmless a vice, then Mandeville's argument would be sound, but in so far as an action is really a vice, Johnson insisted, it cannot be beneficial. While Pope believes in the moral value of good taste, as shown in his advice to Ralph Allen on choosing pictures, he can overlook minor errors of taste as harmless 'luxuries'. But though he can overlook some of Timon's vagaries, his moral judgement remains clear: Timon's charity is 'vanity' and his heart is 'hard'. But as the moral sensibility implicit in the *Epistle to Burlington* is deepened and comes more to the fore in the *Epistle to Bathurst*, Pope has greater difficulty in demonstrating that 'Heav'n's great view . . . counter-works each folly and caprice and . . . disappoints th' effect of ev'ry vice. . .' But we must admire Pope for an instinctive common-sense inconsistency, for insisting that moral effort was still necessary in spite of the logic of his philosophic position. In a world where nature's laws work without fail to balance waste with miserliness, there would of course be little point in exhorting men to imitate the Man of Ross, or to adopt the golden mean in managing their wealth.

From our reading of the *Epistle to Bathurst* it appears that Pope's mature philosophy of nature is less simple than we might suppose from the easy assurance of

"Extremes in Nature equal good produce . . ."

Such easy assertions mar a poem that shows otherwise much less certainty about the ultimate good of actions morally and socially reprehensible. The doings of 'Damn the Poor' Bond and the happily named 'Charitable Corporation' are much less easily accepted than 'extremes of drought and rain', and the picture of 'Corruption like a gen'ral flood' cannot be quickly forgotten. The epistle leaves the reader with impressions far from serene:

"All this is madness," cries a sober sage:
But who, my friend, has reason in his rage?

(153-4)

But the Man of Ross is still there, and if Pope has had a glimpse of the Swiftian apocalypse, his voice is still insistently civilized. Civilization though precarious can be achieved, at least here and there in individual lives or at rare moments in the history of a people.

The *Epistle to Cobham* shows even more painfully Pope's attempt to fit his Horatian causeries into his philosophic scheme, particularly when he will have us believe that the Ruling Passion is the clue to the differences in the characters of men. But the explanation is attempted only in a small number of examples, and then applied quite mechanically and perfunctorily. There is, so to speak, another poem here, on another theme and with a distinct style and rhythm, the poem that Warburton's rearrangements almost completely buried. It starts from a passage expressing the scepticism characteristic of the *Moral Essays*:

Our depths who fathoms, or our shallows finds,
Quick whirls, and shifting eddies, of our minds?

Life's stream for Observation will not stay,
It hurries all too fast to mark their way.
In vain sedate reflections we wou'd make,
When half our knowledge we must snatch, not take.
On human actions reason tho' you can,
It may be reason, but it is not man:
His Principle of action once explore,
That instant 'tis his Principle no more.
Like following life thro' creatures you dissect,
You lose it in the moment you detect.

(29–40)

In imagery, tone, and rhythm typical of most of the poem, Pope is setting forth his central theme, the impossibility of 'observing', of seeing into human nature and of imposing abstract schemes of explanation, impossible because of the swiftly changing and shifting nature of man, which like Heraclitus' river does not remain the same long enough for us to understand it. The character-examples (except for the small group 'explained' by the Ruling Passion) are always showing how the student is deceived by the senses and how human nature veers unpredictably from one direction to another. We hear of the 'observer' who 'eyes the builder's toil', of 'our internal view', of 'Opinion's colors', of 'Darkness' in 'close' natures that 'strikes the sense no less than Light'; and also of the 'wild rotation' of our passions, of 'quick turns of mind', of actions explained as sudden calms or a 'shift' of the wind 'from the east'. Pope seems to have in mind Locke's distinction between primary and secondary qualities and the danger of mistaking 'second qualities for first'. Most of the poem demonstrates the deceptions of appearance, the difficulty of getting at reality.

In keeping with the 'observer's' role, the tone is closer to the more casual parts of the *Epistle to Burlington*, with little of the more public or grandly oratorical qualities of the two earlier epistles. The *Epistle to Cobham* makes quite clear Pope's progress toward the easier Horatian familiarity of *To a Lady* and the *Imitations*:

Yes, you despise the man to Books confin'd,
Who from his study rails at human kind . . .

(1–2)

The rhythmic character of the epistle is somewhat peculiar, in part because of theme and imagery, and in part because of a difference in satirical mode. Aside from the lines on Wharton, there are no full-dress portraits in this epistle. All the other satiric examples are of the rapidly limned type, and two or three at the end are virtuoso performances in fragmentary dialogue, the Horatian art that Pope has now made completely his own:

> The Courtier smooth, who forty years had shin'd
> An humble servant to all human kind,
> Just brought out this, when scarce his tongue could stir,
> "If—where I'm going—I could serve you, Sir?"
> "I give and I devise, (old Euclio said,
> And sigh'd) "My lands and tenements to Ned."
> Your money, Sir; "My money, Sir, what all?
> "Why,—if I must—(then wept) I give it Paul."
> The Manor, Sir?—"The Manor! hold," he cry'd,
> "Not that,—I cannot part with that"—and dy'd.
>
> (252–61)

There is something especially quick and 'shifting' about the movement of this poem (partly due to suggestions of imagery), and there are certainly many choppy, broken lines marked by short phrases and strong pauses, as in the passage just quoted and in:

> But, sage historians! 'tis your task to prove
> One action Conduct; one, heroic Love.
>
> (85–86)

> Is he a Churchman? then he's fond of pow'r:
> A Quaker? sly: A Presbyterian? sow'r:
> A smart Free-thinker? all things in an hour.
>
> (107–9)

The triplet—surprising in Pope at this date—adds to the snappy effect of the passage and brings it roundly to an end. The various sections of the poem, as in the *Epistle to Burlington*, tend to fall into similar patterns of development, some moving from grandly remote observation to low actuality, others falling into a stanza-like form in which Pope keeps running through the same satiric and verse routines. (A strange echo of the sweet repetitions in his early pastoral songs.)

The real distinction of the epistle comes out in the quality of the irony, which is often coolly remote and finely ambiguous. Two passages—easily overlooked in a poem that does not immediately attract most readers—have an urbane elegance worthy of Horace. They exemplify two of the stanzaic patterns, and both use images characteristic of the poem. In the first, the voice of La Rochefoucauld is unmistakable:

> Not always Actions shew the man: we find
> Who does a kindness, is not therefore kind,
> Perhaps Prosperity becalm'd his breast,
> Perhaps the Wind just shifted from the east:
> Not therefore humble he who seeks retreat,
> Pride guides his steps, and bids him shun the great:
> Who combats bravely is not therefore brave,
> He dreads a death-bed like the meanest slave:
> Who reasons wisely is not therefore wise,
> His pride in Reas'ning, not in Acting lies.
>
> (61–70)

In the next passage, the lines on the 'Gem' and 'the Flower', a fine desperation is concealed by a tone of sang-froid and by diction which in pictorial quality and melodiousness goes back to the pastoral-georgic style of Pope's earliest poems:

> 'Tis from high Life high Characters are drawn;
> A Saint in Crape is twice a Saint in Lawn;
> A Judge is just, a Chanc'lor juster still;
> A Gownman, learn'd; a Bishop, what you will;
> Wise, if a Minister; but, if a King,
> More wise, more learn'd, more just, more ev'rything.
> Court-virtues bear, like Gems, the highest rate,
> Born where Heav'n's influence scarce can penetrate:
> In life's low vale, the soil the virtues like,
> They please as Beauties, here as Wonders strike.
> Tho' the same Sun with all-diffusive rays
> Blush in the Rose, and in the Diamond blaze,
> We prize the stronger effort of his pow'r,
> And justly set the Gem above the Flow'r.
>
> (87–100)

The ostensible point of this charming logic is to say that if we want to understand the characters of men in high places, it is quite enough to know their station, just as in studying 'the common mind' it is enough to remember that 'as the Twig is bent, the Tree's inclin'd'. After these and similarly ironic illuminations, and a series of proofs that we cannot judge men from Nature, Actions, Passions, or Opinions, Pope urges us triumphantly to

> Search then the Ruling Passion: There, alone,
> The Wild are constant, and the Cunning known;
> The Fool consistent, and the False sincere;
> Priests, Princes, Women, no dissemblers here.
>
> (174–7)

The clinching example, the character of Wharton, done in the exclamatory manner of the *Essay on Man*, presents a picture of a being half god and half natural wonder:

> This clue once found, unravels all the rest,
> The prospect clears, and Wharton stands confest. . .
>
> Nature well known, no prodigies remain,
> Comets are regular, and Wharton plain.
>
> (178–9, 208–9)

But Pope's analysis is not that plain, and his eye for the inconsistent carries him far beyond his theory. Wharton is a man of parts so various that the concluding strokes give an impression of dazzling conflicts. One couplet is a superb example of Pope's irony of paradoxically close definition:

> A Fool, with more of Wit than half mankind,
> Too rash for Thought, for Action too refin'd . . .
>
> (200–1)

We are inclined to listen to Pope's own caution that 'in this search' for the ruling passion, 'the wisest may mistake'.

The epistle concludes with a series of exempla that are appropriate enough, but the lesson that remains with us is not Pope's short and easy method for understanding human nature, but his sense of its mystery and inscrutability. Pope shows his insight not in his formulas, but in a Proustian awareness of our inner depths and the nature of our confusions and certainties. Anyone who has examined the process by which he arrives at a decision will recognize the truth of Pope's penetrating if discomforting analysis:

> Oft in the Passions' wild rotation tost,
> Our spring of action to ourselves is lost:

Tir'd, not determin'd, to the last we yield,
And what comes then is master of the field.
As the last image of that troubled heap,
When Sense subsides, and Fancy sports in sleep,
(Tho' past the recollection of the thought)
Becomes the stuff of which our dream is wrought:
Something as dim to our internal view,
Is thus, perhaps, the cause of most we do.

(41–50)

In the latest of the *Moral Essays*, the *Epistle to a Lady*,
Pope drops all 'philosophy' except his own, that deep sense
of the variability of all character, the 'amusing study' of
'intricate' characters which delighted Elizabeth Bennet:
'. . . people themselves alter so much, that there is something
new to be observed in them for ever'. But this amusement does
not prevent Pope, any more than Jane Austen, from making
clear judgements and warmly appreciating positive values
when he finds them. His affirmations are all the more convincing for being dramatic and personal rather than systematic and generalized. The *Epistle to a Lady* has little to do
with system, and the charmingly easy art of the poem bears
out the statement by Ruffhead, that Pope 'wrote [it] at once
in a heat not of malice or resentment, but of pure, though
strong, poetical fire'.[1] Along with the *Rape of the Lock*, it is
one of the poems that confirms his comment to Spence:
'The things that I have written fastest, have always pleased
the most'.

The quality of the poetry—its delicacy and variety of irony
and tone, its blending of conversational and earlier more
'poetic' styles—appears in the first twenty lines, the prelude
to the more elaborate set of characters that make up the
main part of the epistle. We can see in this opening section
how the epistle will grow as a poem, and the main lines of the
whole composition:

Nothing so true as what you once let fall,
"Most Women have no Characters at all"
Matter too soft a lasting mark to bear,
And best distinguish'd by black, brown, or fair.

[1] Owen Ruffhead, *The Life of Alexander Pope, Esq.* (London, 1769), p. 293.

How many Pictures of one Nymph we view,
All how unlike each other, all how true!
Arcadia's Countess, here, in ermin'd pride,
Is there, Pastora by a fountain side.
Here Fannia, leering on her own good man,
And there, a naked Leda with a Swan.
Let then the Fair one beautifully cry,
In Magdalen's loose hair and lifted eye,
Or drest in smiles of sweet Cecilia shine,
With simp'ring Angels, Palms, and Harps divine;
Whether the Charmer sinner it, or saint it,
If Folly grows romantic, I must paint it.
Come then, the colours and the ground prepare!
Dip in the Rainbow, trick her off in Air,
Chuse a firm Cloud, before it fall, and in it
Catch, ere she change, the Cynthia of this minute.

(1–20)

The first couplet,

Nothing so true as what you once let fall,
"Most Women have no Characters at all".

the most intimate of all Pope's beginnings, gives a perfect impression of writing to a friend, of talk that needs no introduction. It is both polite and discreetly complimentary, and yet general enough to serve as the basis for a fairly extensive view. The irony is of a kind familiar in Pope and other eighteenth-century writers: a proposition advanced dead-pan as a universal truth slowly begins to effervesce as the reader takes it in and silently applies it to cases. In this example the innocuous illustration in the next couplet accentuates the concealed bleakness of the view and prepares wryly for the irony to be developed later, that most women do indeed have 'Characters' in a less pleasant sense of the term. With the next line,

How many Pictures of one Nymph we view,

the speaker shifts his role by a hidden transition worthy of Horace. From classifying women according to hues, he goes on to talk like a painter-entrepreneur who is taking us on a tour of his favourite pieces. Pope is perhaps also thinking of a seventeenth-century literary type, the 'gallery'[1] in which historical or mythological figures are presented in a series of prose or verse portraits. In Marvell's *The Gallery*, which Pope may have had in mind, the poet's beloved is pictured in a number of different guises. ('Nymph' as a term of gallantry is Marvellian too.) The politely wondering irony of the speaker recalls also the tone of our guide at Timon's villa.

The portrait series, wonderfully evocative of parades of 'Beauties' by Lely and Kneller and their contemporaries,[2] begins with a probable reminiscence of a picture of the Countess of Pembroke. The pastoral note subtly hinted at in 'Nymph' is turned to ironic advantage in the contrast between *'here*, in ermin'd pride' and *'there*, Pastora by a fountain side'. The surface of elegant pastoral compliment is broken by this slight jolt in rhythm, which also makes us feel the absurdity of the Countess's whimsy. In the portrait that Pope had presumably seen she is shown gracefully laying a garland on a lamb cosily resting at her side. The next lady, Fannia (a famous adultress in a Roman plebeian family), is pictured in the ambiguous style of Lely's melting beauties:

> Here Fannia, leering on her own good man,
> And there, a naked Leda with a Swan.

'Leering' is an example of the finely compact irony of Pope's latest satirical style: the woman may be smiling on her husband, as she ought to be; or she may be over-doing it to cover her lack of affection for 'her own good man': or she may be leering in a way that suggests some unmentionable passion like 'naked Leda's'. Thanks to the classical allusion the civilized proprieties are preserved.

With 'her own good man' the speaker strikes the level of domestic gossip, but he soon recovers his role of painter-guide with the impersonal disarmingly sweet

> Let then the Fair one beautifully cry,
> In Magdalen's loose hair and lifted eye . . .

---

[1] See Pierre Le Moyne, *La Gallerie des Femmes Fortes* (Leyden, 1660); *La Galeria del Cavalier Marino distinta in Favole, Historie, Ritratti & Capricci*, ed. G. Batelli (Lanciano, 1926). Cf. Jean Hagstrom, *The Sister Arts* (Chicago, 1958), pp. 100–6.

[2] Lord Killanin, *Sir Godfrey Kneller and his Times, Being a Review of English Portraiture of the Period* (London, 1948), pp. 19, 20, 40–45.

For a moment we have a glimpse of the active melodramatic style of baroque religious painting and sculpture, Magdalen's hair falling loosely in contrition, her eye raised in a mood that 'lifts the soul to heaven' (a phrase Pope had earlier used of Saint Cecilia). But 'loose' and 'lifted', applied to Magdalen, are slippery adjectives, and the lady's saintliness is no more convincing here than in her next guise,

> Or drest in smiles of sweet Cecilia shine,
> With simp'ring Angels, Palms, and Harps divine . . .

This Cecilia—recalling the 'divine' and 'bright Cecilia', of Pope's ode—with her angels and other accoutrements, parodies a familiar type of picture and the 'simpering' piety of the lady. With a shrug of the shoulders, the painter-commentator refuses to take any responsibility for his subjects, as he turns to us in a couplet modish and slangy in tone and comic in rhythm:

> Whether the Charmer sinner it, or saint it,
> If Folly grows romantic, I must paint it.

Assuming an air of grandeur, he now starts off with a high imperative as if announcing a piece in eighteenth-century heroic style, perhaps a fresco by Tiepolo of nobles and allegorical deities reposing on sculptured clouds. But the imagery and the rhythm accompanying his words recall the unsubstantial beauties of the *Rape of the Lock* and indicate that Pope's attitude is equally light and evanescent:

> Come then, the colours and the ground prepare!
> Dip in the Rainbow, trick her off in Air,
> Chuse a firm Cloud, before it fall, and in it
> Catch, ere she change, the Cynthia of this minute.
>
> (17–20)

As often in Dryden the parody is given away by a single inharmonious adjective: 'Chuse a *firm* Cloud' (this Diana may not remain a Diana long). The effect of quickly changing action and instability is increased by the rhythmic pattern with its many breaks in the lines, the shifts in stress to give trochees and dactyls, and the quickness of double rhyme. In the four lines Pope produces four distinctly different metrical patterns by changing the place of the pauses in each and constantly varying the 'sound mass' between pauses: in the first, the pause after two syllables; in the second, after five; in the third, after four syllables, followed by four more and a second pause; and in the last, a line with enjambement plus one pause after the first and another after the fourth. Pope is practising the same art of musical intricacy that he had once used in the sweetly charming songs of the *Pastorals*.

The poetic design of the *Epistle* and its satirical power are clearly revealed in these first twenty lines of seemingly whimsical chit-chat. In politer phases of the poem we shall hear again the '*Spectator*' tone that combines so easily, as in the *Rape of the Lock*, with pastoral and heroic parody. (The *Epistle to a Lady* often recalls also the early epistles to the Misses Blount.) The painting metaphor—by now we might call this a key metaphor in Pope's poetry—is kept up in various ways, especially through the speaker's role, but also by small hints of pictorial quality in visual imagery, and by the use of technical terms from painting. A few instances may be cited from different points in the poem:

> See Sin in State, majestically drunk . . .
>
> (69)

> Turn then from Wits; and look on Simo's Mate,
> No Ass so meek, no Ass so obstinate . . .
>
> (101–2)

> Pictures like these, dear Madam, to design,
> Asks no firm hand, and no unerring line;
> Some wand'ring touches, some reflected light,
> Some flying stroke alone can hit 'em right:
> For how should equal Colours do the knack?
> Chameleons who can paint in white and black?
>
> (151–6)

> One certain Portrait may (I grant) be seen,
> Which Heav'n has varnish'd out, and made a *Queen*:
> The same for ever! and describ'd by all
> With Truth and Goodness, as with Crown and Ball:

Poets heap Virtues, Painters Gems at will,
And show their zeal, and hide their want of skill.
'Tis well—but, Artists! who can paint or write,
To draw the Naked is your true delight.
That Robe of Quality so struts and swells,
None see what Parts of Nature it conceals.
Th' exactest traits of Body or of Mind,
We owe to models of an humble kind . . .

Alas! I copy (or my draught would fail) . . .

(181–92, 197)

The fiction of mythological portraiture (to which there are analogues in Horace) is maintained also by the use of ironically appropriate names. There is Calista (the name of a nymph made pregnant by Zeus) who 'proves her conduct nice'; Calypso, who bewitches by being loathsome and fascinating; Narcissa, seemingly so sweet, but really self-centred; and terrible Atossa, whose name comes from the sister of Cambyses, the king with a terrible temper. In the poem as in the prelude, 'ladies, like variegated Tulips' show their charms in contrasting portraits of some historical or mythical type, each portrait having a central theme enriched by the play of ever changing ironies. There are the more charming characters, pastorally sweet on the surface, who betray absurd inconsistencies or even brutalities. The prettiest of this type is butterfly-Papillia, the lover of rural 'shades' and 'parks':

Papillia, wedded to her doating spark,
Sighs for the shades—"How charming is a Park!"
A Park is purchas'd, but the Fair he sees
All bath'd in tears—"Oh odious, odious Trees!"

(37–40)

Seemingly sweet Narcissa is introduced in a couplet of politely terrible irony worthy of Swift,

Narcissa's nature, tolerably mild,
To make a wash, would hardly stew a child . . .

(53–54)

The rest of the portrait like Chloe's falls into a more conversational piece of 'telling-off', the 'Atticus' type, as we might call it. The other satirical characters are done in the nobly oratorical, at times heroic, manner of the Villiers portrait. Philomede, whose Hellenic name suggests a passion for the barbarous and exotic, is first presented in lines far removed from insinuating politeness,

> See Sin in State, majestically drunk,
> Proud as a Peeress, prouder as a Punk...
>
> (69–70)

This pompous address, of the kind associated with attacks on greatness and pride in the *Essay on Man*, brings forward a tremendous allegorical personage, 'the *Lewd* and *Vicious*' (so Pope describes her in his note). Her high manners and rare tastes are symbolized on the sublime level by 'Caesar', 'Charlema'ne', and 'Helluo', the Roman glutton, 'late Dictator of the Feast'. We have another heroic figure with an imperial Roman name in the witty Flavia, who may recall Catullus' Lesbia-Clodia in her echo of '*vivamus atque amemus*'.

> Nor asks of God, but of her Stars to give
> The mighty blessing, "while we live, to live."
>
> (89–90)

'Great Atossa' is the most morally frightening of these creatures, and her picture the most concentrated piece of imaginative portraiture because of the way in which it is composed and because of its large symbolic quality. But to understand its *poetic* character, we must give our attention to Pope's language rather than to eighteenth-century gossip. If we do, what do we find? First we note the repeated stress on the theme of 'one warfare upon earth': on 'Rage', 'Fury', 'Hate', 'Violence', and 'death'. With these motifs go qualifying images of suddenly changing motion and destruction: 'Eddy', 'whisks', 'Down it goes', 'out-ran', 'Miss'd', 'Hit', 'turn', and 'storm'. An increasing speed and roughness of movement is heard as similar expressions and images accumulate and fuse in a complex impression of a monster of feminine violence, all darting-whisking and eddying motion. Like some swiftly developing organism, this creature of incalculable loves and hates, consistent only in her violence, of preposterous egotism expressing itself in every extreme of passion, ends in the horror of disease and sterility both physical and moral. It seems almost comic to ask whether we should read the passage with a limited personal reference[1] to the Duchess of Marlborough or the Duchess of Buckinghamshire, as if the character was primarily a biographical record of Pope's feelings toward one or both of these women. (The Twickenham editor concludes in favour of the Duchess of Buckinghamshire, but the portrait was long thought to refer to the other Duchess.) The question of whether we read 'Atossa' as a biographical piece is worth answering, since the portrait is fairly typical of Pope's more elaborate 'personal' attacks, and since it raises general questions about the nature of his satirical poetry and how we are to read it. We can certainly refer various points in the portrait to one or the other of the women and to Pope's not too well ascertained difficulties in his relations with both of them. While it would be absurd to deny that such references are among the meanings of the passage, it would be equally absurd to say that these meanings occupy a prominent place in our reading. We hardly read *the poem* saying, 'This line refers to one duchess; and that to another'. Even if we agree that the portrait includes references only to the Duchess of Buckinghamshire, we do not reduce our response to fitting the details to the facts about the actual woman. Take as an instance a feature that almost certainly refers to a matter of fact:

> Atossa . . .
> Childless with all her Children, wants an Heir.

It is well known that the Duchess of Buckinghamshire lost all five of her own children and that she had disputes with the illegitimate children of the Duke as to who was his 'heir-at-law'. But is the detail without dramatic and symbolic relation to the imaginatively composed picture of Atossa, is

---

[1] Cf. J. M. Osborn, 'Pope, the Byzantine Empress, and Walpole's Whore', *Review of English Studies* (new series), vi. 372–82, for an example of a symbolic figure ('Vice' in the *Epilogue to the Satires,* Dialogue I) that can be identified with at least two persons. Osborn's conclusion is excellent: 'Pope's skill at the multiple keyboard of Horatian "elegant ambiguity" may be valued even more highly than his *saeva indignatio*'. p. 382.

it only a biographical hit at a woman whom Pope hated? Hardly so. As presented in the poem the detail is the fitting climax to the whole picture of selfishness and incapacity for love (love always turning into violence), the final example of horrible contrariety: a woman of such violent power produces nothing. Pope was doing something more than record biographical fact or express a private emotion. As soon as he sensed the kind of portrait he was creating, he was governed as most writers are by another ordering than the factual and the personal, by his sense of the form he was creating in the line and in the portrait. Something marvellous happened in the poetic process of 'stating a fact':

> Atossa, curs'd with ev'ry granted pray'r,
> Childless with all her Children, wants an Heir.
>
> (147–8)

We respond less to the fact than to the shock of likeness and unlikeness in '*Childless* with *all* her *Children*', to the generalizing effect of this paradoxical formula, to the balancing of fertility and sterility, and to the 'retroactive' allusion to earlier impressions of power and passion.

We must not then confuse the history of Pope's portraits with the poetry. Pope's own fury may have set him writing, but as he wrote he transformed his victims—if that is the word—into something quite unreal. Like Yeats's familiar revolutionaries, they are

> . . . changed, changed utterly:
> A terrible beauty is born.

Sometimes as in the Atossa portrait they became monsters; and people who recognized themselves in certain details cried out in anguish, 'But I was never like that!' And they were perfectly right. Sometimes, the familiar person became something more heroic than in fact he was. The Man of Ross, as Dr. Johnson observed, was not the miraculous financier of Pope's *Epistle to Bathurst*. 'If any man shall ever happen to endeavour to emulate the Man of Ross', Pope wrote to old Jacob Tonson,

'twill be no manner of harm if I make him think he was something more charitable and more beneficent than really he was, for so much more good it would put the imitator upon doing.[1]

The Man of Ross like Atossa is a symbolic figure inhabiting a poetic world, not a citizen of the actual world in which Pope lived.

All the portraits of the poem (including Sappho's) are examples of symbolic remaking of this sort. The unity of effect, more perfect than in any other satirical poem by Pope except the *Epistle to Burlington*, depends on Pope's 'fixing' all these creatures at the same level of reality. He achieves his end by using certain common modes of symbolic portraiture, and as in the Burlington essay, by a similar manner of proceeding in the individual portraits and the more general satirical tirades. Whether the portraits open with sweetly charming compliments or with high oratorical announcements, they come down at the end to bathos or a biting piece of wit that deflates any impression of charm or nobility. The lines between, with all their varying tactics of irony and innuendo, usually show some type of rhetorical and rhythmic pattern peculiar to the individual portrait. Often toward the end of a portrait, as Pope gathers force for his final blow, he will fall into the identical pattern for two or more lines at a time. All these features can be seen very clearly in the lines on Narcissa:

> Narcissa's nature, tolerably mild,
> To make a wash, would hardly stew a child;
> Has ev'n been prov'd to grant a Lover's pray'r,
> And paid a Tradesman once to make him stare,
> Gave alms at Easter, in a Christian trim,
> And made a Widow happy, for a whim.
> Why then declare Good-nature is her scorn,
> When 'tis by that alone she can be born?
> Why pique all mortals, yet affect a name?
> A fool to Pleasure, yet a slave to Fame:
> Now deep in Taylor and the Book of Martyrs,
> Now drinking citron with his Grace and Chartres.
> Now Conscience chills her, and now Passion burns:
> And Atheism and Religion take their turns;
> A very Heathen in the carnal part,
> Yet still a sad, good Christian at her heart.   (53–68)

[1] Let. iii. 290.

For similarity in general form and contrasts in the particular patterns, consider the portrait of Flavia:

> Flavia's a Wit, has too much sense to Pray,
> To Toast our wants and wishes, is her way:
> Nor asks of God, but of her Stars to give
> The mighty blessing, "while we live, to live."
> Then all for Death, that Opiate of the soul!
> Lucretia's dagger, Rosamonda's bowl.
> Say, what can cause such impotence of mind?
> A Spark too fickle, or a Spouse too kind.
> Wise Wretch! with Pleasures too refin'd to please,
> With too much Spirit to be e'er at ease,
> With too much Quickness ever to be taught,
> With too much Thinking to have common Thought:
> You purchase Pain with all that Joy can give,
> And die of nothing but a Rage to live.
>
> (87–100)

Similar patterns and much the same line of development can be traced in the pictures of Silia, Papillia, and Calypso, of 'Sin in State', and the lady 'Wits'. A web of less obvious connexions is created through recurrent modes of irony: alternate shocks of classic allusion with modern realism, politely exaggerated wonder, delicate 'under-praise' and 'under-damnation', confidential asides of social gossip, the concentrated blow of multiple ironies flowering in a single word.

No satire by Pope shows greater skill in attaining a unity of effect through tone and parody or near-parody of other styles, including earlier styles used by Pope himself. And yet Pope's manner in the *Epistle* is quite distinct. It might be described as cosy small talk 'perplexed' with strains of the fanciful pictorial and the heroic, a combination of styles that goes back to the epistles to the Misses Blount and the *Rape of the Lock*. For a beautiful example of the manner, consider the passage following the bleak lines on 'the fate of a whole Sex of Queens':

> Pleasures the sex, as children Birds, pursue,
> Still out of reach, yet never out of view,
> Sure, if they catch, to spoil the Toy at most,
> To covet flying, and regret when lost:

> At last, to follies Youth could scarce defend,
> It grows their Age's prudence to pretend;
> Asham'd to own they gave delight before,
> Reduc'd to feign it, when they give no more:
> As Hags hold Sabbaths, less for joy than spight,
> So these their merry, miserable Night;
> Still round and round the Ghosts of Beauty glide,
> And haunt the places where their Honour dy'd.

> (231–42)

The first two lines are based on a couplet from an early poem, *Stanza's. From the french of MALHERBE*,[1] a dignified lyric on the vanity of human wishes:

> As children birds, so men their bliss pursue,
> Still out of reach, tho' ever in their view.

> (5–6)

In fitting this harmless couplet into a more worldly context thought and tone have been modified in a manner that is polite but cutting. A superficial comment on 'the Sex', made in a tone of 'good society' and given an air of pastoral innocence by comparing feminine flights and frolics with a children's game, leads unexpectedly into a scene of mingled horror and charm. The final couplet of the passage has a satiric sting all the more telling because of the deftness with which it is introduced:

> Still round and round the Ghosts of Beauty glide,
> And haunt the places where their Honour dy'd.

The union of this mocking tone with a picture of ghostly beauties may be traced to the *Rape of the Lock*:

> As now your own, our Beings were of old,
> And once inclos'd in Woman's beauteous Mold;
> Thence, by a soft Transition, we repair
> From earthly Vehicles to these of Air.
> Think not, when Woman's transient Breath is fled,
> That all her Vanities at once are dead:
> Succeeding Vanities she still regards,
> And tho' she plays no more, o'erlooks the Cards.
> Her Joy in gilded Chariots, when alive,
> And Love of *Ombre*, after Death survive.

[1] TE vi. 71.

For when the Fair in all their Pride expire,
To their first Elements their Souls retire . . .

The light Coquettes in *Sylphs* aloft repair,
And sport and flutter in the Fields of Air.
                    (I. 47–58, 65–66)

In the later 'inversion' of this theme, the moral evaluation is much more deeply disturbing, but it is made by similar poetic means and by a natural extension of Pope's earlier styles. The witches' dance is beguilingly beautiful in the melodiously 'choreographic', faintly sensuous, and romantic manner of the *Pastorals*:

And chaste Diana haunts the forest-shade.
                    (*Summer*, 62)

And the fleet shades glide o'er the dusky green.
                    (*Autumn*, 64)

A youthful Romantic poet, a lesser Keats, might have written the couplet up to 'their *Honour* died'. A wit, a more elegant Byron, might have written the last line. It is Pope's peculiar genius to have written both.

The judgement passed on these Beauties is far from pretty, but it arises easily out of elegant fancy and light social talk. The witches' sabbath is a 'merry, miserable Night', a more devastating remark just because it is the 'visiting night' of society 'queens'. Like Proust, Pope had been granted his revelation of the hell of mechanical social 'activity' and the slavery of pretended passion. We have amusing proof of how close the tone of these lines was to the social world in which Pope and his friends moved. In a letter written two or three years earlier, Pope quotes a version of the 'ghosts of Beauty' couplet (from an *Epigram* of 1730):

I am stuck at Twit'nam, as fast as my own Plants, scarce removeable at this season. So is Mrs Patty Blount, but not stuck with me, but removeable to all other Gardens hereabouts. Women seldom are planted in the Soil that would best agree with them, you see Carnations fading & dirty in Cheapside, which would blush and shine in the Country. Mrs Cornish is (just now) going to some such soft Retreat, at Hampsted, or Richmond, or Islington, having read the following Epigram,

When other Fair ones to the Shades go down,
Still Cloë, Flavia, Delia, stay in Town.

> Those Ghosts of Beauty wandring here reside
> And haunt the places where their Honor dy'd.[1]

In this coarse talk of women and gardening, we get a first
glimpse of the 'variegated tulips' and other *fleurs du mal* of
the *Epistle to a Lady*. In much the same worldly tone, Pope
makes his harshest judgement of 'veteran' beauties:

> Fair to no purpose, artful to no end,
> Young without Lovers, old without a Friend,
> A Fop their Passion, but their Prize a Sot,
> Alive, ridiculous, and dead, forgot!

(245–8)

Starting from this hardboiled level he rises without embarrassment to praise the woman of ideal constancy. The art
with which Pope makes his way from the familiar to the
noble by parody and reminiscence of his earlier styles was
never clearer than in these lovely lines:

> Ah Friend! to dazzle let the Vain design,
> To raise the Thought and touch the Heart, be thine!
> That Charm shall grow, while what fatigues the Ring
> Flaunts and goes down, an unregarded thing.
> So when the Sun's broad beam has tir'd the sight,
> All mild ascends the Moon's more sober light,
> Serene in Virgin Modesty she shines,
> And unobserv'd the glaring Orb declines.

(249–56)

The fashionable drive around the Ring is referred to in a
Virgilian idiom, *silvas fatigant*, and the picture of the vain
and dazzling beauty is almost a revision of the Pamela portrait in the *Epistle to Miss Blount, With the Works of Voiture*:

> The Gods, to curse *Pamela* with her Pray'rs,
> Gave the gilt Coach and dappled *Flanders* Mares,
> The shining Robes, rich Jewels, Beds of State,
> And to compleat her Bliss, a Fool for Mate.
> She glares in *Balls, Front-boxes,* and the *Ring,*
> A vain, unquiet, glitt'ring, wretched Thing!
> Pride, Pomp, and State but reach her outward Part,
> She sighs, and is no *Dutchess* at her Heart.

(49–56)

---

[1] Let. iii. 123.

In the later version, the elevation of 'fatigues the Ring' leads
to a Homeric simile that revives one of the most tranquil
images of the *Pastorals*,

> The moon, serene in glory, mounts the sky . . .
>
> (*Winter*, 6)

The simile originally appeared in some lines addressed to
another Lady, 'Erinna', Judith Cowper (a pleasant illustration of Pope's poetic economy). They were written, he tells
her, on the day 'you sate for your picture'. The pictorial
quality of the later poem may perhaps be traced to a vague
association of these lines with Miss Cowper's sitting for her
portrait.

The idyllic quality of the 'painting' in the *Epistle* is wisely
steadied by a ballast of social experience and secure friendship of the kind that makes for frankness. Warmth of affection and admiration combine as in the *Rape of the Lock* with
sound advice and mockery:

> Oh! blest with Temper, whose unclouded ray
> Can make to morrow chearful as to day;
> She, who can love a Sister's charms, or hear
> Sighs for a Daughter with unwounded ear;
> She, who ne'er answers till a Husband cools,
> Or, if she rules him, never shows she rules;
> Charms by accepting, by submitting sways,
> Yet has her humour most, when she obeys;
> Let Fops or Fortune fly which way they will;
> Disdains all loss of Tickets, or Codille;
> Spleen, Vapours, or Small-pox, above them all,
> And Mistress of herself, tho' China fall.
>
> (257–68)

It is not surprising that the language recalls a remark of
Addison's about 'fair Readers' who were not 'Philosophers
enough to keep their Temper at the fall of a Tea Pot or a
China Cup', behaviour ridiculed in the lines on Belinda's
outcry:

> Not louder Shrieks to pitying Heav'n are cast,
> When Husbands or when Lap-dogs breathe their last,
> Or when rich *China* Vessels, fal'n from high,
> In glittring Dust and painted Fragments lie!
>
> (III. 157–60)

There is a final agreeable irony in the character of the perfect woman: like the others she, too, is 'a Contradiction still'. But her compensating virtues, 'Sense' and 'Good-humour', are implied in the relation that makes joking possible. The virtues once praised in the *Rape of the Lock* are also the positive allegiances that lie behind the *Epistle*, the 'ideas' that rise from an appreciation of personal integrity and from affection based on long experience and long discipline of feeling. Their poetic importance can be measured best by the indirect evidence of the depth and complexity of feeling they evoke. In poetry, as in life, 'the less said about them the better'. As we must not be taken in by Pope's more solemn moralizing in other poems, we need not be misled by his lightness of touch here. If we remember—along with the perfect woman—Atossa,

> Sick of herself thro' very selfishness!
> (146)

or Chloe,

> Virtue she finds too painful an endeavour,
> Content to dwell in Decencies for ever . . .
> (163-4)

we may agree that the *Epistle* which seems least a 'moral essay' is not the least serious morally.

We cannot of course rule out direct moral statement from poetry, least of all from the poetry of Pope; but there are ways and ways of stating in poetry, and much depends on what happens elsewhere in the poem in which statements occur, on the kind of commerce set up as in Shakespeare between 'truth' and drama, including the quiet drama of the Horatian epistle. In the *Epistle to Burlington*, the commerce is active and unforced, since the voice of the aesthetic and social philosopher is recognizably the same as that of the amused observer of Timon and his kind. The *Epistle to Bathurst* offers important social and moral criticism made through symbolic portraits of such power as to undercut the avowed philosophy of the epistle. In the *Epistle to Cobham*, Pope's most serious concern, the inscrutability of human nature, is expressed in lively exempla or in finely ironic poses and symbolic imagery. As in Horace the beliefs that lie deepest in the epistle are continually being enacted in the fine 'gestures' of style. But the official doctrine of the ruling passions has only a slight connexion with Pope's dominant attitudes and modes of expression in the poem. In the *Epistle to a Lady* Pope approaches the view of human nature implicit in the *Epistle to Cobham*, but he has now fully recovered his integrity of vision and expression: he will write no more *Essays on Man*.

It seems inevitable and right to invoke the image of Horace in connexion with the poem that in total effect comes nearer to an Horatian epistle than anything Pope has yet written. In writing of the characters of women Pope is philosophic in Horace's most characteristic manner, and the burden of the poem is thoroughly Horatian—an expression of mingled amusement and horror at the muddle most people make of their lives and of rare satisfaction in finding one life, like Horace's Ofellus or Volteius, that seems to make sense. It is Horatian too in Pope's refusal to be dazzled by social prestige or pretension to wisdom, and in his quiet testimony to deep but free and easy friendship. The epistle is also Horatian in its poetic art, in the placing of contrasting cases that culminate in a winning yet not over-serious portrait of an ideal, in establishing a tone of casual talk that can embrace literary parody and high allusion, and finally in the skilful handling of transitions, which for Pope as for Horace is not only a technique of style, but a technique of moving freely among moral and emotional possibilities.

IX

AN ANSWER FROM HORACE

> The Occasion of publishing these Imitations was the
> Clamour raised on some of my Epistles. An Answer from
> Horace was both more full, and of more Dignity, than any
> I cou'd have made in my own person . . .
> (Pope, 'Advertisement' to the *Imitations of Horace*)

THE drift from philosophy as system to the satirical
study of man, clear enough in the epistles *To Bathurst*
and *To Cobham*, is completed with the *Epistle to a
Lady*. In that 'ethic epistle' and in the best parts of the
companion poems, Pope's poetry becomes more philosophical in the relevant sense. His language bears witness to a
vision illuminated and extended by 'truths of general nature',
by a belief in certain moral and social values, and by insights
into the way men act and feel in solitude and society. Pope
has returned to the less systematic philosophy of the *Essay
on Criticism*,

> Unerring NATURE, still divinely bright,
> One clear, unchanged, and universal light,
> Life, force, and beauty, must to all impart,
> At once the source, and end, and test of Art.

The great frame of Nature, implied in the epithets Pope uses
here, is also present by implication in the *Moral Essays*, but
increasingly in Pope's later poems[1] there are glimpses of
chaos, of the uncreating word that will replace *fiat lux* with
fiat nox. The return from abstractions to the minute particulars of mankind seems less unexpected if we remember that
while Pope's right hand was completing the *Essay on Man*,[2]
his left was occupied with the casual imitations of Horace,
which he first undertook in late January of 1732–3. By 20
March he had already completed his second imitation of
Horace. It is worth noting also that Pope was almost certainly

---

[1] I owe this point to T. R. Edwards, Jr., *Pope's Versions of Nature: the Progression
from Neo-Classic to Grotesque Poetic Style* (unpublished doctoral dissertation, Harvard
University, 1956).   [2] TE iii (i), p. xiv.

revising his early *Satires of Donne* in this same year of 1733. The example of Donne may have had its part in bringing Pope back to his proper poetic 'study', to the use of the talent that Atterbury had recognized years before in the lines on Addison. In Pope's next original poem after the *Epistle to a Lady*, the *Epistle to Dr. Arbuthnot*, Pope easily found a place for this fragment of 1715. But 'original' is always a relative term when used of Pope: his latest successes like his earliest were all more or less 'imitations'.

'Imitation' (unlike 'original') was not a lovely word to nineteenth-century readers and critics, and it was already becoming odious by the second half of the eighteenth century. Although twentieth-century criticism has made 'mimesis' acceptable and even attractive to the present generation, no one has quite dared use its older synonym without apology. Perhaps a minor product of this study may be to restore to the word some of its Renaissance dignity. The most characteristic achievements of Renaissance architecture—think of Bramante's temple on the Janiculum or of a villa by Palladio—were imitations, and the liveliest currents of art flowed through artists who were attempting to make ancient forms aesthetically satisfying and useful in the modern world. Pope and Burlington were fellow workers in the latest phase of the Renaissance: the Horatian epistles and the villa at Chiswick are successful imitations of Graeco-Roman originals. In a broad sense the term fits all of Pope's best work, from *Windsor Forest* and the *Rape of the Lock* to the *Epistle to Dr. Arbuthnot* and the *Dunciad*. The line between translation and imitation is hard to draw in his *Iliad*, and it is often no clearer in more original poems, since Pope is constantly reworking some remembered line or phrase or motif from another poet to express attitudes often quite alien to the context in which they first occurred. The 'imitation', as used more narrowly of a poem based on a specific text in a foreign language, had been recognized by Dryden as a distinct type of translation

. . . where the translator (if now he has not lost that name) assumes the liberty, not only to vary from the words and sense, but to forsake them both as he sees occasion; and taking only some general hints from the original, to run division on the groundwork, as he pleases.

Imitation of this type assumes familiarity with the original, and part of the meaning and much of the pleasure depend on the play of the version against the original. Pope himself referred twice to the process as 'parody', obviously meaning parody in the eighteenth-century sense of more or less faithful reproduction of a writer's style without lowering or burlesquing it.

As in Pope's style of living and in many of his poems, the 'imitation' of Horace went well beyond mimicking a style. Like Horace, Pope had been criticized by people who had been satirized (or imagined they had been) in earlier poems, and following Horace he set out to make a defence of his own satires and of satire in general. Both poets disclaimed interest or influence in affairs of state, although their friendship with 'the great' made their role and their poetry seem politically significant to others. John Butt[1] points out the close connexion between the *Imitations* and Pope's interest (evident from his letters) in the attempts of the Opposition to check Walpole's career and if possible oust him from his place as 'First Minister'. The poems also picture the conflict—noted already in the *Epistle to Bathurst*—between the forces of Court and City and the old country aristocracy, a conflict that Pope could easily translate in Horatian terms of 'the old Roman simplicity of a secluded villa' opposed to the corruption and luxury of the capital. National life as well as private seemed quite conveniently to be imitating art and history.

What interests us is not whether Pope's imitations are accurate, in the sense of being true to the original text or to the facts of Pope's life and time, but what Pope made out of Horace and what Horace made out of Pope, 'Pope' here meaning not the man, but the poetry and the dramatic figure of the poet in the works of his youth and his maturity. The biographer and the historian may determine in how far the actual man and the actual England resemble the poet's image.

The first of the *Imitations* (*Satires*, Book ii. i), *To Mr. Fortescue*, is an excellent example to begin with because the process of reciprocal transformation is so complete. Imita-

---

[1] TE iv, pp. xxxi–xli.

tion is here creation, and there is no point where we feel that
dependence on the original is a weakness. The satire is a rich
poem in its own right, and has as a whole a rush and liveliness
rare in Pope's longer satirical pieces, perhaps because, like
the *Rape of the Lock* and the *Epistle to a Lady*, it was written
in a comparatively short time. From start to finish there is
no break in rhythmic energy, a fair sign as usual that Pope
is in his vein. In defending his position as poet he has a
subject he can warm to, and he is happy in giving expression
to themes that have been constant throughout his poetry—
his disgust with dullness and folly, his feeling that he *must*
write, his high appreciation of moral independence, his irritation at solemnity in art and manners and his impatience
with lack of art, his antipathy to pretentiousness and corruption in high places (while acknowledging the splendours of
'high life'), and his fondness for a life of retreat and elegant
companionship. Taken as a whole, the poem is a 'realization
of the poet's life as Pope sees it through the image of Horace.

At each stage in the satire, we see Pope starting from a
theme or a turn of style in the original and going on to create
fresh variations true to the hint with which he began. It is
always very clear what Pope 'saw' in Horace. For example,
the opening section, though in comparison with the original
jauntier and more cunning in its tone of self-depreciation,
is a piece of well-bred spoofing in the same vein:

> *P.* There are (I scarce can think it, but am told)
> There are to whom my Satire seems too bold,
> Scarce to wise *Peter* complaisant enough,
> And something said of *Chartres* much too rough.
> The Lines are weak, another's pleas'd to say,
> Lord *Fanny* spins a thousand such a Day.
> Tim'rous by Nature, of the Rich in awe,
> I come to Council learned in the Law.
> You'll give me, like a Friend both sage and free,
> Advice; and (as you use) without a Fee.
> *F.* I'd write no more.
>   *P.* Not write, but then I *think*,
> And for my Soul I cannot sleep a wink.
> I nod in Company, I wake at Night,
> Fools rush into my Head, and so I write.
>   (1–14)

Pope moves exactly in Horace's way from casual reflection to friendly address and sharp repartee:

> Sunt quibus in satira videar nimis acer et ultra
> legem tendere opus . . .
>
>   Trebati,
> quid faciam praescribe. 'quiescas.' ne faciam, inquis,
> omnino versus? 'aio.'. . .

$$(1-2, 4-6)$$

As many readers have noticed, Pope works in attacks on individuals where Horace speaks in general terms. But this criticism is less damaging if we consider the whole of Horace's poem and Pope's method of imitating. Horace is in fact defending the personal attacks made in his early poems, and later in this satire he too names names (the 'witch' Canidia, the informer Cervius, and probably others no longer identifiable). Pope takes the liberty of doing in one place what Horace does in another, and introduces particular cases in his opening speech. But 'Lord Fanny' is something more than Lord Hervey. He is a metamorphosed Horatian character, the self-satisfied poet, Fannius (*Satires*, I. iv. 21), and he is reminiscent too of Horace's Lucilius, who 'often composed two hundred verses in an hour while standing on one foot' (*Satires*, I. iv. 9–10). The transformation of Hervey and Fannius goes further: the artless courtier poet becomes one of those subtly Popeian spiders, spinning 'a vast extent of flimsy lines'. The transition to the example via 'lines' is Horatian in finesse but thoroughly like Pope in being metaphorical:

> The Lines are weak, another's pleas'd to say,
> Lord *Fanny* spins a thousand such a Day.

Here and often in the poem, Pope particularizes not only by using actual or thinly disguised names but by evolving vivid satirical images. 'Particularizing' even in these satires that insist on the right to name individuals is an imaginative process.

This opening dialogue also shows how Pope transforms a personal reference and the Horatian original by semi-parody and economical reminiscence of his own earlier expressions.

For Horace's *verum nequeo dormire* there is the sharply out-
lined portrait of the insomniac and a new variation on

   . . . Fools rush in where Angels fear to tread.

The hint that the satirist should try less dangerous subjects
comes out as a parody of Pope's pastoral 'lays' and his lines
on sound and sense in the *Essay on Criticism*:

> Then all your Muse's softer Art display,
> Let *Carolina* smooth the tuneful Lay,
> Lull with *Amelia*'s liquid Name the Nine,
> And sweetly flow through all the Royal Line.
>
>   (29–32)

> Soft is the strain when Zephyr gently blows,
> And the smooth stream in smoother numbers flows . . .
>   (*Essay on Criticism*, 366–7)

A subtle hint of epic exaggeration in Horace's coy refusal to
sing of 'hosts bristling with spears' gives Pope an opportunity to burlesque Sir Richard Blackmore's epic style and
the kind of 'historical painting' he had once described so
solemnly in his notes to his *Iliad*: .

> What? like Sir *Richard*, rumbling, rough and fierce,
> With ARMS, and GEORGE, and BRUNSWICK crowd the Verse?
> Rend with tremendous Sound your ears asunder,
> With Gun, Drum, Trumpet, Blunderbuss & Thunder?
> Or nobly wild, with *Budgell*'s Fire and Force,
> Paint Angels trembling round his *falling Horse*?
>
>   (23–28)

The tone of impatient ironic exclamation in 'What? like
Sir *Richard* . . .' is most like Pope and quite typical of the
whole imitation. It is perhaps this tone that led Elwin and
Courthope to describe a later passage as 'much more in the
manner of Juvenal than of Horace':

> What? arm'd for *Virtue* when I point the Pen,
> Brand the bold Front of shameless, guilty Men,
> Dash the proud Gamester in his gilded Car,
> Bare the mean Heart that lurks beneath a Star;
> Can there be wanting to defend Her Cause,
> Lights of the Church, or Guardians of the Laws?
>
>   (105–10)

But Horace's tone in this satire is often boldly declarative

and in this particular passage almost as rhetorical as Pope's.
He opens his defence with exactly the same idiom:

> . . . quid, cum est Lucilius ausus
> primus in hunc operis componere carmina morem,
> detrahere et pellem, nitidus qua quisque per ora
> cederet, introrsum turpis . . .

(62–65)

The contrast with Horace comes out in Pope's splendidly
pictorial metaphors, and in his transferring the praise of the
satirist from Lucilius to himself:

> Yes, while I live, no rich or noble knave
> Shall walk the World, in credit, to his grave.
> TO VIRTUE ONLY and HER FRIENDS, A FRIEND,
> The World beside may murmur, or commend.

(119–22)

But Pope's tone in more personal moments of this kind
is certainly more public than Horace's. As in the *Essay on
Criticism*, the club and the coffee-house are almost always
in view. But within his range—admittedly narrower than
Horace's—he can modulate from the public to the relatively
private with similar assurance and rhythmic skill:

> Know, all the distant Din that World can keep
> Rolls o'er my *Grotto*, and but sooths my Sleep.
> There, my Retreat the best Companions grace,
> Chiefs, out of War, and Statesmen, out of Place.
> There *St. John* mingles with my friendly Bowl,
> The Feast of Reason and the Flow of Soul:
> And He, whose Lightning pierc'd th' *Iberian* Lines,
> Now, forms my Quincunx, and now ranks my Vines,
> Or tames the Genius of the stubborn Plain,
> Almost as quickly, as he conquer'd *Spain*.

(123–32)

This scene of sociable rural retreat, in Popeian pastoral song,
is touched off by Horace's brief mention of Scipio and 'wise'
Laelius joking with Lucilius as they cooked dinner in true
heroic simplicity. The biographical parallels are in this instance too good to be passed over: the Roman great are
replaced by St. John, philosopher and friend, and Peterborough, the conquerer of Barcelona, who was famed for his

skill in cookery! Pope gives us a vivid picture of the general's heroic character in the letters describing his last illness. Peterborough suffered the tortures of eighteenth-century surgery with Roman fortitude, and in the intervals between bouts of pain he conversed with his friends and relations, who visited him in large numbers. In turning fact into a lyric of country life, Pope has not translated the Latin text, but written as Horace wrote of life on his Sabine farm: *o noctes cenaeque deum.*

In another passage Pope again brings his self-portrait closer to the Horatian image by introducing motifs from other poems by Horace:

> My Head and Heart thus flowing thro' my Quill,
> Verse-man or Prose-man, term me which you will,
> Papist or Protestant, or both between,
> Like good *Erasmus* in an honest Mean,
> In Moderation placing all my Glory,
> While Tories call me Whig, and Whigs a Tory.
>
> (63–68)

Horace humorously explains that his defensive position as a poet comes from his being born of frontier stock, 'Lucanian or Apulian—I'm not sure which'. Pope's lines are closer to two passages on 'Moderation' that we noted in an earlier chapter,[1] both from satires Pope also imitated: Horace's definition of his middling state,

> Behind the foremost, and before the last.
> (*The Second Epistle of the Second Book*, 303)

and his picture of how he steers his course between Stoic and Epicurean,

> But ask not, to what Doctors I apply?
> Sworn to no Master, of no Sect am I:
> As drives the storm, at any door I knock,
> And house with Montagne now, or now with Lock.
> Sometimes a Patriot, active in debate,
> Mix with the World, and battle for the State,
> Free as young Lyttelton, her cause pursue,
> Still true to Virtue, and as warm as true:

---

[1] Cf. Ch. VI, pp. 186–7, 178–9.

> Sometimes, with Aristippus, or St. Paul,
> Indulge my Candor, and grow all to all;
> Back to my native Moderation slide,
> And win my way by yielding to the tyde.
> (*The First Epistle of the First Book of Horace Imitated*, 23–34)

In imagery and movement Pope gives a good equivalent for
Horace's playful balancing of loyalties, but he makes us feel
much less keenly the span between the contrasting positions.
Horace takes us *into* the Stoic seriousness, in a way that Pope
does not take us into the moral or political positions of Locke
or St. Paul. It must be admitted that there is a degree of
personal seriousness in Horace that Pope rarely ever reaches
in his *Imitations*. What he expresses admirably is the Horatian attitude of light, civilized moderation, an easy moderation that includes amusement at one's lightness. But Pope
misses the smile within the seriousness, the subtle amusement with which Horace regards himself in moments of
speculation and moral resolve.

Pope's success in domesticating Horatian *mediocritas* is
characteristic: he takes from Horace what he can best assimi-
late and what he is best fitted to express. The result is a kind
of conversational poetry that comes as near to Horace's as
anything in English (with the possible exception of Ben
Jonson's poetical 'letters'). With similar virtuosity he can
give a completely convincing impression of friend talking to
friend, while he is keeping a surprisingly precise metrical
pattern:

> [*F.*] It stands on record, that in *Richard*'s Times
> A man was hang'd for very honest Rhymes.
> Consult the Statute: *quart.* I think it is,
> *Edwardi Sext.* or *prim. & quint. Eliz*:
> See *Libels*, *Satires*—here you have it—read.
>   *P. Libels* and *Satires*! lawless Things indeed!
> But grave *Epistles*, bringing Vice to light,
> Such as a *King* might read, a *Bishop* write,
> Such as Sir *Robert* would approve—
>   *F.* Indeed?
> The Case is alter'd—you may then proceed.
>   (145–54)

In variety of poetic roles and of idiom and rhythm, Pope

easily equals the ideal satirist described by Horace.[1] We need only recall examples from this poem: the pleasant joking of the opening and the close, the ironic lyrics in heroic and pastoral styles, the praise of a rural retreat, the confession of faith in the golden mean, the grand exclamations of the satirist and moralist, and the sharp personal thrusts, whether merely personal or transformed by allusion and symbolic imagery. Pope also gives an overall impression of the Horatian movement from role to role and from attitude to attitude, though he moves on a larger scale rhetorically and rhythmically. There are fewer fine shifts of feeling and rhythm, fewer subtle transitions than in Horace or in Pope's more original Horatian poems, such as the epistles *To Burlington* or *To a Lady*. Though nearly every feature in Pope's portrait of the poet-satirist has an Horatian counterpart, the selection and emphasis are significant. Pope's 'Horatian' poet is more deliberately moral, more loudly declamatory in his defence, and more often shrewdly personal or cuttingly ironic.

But while Pope is surely among the more urbane English poets, comparison with Horace will always make us feel the gap between Latin and English urbanity. Take, for example, his next imitation, *The Second Satire of the Second Book . . . ,* 'To Mr. Bethel' (Horace's 'Ofellus'), and compare the gravity and decorum of Horace's first line,

> Quae virtus et quanta, boni, sit vivere parvo . . .

with Pope's opening couplets:

> What, and how great, the Virtue and the Art
> To live on little with a chearful heart,
> (A Doctrine sage, but truly none of mine)
> Lets talk, my friends, but talk before we dine . . .
> (1–4)

Pope has a manner and dignity, but after Horace he seems bluff and British with his 'chearful heart' and 'Lets talk, my friends . . .' And even more so in:

> Go work, hunt, exercise! (he thus began)
> Then scorn a homely dinner, if you can.
> (11–12)

[1] Cf. Ch. VI, pp. 167–8.

As in the first of the *Imitations*, Pope selects certain notes in Horace's repertoire—the rugged country character of Ofellus and his direct didactic speech—and misses others, especially the high exhortation and the Stoic nobility, which lift Horace's poem to quite a different dramatic and moral plane. Pope approached these nobler qualities more nearly in the Fourth Epistle of the *Essay on Man*.[1] In his imitation he is more at home when giving hearty advice on the simple life, though the satiric edge is more in evidence than in Horace. We occasionally catch a coarse Swiftian accent:

> By what *Criterion* do ye eat, d'ye think,
> If this is priz'd for *sweetness*, that for stink?
>
> (29–30)

> *Avidien* or his Wife (no matter which,
> For him you'll call a dog, and her a bitch) . . .
>
> (49–50)

The tone may have an easy explanation, since the 'Ofellus' Pope originally had in mind may have been Swift rather than Bethel. Pope was curiously ambiguous in writing to Swift about the satire, leaving him with the distinct impression that he was to be the hero of the piece. But in the final version Swift was assigned only a single speech and a role that did not altogether please him. The conclusion of the poem is certainly Scriblerian, though there is surprising, almost Horatian depth of melancholy in the simple question, 'What's *Property?* dear Swift!' And the impulse that gives the imitation life and character, Pope's admiration for two of his closest friends, is definitely Horatian. The latter half of the poem especially is less like the 'Ofellus' and more like one of Horace's letters in which a friend is bantered and scolded with affectionate freedom. The charm of the poetry—of no common sort in English—can be felt in a passage that includes motifs from other poems by Horace:

> Thus Bethel spoke, who always speaks his thought,
> And always thinks the very thing he ought:
> His equal mind I copy what I can,
> And as I love, would imitate the Man.

[1] Cf. Ch. VII. ii, pp. 234–5.

In *South-sea* days not happier, when surmis'd
The Lord of thousands, than if now *Excis'd*;
In Forest planted by a Father's hand,
Than in five acres now of rented land.
Content with little, I can piddle here
On Broccoli and mutton, round the year:
But ancient friends, (tho' poor, or out of play)
That touch my Bell, I cannot turn away.
'Tis true, no Turbots dignify my boards,
But gudgeons, flounders, what my Thames affords.
To Hounslow-heath I point, and Bansted-down,
Thence comes your mutton, and these chicks my own:
From yon old wallnut-tree a show'r shall fall;
And grapes, long-lingring on my only wall,
And figs, from standard and Espalier join:
The dev'l is in you if you cannot dine.
Then chearful healths (your Mistress shall have place)
And, what's more rare, a Poet shall say *Grace*.

                                        (129–50)

The praise of the Sabine Farm has been perfectly transposed
into the idiom of Twit'nam, with echoes of Ben Jonson's
epistle, *Inviting a friend to supper*. (Pope's amiable picture of
cosy friendship seems to have been startlingly like and unlike the reality, as the reader may discover from the notes in
the Elwin and Courthope and Twickenham editions.)

   In 1734, the year in which he published his 'Ofellus',
Pope also printed his fairly nasty imitation of Horace's
second satire of Book I, *Sober Advice from Horace*. The
Latin and English poems might serve as apt illustrations of
E. M. Forster's remark that 'Coarseness reveals something,
vulgarity conceals something'. Horace's piece is grossly
Roman, where Pope is insinuating and, in the notes if not
in the text, pornographic. Viewed biographically, *Sober Advice* is not an admirable performance, as Pope half-confessed
by publishing it anonymously and by equivocating about it
in letters to Caryll and others. But early in the next year,
1735, Pope published two poems of which he was justly
proud, the epistles *To a Lady* and *To Dr. Arbuthnot*.

   In both poems Pope shows that he could be most Horatian
when he was being most fully himself and under no obliga-
tion to imitate a particular poem by Horace. Addressing

Arbuthnot almost as a personified literary conscience, he displays the freedom of the ideal conversationalist in a poem combining satire with poetic biography. The epistle is not a 'composition in irony' of the same type as the *Moral Essays*, not focused on a single theme rich in ironies brought out through symbolic portraits or stanzaic meditations. There is not as in most of the *Moral Essays* any direct statement of positive values, but the ideal is presented dramatically through the poet's talk and through narrative. There is also no dominant kind of image like the gardening and pictorial imagery of the epistles *To Burlington* and *To a Lady*. The metaphor of the poem is quite simply 'Horace', the image of the poet in the *Satires* and *Epistles* as Pope has reshaped it in his *Imitations*. Attempting to do in one poem what Horace does in a number of poems, Pope makes an apologia for his whole career and defends himself against poetasters, critics, and personal enemies while expressing his affection for his parents and friends, especially for 'the Doctor', a man who was learned, witty, and good. The poem is a poetic biography, 'poetic' in the obvious sense of the literary form Pope is using, and also in a less obvious Aristotelian sense. The *Epistle to Dr. Arbuthnot* is 'the life of a poet', not of an individual poet, but the epitome of a satirist's career as Pope saw it.

Like the best of Horace's *Epistles*, it is the kind of letter we dream of writing, our own talk brought to paper without any obvious plan or artifice, yet capable of embracing whatever concerns or amuses us. To give talk of this sort the finality of verse is surely among the rarest of poetic feats. In Pope's handling, the imagined dialogue becomes unexpectedly beautiful, a wonderful example of how he can transform the commonplace into the lyric and the fantastic:

> Shut, shut the door, good *John*! fatigu'd I said,
> Tye up the knocker, say I'm sick, I'm dead,
> The Dog-star rages! nay 'tis past a doubt,
> All *Bedlam*, or *Parnassus*, is let out:
> Fire in each eye, and Papers in each hand,
> They rave, recite, and madden round the land.
>   What Walls can guard me, or what Shades can hide?
> They pierce my Thickets, thro' my Grot they glide,

By land, by water, they renew the charge,
They stop the Chariot, and they board the Barge . . .
(1–10)

The lines draw their energy from many sources, from memories of a London August and scenes in Horace and Juvenal, from cosy familiarity with 'good *John*' and long affection for Arbuthnot, and from disgust with the *genus irritabile*, of which the speaker is obviously a good specimen. The technical mastery is so fine that we barely see how talk becomes in the musical sense *bien rhythmé*, reaching an almost ragtime effect in

> They rave, recite, and madden round the land.

Note, for example, how 'shut the door, good *John*!' is thrown into quite a different pattern by starting the line with 'Shut, *shut*', and how the inversion of 'fatigu'd' increases the swing of the whole line. Trochaic openings in four verses and the use of something like the ancient choriamb ($-\cup\cup-$),

> Fire in each eye, and Papers in each hand,

also suggest a song and dance movement. The imagery is comically mad and charmingly real and unreal. The poetasters seem both like walking fireworks and ghosts in a pastoral scene, but through the farcical exaggeration we get amusing glimpses of Pope playing with his grotto and making pleasant journeys up and down the Thames. Pope has now attained the ultimate in freedom of movement and feeling; and changes of tone and role, with small Horatian shocks of contrast, appear almost everywhere. He turns easily from pitying sarcasm to simple affection and warm but playful compliment,

> Poor *Cornus* sees his frantic Wife elope,
> And curses Wit, and Poetry, and *Pope*.
> Friend to my Life, (which did not you prolong,
> The World had wanted many an idle Song)
> What *Drop* or *Nostrum* can this Plague remove?
(25–29)

or from bluntness and cynicism to the mockery of heroic oath,

> You think this cruel? take it for a rule,
> No creature smarts so little as a Fool.

> Let Peals of Laughter, *Codrus*! round thee break,
> Thou unconcern'd canst hear the mighty Crack.
>
> (83–86)

from broad comedy to the slyly smiling humour of Horace,

> This prints my Letters, that expects a Bribe,
> And others roar aloud, "Subscribe, subscribe."
>   There are, who to my Person pay their court,
> I cough like *Horace*, and tho' lean, am short,
> *Ammon*'s great Son one shoulder had too high,
> Such *Ovid*'s nose, and "Sir! you have an *Eye*—"...
>
> (113–18)

and from his own familiar kind of ironic praise to decorous elegy,

> Blest be the *Great*! for those they take away,
> And those they left me—For they left me GAY,
> Left me to see neglected Genius bloom,
> Neglected die! and tell it on his Tomb...
>
> (255–8)

As the quotations show, the *Epistle to Dr. Arbuthnot* is 'poetic biography' in a rather special sense, a kind of résumé of modes Pope had perfected while 'imitating' Dryden and Horace. The most famous passage, the portrait of Atticus, dating in its first form from 1715, is a character in the seventeenth-century tradition that Dryden had adapted to suit his heroic manner. This mock-heroic 'Cato' in 'his little Senate' is linked with Dryden's heroes and Horace's symbolic Romans. Pope's individual quality comes out in the insidiously intimate tone, evoking so perfectly the whispered gossip of the coterie he is satirizing. But the control exercised in moulding an unforgettable type of the petty and cautious literary dictator lifts the passage from gossip to art. The magnificent inflation of the picture of Bufo starts off in a style reminiscent of *Absalom and Achitophel*,

> Proud, as *Apollo* on his forked hill,
> Sate full-blown *Bufo*, puff'd by ev'ry quill...
>
> (231–2)

and includes the handsome tribute,

> *Dryden* alone (what wonder?) came not nigh,
> *Dryden* alone escap'd this judging eye...
>
> (245–6)

The remark, as John Butt notes, does not fit the supposed originals of the character, either Halifax or Dodington. The figure of this soft-fed creature puffed out like the toad in Horace's fable, is more symbolic than biographical, an imaginative blend of the disgusting and the splendidly classical. The sketch of

> That Fop whose pride affects a Patron's name,
> Yet absent, wounds an Author's honest fame;
> Who can your Merit selfishly approve,
> And show the Sense of it, without the Love;
> Who has the Vanity to call you Friend,
> Yet wants the Honour injur'd to defend;
> Who tells whate'er you think, whate'er you say,
> And, if he lye not, must at least betray . . .
>
> (291–8)

is a refined version[1] of an earlier 'paraphrase of four lines and a half of Horace', a sharp warning against the satirist who attacks his victims behind their backs. The lines introduce the most original portrait in the epistle. It is the most Popeian not because it was intensely personal in origin, but because the art is unmistakably Pope's and not Dryden's or Horace's:

> A Lash like mine no honest man shall dread,
> But all such babling blockheads in his stead.
>   Let *Sporus* tremble—"What? that Thing of silk,
> "*Sporus*, that mere white Curd of Ass's milk?
> "Satire or Sense alas! can *Sporus* feel?
> "Who breaks a Butterfly upon a Wheel?"
> Yet let me flap this Bug with gilded wings,
> This painted Child of Dirt that stinks and stings;
> Whose Buzz the Witty and the Fair annoys,
> Yet Wit ne'er tastes, and Beauty ne'er enjoys,
> So well-bred Spaniels civilly delight
> In mumbling of the Game they dare not bite.
> Eternal Smiles his Emptiness betray,
> As shallow streams run dimpling all the way.
> Whether in florid Impotence he speaks,
> And, as the Prompter breathes, the Puppet squeaks;
> Or at the Ear of *Eve*, familiar Toad,
> Half Froth, half Venom, spits himself abroad,

[1] TE vi. 338.

In Puns, or Politicks, or Tales, or Lyes,
Or Spite, or Smut, or Rymes, or Blasphemies.
His Wit all see-saw between *that* and *this*,
Now high, now low, now Master up, now Miss,
And he himself one vile Antithesis.
Amphibious Thing! that acting either Part,
The trifling Head, or the corrupted Heart!
Fop at the Toilet, Flatt'rer at the Board,
Now trips a Lady, and now struts a Lord.
Eve's Tempter thus the Rabbins have exprest,
A Cherub's face, a Reptile all the rest;
Beauty that shocks you, Parts that none will trust,
Wit that can creep, and Pride that licks the dust.

(303–33)

This may be horror, but the horror of a vision of the epicene
in its essence is hardly personal. The passage can be defended—if defence seems necessary—on Byron's principle
that 'one should see every thing, once, with attention'.[1] Our
'liking' or 'disliking' do not seem particularly relevant, just
as when we are faced with Lear's horrible nightmare of
adultery and lechery. The integrity of vision and effect in
the portrait of Sporus is in a definable sense Shakespearian:
dramatic speech brings a character to life through continuously evolving metaphors, 'modified', as Coleridge would
say, 'by a predominant passion', the revulsion from physical
and moral ambiguity. From the name 'Sporus', associated
(in Gibbon's phrase) with the 'scarcely correct' love of Roman
emperors, to the innocent delicacy and disgust of 'silk' and
'Curd of Ass's milk', the satirical current passes through
another inversion of the *Rape of the Lock* (via the images of
'a Butterfly upon a Wheel', the 'Bug with gilded wings', and
the 'painted Child of Dirt'). By a transition very much in
Shakespeare's style, from 'Buzz' to 'mumbling', the insect
becomes a 'Spaniel' with a smile so sweet that only a pastoral
simile can describe it,

As shallow streams run dimpling all the way.

This flowery-speaking, painted doll expands with the impo-
tent puffings of the 'familiar Toad'. The 'Toad', one of the

[1] *Byron, a Self-Portrait*, ed. Peter Quennell (London, 1950), vol. ii, Letter to
John Murray, 30 May 1817, 409.

metamorphoses of Milton's serpent-Satan, 'half Froth, half Venom', exuding triviality and evil by turns in true 'amphibious' fashion, is finally reduced to 'one vile Antithesis', a mere figure of wit. The closing lines with their bright contradictions are also a marvel of coalescing opposites—of the flutteringly angelic and the satanically reptilian—which sum up in little the alternates of moral and sensuous impression of the whole passage.

But we do not find the attacking 'English' satirist in all parts of the poem. The more autobiographical phases remind us of Horace's most humorous and temperate moods, as, for example, when Pope describes how he 'sits with sad Civility' listening to bad poetry, or when he recalls the flattering comparisons of his 'Person' to Horace or Alexander the Great, or when he drops all irony to praise his father and Arbuthnot. In other passages Pope is heard like Ovid 'lisping in Numbers', or gently parodying his pastoral style while defending the innocence of his early works:

> Soft were my Numbers, who could take offence
> While pure Description held the place of Sense?
> Like gentle *Fanny*'s was my flow'ry Theme,
> A painted Mistress, or a purling Stream.
>
> (147–50)

There is also the forthright champion of satire of the first *Imitation*, who enunciates his principles and defends himself in terms politely general in form but decidedly particular in application,

> The Blow unfelt, the Tear he never shed;
> The Tale reviv'd, the Lye so oft o'erthrown . . .
>
> (349–50)

and who also descends to name individuals and their crimes:

> Let *Budgel* charge low *Grubstreet* on his quill,
> And write whate'er he pleas'd, except his *Will*;
> Let the *Two Curls* of Town and Court, abuse
> His Father, Mother, Body, Soul, and Muse.
>
> (378–81)

Here certainly truth breaks in with her matter of fact, and poetic biography ceases to be poetic except for the smartness of the rhyme (not altogether a slight difference).

In the preface to the poem, Pope had raised the ugly question of truth and satire, and, like many of his critics, he is soon caught in the snares of the meaning of 'truth' and its application to literature:

> *If it* [this Epistle] *have any thing pleasing, it will be That by which I am most desirous to please, the* Truth *and the* Sentiment; *and if any thing offensive, it will be only to those I am least sorry to offend, the* Vicious *or* the Ungenerous.
>
> *Many will know their own Pictures in it, there being not a Circumstance but what is true; but I have, for the most part spar'd their* Names, *and they may escape being laugh'd at, if they please.*

In the second sentence Pope makes a claim to truth in the most limited factual sense. Certain criticisms he makes of individuals are undoubtedly true in this sense, though all that purport to be are not, for example, the comment on Dryden's relations to Halifax. But even if Pope's poem were true in each 'Circumstance', even if every item of a portrait could be traced to a fact observed by Pope or reported to him, the portrait as a whole, the portrait created by Pope's language, may not be true in this sense, though true in quite another. Pope indicates the relevant meaning, though not without ambiguity, in the first sentence we have quoted. 'Truth' and 'Sentiment' go closely together, and 'Sentiment' is more than feeling, as we may see from his many Observations on the 'sentiments' of the *Iliad*. It is the kind of feeling that approaches wisdom, most often expressed in *sententiae*, Dr. Johnson's 'sentiments to which every bosom returns an echo'. The Horatian pleasure that Pope is speaking of, and that his satire gives to intelligent readers, arises not from truth 'individual and local'—the recognition that Sporus is Hervey or that Atticus is Addison—but from truth 'general, and operative . . . carried alive into the heart by passion'. Although in the first *Imitation* and in a well-known letter to Arbuthnot Pope defended naming individuals, he fortunately did not follow the principle consistently. There is some confusion in his remark to the Doctor about 'hunting One or two from the Herd',[1] as becomes clear from his more elaborate version of the same letter:

To attack Vices in the abstract, without touching Persons, may

[1] Let. iii. 423.

be safe fighting indeed, but it is fighting with Shadows. General propositions are obscure, misty, and uncertain, compar'd with plain, full,
and home examples: Precepts only apply to our Reason, which in
most men is but weak: Examples are pictures, and strike the Senses,
nay raise the Passions, and call in those (the strongest and most general
of all motives) to the aid of reformation. Every vicious man makes
the case his own; and that is the only way by which such men can be
affected, much less deterr'd.[1]

The contrast between 'general propositions' and 'examples'
is ambiguous since 'examples' may mean both *particular*
cases and *representative* cases (the latter almost certainly
here). But as soon as Pope talks of cases as 'pictures' that
'strike the Senses' and 'raise the Passions', he is no longer
talking of 'fact', but of metaphor and the persuasive power
of poetry. (His argument resembles Sidney's in the *Defence
of Poesie*.) The case viewed as example and described in a
way to make us see it as Vice or Virtue is very different from
a report of the acts of a particular man. Fortunately for his
poetry Pope's instinct as a poet got the better of the reformer, and in practice Pope, like Horace, freely mingled
actual names and items of fact with symbolic figures and
fiction.

Though in *Arbuthnot* Pope did not 'make as free use' of
names as he apparently was inclined to do, he often worked
in attacks on persons (either by name or under transparent
pseudonyms) which have little general significance, moral or
dramatic. But the great cases are always more than personal;
all have become like Atossa creatures of satiric imagination
belonging to the same realm of experience as Thersites or
Caliban. If a literary detective should discover tomorrow that
the speech of either of these characters closely echoed the
talk of Greene or Nash and if letters were found showing that
contemporaries recognized the portrayal as a personal attack,
what would happen to Thersites and Caliban? Very little,
at least for a reader or listener who was responding properly
to *Troilus and Cressida* or *The Tempest*. Only a Parson Adams
would reduce Caliban to the man whom Shakespeare knew
and disliked. The character of Sporus does undoubtedly have
a bitter personal application, but to the qualified reader of

[1] Let. iii. 419.

the poem, the reference comes in afterward or on the side, as
a further relation he may make with the actual Pope and his
sometimes despicable, sometimes deeply affectionate personal
relationships.

Pope's poetic biography, which occupies so large a place
in the *Epistle to Dr. Arbuthnot*, is continued in the next
imitation, *The Second Epistle of the Second Book*. The lines
that especially pleased Swift, and that he perhaps inspired,
are written in the lyric and allusive style of similar passages
in other imitations:

> Years foll'wing Years, steal something ev'ry day,
> At last they steal us from our selves away;
> In one our Frolicks, one Amusements end,
> In one a Mistress drops, in one a Friend:
> This subtle Thief of Life, this paltry Time,
> What will it leave me, if it snatch my Rhime?
> If ev'ry Wheel of that unweary'd Mill
> That turn'd ten thousand Verses, now stands still.
>
> (72–79)

By echoing the youthful Milton, Pope has caught exactly the
light melancholy (*eheu fugaces*) and quick movement of the
lines in Horace. But in other parts of this imitation Pope
misses the religious feeling and inner seriousness of Horace's
most noble epistle.[1] The mystery of the Genius and the
presence of death, which Horace expresses with immediacy,
is transposed into a coarser, more masculine and more public
irony:

> *Man?* and *for ever?* Wretch! what wou'dst thou have?
> Heir urges Heir, like Wave impelling Wave:
> All vast Possessions (just the same the case
> Whether you call them Villa, Park, or Chace)
> Alas, my Bathurst! what will they avail?
> Join *Cotswold* Hills to *Saperton's* fair Dale,
> Let rising Granaries and Temples here,
> There mingled Farms and Pyramids appear,
> Link Towns to Towns with Avenues of Oak,
> Enclose whole Downs in Walls, 'tis all a joke!
> Inexorable Death shall level all,
> And Trees, and Stones, and Farms, and Farmer fall.
>
> (252–63)

[1] Cf. Ch. VI, pp. 186-7.

The conclusion of the epistle, Horace's remarkable examina-
tion of himself and his friend that we quoted earlier, loses
sharpness of application and moral grandeur:

> Has Life no sourness, drawn so near its end?
> Can'st thou endure a Foe, forgive a Friend?
> Has Age but melted the rough parts away,
> As Winter-fruits grow mild e'er they decay?
> Or will you think, my Friend, your business done,
> When, of a hundred thorns, you pull out one?
>   Learn to live well, or fairly make your Will;
> You've play'd, and lov'd, and eat, and drank your fill:
> Walk sober off; before a sprightlier Age
> Comes titt'ring on, and shoves you from the stage:
> Leave such to trifle with more grace and ease,
> Whom Folly pleases, and whose Follies please.
>
> (316–27)

Admirable advice from Pope, but hardly 'out of Horace'.
The subject of Pope's poetry is not the private drama of the
soul, and he is accordingly much less convincing than Horace
when he says,

> To Rules of Poetry no more confin'd,
> I learn to smooth and harmonize my Mind,
> Teach ev'ry Thought within its bounds to roll,
> And keep the equal Measure of the Soul.
>
> (202–5)

Horace says less and means more,

> ac non verba sequi fidibus modulanda Latinis,
> sed verae numerosque modosque ediscere vitae.
>
> (143–4)

and he supports his high resolve by 'schooling his soul' in
the meditation with which the poem ends. On the other
hand, in the lines on the guardianship of the language, Pope
is very much at home as a moralist and a poet:

> But how severely with themselves proceed
> The Men, who write such Verse as we can read?
> Their own strict Judges, not a word they spare
> That wants or Force, or Light, or Weight, or Care,
> Howe'er unwillingly it quits its place,
> Nay tho' at Court (perhaps) it may find grace:

Such they'll degrade; and sometimes, in its stead,
In downright Charity revive the dead;
Mark where a bold expressive Phrase appears,
Bright thro' the rubbish of some hundred years;
Command old words that long have slept, to wake,
Words, that wise *Bacon*, or brave *Raleigh* spake;
Or bid the new be *English*, Ages hence,
(For Use will father what's begot by Sense)
Pour the full Tide of Eloquence along, ⎫
Serenely pure, and yet divinely strong, ⎬
Rich with the Treasures of each foreign Tongue; ⎭
Prune the luxuriant, the uncouth refine,
But show no mercy to an empty line;
Then polish all, with so much life and ease,
You think 'tis Nature, and a knack to please:
"But Ease in writing flows from Art, not Chance,
"As those move easiest who have learn'd to dance."
                                      (157–79)

It is in a passage like this that Pope's soul shows itself, if we
mean by 'soul' mind working in harmony with moral feeling,
the area of the inner life in which accurate thinking and fine
feeling are one and indistinguishable. But Pope rarely dramatizes this area directly except for brief moments here and
there:

Oft in the Passions' wild rotation tost,
Our spring of action to ourselves is lost:
Tir'd, not determin'd, to the last we yield,
And what comes then is master of the field.
                (Epistle to Cobham, 41–44)

A man's true merit 'tis not hard to find,
But each man's secret standard in his mind,
That Casting-weight Pride adds to Emptiness,
This, who can gratify? for who can *guess?*
                (Epistle to Dr. Arbuthnot, 175–8)

In plenty starving, tantaliz'd in state,
And complaisantly help'd to all I hate,
Treated, caress'd, and tir'd, I take my leave,
Sick of his civil Pride from Morn to Eve;
I curse such lavish cost, and little skill,
And swear no Day was ever past so ill.
                (Epistle to Burlington, 163–8)

In the last example, as in the present one, we catch a glimpse of the sensitive point in Pope's inner life, the meeting-place of aesthetic sensibility ('taste') and moral judgement. When reading Pope's more obvious declarations of principle in the *Essay on Man* or the *Morals Essays*, we are tempted to adopt Wilson Knight's comment on Dryden and say that Pope 'lacked a personal core to his life's work'. But the judgement is hardly charitable or sound. Men are not equally 'soulful' in all areas of experience, and the expression of the inner life may take different forms in different men. Except in the lines on Oldham, Dryden almost always reveals his deepest concerns on great public occasions. Pope's occasions—those on which he is most surely 'touched'—belong more commonly to smaller social worlds, but in his later *Imitations* and satires (from 1737 on) he speaks more often for the nation and the age. (*Windsor Forest* is the 'prophetic' exception among his early poems.) In the noble lines on language of this epistle to '*Cobham's*' and his 'Country's Friend', we hear the true voice of Augustan taste, the morality of language practised by poet and lexicographer. Johnson in fact chose the original lines in Horace as an epigraph on the title-page of his dictionary. By quoting in this context the couplet from the *Essay on Criticism*, Pope gives a new weight to 'art', and he reminds us at the same time of the continuity between his youthful and his mature expression of the Horatian belief in both *studium* and *ingenium*.

For all its irony, the *Epistle to Augustus* is Pope's ultimate evaluation of the Augustan age and its standards in art and life. Although the praise is more sober than in the *Essay on Criticism* and *Windsor Forest*, the spirit of the age as depicted by Pope is admirable, admirable in part because of the sophisticated level of the irony and the independence implied in well-considered praise. The sophistication is that of a man who has deep loyalties to poetry and to the past, but who talks in a well-bred half-deprecating manner:

> Shakespear, (whom you and ev'ry Play-house bill
> Style the divine, the matchless, what you will)
> For gain, not glory, wing'd his roving flight,
> And grew Immortal in his own despight.
>
> (69–72)

Pope has happily caught Horace's attitude of humorous reverence and affectionate mockery of the classics, and he is surpassed only by Dr. Johnson in the sanity and lack of unction with which he speaks of Shakespeare and Milton. The Restoration never received more charming or more devastating praise:

> In Days of Ease, when now the weary Sword
> Was sheath'd, and *Luxury* with *Charles* restor'd;
> In every Taste of foreign Courts improv'd,
> "All, by the King's Example, liv'd and lov'd."
> Then Peers grew proud in Horsemanship t' excell,
> New-market's Glory rose, as Britain's fell;
> The Soldier breath'd the Gallantries of France,
> And ev'ry flow'ry Courtier writ Romance.
> Then Marble soften'd into life grew warm,
> And yielding Metal flow'd to human form:
> Lely on animated Canvas stole
> The sleepy Eye, that spoke the melting soul.

> (139–50)

The later lines on the 'Augustanization' of England are not quite true to political or literary history, but they show Pope's remarkable skill in balancing the claims of correctness and of more positive poetic values. The evaluations of individual writers—classic in every sense of the word—give a substance to the adjustment of values that was lacking in the *Essay on Criticism*:

> We conquer'd France, but felt our captive's charms;
> Her Arts victorious triumph'd o'er our Arms:
> Britain to soft refinements less a foe,
> Wit grew polite, and Numbers learn'd to flow.
> Waller was smooth; but Dryden taught to join ⎫
> The varying verse, the full resounding line, ⎬
> The long majestic march, and energy divine. ⎭
> Tho' still some traces of our rustic vein
> And splay-foot verse, remain'd, and will remain.
> Late, very late, correctness grew our care,
> When the tir'd nation breath'd from civil war.
> Exact Racine, and Corneille's noble fire
> Show'd us that France had something to admire.
> Not but the Tragic spirit was our own,
> And full in Shakespear, fair in Otway shone:

But Otway fail'd to polish or refine
And fluent Shakespear scarce effac'd a line.
Ev'n copious Dryden, wanted, or forgot,
The last and greatest Art, the Art to blot.

(263–81)

Though these lines are flattering enough to the small class of writers and readers who were the true Augustans, much of the epistle is sharply critical of George Augustus II and his court and the stout British public that was as eager for a good show as the citizenry of Horace's Rome. W. K. Wimsatt has said very well that '... Pope's tribute *To Augustus* ... is reflected against the more forthright epistle of Horace, so that Horace is not only a model for Pope's poem, but a part of its main ironic metaphor'.[1] Pope adapts Horace to his purpose in ways now familiar from earlier *Imitations*, and as usual he uncovers every possible hint of irony in the original. Horace's epistle is not simply admiring, and if it is not certainly ironic, all the materials of irony are present.[2] The grandeur of the praise is matched by a reluctance to give Augustus the epic he had asked for and by oddly giving him something he may not have wanted, an encomium on the Augustan poets and caustic criticism of the Roman literary and theatrical public. There is just enough ambiguity in Augustus' relations with the writers of his age (as may be seen in Suetonius), for Pope to take off on his un-'Maeonian wing'.

While You, great Patron of Mankind, sustain
The balanc'd World, and open all the Main;
Your Country, chief, in Arms abroad defend,
At home, with Morals, Arts, and Laws amend;
How shall the Muse, from such a Monarch, steal
An hour, and not defraud the Publick Weal?

(1–6)

In his 'Advertisement', Pope with tongue-in-cheek exploits hints from Suetonius and Horace so as to satirize George II's lack of interest in the arts and draw the contrast with conditions under Augustus:

This Epistle will show the learned World to have fallen into two

---

[1] Wimsatt, 'Rhetoric and Poems', *English Institute, 1948*, p. 183.
[2] Cf. Ch. VI, p. 183.

mistakes; one, that Augustus was a Patron of Poets in general; *whereas he not only prohibited all but the Best Writers to name him, but recommended that Care even to the Civil Magistrate . . .*[1]

We hear Pope's opening lines against Horace's noble yet polite praise of Augustus:

> Cum tot sustineas et tanta negotia solus,
> res Italas armis tuteris, moribus ornes,
> legibus emendes . . .

Pope echoes the nobility and the politeness, but by shrewdly selecting his facts he brings out the differences between the *Pax Augustana* and the peace policy of Walpole (which 'opens' the British main to the attacks of Spanish ships), and he quietly contrasts Augustus' defence of the imperial frontiers with George's visits to Hanover and Mme Walmoden. It is Pope's grand historical manner that gives the poem unity of tone and feeling, whether he is attacking writers and noble patrons, as here, or whether with less obvious irony he surveys the accomplishments of British poets in earlier ages or the immediate past. The concluding praise of George Augustus combines the mockery of the historian with fine responsiveness to the plastic arts and poetic styles:

> Not with such Majesty, such bold relief,
> The Forms august of King, or conqu'ring Chief,
> E'er swell'd on Marble; as in Verse have shin'd
> (In polish'd Verse) the Manners and the Mind.
> Oh! could I mount on the Maeonian wing,
> Your Arms, your Actions, your Repose to sing!
> What seas you travers'd! and what fields you fought!
> Your Country's Peace, how oft, how dearly bought!
> How barb'rous rage subsided at your word,
> And Nations wonder'd while they dropp'd the sword!
> How, when you nodded, o'er the land and deep,
> Peace stole her wing, and wrapt the world in sleep;
> Till Earth's extremes your mediation own,
> And Asia's Tyrants tremble at your Throne—
>
> (390–403)

The points are made by deft allusion to Homer, Virgil, Milton, and Pomfret (!), and the rhythm has a scale that

[1] TE iv. 191.

anticipates Pope's return to Dryden in his latest poems. As in other passages reminiscent of Dryden the irony focuses in a single word of elevated tone and seemingly innocuous intent,

> Your Arms, your Actions, your *Repose* to sing!

The conclusion with its Homeric and Miltonic associations anticipates the less lightly ironic vision in the *Dunciad* of a world also 'wrapt in sleep'. Pope will not write again in such high spirits of the Age of George II.

The pointed satire on the king may reflect the hopes of Pope's friends that the Opposition might soon succeed in their long fight against Walpole and 'Corruption like a gen'ral flood'. The next two imitations of Horace indicate that Pope shared their hopes, but both poems present an even darker view of England than the *Epistle to Augustus*, though the judgement implied is characteristically moral rather than political. Pope's version of *Nil Admirari* (To Mr. Murray) is after the epistle to Fortescue the most unified of the *Imitations*, although the character that Pope imposes on the satire is decidedly his own. Horace's poem is a much tighter composition, held together by a fine consistency in its tone of ironic advice. Pope seizes on the least polite tones in Horace—the more exalted commands and the lofty rhetorical questions—and introduces a strain of splendour barely suggested by Horace's lines on the philosopher who 'beholds the sun and the stars and the seasons' regular change'. Pope's rendering, reminiscent of Hamlet's apostrophe, is more magniloquent and more splendid:

> This Vault of Air, this congregated Ball,
> Self-centred Sun, and Stars that rise and fall,
> There are, my Friend! whose philosophic eyes
> Look thro', and trust the Ruler with his Skies,
> To him commit the hour, the day, the year,
> And view this dreadful All without a fear. (5–10)

Images of exotic wealth and hints of heroic grandeur are ironically apt for the lordly types whose ambition and corruption are being satirized:

> Go then, and if you can, admire the state
> Of beaming diamonds, and reflected plate;

> Procure a *Taste* to double the surprize,
> And gaze on Parian Charms with learned eyes:
> Be struck with bright Brocade, or Tyrian Dye,
> Our Birth-day Nobles splendid Livery . . .
>
> (28–33)

The glories of British trade, once praised so cheerfully in *Windsor Forest*, are now the subject of mockery,

> Admire we then what Earth's low entrails hold,⎫
> Arabian shores, or Indian seas infold?   ⎬
> All the mad trade of Fools and Slaves for Gold? ⎭
>
> (11–13)

and bitter irony,

> Is Wealth thy passion? Hence! from Pole to Pole,
> Where winds can carry, or where waves can roll,
> For Indian spices, for Peruvian gold,
> Prevent the greedy, and out-bid the bold:
> Advance thy golden Mountain to the skies;
> On the broad base of fifty thousand rise,
> Add one round hundred, and (if that's not fair)
> Add fifty more, and bring it to a square.
>
> (69–76)

The roughness of this heroic advice again connects Pope with Dryden, whose translation of Persius he is apparently recalling.

The imitation addressed to Bolingbroke, the ageing hero of the Opposition, has in its broad outlines an Horatian movement, but Pope does not make us feel strongly the underlying concern of Horace's poem, the desire to find the good life. Pope's animus is more obviously directed 'against something', particularly against the feverish pursuit of wealth that Horace also deplores and that becomes the central motif in the pictures of 'Old England' in the later satires. Horace's mild if damning inventory of the pursuits of the *populus Romanus* is turned into the kind of tom-tom assault typical of Pope when he is going at full force:

> The rest, some farm the Poor-box, some the Pews;
> Some keep Assemblies, and wou'd keep the Stews;
> Some with fat Bucks on childless Dotards fawn;
> Some win rich Widows by their Chine and Brawn;

> While with the silent growth of ten per Cent,
> In Dirt and darkness hundreds stink content.
>
> (128–33)

In the last couplet—which Ezra Pound might envy—Pope realizes with horrid and truthful vividness the picture compressed in Horace's *multis occulto crescit res faenore*.

After such knowledge, pretence to Horatian good temper could only be shrewdly ironic: the *Epilogue to the Satires* was first called *One Thousand Seven Hundred and Thirty Eight. A Dialogue Something like Horace.* Spelling out the date drew attention to the year that saw the end of the Patriots' effort to return to power. 'Horace', we hear the Friend say in *Dialogue* I, 'was delicate, was nice'; but Pope is too exasperated to keep within the Horatian role. He referred to *Dialogue* II as his 'Protest', and the tone of his attack is loud and impatient. On a first reading both poems, especially the second, seem too close to biography in a restricted sense, and occasional passages of noble poetry suffer by suddenly coming down to actual cases so insignificant or local that the effect is near to bathos:

> Not so, when diadem'd with Rays divine,
> Touch'd with the Flame that breaks from Virtue's Shrine,
> Her Priestess Muse forbids the Good to dye,
> And ope's the Temple of Eternity;
> There other *Trophies* deck the truly Brave,
> Than such as *Anstis* casts into the Grave;
> Far other *Stars* than * and ** wear,
> And may descend to *Mordington* from *Stair* . . .
>
> (*Dialogue* II. 232–9)

We do not object that Pope uses contemporary examples, but that he makes so little out of them poetically. Consider by contrast his praise of statesmen who were members or supporters of the Opposition:

> Oft in the clear, still Mirrour of Retreat,
> I study'd SHREWSBURY, the wise and great:
> CARLETON's calm Sense, and STANHOPE's noble Flame,
> Compar'd, and knew their gen'rous End the same:
> How pleasing ATTERBURY's softer hour!
> How shin'd the Soul, unconquer'd in the Tow'r!

How can I PULT'NEY, CHESTERFIELD forget,
While *Roman* Spirit charms, and *Attic* Wit:
ARGYLE, the State's whole Thunder born to wield,
And shake alike the Senate and the Field:
Or WYNDHAM, just to Freedom and the Throne,
The Master of our Passions, and his own.

(II. 78–89)

or the tribute to Pelham,

Pleas'd let me own, in *Esher*'s peaceful Grove
(Where *Kent* and Nature vye for PELHAM's Love)
The Scene, the Master, opening to my view,
I sit and dream I see my CRAGS anew!

(*Dialogue* II. 66–69)

In the first passage idiom and allusion impart to these statesmen, not undeservedly, Roman and heroic stature. In the
second, the reference to 'Kent and Nature' and the touches
of the pastoral-descriptive style neatly suggest that Pelham
is one of Pope's ideal country-gentlemen landscapists. In
the course of the *Epilogue* Pope manages to rise from the
occasion with its personalities to the most general and most
eloquent affirmation of the value of satire and to a vision of
Vice triumphant that is anything but local.

The two dialogues are both defences of satirical poetry,
the second more directly and obviously. The question for the
poet as before is how to follow his friend's advice:

Spare then the Person, and expose the Vice.

Pope answers with a fine desperation (a prominent note in
both poems):

P. How Sir! not damn the Sharper, but the Dice?
Come on then Satire! gen'ral, unconfin'd,
Spread thy broad wing, and sowze on all the Kind.
Ye Statesmen, Priests, of one Religion all!
Ye Tradesmen vile, in Army, Court, or Hall!
Ye Rev'rend Atheists!—*F.* Scandal! name them, Who?

(II. 13–18)

Through the Horatian trickery of the dialogue we feel the
frustration of a man who sees and must speak out: 'The
Emperor *has* no clothes!' The argument explores every possible tactic for avoiding particular examples: blaming 'no

Rogues at all', praising friends and virtue, giving 'random
Praise', or damning in advance men as yet uncorrupted.
With great address Pope defends various attacks he has
made, reaching a climax in the 'filthy Simile' for flat-
terers:

> As Hog to Hog in Huts of *Westphaly* . . .
> (II. 172)

The vileness is there because it is necessary, because Pope
like Swift has caught the scent of the subhuman and is sick
with moral disgust. Pope's bitter and proud affirmation comes
as an explosion of anger that has been accumulating in the
course of the poem. It is dramatically right and humanly
justified:

> *Fr.* You're strangely proud.
> 　　　　　　　　　*P* So proud, I am no Slave:⎞
> So impudent, I own myself no Knave:　　　　⎟
> So odd, my Country's Ruin makes me grave.⎠
> Yes, I am proud; I must be proud to see
> Men not afraid of God, afraid of me:
> Safe from the Bar, the Pulpit, and the Throne,
> Yet touch'd and sham'd by *Ridicule* alone.
> 　O sacred Weapon! left for Truth's defence,
> Sole Dread of Folly, Vice, and Insolence!
> To all but Heav'n-directed hands deny'd,
> The Muse may give thee, but the Gods must guide.
> Rev'rent I touch thee! but with honest zeal;
> To rowze the Watchmen of the Publick Weal,
> To Virtue's Work provoke the tardy Hall,
> And goad the Prelate slumb'ring in his Stall.
> (II. 205–19)

The voice is larger than life, eloquent with the ring of a
great tradition, the humanity of Terence's

> Homo sum: humani nil a me alienum puto

and the defensive pride of Horace asserting his accomplishments and comparing his pen to a sword ready to protect
him from attack (*Satires* I. iv and x; II. i, 40, 41). But now
it is Pope and not Horace who seems fully serious. Urbanity
is out of place, and the tone is nearer to that of the prophet
than the civilized conversationalist. A very English voice
breaks through the classic decorum,

> The Muse may give thee, but the Gods must guide.
> Rev'rent I touch thee! but with honest zeal;
> To rowze the Watchmen of the Publick Weal . . .

What the satirist had 'seen' is clear from the first *Dialogue*, a 'Praise of Folly' that anticipates the *Dunciad*. The theme may have been suggested by Horace's 'Damasippus' (*Satires* II. iii), but the mad quality of the irony is more Swiftian than Horatian, with the poet happily embracing the inversion of all values in the Court, the City, and English society generally. Displaying his old versatility, Pope describes this moral topsy-turvydom in many contrasting modes, from the jocular and the elegant to the apocalyptic. At first he seems almost at one with his good-natured interlocutor,

> [*P*]. Come, come, at all I laugh He laughs, no doubt,
> The only diff'rence is, I dare laugh out.
> *F*. Why yes: with *Scripture* still you may be free;
> A Horse-laugh, if you please, at *Honesty* . . .
>
> (*Dialogue* 1. 35–38)

But as the friend drives the point home, the tone becomes more polite and the irony more searing:

> To Vice and Folly to confine the jest,
> Sets half the World, God knows, against the rest;
> Did not the Sneer of more impartial men
> At Sense and Virtue, balance all agen.
>
> (1. 57–60)

For a moment Pope adopts his friend's politeness,

> *P*. Dear Sir, forgive the Prejudice of Youth:

and launches gaily into one of his sweet half-pastoral songs,

> Adieu Distinction, Satire, Warmth, and Truth!
> Come harmless *Characters* that no one hit,
> Come *Henley*'s Oratory, *Osborn*'s Wit!
> The Honey dropping from *Favonio*'s tongue,
> The Flow'rs of *Bubo*, and the Flow of *Y*—*ng*!
> The gracious Dew of Pulpit Eloquence;
> And all the well-whipt Cream of Courtly Sense,
> That first was *H*—*vy*'s, *F*—'s next, and then
> The *S*—*te*'s, and then *H*—*vy*'s once agen.
>
> (1. 63–72)

But in the friend's next reply there is a bitterness that anticipates the last phase of the poem:

> *F.* Why so? if Satire know its Time and Place,
> You still may lash the Greatest—in Disgrace:
> For Merit will by turns forsake them all;
> Would you know when? exactly when they fall.
>
> (1. 87–90)

In the lines that follow, Pope lifts the pastoral strain to a
higher level as he sings of two courtiers wafted to their
proper realm:

> Silent and soft, as Saints remove to Heav'n,
> All Tyes dissolv'd, and ev'ry Sin forgiv'n,
> These, may some gentle, ministerial Wing
> Receive, and place for ever near a King!
> There, where no Passion, Pride, or Shame transport,
> Lull'd with the sweet *Nepenthe* of a Court;
> There, where no Father's, Brother's, Friend's Disgrace
> Once break their Rest, or stir them from their Place;
> But past the Sense of human Miseries,
> All Tears are wip'd for ever from all Eyes;
> No Cheek is known to blush, no Heart to throb,
> Save when they lose a Question, or a Job.
>
> (1. 93–104)

The sanctimonious elevation of tone, the lingering on 'all',
are Miltonic and echo the lines from *Lycidas* imitated earlier
in the *Messiah*,

> There entertain him all the Saints above,
> In solemn troops, and sweet Societies
> That sing, and singing in their glory move,
> And wipe the tears for ever from his eyes.
>
> (178–81)

But even tongue-in-cheek sweetness disappears from the
last great speech of the epistle, which raises the Biblical tone
to the heroic and prophetic:

> *P.* Good Heav'n forbid, that I shou'd blast their Glory,
> Who know how like Whig-Ministers to Tory,
> And when three Sov'reigns dy'd could scarce be vext,
> Consid'ring what a Gracious Prince was next.
> Have I in silent wonder seen such things
> As Pride in Slaves, and Avarice in Kings,

> And at a Peer, or Peeress shall I fret,
> Who starves a Sister, or forswears a Debt?
> *Virtue*, I grant you, is an empty boast;
> But shall the Dignity of *Vice* be lost?
>
> (1. 105–14)

As Pope pursues the bitter logic of his irony, his emphasis is more rhetorical, and the sarcasm becomes a measure of moral despair:

> This, this, my friend, I cannot, must not bear:
> Vice thus abus'd, demands a Nation's care;
> This calls the Church to deprecate our Sin,
> And hurls the Thunder of the Laws on *Gin*.
>
> (1. 127–30)

A similar irony, the dignity of Vice in 'high life', was the theme of 'the Gem and the Flower' lines in *Moral Essay* 1; but there Pope was able to maintain a surface impression of charm and polite amusement. By contrast, the passage on the triumph of Vice in *Dialogue* 1 has a Dantesque quality of dreadful splendour and infernal exultation:

> *Vice* is undone, if she forgets her Birth,
> And stoops from Angels to the Dregs of Earth:
> But 'tis the *Fall* degrades her to a Whore;
> Let *Greatness* own her, and she's mean no more:
> Her Birth, her Beauty, Crowds and Courts confess,
> Chaste Matrons praise her, and grave Bishops bless:
> In golden Chains the willing World she draws,
> And hers the Gospel is, and hers the Laws:
> Mounts the Tribunal, lifts her scarlet head,
> And sees pale Virtue carted in her stead!
> Lo! at the Wheels of her Triumphal Car,
> Old *England*'s Genius, rough with many a Scar,
> Dragg'd in the Dust! his Arms hang idly round,
> His Flag inverted trails along the ground!
> Our Youth, all liv'ry'd o'er with foreign Gold,
> Before her dance; behind her crawl the Old!
> See thronging Millions to the Pagod run,
> And offer Country, Parent, Wife, or Son!
> Hear her black Trumpet thro' the Land proclaim,
> That "Not to be corrupted is the Shame."
> In Soldier, Churchman, Patriot, Man in Pow'r,
> 'Tis Av'rice all, Ambition is no more!

See, all our Nobles begging to be Slaves!
See, all our Fools aspiring to be Knaves!
The Wit of Cheats, the Courage of a Whore,
Are what ten thousand envy and adore.
All, all look up, with reverential Awe,
On Crimes that scape, or triumph o'er the Law:
While Truth, Worth, Wisdom, daily they decry—
"Nothing is Sacred now but Villany."

(141–70)

The moral and satiric power is felt in the rising tempo of the
lines and in the increasing grandeur of pace and sound up
to the blast of 'Not to be corrupted is the Shame'. The
ultimate and complete reduction of decency strikes with
greater intensity because of the sudden focusing of sound
and sight in

Hear her *black* Trumpet thro' the Land proclaim . . .

Pope has prepared for the effect through a telling and
economical piece of allegorical-historical 'painting', with
salient details in striking colour—'golden', 'scarlet', 'pale',
'liv'ry'd o'er with Gold', and 'black'—and with every figure
and gesture sharply drawn.

The passage is rich too in apt reminiscence of other poetic
styles. There is the overall effect of classical-Biblical prophecy
(suggested by the exclamatory rhetoric), which goes back
to the Fourth *Eclogue* and the *Messiah*. There is also the
Spenserian quality of the pictorial allegory, with at least one
image that comes from the book of Revelation:

. . . the great whore that sitteth upon many waters . . .
. . . and I saw a woman sit upon a scarlet coloured beast . . .
And the woman was arrayed in purple and scarlet colour,
and decked with gold and precious stones and pearls, having
a golden cup in her hand . . .

(XVII. 1, 3, 4)

Homer's gold chain is given a new turn, and the 'dragging
of Hector after Achilles' car' is recalled in the picture of
'Old *England*'s Genius' (Pope's *Iliad*, xxii. 500–4). The
image of Vice in 'her Triumphal Car' is a counterpart of
Horace's *Gloria*, his *ventoso Gloria curru* who lures poets to

seek popularity in the theatre, 'who drags all, bound to her glittering car, unknown no less than the well-known':

> sed fulgente trahit constrictos Gloria curru
> non minus ignotos generosis . . .
>
> (*Satires*, I. vi. 23–24)

But in Pope's scene,[1] even ambition is extinct: "'Tis Avr'ice all.'

It is Pope's vision, his power of seeing in both the moral and aesthetic senses of the word, that combines the many reminiscences into a single expression. The prophecy mockingly attributed to Blunt in the *Epistle to Bathurst* has been fulfilled:

> "At length Corruption, like a gen'ral flood,
> "(So long by watchful Ministers withstood)
> "Shall deluge all; and Av'rice creeping on,
> "Spread like a low-born mist, and blot the Sun . . ."
>
> (137–40)

The confident prophecies of *Windsor Forest*—already badly shaken, as we saw in the *Epistle to Augustus*—have now come full circle: the Great Age that begins anew is an age of corruption in state and church, in public and private life. The 'Augustan twilight'—a small event if viewed as the failure of the Tories, the disappointments of Pope and his friends, the death of the men who had created the brief illusion of a new literature and a new culture—has become a timeless image of decline and fall.

---

[1] For further references see Osborn, 'Pope, the Byzantine Empress and Walpole's Whore'.

X

THIS INTELLECTUAL SCENE:
THE TRADITION OF POPE

A Train of Phantoms in wild Order rose,
And, join'd, this Intellectual Scene compose.
(The Temple of Fame)

Yet the panorama of despair
Cannot be the specialty
Of this ecstatic air.
(Wallace Stevens, *Botanist on Alp (No. 1)*)

THE prophecy of the *Epilogue to the Satires* comes in
the *Dunciad* to its almost necessary conclusion, the
blotting out of all intelligence and order in a return
to original darkness and chaos. In the closing lines of Book
IV, political and financial corruption take their place in a
panorama of the decay of public and private morality, learning, and religion. Pope sees the decline as the triumph of
'dullness', or as we might say of mindlessness. Although the
vision of imminent disorder and death fulfils the promise at
the beginning of Book I,

Say how the Goddess bade Britannia sleep,
And pour'd her Spirit o'er the land and deep . . .
(7, 8)

many readers have doubted whether the intervening books
could be seriously regarded as a poetic whole of any sort.
But since in 1743 Pope presented the revised earlier versions
as a single work, it is our business to read the poem he finally
composed, without confusing it with its incredibly complex
history. As always in literary criticism, the unity we find
depends in part on the unity we look for, on the poem we
are reading and trying to grasp. The *Dunciad* in which we
are interested here is the one to which the Fourth Book is a
conclusion, the poem that Pope tried to revise into coherence,
as his numerous changes show. The couplet quoted above,

for example, belongs to the new introduction to the *Dunciad*
added by Pope in 1743.

To think of the special quality of Pope's poetry in the last
book is to think of the Yawn of Dulness and the epilogue to
the poem. But if we are to understand the poetic mode of
these lines and of the whole *Dunciad*, we should begin a
little earlier, with the charge of the Queen to her subjects:

> Then blessing all, "Go Children of my care!
> To Practice now from Theory repair.
> All my commands are easy, short, and full:
> My Sons! be proud, be selfish, and be dull.
> Guard my Prerogative, assert my Throne:
> This Nod confirms each Privilege your own.
> The Cap and Switch be sacred to his Grace;
> With Staff and Pumps the Marquis lead the Race;
> From Stage to Stage the licens'd Earl may run,
> Pair'd with his Fellow-Charioteer the Sun;
> The learned Baron Butterflies design,
> Or draw to silk Arachne's subtile line;
> The Judge to dance his brother Sergeant call;
> The Senator at Cricket urge the Ball;
> The Bishop stow (Pontific Luxury!)
> An hundred Souls of Turkeys in a pye;
> The sturdy Squire to Gallic masters stoop,
> And drown his Lands and Manors in a Soupe.
> Others import yet nobler arts from France,
> Teach Kings to fiddle, and make Senates dance.
> Perhaps more high some daring son may soar,
> Proud to my list to add one Monarch more;
> And nobly conscious, Princes are but things
> Born for First Ministers, as Slaves for Kings,
> Tyrant supreme! shall three Estates command,
> And MAKE ONE MIGHTY DUNCIAD OF THE LAND!"
>
> (579–604)

This passage, written in a strain fairly characteristic of the
Dunciad, is a kind of fantastic *mélange* in which orders of
being and behaviour combine in a pattern of superficially
rigorous logic and rhythm. At first we seem to be proceeding
in a quite systematic way through various degrees of society,
past dukes, marquises, earls, judges, senators, bishops, kings,
each like an epic hero provided with a special function and an

appropriate symbol. But the order has the perverse regularity of *Alice in Wonderland*, where the symbols of office and the actions of kings, queens, and duchesses are conventionally wrong and yet actually right since they fit the well-known unregal behaviour of actual noble persons. Absurdities such as earls who drive mail coaches and barons who try to spin silk from spiders, or bishops who 'stow an hundred Turkeys in a Pye', do exist, Pope is saying, and he gives notes to support most of his examples. But in the poetic 'reporting' the factual details are given strange and wonderful twists through imagery and rhythmic surprises. The 'licens'd Earl', having been exalted to the level of Hyperion, is 'all at once let down' by the exaggeration of a final monosyllable:

> Pair'd with his Fellow-Charioteer the Sun . . .

(This seems to be bathos by hypsos!) Spinning spiders' silk sounds like the most charming of occupations in the liquid and sibilant flow of

> Or draw to silk Arachne's subtile line . . .

A few lines later, when the metre seems to be freezing into a mechanical swing, a magniloquent aside and enjambement comically break the pattern:

> The Bishop stow (Pontific Luxury!)
> An hundred Souls of Turkeys in a pye . . .

The sacrilegious solemnity of 'an hundred *souls*'—both nicely right and wrong—is another piece of logical topsy-turvy-dom, while 'fiddling Kings' and 'dancing Senates' prepare us for a 'First Minister' who overturns the constitution and commands all 'three Estates'. The social confusion, implying worse moral and intellectual disorders, is pictured as a kind of fancy-dress ball of all the best people, their antics dignified by heroic and religious associations and made delightful by imagery and rhythms subtly poised between rigidity and freedom.

This joyous preview of a land become 'ONE MIGHTY DUNCIAD' is the imaginative 'platform' for Pope's magnificent epic joke, the Yawn of Dulness:

> More she had spoke, but yawn'd—All Nature nods:
> What Mortal can resist the Yawn of Gods?

Churches and Chapels instantly it reach'd;
(St. James's first, for leaden Gilbert preach'd)
Then catch'd the Schools; the Hall scarce kept awake;
The Convocation gap'd, but could not speak:
Lost was the Nation's Sense, nor could be found,
While the long solemn Unison went round:
Wide, and more wide, it spread o'er all the realm;
Ev'n Palinurus nodded at the Helm:
The Vapour mild o'er each Committee crept;
Unfinish'd Treaties in each Office slept;
And Chiefless Armies doz'd out the Campaign;
And Navies yawn'd for Orders on the Main.

(605–18)

If we remember Homer, the burlesque is of course tremendous. But Pope gets a positive force from the image
which sets the passage above mechanical mock-epic and the
easy laughter that Dryden deplored in *Hudibras*. Exactly as
in Dryden (whose influence is often very strong in the *Dunciad*), magniloquence of tone and largeness of rhythm raise
mockery to epic seriousness. Like Dryden and 'his master'
Virgil, Pope moves easily through a long verse paragraph,
pausing for asides and rhetorical questions, building up
sonorities through assonance and repetition. (Sound without
sense becomes a kind of metaphor in the *Dunciad*, as many
finely resonant passages will show.) But whatever his models
may have been, the mastery, especially the artful interweaving of imagery and metrical pattern, is all Pope's. As the
images become increasingly soporific, pauses increase and
the pace slows down to the expected full stop,

And Chiefless Armies doz'd out the Campaign;
And Navies yawn'd for Orders on the Main.

We get a distinct sense of the half-comic somnolence of the
eighteenth-century governmental machine, as the vista opens
into a world well beyond the actual, a realm beautifully described by F. R. Leavis: 'The "Chiefless Armies" doze in an
immensely fantastic dream-comedy, and the Navies yawn
vastly on an enchanted sea.'[1]

Movement and tone and the immensity of the scene
make it easy to bring in Palinurus and address the Muse in

[1] F. R. Leavis, *Revaluation* (London, 1949: first published, 1936), p. 88.

language echoing both the *Aeneid* and the *Iliad*. For a moment Pope seems to be launching on an epic catalogue like Dryden's in *Absalom and Achitophel*:

> O Muse! relate (for you can tell alone,
> Wits have short Memories, and Dunces none)
> Relate, who first, who last resign'd to rest;
> Whose Heads she partly, whose completely blest;
> What Charms could Faction, what Ambition lull,
> The Venal quiet, and intrance the Dull;
> 'Till drown'd was Sense, and Shame, and Right, and Wrong—
> O sing, and hush the Nations with thy Song!
>
> (619–26)

As the epic address turns into a lullaby so potent that even the Muse succumbs, we are almost beguiled into believing that complete damnation is harmless and desirable. The joke is introduced with a kind of punning wit not uncommon in the *Dunciad*:[1]

> In vain, in vain,—the all-composing Hour
> Resistless falls: The Muse obeys the Pow'r.
>
> (627–8)

The poetic hour that should harmonize ('compose') all 'Heads' through song, puts everyone to sleep. But the poet himself is terribly awake, ready to see well beyond the present moment:

> She comes! she comes! the sable Throne behold
> Of *Night* Primaeval, and of *Chaos* old!
> Before her, *Fancy*'s gilded clouds decay,
> And all its varying Rain-bows die away.
> *Wit* shoots in vain its momentary fires,
> The meteor drops, and in a flash expires.
> As one by one, at dread Medea's strain,
> The sick'ning stars fade off th' ethereal plain;
> As Argus' eyes by Hermes' wand opprest,
> Clos'd one by one to everlasting rest;
> Thus at her felt approach, and secret might,
> *Art* after *Art* goes out, and all is Night.
> See skulking *Truth* to her old Cavern fled,
> Mountains of Casuistry heap'd o'er her head!
> *Philosophy*, that lean'd on Heav'n before,
> Shrinks to her second cause, and is no more.

---

[1] On Pope's puns, see Leavis, pp. 96–100.

Physic of *Metaphysic* begs defence,
And *Metaphysic* calls for aid on *Sense*!
See *Mystery* to *Mathematics* fly!
In vain! they gaze, turn giddy, rave, and die.
Religion blushing veils her sacred fires,
And unawares *Morality* expires.
Nor *public* Flame, nor *private*, dares to shine;
Nor *human* Spark is left, nor Glimpse *divine*!
Lo! thy dread Empire, C H A O S! is restor'd;
Light dies before thy uncreating word:
Thy hand, great Anarch! lets the curtain fall;
And Universal Darkness buries All.

(629–56)

Although the 'dread empire' is all but restored, the tone of the epilogue remains prophetic and visionary. The first line in the 1729 version of the passage alluded—almost inevitably, we now may feel—to the Fourth *Eclogue*:

"Signs following signs lead on the Mighty Year . . ."
(III (A), 335)
magnus ab integro saeclorum nascitur ordo.

This line came soon after another allusion to the Great Year of Plato that also echoed Virgil's poem:

"Proceed great days! till Learning fly the shore . . ."
(III (A), 329)
. . . et incipient magni procedere menses . . .

But the prophetic in Pope is almost always composed of several styles. From the allusion to Virgil, we expect the heroic, and in typical fashion Pope parodies his own heroic manner. The original of 'She comes! she comes!' appears in a couplet describing Achilles:

For lo! he comes, with unresisted Sway;
He comes, and Desolation marks his Way!
(*Iliad* xxi. 624–5)·

The heroic for Pope is also Miltonic, and much of the conclusion, as Aubrey Williams[1] has shown, depends on

[1] Aubrey L. Williams, *Pope's 'Dunciad'* (London, 1955), pp. 139–41; see footnotes to p. 139.

Miltonic themes of 'chaos', and 'night', and their association with evil and non-being. The throne of Dulness recalls

> the Throne
> Of *Chaos*, and his dark Pavilion spred
> Wide on the wasteful Deep; with him Enthron'd
> Sat Sable-vested *Night*, eldest of things . . .
> (*Paradise Lost*, ii. 959–62)

But 'sable' also suits very well the dark-light imagery of the whole scene, with its pictorial contrasts between the night sky and 'gilded clouds', 'varying Rainbows', and flashing or fading stars. The astronomical metaphors lend a sense of nightmarish confusion to the apocalypse, as if the death of fancy and wit and of the arts and sciences had a real con-nexion with disturbances in the cosmos. The degeneration of learning becomes a mad ballet of half-human forms that 'turn giddy, rave, and die'. In the final lines Virgilian and Biblical prophetic themes and styles coalesce in a parody of *Fiat lux*:

> Lo! thy dread Empire, C h a o s! is restor'd:
> Light dies before thy uncreating word . . .

The promise of life and growth in the myths of the Golden Age and the Garden of Eden is fulfilled in sterility and death.

The poetic mode through which Pope expresses this re-versal is not a style belonging to some single tradition or genre, but a fresh fusion of several styles into a complex in-strument of vision and expression. The greatness and beauty of the mode lies in its 'embrace', the imaginative excitement of the Fourth Book coming in large part from our sense of Pope's complete adequacy to his subject, his power of com-posing an ideal order from the 'phantoms' of dullness. Though there are many signs of styles used in earlier works —the heroic and the prophetic, the pictorial and pastoral, the charmingly fanciful and the madly fantastic—the lines be-tween the styles are constantly dissolving, and transitions are even less perceptible than in the *Moral Essays*. If Pope had written the whole of the *Dunciad* in a mode of such com-plexity and such inclusive moral and intellectual implication, he would indeed have produced an ironic 'long poem'—epic seems hardly the term—that might rank with *Paradise Lost* in integrity of vision and design. And there are enough traces of this poem in earlier books to tempt us into believing that he really succeeded.

In the first and third books, anticipations of the complex later mode are many and obvious. In Book I they are especially well woven into the series of speeches and scenes, more pictorial than dramatic, that Pope makes do for narrative. (We recall in his *Iliad* how pictorial effect dominates over action.) After 'the Proposition, the Invocation, and the Inscription', passages that remind us in turn of Virgil, Milton, and Horace, we are shown the cavern of Dulness and her 'wild creation', a scene followed soon by a more elaborate picture of her hero-poet Cibber sitting 'pensive among his Books'. Presently he makes a sacrifice to his patroness, invoking her aid in a prayer of truly epic length. 'Great in her charms', the Queen flies to his call and leads the hero to her 'sacred Dome' where he is proclaimed laureate in an encomium echoed throughout London.

In the 'Proposition' that Pope wrote for the 1743 version to prepare for replacing Theobald by Cibber and the final triumph of Dulness, we hear at once the exalted tone and Miltonic rhythm of Book IV:

> The Mighty Mother, and her Son who brings
> The Smithfield Muses to the ear of Kings,
> I sing. Say you, her instruments the Great!
> Call'd to this work by Dulness, Jove, and Fate;
> You by whose care, in vain decry'd and curst,
> Still Dunce the second reigns like Dunce the first;
> Say how the Goddess bade Britannia sleep,
> And pour'd her Spirit o'er the land and deep.
>
> (I. 1–8)

Note the Miltonic imbalance of rhythm and the strong pause in the third line. In comparison with this opening, the first couplet in the 1729 version is a piece of machine-made mock-epic:

> Books and the Man I sing, the first who brings
> The Smithfield Muses to the Ear of Kings.

The Miltonic themes of the last book are anticipated im-

mediately in a passage common to both the earlier and final
versions:

> In eldest time, e'er mortals writ or read,
> E'er Pallas issu'd from the Thund'rer's head,
> Dulness o'er all possess'd her ancient right,
> Daughter of Chaos and eternal Night:
> Fate in their dotage this fair Ideot gave,
> Gross as her sire, and as her mother grave,
> Laborious, heavy, busy, bold, and blind,
> She rul'd, in native Anarchy, the mind. (9–16)

Dryden is present in the distinct echo of the first lines of
Absalom and Achitophel,

> In pious times, ere priestcraft did begin,
> Before polygamy was made a sin . . .

and Pope's 'fair Ideot' is related to the jolly numskull of
Cymon and Iphigenia:

> Fair, tall, his limbs with due proportion join'd,
> But of a heavy, dull, degenerate mind.
>
> (52–53)

The 'rude chaos' of Cymon's mind in its 'native night', and
his so-called processes of thought, were described by Dryden
in Cibberian imagery:

> The more inform'd, the less he understood,
> And deeper sunk by flound'ring in the mud.
>
> (63–64)

Cibber is seen

> Sinking from thought to thought, a vast profound!
> Plung'd for his sense, but found no bottom there,
> Yet wrote and flounder'd on, in mere despair.
>
> (118–20)

The Miltonic manner of the *Dunciad* combines easily with
the gusty humour of Dryden, and is quite unlike the solemn
eighteenth-century Miltonic of Thomson and his successors.
Transition to parody of Metaphysical wit is accordingly not
difficult, as in the lines describing the Queen's 'wild creation':

> Here she beholds the Chaos dark and deep,
> Where nameless Somethings in their causes sleep,
> 'Till genial Jacob, or a warm Third day,
> Call forth each mass, a Poem, or a Play:

How hints, like spawn, scarce quick in embryo lie,
How new-born nonsense first is taught to cry,
Maggots half-form'd in rhyme exactly meet,
And learn to crawl upon poetic feet.
Here one poor word an hundred clenches makes,
And ductile dulness new meanders takes;
There motley Images her fancy strike,
Figures ill pair'd, and Similies unlike.
She sees a Mob of Metaphors advance,
Pleas'd with the madness of the mazy dance:
How Tragedy and Comedy embrace;
How Farce and Epic get a jumbled race;
How Time himself stands still at her command,
Realms shift their place, and Ocean turns to land.
Here gay Description Ægypt glads with show'rs,
Or gives to Zembla fruits, to Barca flow'rs;
Glitt'ring with ice here hoary hills are seen,
There painted vallies of eternal green,
In cold December fragrant chaplets blow,
And heavy harvests nod beneath the snow.   (55–78)

In the 'madness of the mazy dance', Pope gives us our first taste of the *mélange*-fantasy of the epilogue and of many later scenes in the poem. The concluding lines of the passage are a paradoxical parody of Pope's early style where 'pure Description held the place of Sense'. Although the landscape is decidedly surrealist, the charm of the images and the musical delight of the verse lull us (as in the *Pastorals*) into accepting the absurd and the impossible. The language of the dance is especially worth noting: 'nameless Somethings', 'spawn', 'maggots half-form'd', 'meanders', 'a Mob', and 'a jumbled race'. Hints of confusion and abortion point to the metaphorical centre of the poem in the pervading image of chaos, 'the mighty maze without a plan', which stands in contrast to the Great Order of Nature. The 'maze' of the *Dunciad* is constantly associated with muddledom and abuse of mind, the result of too much education of the kind described in the *Essay on Criticism*:

So by false learning is good sense defaced:
Some are bewildered in the maze of schools,
And some made coxcombs Nature meant but fools.
                                    (25–27)

The theme and the metaphor flower in unexpected forms in later passages:

> Or quite unravel all the reas'ning thread,
> And hang some curious cobweb in its stead!
>
> (I. 179–80)

> The mind, in Metaphysics at a loss,
> May wander in a wilderness of Moss . . .
>
> (IV. 449–50)

The 'uncreating' process of Cibber's plunging intellect is symbolized in another passage of fanciful disorder:

> Round him much Embryo, much Abortion lay,
> Much future Ode, and abdicated Play;
> Nonsense precipitate, like running Lead,
> That slip'd thro' Cracks and Zig-zags of the Head;
> All that on Folly Frenzy could beget,
> Fruits of dull Heat, and Sooterkins of Wit.
>
> (I. 121–6)

The *disiecta membra* of the poets Cibber has 'plundered'

> And suck'd all o'er, like an industrious Bug . . .
>
> (130)

are part of

> A Gothic Library! of Greece and Rome
> Well purg'd, and worthy Settle, Banks, and Broome.
>
> (145–6)

The description of the library (not at all appropriate to the actual Cibber) gives us the first of the historic vistas that complement the prophecies of the poem. As in the *Essay on Criticism* and the satires, they accentuate the barbarous state of learning in eras not illuminated by the Graeco-Roman tradition.

The hero's prayer with its epic address, 'Great Tamer of all human art!' anticipates many solemn petitions of later scenes. But the prayers, like the poet's address to his Muse at the end of Book IV, are always being 'confused' by witty deviations. Cibber's sacrifice recalls the Baron's in the *Rape of the Lock*, and his plea for witlessness is a parody of conceits Pope had used when improving Wycherley's *A Panegyrick on Dulness*:

> "O thou! of Bus'ness the directing soul!
> To this our head like byass to the bowl,
> Which, as more pond'rous, made its aim more true,
> Obliquely wadling to the mark in view . . .
>
> (169–72)

> As, forc'd from wind-guns, lead itself can fly,
> And pond'rous slugs cut swiftly thro the sky;
> As clocks to weight their nimble motion owe,
> The wheels above urg'd by the load below:
> Me Emptiness, and Dulness could inspire,
> And were my Elasticity, and Fire."
>
> (181–6)

Dryden's toughness comes again to the fore, but the crowning lines in each conceit are in Pope's best Metaphysical style. We can feel the gaucherie of that 'mind' in its rolling ducklike progress, and the perverse bounce of its ineptitudes.

The prayer ends with a hushed, lulling strophe of a kind Pope uses with beautifully soporific effect at other points in the *Dunciad*. (We have here another similarity to the prayer to the Muse of Book IV.) As the hero's works ascend in flames to the sky, he tearfully sings:

> "O! pass more innocent, in infant state,
> To the mild Limbo of our Father Tate:
> Or peaceably forgot, at once be blest
> In Shadwell's bosom with eternal Rest!
> Soon to that mass of Nonsense to return,
> Where things destroy'd are swept to things unborn."
>
> (237–42)

The goddess, appearing with the cloudy magnificence and awful look of Venus coming to Aeneas, now takes her favourite to 'her sacred dome'. The description of her works is a blurred fantastic dance:

> Here to her Chosen all her works she shews;
> Prose swell'd to verse, verse loit'ring into prose:
> How random thoughts now meaning chance to find,
> Now leave all memory of sense behind:
> How Prologues into Prefaces decay,
> And these to Notes are fritter'd quite away:

How Index-learning turns no student pale,
Yet holds the eel of science by the tail . . .
(273–80)

The Queen addresses the laureate with a Virgilian salute to the new era:

. . . "All hail! and hail again,
My son! the promis'd land expects thy reign."
(291–2)

But the semi-epic Biblical address turns into an unseemly romp, the first of the resounding songs of the *Dunciad*:

"Lift up your gates, ye Princes, see him come!
Sound, sound ye Viols, be the Cat-call dumb!
Bring, bring the madding Bay, the drunken Vine;
The creeping, dirty, courtly Ivy join."
(301–4)

Within a few lines, a prophetic prayer gently modulates into a true lullaby, heroically grand and yet grotesque:

"O! when shall rise a Monarch all our own,
And I, a Nursing-mother, rock the throne,
'Twixt Prince and People close the Curtain draw,
Shade him from Light, and cover him from Law;
Fatten the Courtier, starve the learned band,
And suckle Armies, and dry-nurse the land:
'Till Senates nod to Lullabies divine,
And all be sleep, as at an Ode of thine."
(311–18)

The book ends with rolling echoes of ' "God save king Cibber!" ' that degenerate into burlesque Jovian thunder and the croaking of frogs. The Queen's lullaby and its batrachian echo bring to a close an appropriate first book for a poem that will conclude with the apocalypse of Book IV. We see everything as epically grand and yet in cloudy confusion, with 'momentary monsters rising and falling' in mazy dances and songs. Prayers seem to point to some far-off divine event to which this 'wild creation' moves, and revelations are punctured by wit or damped in soporific melody. Soon, we feel, everything will like Cibber's works return to 'that mass of Nonsense',

Where things destroy'd are swept to things unborn.

Readers familiar with the 1728 and 1729 versions of the *Dunciad* are aware that the verse just quoted, along with the Queen's lullaby and a number of passages closest to the poetry of *Dunciad* IV, are additions made by Pope in 1743. But other passages equally in key with the last book, such as the lines on 'Chaos and eternal Night' or the dance of motley poetic images, belong also to the 1728 version. Pope, we might say, found in *The New Dunciad* the poem he had been half-consciously writing 'toward' for some ten or fifteen years. In 1743 he attempted to bring this poem to light, though with results that are far from perfect. The revision of Book I is by and large very successful. Local hits at now forgotten writers and their works do not for long keep us from seeing the 'Greater *Dunciad*' in the lesser.

No one can speak so cheerfully of Book II, the 'Games' of the authors, which is a piece of deliberate Scriblerian burlesque. Aeneas' lament before the pictured story of Troy becomes:

> "And oh! (he cry'd) what street, what lane but knows,
> Our purgings, pumpings, blankettings, and blows?
> In ev'ry loom our labours shall be seen,
> And the fresh vomit run for ever green!"
>
> (153-6)

This is crudely comic and undoubtedly appropriate to the victims, but unlike Pope's subtler parodies it hardly gives us a truly heroic measure of the little world of the poem, or a sense of a more complex evaluation of any sort. But there are scattered passages, especially near the beginning and the end, where the poetic mode of the better poem comes in view. The opening scene with its splendid evocation of *Paradise Lost* ('High on a gorgeous seat . . .') and its metamorphosis of the vile into something rich and strange, is equal to the best pieces of grotesque 'heroic painting' in the first and last books. The summoning of the sons of Dulness is one of those 'motley mixtures' that we find in almost every great scene of the poem:

> They summon all her Race: An endless band
> Pours forth, and leaves unpeopled half the land.

A motley mixture! in long wigs, in bags,
In silks, in crapes, in Garters, and in rags,
From drawing rooms, from colleges, from garrets,
On horse, on foot, in hacks, and gilded chariots:
All who true Dunces in her cause appear'd,
And all who knew those Dunces to reward.   (19–26)

The picture of 'shameless Curl's' display could pass in
another context for one of Pope's descriptions in baroque
sculptural style:

                    . . . impetuous spread
The stream, and smoking flourish'd o'er his head.
So (fam'd like thee for turbulence and horns)
Eridanus his humble fountain scorns;
Thro' half the heav'ns he pours th' exalted urn;
His rapid waters in their passage burn.

                            (179–84)

We find much of the same dreadful grandeur in the diving
scenes, passages that have the true 'Dunciad' character.
Images combine monstrosity with moral outrage, and yet remain splendid; diction and rhythm are majestic in Dryden's
Virgilian epic manner (note especially the line endings:
'precipitately dull', 'gravitation blest'), and the wit con-
centrates in puns that are weighty yet elegant: 'the plunging
Prelate'. The total effect is grandly comic:

        Not so bold Arnall; with a weight of skull,
    Furious he dives, precipitately dull.
    Whirlpools and storms his circling arm invest,
    With all the might of gravitation blest.
    No crab more active in the dirty dance,
    Downward to climb, and backward to advance.
    He brings up half the bottom on his head,
    And loudly claims the Journals and the Lead.
        The plunging Prelate, and his pond'rous Grace,
    With holy envy gave one Layman place.
    When lo! a burst of thunder shook the flood.
    Slow rose a form, in majesty of Mud;
    Shaking the horrors of his sable brows,
    And each ferocious feature grim with ooze.
    Greater he looks, and more than mortal stares:
    Then thus the wonders of the deep declares.

                            (315–30)

Another diving episode ends with a couplet of Keatsian serenity:

> No noise, no stir, no motion can'st thou make,
> Th' unconscious stream sleeps o'er thee like a lake.
>
> (303–4)

There is also a brilliant passage in which sounds of actual names and terms in logic produce noisy and oddly charming nonsense:

> Now thousand tongues are heard in one loud din:
> The Monkey-mimics rush discordant in;
> 'Twas chatt'ring, grinning, mouthing, jabb'ring all,
> And Noise and Norton, Brangling and Breval,
> Dennis and Dissonance, and captious Art,
> And Snip-snap short, and Interruption smart,
> And Demonstration thin, and Theses thick,
> And Major, Minor, and Conclusion quick.
>
> (235–42)

There are some beautiful lines of melodiously drowsy song in the contest that closes like others with 'the soft gifts of Sleep':

> The clam'rous crowd is hush'd with mugs of Mum,
> 'Till all tun'd equal, send a gen'ral hum.
> Then mount the Clerks, and in one lazy tone
> Thro' the long, heavy, painful page drawl on;
> Soft creeping, words on words, the sense compose,
> At ev'ry line they stretch, they yawn, they doze.
> As to soft gales top-heavy pines bow low
> Their heads, and lift them as they cease to blow:
> Thus oft they rear, and oft the head decline,
> As breathe, or pause, by fits, the airs divine.
> And now to this side, now to that they nod,
> As verse, or prose, infuse the drowzy God.
>
> (385–96)

The richness of texture here depends on familiar arts—the parody of pastoral and descriptive-heroic styles (of Virgil, Ovid, Milton, and Pope himself), the apt use of assonance and rhyme to create sleepy Spenserian effects, and the fine harmonizing of image and rhythm, all beautifully illustrated in

> As to soft gales top-heavy pines bow low
> Their heads, and lift them as they cease to blow . . .

The main weakness of Book II is obvious. We find it hard to care about the objects of the satire, in part, as Aubrey Williams suggests, because they are so inadequately dramatized and so little 'present' in the poetry. In part, too, because Pope rarely lifts our attention to the large moral and aesthetic concerns that give dignity and meaning to the satire of Book IV (where, it is worth noting, the characters are more often fictional and symbolic). In the second book Pope suffers the ironic consequence of attacking dullards: he becomes almost as dull and petty as his victims.

With Book III, a Virgilian journey to the underworld, we are again in the 'better' *Dunciad* of grander style and more serious moral scope. The first few lines take us back to the world of Book I of dark mistiness and chaotic intelligence. The rhythm moves forward through longer verse paragraphs, and the language is more exciting to the senses and enriched by allusions to literature and popular fancies:

> But in her Temple's last recess inclos'd,
> On Dulness' lap th' Anointed head repos'd.
> Him close she curtains round with Vapours blue,
> And soft besprinkles with Cimmerian dew.
> Then raptures high the seat of Sense o'erflow,
> Which only heads refin'd from Reason know.
> Hence, from the straw where Bedlam's Prophet nods,
> He hears loud Oracles, and talks with Gods:
> Hence the Fool's Paradise, the Statesman's Scheme,
> The air-built Castle, and the golden Dream,
> The Maid's romantic wish, the Chemist's flame,
> And Poet's vision of eternal Fame.
>
> (1–12)

'The narrow sound of satire' (in W. P. Ker's phrase), which rises from strict parody of epic, widens out into poetry Dantesque in precision of image and suggestiveness:

> Here, in a dusky vale where Lethe rolls,
> Old Bavius sits, to dip poetic souls,
> And blunt the sense, and fit it for a skull
> Of solid proof, impenetrably dull:
> Instant, when dipt, away they wing their flight,
> Where Brown and Mears unbar the gates of Light,

> Demand new bodies, and in Calf's array,
> Rush to the world, impatient for the day.
> Millions and millions on these banks he views,
> Thick as the stars of night, or morning dews,
> As thick as bees o'er vernal blossoms fly,
> As thick as eggs at Ward in Pillory.

(23–34)

A satirical thrust

> and fit it for a skull
> Of solid proof, impenetrably dull . . .

gains in surprise and power from the richness of the poetic context. Vulgar cracks like 'in Calf's array' or 'thick as eggs' become almost splendid in lines alluding to Miltonic and Platonic heavens or Virgilian underworlds where souls gather 'as thick as leaves that fall with the first frost of autumn':

> quam multa in silvis autumni frigore primo
> lapsa cadunt folia . . .
>
> (*Aeneid* VI. 309–10)

The echoes of Pope's earlier poems are as usual significant. We hear again in these lines the solemn prophecy of the *Messiah*,

> See, a long race thy spacious courts adorn;
> See future sons, and daughters yet unborn,
> In crowding ranks on every side arise,
> Demanding life, impatient for the skies!

(87–90)

and the ironic vision of 'ripened' lies in *The Temple of Fame*,

> When thus ripe Lyes are to perfection sprung,
> Full grown, and fit to grace a mortal Tongue,
> Thro thousand Vents, impatient forth they flow,
> And rush in Millions on the World below.

(479–82)

The style of the book is often reminiscent of the *Messiah* and the Virgilian prophecies of *Windsor Forest*, but the 'See's' and 'Behold's' that were liable to misfire in the *Messiah* are now appropriately ambiguous, sufficiently awful but comically exaggerated. Behind the scenes loom two great epic prophecies, the sixth book of the *Aeneid* and the eleventh and twelfth books of *Paradise Lost*. The metaphorical effect is

more powerful because the parallels are not worked out completely, but suggested indirectly and continuously by the
style. As in translating the *Iliad*, Pope does not attempt close
paraphrase, but uses instead the handiest analogue in poetic
tradition, which now includes the tradition of Pope. The
satirical strength of the manner comes out most clearly when
Pope, like Virgil and Milton, uses a prophetic occasion to
extend his drama in space and time:

> "Ascend this hill, whose cloudy point commands
> Her boundless empire over seas and lands.
> See, round the Poles where keener spangles shine,
> Where spices smoke beneath the burning Line,
> (Earth's wide extremes) her sable flag display'd,
> And all the nations cover'd in her shade!
> "Far eastward cast thine eye, from whence the Sun
> And orient Science their bright course begun:
> One god-like Monarch all that pride confounds,
> He, whose long wall the wand'ring Tartar bounds;
> Heav'ns! what a pile! whole ages perish there,
> And one bright blaze turns Learning into air.
> "Thence to the south extend thy gladden'd eyes;
> There rival flames with equal glory rise,
> From shelves to shelves see greedy Vulcan roll,
> And lick up all their Physic of the Soul.
> "How little, mark! that portion of the ball,
> Where, faint at best, the beams of Science fall:
> Soon as they dawn, from Hyperborean skies
> Embody'd dark, what clouds of Vandals rise!
> Lo! where Maeotis sleeps, and hardly flows
> The freezing Tanais thro' a waste of snows,
> The North by myriads pours her mighty sons,
> Great nurse of Goths, of Alans, and of Huns!
> See Alaric's stern port! the martial frame
> Of Genseric! and Attila's dread name!
> See the bold Ostrogoths on Latium fall;
> See the fierce Visigoths on Spain and Gaul!
> See, where the morning gilds the palmy shore
> (The soil that arts and infant letters bore)
> His conqu'ring tribes th' Arabian prophet draws,
> And saving Ignorance enthrones by Laws.
> See Christians, Jews, one heavy sabbath keep,
> And all the western world believe and sleep."
>   (67–100)

The passage is highly characteristic of Popeian description in
the way large pictorial impressions are combined with precise
visual details. Within the vast prospect of the first few lines
'keener spangles shine', 'spices smoke', and earth's 'sable
flag' is 'display'd'. The extensiveness of the scene makes us
feel more powerfully the spreading inertia of mindlessness,
and the fineness of detail assures us of the perceptiveness of
the prophet. Pope—here he has much in common with Yeats
and with Lawrence—can respond to the fascination of Van-
dalism and of sterile northern purity, but his ironic joy is a
sign of sanity and faith in intelligence. Two lines that equal
Donne in compression of wit and in the sensuous 'action' of
the imagery express with beauty and irony ultimate concerns
of the poem:

> And one bright blaze turns Learning into air.
> And lick up all their Physic of the Soul.

The vision of the Middle Ages, like other visions in the
poem, comes to a close in sleep. In the lines immediately following that 'heavy sabbath', a picture of Roman decay anticipates the scene of Italy's decline in the Grand Tour passage
of Book IV. The later renewal of the ancient world in Renaissance Rome is hinted at through subtly ambiguous contrasts:

> "Lo! Rome herself, proud mistress now no more
> Of arts, but thund'ring against heathen lore;
> Her grey-hair'd Synods damning books unread,
> And Bacon trembling for his brazen head.
> Padua, with sighs, beholds her Livy burn,
> And ev'n th' Antipodes Vigilius mourn.
> See, the Cirque falls, th' unpillar'd Temple nods,
> Streets pav'd with Heroes, Tyber choak'd with Gods:
> 'Till Peter's keys some christ'ned Jove adorn,
> And Pan to Moses lends his pagan horn;
> See graceless Venus to a Virgin turn'd,
> Or Phidias broken, and Apelles burn'd."

(101–12)

This Piranesi-like scene approaches the finest lyric of utter
confusion in the poem, the dance of theatrical wonders revealed to the astonished hero:

> [He] look'd, and saw a sable Sorc'rer rise,
> Swift to whose hand a winged volume flies:

All sudden, Gorgons hiss, and Dragons glare,
And ten-horn'd fiends and Giants rush to war.
Hell rises, Heav'n descends, and dance on Earth:
Gods, imps, and monsters, music, rage, and mirth,
A fire, a jigg, a battle, and a ball,
'Till one wide conflagration swallows all.
 Thence a new world to Nature's laws unknown,
Breaks out refulgent, with a heav'n its own:
Another Cynthia her new journey runs,
And other planets circle other suns.
The forests dance, the rivers upward rise,
Whales sport in woods, and dolphins in the skies;
And last, to give the whole creation grace,
Lo! one vast Egg produces human race.

(233–48)

The poetry of this latter-day Genesis revives the pastoral and cosmological hyperboles of the *Messiah*:

> See lofty Lebanon his head advance,
> See nodding forests on the mountains dance . . .
>
> Sink down ye mountains, and ye valleys rise,
> With heads declined, ye cedars homage pay:
> . Be smooth ye rocks, ye rapid floods give way!

(25–26, 34–36)

> No more the rising Sun shall gild the morn,
> Nor evening Cynthia fill her silver horn;
> But lost, dissolved in thy superior rays,
> One tide of glory, one unclouded blaze
> O'erflow thy courts: the light himself shall shine
> Revealed, and God's eternal day be thine!
> The seas shall waste, the skies in smoke decay,
> Rocks fall to dust, and mountains melt away . . .

(99–106)

Pope describes the god of his theatrical chaos (John Rich) in language reminiscent of Jove and the deity of the Old Testament, the perversion of both Classic and Christian traditions being neatly implied as later in the frolics of the student-Aeneas. The book ends with a Virgilian vision of the Age of Lead, announced by wondrous signs in the heavens, and declining into an exultant song of decay in the arts and learning. The climax comes with a tremendous pun, which is followed by a last reminder that Pope's prophetic book is an

ironic variation on the sixth book of the *Aeneid* and that all
the revelations belong to the world of sleep and false dreams,

> "Proceed, great days! 'till Learning fly the shore,
> 'Till Birch shall blush with noble blood no more,
> 'Till Thames see Eaton's sons for ever play,
> 'Till Westminster's whole year be holiday,
> 'Till Isis' Elders reel, their pupils' sport,
> And Alma mater lie dissolv'd in Port!"
>   "Enough! enough!" the raptur'd Monarch cries;
> And thro' the Iv'ry Gate the Vision flies.

$$(333-40)$$

We need hardly 'prove' that the poetic mode we have been
tracing in earlier books is dominant in Book IV. *The New
Dunciad*, as it was first called, is permeated with the 'felt
approach' of darkness and disorder, the parade of dunces
coming to fulfil the prophecies of the preceding book:

> Yet, yet a moment, one dim Ray of Light
> Indulge, dread Chaos, and eternal Night!
> Of darkness visible so much be lent,
> As half to shew, half veil the deep Intent.
> Ye Pow'rs! whose Mysteries restor'd I sing,
> To whom Time bears me on his rapid wing,
> Suspend a while your Force inertly strong,
> Then take at once the Poet and the Song. $(1-8)$

The bard's prophetic prayer, in which Miltonic grandeur is
barely ruffled by urbane absurdities, sets the tone for the
book. Many speeches of the Goddess and her creatures take
the form of ironic prayers or joyful glimpses into the future,
from the spirit of opera's revelation,

> One Trill shall harmonize joy, grief, and rage,
> Wake the dull Church, and lull the ranting Stage . . .

$$(57-58)$$

to the Queen's happy cry,

> "Oh (cry'd the Goddess) for some pedant Reign!
> Some gentle J A M E s, to bless the land again . . ."

$$(175-6)$$

and the forger's petition,

> "O may thy cloud still cover the deceit!
> Thy choicer mists on this assembly shed,
> But pour them thickest on the noble head.

So shall each youth, assisted by our eyes,
See other Caesars, other Homers rise;
Thro' twilight ages hunt th' Athenian fowl,
Which Chalcis Gods, and mortals call an Owl,
Now see an Attys, now a Cecrops clear,
Nay, Mahomet! the Pigeon at thine ear;
Be rich in ancient brass, tho' not in gold,
And keep his Lares, tho' his house be sold;
To headless Phoebe his fair bride postpone,
Honour a Syrian Prince above his own;
Lord of an Otho, if I vouch it true;
Blest in one Niger, till he knows of two."
                                        (356–70)

The scenes of the book, like the scenes in this pedant's prayer, are constantly being extended into the past by learned reference and epic allusion, and the misty darkness of Dulness's 'other Kingdom' appears in many speeches and descriptions, especially in the huddled processions and confused dances of the Queen and her followers. One example shows supremely how Pope combines the grotesque with epic magnificence and picturesque 'georgic' song:

And now had Fame's posterior Trumpet blown,
And all the Nations summon'd to the Throne.
The young, the old, who feel her inward sway,
One instinct seizes, and transports away.
None need a guide, by sure Attraction led,
And strong impulsive gravity of Head:
None want a place, for all their Centre found,
Hung to the Goddess, and coher'd around.
Not closer, orb in orb, conglob'd are seen
The buzzing Bees about their dusky Queen.
                                        (71–80)

Another processional scene closes with a Spenserian lullaby and a second version of the pun which graced the final prophecy of Book III:

Prompt at the call, around the Goddess roll
Broad hats, and hoods, and caps, a sable shoal:
Thick and more thick the black blockade extends,
A hundred head of Aristotle's friends.
Nor wert thou, Isis! wanting to the day,
[Tho' Christ-church long kept prudishly away.]

> Each staunch Polemic, stubborn as a rock,
> Each fierce Logician, still expelling Locke,
> Came whip and spur, and dash'd thro' thin and thick
> On German Crouzaz, and Dutch Burgersdyck.
> As many quit the streams that murm'ring fall
> To lull the sons of Marg'ret and Clare-hall,
> Where Bentley late tempestuous wont to sport
> In troubled waters, but now sleeps in Port.
>
> (189–202)

In imagery and rhythm these passages have the proper grandeur for a poem which has the scope of scene and underlying seriousness of 'true Heroick poetry'. What is novel in the Fourth Book—and in parts of earlier books that resemble it most—is greatness of subject. Pope sees the human drama, absurd and miserable as it is, against the 'huge scenic background of the stars', and his feeling of the connexion between human folly and larger orders and disorders is religious in a quite primitive sense. The heroic—the anti-mask of dullness —is present constantly in the Miltonic tone and in allusions to Virgil and Homer and their successors. Though the Fourth Book is a kind of witty 'panorama of despair', the underlying assumptions and acceptances are exactly those of Pope's *Iliad*. Both the poem and the translation depend on a belief that the essence of divinity and nature is order, that civilization and order are one. Book IV is the poem of a man acutely sensitive to disorder in a work of art, a life, a society. Pope has had his glimpse into chaos, and he now gives more convincing testimony to his sensitivity and his beliefs than in the tranquil and more facile salutes to the universe of the *Essay on Man*. E. M. Forster's comment on Mrs. Moore's state of mind before hearing the echo is apropos:

Mrs. Moore had always inclined to resignation. As soon as she landed in India it seemed to her good, and when she saw the water flowing through the mosque-tank, or the Ganges, or the moon, caught in the shawl of night with all the other stars, it seemed a beautiful goal and an easy one. To be one with the universe! So dignified and simple.

(*A Passage to India*)

But if Pope's second epic of the mind is full of echoing madness, the madness is controlled and clearly expressed, and if there are hints of anarchy in the universe and in society, there is no anarchy in the poetry. With the Fourth Book of the *Dunciad* Pope returns surely to the central theme of all his poetry—intelligence—or to use his own terms, 'good sense' and 'right reason'. The main concern behind the Fourth Book is with man knowing himself and his world. Hence the exasperation felt when man substitutes antiquarianism, touring, logic-chopping, or virtuoso science for humane knowledge. We must remember that Pope was ridiculing amateurs who 'wandered in a wilderness of moss', not Newton; fashionable coin collectors, not historians of the order of Gibbon. If he was unjust to Bentley, it should be said in Pope's defence that the Bentley of his imagination, dealing only in grammatical minutiae, has haunted the classroom and the textbook ever since. Pope is asking for an education in life, not words.

With his delight in the absurd and his sure sense of musical form, Pope created in the Fourth Book no mock-*Iliad* or mock-*Paradise Lost*, but something new, an epic fantasia, a series of free variations on the Miltonic theme of 'right reason obscured'. Though he usually starts from a hint of the heroic, he plays lightly with epic conventions and style and often goes off on a flight of fancy that is truly charming or beautifully grotesque, yet satirically apt. The exploits of the travelling student become an agreeable saunter through a pastoral world of utter decadence; the pursuit of knowledge (civilized substitute for the hero's pursuit of an enemy) turns into a sylph-like chase of a butterfly: a school-master ('the Genius of the place') rises 'a Spectre . . . dropping with Infant's blood' like Milton's Moloch, only to utter a jingle worthy of an inspired Gradgrind:

> "Plac'd at the door of Learning, youth to guide,
> We never suffer it to stand too wide.
> To ask, to guess, to know, as they commence,
> As Fancy opens the quick springs of Sense.
> We ply the Memory, we load the brain,
> Bind rebel Wit, and double chain on chain,
> Confine the thought, to exercise the breath;
> And keep them in the pale of Words till death."
> (153–60)

In general the parallels to epic inductions, speeches, and

catalogues of heroes and their deeds are of the vaguest sort. The heroic quality like the fantastic is not produced by a literary receipt or by rigorous parody of epic, but by continuous poetic 'hints' of the kind we have been describing in the fourth and earlier books. The Miltonic-prophetic accent, the dark and mazy confusion and the murky vastness of scenes and processions, the soothing and mysteriously infectious songs, and the deft telescoping of wit and image often implying extensive and incisive evaluations, are surer signs than any systematic imitation could give, of heroic seriousness and epic range in the satire of the *Dunciad*. The minute indications of a 'misty' adjective, a prophetic 'See!', a lulling rhyme or a heroic allusion, a fanciful or grotesque image, a characteristic turn of wit, are evidence of felt analogies between experiences and of an integrity of vision that goes well beyond deliberate daylight planning.

It is through these minute indications that the earlier books are linked imaginatively with the fourth and that they take their place in the epic fantasia of the *Dunciad*. When the vision wavers or fails, as it does in much of Book II, then systematic imitation takes over and the language loses the resonance on which poetic unity so largely depends. But even in Book II there are echoes of the monstrous grandeur and the confused or lulling nonsense of the better books. Although various traditional and dramatic patterns have been pointed out in the *Dunciad*, it must be admitted that most of them do not enter continuously into the language of the poem. Aubrey Williams sees 'the action' of the poem as '. . . the removal of the empire of Dulness from the City of London to the polite world, Westminster, just as the action of the "Æneid is the Removal of the empire of *Troy* to *Latium*." In other words, we have the destruction of one empire, in Pope's poem as in Virgil's, and the establishment of another.'[1] The analogy is clear enough in Book I, but there are few signs of it in Books II and III and none at all in Book IV. The 'removal of the empire of Dulness' occupies a minor place on a count of specific references, and the Lord Mayor's procession, on which the action seems to be based, is mentioned sparingly and obscurely. By contrast, the prophetic

[1] Op. cit., pp. 17–18.

quality of Virgilian and Miltonic epic does enter into the texture of the poem at many points in all books except the second. Other analogies that have been suggested—with the war between good and evil in *Paradise Lost* and with the theatre—have a more pervasive effect on language and meaning. As George Sherburn has shown,[1] it is likely that the free dramatic form of Book IV owes something to the farcical entertainments of Fielding. If we are considering design and effect rather than origins, we may learn more from Sherburn's apt suggestion that the diversity of episodes is analogous to the variety of movements in a suite by Purcell or Handel. But it is still well to remember that the obvious model for Pope's poem was the first 'epic' of dullness, *Mac Flecknoe*. The narrative of *Mac Flecknoe* like the *Dunciad* is vague and meagre, and in both poems epic situations arise suddenly to be used solely as occasions for satirical announcements and prophecies. Both also have grandly mocking descriptions of actors and scene quite out of proportion to anything that happens. But more important than such similarities is the 'prophetic mood' of the narrator and the ageing Flecknoe, the tone that Pope adopts so frequently in the *Dunciad*. The style that shapes the tone is like Dryden's a compound of Virgilian, Miltonic, and Biblical elements. Parody is common, and the irony is continually allusive. Even the atmosphere of murky mystery and fantasy has its beginnings in Dryden:

> Where their vast courts the mother-strumpets keep,
> And, undisturb'd by watch, in silence sleep.
> *(Mac Flecknoe, 72–73)*

> The sire then shook the honors of his head,
> And from his brows damps of oblivion shed . . .
> (134–5)

> Leave writing plays, and choose for thy command
> Some peaceful province in acrostic land.
> (205–6)

The lightness of fancy and rhythm in the last couplet are worthy of Pope.

---

[1] 'The *Dunciad*, Book IV', *Studies in English, University of Texas*, 1944, pp. 174–90.

But however much Pope owes to literature of the past, he owes more to his own past, to his growth through a long career. In the Fourth Book of the *Dunciad* Pope wears 'the ecstatic air' of a poet who has found full and harmonious expression of all his poetic selves. He unites now—to borrow his sacrilegious phrase—'three essential Popes in one'; the poet of picture and song, the heroic poet, and the Horatian 'philosopher'. The reader may well wonder at the last of these personae, since the prophetic voice of the last book and the mood of near-despair felt even in amusing scenes seem to leave little place for the relaxed urbane conversationalist of Twickenham or the Sabine Farm. The dropping of the intimate essay tone of his youthful mock-epic style marks the distance between the poet of the *Dunciad* and the Pope of polite small-talk. But in basic outlook and in satiric mode, *The New Dunciad* shows a clear relation with Pope's poetry in the Horatian manner, from the *Essay on Criticism* and the *Essay on Man* through the *Moral Essays* and the *Imitations*. The definition of the whole duty of man as self-knowledge, scepticism toward the philosophy of the schools, and amusement at every sort of pretence—all Horatian attitudes as well as Socratic—underlie the *Essay on Man*, parts of the *Essay on Criticism*, and most of the purely Horatian poems. The connexion between the last book of the *Dunciad* and the epistles belonging to Pope's *Opus Magnum* is obviously close. To the projected piece 'Of the Use of Education' belong some two hundred lines (139–336), a passage that includes a number of the best things in the poem—the portraits of the schoolmaster, of Bentley, and of the youth who has returned from the Grand Tour. While more fully dramatized than most of Horace's portraits, all are Horatian 'examples' in which the victim satirizes himself by his speech and antics. The sketches introducing these and other characters in the *Dunciad* are hardly distinguishable from similar sketches in the satires and *Moral Essays*. The easy freedom with which Pope shifts from type to type, setting off one figure against another, is Horatian too and typical of Pope's usual manner of proceeding in satire.

Most remarkable is the way in which Pope reshaped the Horatian mode to suit a new poetic occasion. The 'characters' of the *Dunciad* IV remind us of Quince's 'Lamentable Comedy': they are heroic-pastoral-pictorial-Horatian. We saw earlier that the youthful traveller through scenes of pastoral harmony and georgic fruitfulness had affinities with Aeneas and the wondrous child of the Fourth *Eclogue*. We should also add that his portrait includes an Ovidian metamorphosis, that its wittiest lines are close to Pope's Horatian style in urbanity of tone and compact poising of opposites, and that the whole character is an Horatian satirical exemplum. Aubrey Williams suggests that the young voyager is really Ulysses in the guise of Aeneas and cites Horace's epistle to young Lollius, *Troiani belli scriptorem* (I. ii), as the probable source of the metaphor. The Renaissance tradition of travel as education seems to have started with the Ulysses analogy, and Bacon's advice to the young Lord Rutland (1596) may remind us again of the noble aims with which the Grand Tour was first conceived. The purpose of travel abroad, says Bacon, is to

... see the beauty of many cities, know the manners of the people of many countries, and learn the language of many nations. Some of these may serve for ornaments, and all of them for delights: but your Lordship must look further than these; for the greatest ornament is the inward beauty of the mind, and when you have known as great variety of delight as the world will afford, you will confess that the greatest delight is *sentire te indies fieri meliorem*; to feel that you do every day become more worthy; therefore your Lordship's end and scope should be that which in moral philosophy we call *cultum animi*, the tilling and manuring of your own mind.[1]

Nothing could be more Horatian than the *cultum animi* described by Bacon as 'end and scope' for the young man's journey abroad. Pope's portrait in Book IV assumes the complete Baconian ideal, embracing both the outward 'ornaments' and 'inward beauty'. 'All Classic learning lost on Classic ground' is present by implication in the passage that so wonderfully describes the loss.

But Pope's greatness, his poetic feat, lies in the 'implying', in writing verse that looks like poetry of the surface and merely local interest, but which carries this richness of liter-

---

[1] *The Works of Francis Bacon*, ed. James Spedding, vol. ix, *The Letters and the Life*, ii. 7. Quoted in Parks, 'Travel as Education', p. 266.

ary allusion and depth of moral and intellectual criticism.
The result is amusement of the highest and most effortless
sort. Let me quote again the most Horatian lines of the portrait, which reach a climax in the miraculous change of
Narcissus and end with a sublime parody of Virgilian
prophecy:

> "Led by my hand, he saunter'd Europe round,
> And gather'd ev'ry Vice on Christian ground;
> Saw ev'ry Court, heard ev'ry King declare
> His royal Sense, of Op'ra's or the Fair;
> The Stews and Palace equally explor'd,
> Intrigu'd with glory, and with spirit whor'd;
> Try'd all *hors-d'oeuvres*, all *liqueurs* defin'd,
> Judicious drank, and greatly-daring din'd;
> Dropt the dull lumber of the Latin store,
> Spoil'd his own language, and acquir'd no more;
> All Classic learning lost on Classic ground;
> And last turn'd *Air*, the Echo of a Sound!
> See now, half-cur'd, and perfectly well-bred,
> With nothing but a Solo in his head;
> As much Estate, and Principle, and Wit,
> As Jansen, Fleetwood, Cibber shall think fit;
> Stol'n from a Duel, follow'd by a Nun,
> And, if a Borough chuse him, not undone;
> See, to my country happy I restore
> This glorious Youth, and add one Venus more.
> Her too receive (for her my soul adores)
> So may the sons of sons of sons of whores,
> Prop thine, O Empress! like each neighbour Throne,
> And make a long Posterity thy own."
>
> (311–34)

Of all the satirical characters in the last book, the portrait
of the Grand Tour Ulysses shows the finest balance between
Pope's various poetic selves and styles. In other portraits
some one style usually prevails, although the heroic note can
be heard in most. The student of statesmanship, after being
introduced with heroic pomp, is polished off in the Horatian
style of the satires: (One line is almost identical with a line in
the *Epistle to Dr. Arbuthnot*.)

> "First slave to Words, then vassal to a Name.
> Then dupe to Party; child and man the same;

Bounded by Nature, narrow'd still by Art,
A trifling head, and a contracted heart.
Thus bred, thus taught, how many have I seen,
Smiling on all, and smil'd on by a Queen."

                              (501–6)

The freethinkers are sketched in a similar style and rhythm
of sharply pointed contrasts:

"We nobly take the high Priori Road,
And reason downward, till we doubt of God:
Make Nature still incroach upon his plan;
And shove him off as far as e'er we can:
Thrust some Mechanic Cause into his place;
Or bind in Matter, or diffuse in Space.
Or, at one bound o'er-leaping all his laws,
Make God Man's Image, Man the final Cause,
Find Virtue local, all Relation scorn,
See all in *Self*, and but for self be born:
Of nought so certain as our *Reason* still,
Of nought so doubtful as of *Soul* and *Will*."

                              (471–82)

Two of the most annihilating portraits are done in Pope's
innocent pastoral manner, melodious and visually exquisite.
The Sarpedon and Glaucus of the virtuosi, they appear in
'the foremost' ranks with 'aspect ardent', moving in a scene
of the strange confusion typical of the *Dunciad*:

Then thick as Locusts black'ning all the ground,
A tribe, with weeds and shells fantastic crown'd,
Each with some wond'rous gift approach'd the Pow'r,
A Nest, a Toad, a Fungus, or a Flow'r.
But far the foremost, two, with earnest zeal,
And aspect ardent to the Throne appeal.
    The first thus open'd: "Hear thy suppliant's call,
Great Queen, and common Mother of us all!
Fair from its humble bed I rear'd this Flow'r,
Suckled, and chear'd, with air, and sun, and show'r,
Soft on the paper ruff its leaves I spread,
Bright with the gilded button tipt its head,
Then thron'd in glass, and nam'd it C A R O L I N E:
Each Maid cry'd, charming! and each Youth, divine!
Did Nature's pencil ever blend such rays,
Such vary'd light in one promiscuous blaze?

Now prostrate! dead! behold that Caroline:
No Maid cries, charming! no Youth, divine!
And lo the wretch! whose vile, whose insect lust
Lay'd this gay daughter of the Spring in dust.
Oh punish him, or to th' Elysian shades
Dismiss my soul, where no Carnation fades."
    He ceas'd, and wept. With innocence of mien,
Th' Accus'd stood forth, and thus address'd the Queen.
    "Of all th' enamel'd race, whose silv'ry wing
Waves to the tepid Zephyrs of the spring,
Or swims along the fluid atmosphere,
Once brightest shin'd this child of Heat and Air.
I saw, and started from its vernal bow'r
The rising game, and chac'd from flow'r to flow'r.
It fled, I follow'd; now in hope, now pain;
It stopt, I stopt; it mov'd, I mov'd again.[1]
At last it fix'd, 'twas on what plant it pleas'd,
And where it fix'd, the beauteous bird I seiz'd:
Rose or Carnation was below my care;
I meddle, Goddess! only in my sphere.
I tell the naked fact without disguise,
And, to excuse it, need but shew the prize;
Whose spoils this paper offers to your eye,
Fair ev'n in death! this peerless *Butterfly*."

(397–436)

In this picture of the last of the sylphs as in Pope's earliest
poems, the pictorial and the mythological are one. As the
butterfly-minded youth turns in Ovidian fashion into the
creature he pursues, the beauty of the imagery increases
rather than diminishes the symbolic and satirical effect. The
entomologist's pretty boast is a shrewd appraisal of frivolous
and blind specialists:

I meddle, Goddess! only in my sphere.

We have heard that voice before, in the laboratory and
the faculty room, in the government bureau, replying to the
commonsense man who stubbornly insists with Pope that the
hero as expert should see beyond his sphere. Because of such
larger resonances, the main symbolic figures of the *Dunciad*
are more than pet peeves of the poet or bits of décor in a

---

[1] There is a nice irony in the parody in this couplet of *Paradise Lost*, IV. 462–3,
especially since Book IV is the most pastoral book in Milton's epic.

period piece. The *Dunciad* has 'period' significance, surely enough, but also critical significance of a large historical sort. In the Queen of Dulness and her court and in the coming wonders described in the third and fourth books, Pope gave the mid-century a view of itself that neatly balances the serene vision of *Windsor Forest*. (The view is still illuminating and salutary for uncritical admirers of this 'delightful' period.) Pope sets before us in symbolic figure and speech almost everything that later critics have deplored in the eighteenth century. He shows us its dreadful *longueurs*, its boredom and frivolousness, both moral and intellectual. In the world of letters he sees the interminable sermon and the equally interminable epic, the deadly descriptive poem, the made-to-order occasional ode and the hyperbolical encomium, the vulgarity and stupidity of dramatic and operatic spectacles, the horror of critics 'forever reading, never to be read' and of editors darkening and hacking the classics, the nastiness and irresponsibility of Grub-street journalists and their shameless publishers. In the speech given to Bentley there is poignancy as well as comedy:

> "Ah, think not, Mistress! more true Dulness lies
> In Folly's Cap, than Wisdom's grave disguise.
> Like buoys, that never sink into the flood,
> On Learning's surface we but lie and nod.
> Thine is the genuine head of many a house,
> And much Divinity without a *Noûs*."
>
> (239–44)

Here and elsewhere, Pope catches exactly the decadent atmosphere of the universities, in one of which Gibbon was shortly to endure a brief period of 'education'. The schools, seen with Dickensian clarity, offer a spectacle of physical cruelty and deadly routine where masters 'ply the Memory' and 'load the brain'. The mechanical art of versifying as taught in the classroom was not criticized more effectively by Coleridge:

> "Whate'er the talents, or howe'er design'd,
> We hang one jingling padlock on the mind:
> A Poet the first day, he dips his quill;
> And what the last? a very Poet still."
>
> (161–4)

Among the amateurs, the sterility and narrowness of the elegant botanist and his fellow naturalists are matched in the quaint delights of the coin-collectors and the antiquarians.

The decadence of learning is equalled by the low state of public morality, which is finely displayed in the education of young statesmen, in the tragedy of Swift's wasted efforts to help Ireland, and in the vast success of Walpole's 'tyranny' with its kept press. Although Pope's religious position may seem too skilfully trimmed between enlightenment and orthodoxy, he sees very clearly the death of religion without mystery, and the confusion of a culture that makes dining a 'solemn sacrifice'. Put in the simplest terms, Pope sees a society without humility, sick and lost through 'dulness', suffering from an absurd confidence in self and 'wit' (reason without complete education).[1] He had made the point years before in the *Essay on Criticism*:

> Pride, where wit fails, steps in to our defence,
> And fills up all the mighty Void of sense.
> If once right reason drives that cloud away,
> Truth breaks upon us with resistless day.
>
> (209–12)

For Pope full exercise of intelligence is inseparable from moral discipline and wide learning, and hence to substitute for 'right reason' the frivolity of verbalism and of specialization is to lose the power of ordering the inner life, on which order in society depends. The *Dunciad* like the *Essay on Man* is a criticism of naïve trust in 'reason' (in the pejorative sense indicated) by the poet of reason in the larger and more humane sense.

We need hardly argue that Pope's vision was wholly adequate to his age or entirely just to particular groups and individuals in order to agree that it was and is of value. His criticism of the century, like that of Johnson and Burke, and later of Wordsworth and Coleridge, was among the criticisms necessary to be made. It is translatable into terms that have present meaning and application, at least for readers who feel the living continuity between our civilization and the Graeco-Roman. For Pope's moral evaluation is inseparable

---

[1] Cf. Ch. VII. ii, pp. 235–7.

from his historical sense of an inherited culture traceable to
Greece and Rome. But he was a poet, not an historian, and
being a poet the past lived for him in expressions, in the language and the design of poems by Homer, Virgil, Ovid, and
Horace, and by later writers who had renewed their poetry in
French and English. The English poets who live again most
certainly in Pope's verse are Dryden, Milton, and Spenser.
(For both Homer and Virgil, we must often read Dryden
and Milton.) Donne and other poets in the Metaphysical
line, Marvell, Crashaw, Cowley, have left their mark on
Pope's poetry, too, but the tradition of Donne was scarcely
separable in Pope's mind from the central Renaissance and
Classical tradition. Indications of this view can be found in
his imitations of Donne, which are barely distinguishable in
style from his Horatian imitations, and in the ease with
which he combines Metaphysical wit with neo-classical wit
and the heroic eloquence of Dryden and Milton. It is also
plain from Pope's early imitations and from quotations and
remarks in his letters that Chaucer was a congenial author
for him as for Dryden. He shares Spenser's and Dryden's
taste for both Chaucer and Ovid. While the direct effect[1] of
French poetry on Pope's verse can be exaggerated, his indebtedness to Boileau in the *Essay on Criticism* and the *Imitations* is obvious enough, and there are traces of his admiration for Voiture, Racine, and Corneille.

Pope is thus perhaps the last major English poet to feel at
home with the whole European and English tradition in
poetry. The lines of the Romantic division had not been
drawn decisively, and Homer and Spenser had not become
definitely members of one camp, with Virgil, Milton, and
Dryden in another. (There are hints of the later division in
Pope's Preface to the *Iliad*.) We are familiar with Keats's
attempt to recover this relationship in spite of accepting the
common prejudice against Pope, and in our own century we
have seen Eliot and Yeats aspiring to reach a more catholic
attitude toward the poetry of the past. Though feeling
obliged to reject Milton and Shelley, Eliot found a fruitful
relation as critic and poet with Donne and with Dryden,

---

[1] See the exhaustive study of E. Audra, *L'Influence française dans l'œuvre de
Pope* (Paris, 1931), especially pp. 315–82; 139, 140, 144, 145.

and Yeats, although so close to the Romantics and their
successors, re-established in his later poetry a connexion with
the poets of the eighteenth century and the Metaphysicals:

> And I may dine at journey's end
> With Landor and with Donne.

We have a forecast of Pope's allegiances in poetry, especially to the Greek and Roman poets who were the 'heroes' of
Renaissance poetry and criticism, in one of his most interesting early works, *The Temple of Fame*. In style and attitude the
poem is prophetic of the lines along which Pope will develop,
and it anticipates in a curious fashion 'The Temple of In-
famy' with which his career closed. Pope's more obvious
literary heroes in the poem are Chaucer, whom he is imitating, and the ancient poets whom he honours in his temple.
Equally significant are the writers not named, whose effect
appears indirectly through allusion and through the manner
in which Pope refashions his original.

Homer naturally comes first in the pantheon, and the
qualities in his poetry that Pope admires, and which he expresses with eloquence, are the ones stressed in the Preface
to the *Iliad*:

> Tho' blind, a Boldness in his Looks appears,
> In Years he seem'd, but not impair'd by Years.
> The Wars of *Troy* were round the Pillar seen:
> Here fierce *Tydides* wounds the *Cyprian* Queen;
> Here *Hector* glorious from *Patroclus*' Fall,
> Here dragg'd in Triumph round the *Trojan* Wall.
> Motion and Life did ev'ry Part inspire,
> Bold was the Work, and prov'd the Master's Fire;
> A strong Expression most he seem'd t'affect.
> And here and there disclos'd a brave Neglect.
>
> (186–95)

The terms of the praise tell us a good deal about the qualities
that Pope tried to reproduce in translation and something
about the literary ideal represented to him by Homer. The
'Fire' which Pope admires in Homer is inventive power, the
remarkable talent for presenting action so that the reader not
only sees it, but feels himself engaged in it. 'Fire' is also
'prov'd' as Douglas Knight has noted, by the ability to

infuse life and order into the whole work. The familiar analogies with Nature and with the art of the painter are again
assumed, as in the *Essay on Criticism*:

> In some fair body thus th' informing soul
> With spirits feeds, with vigour fills the whole . . .
>
> (76–77)

In both the portrait and the *Essay* order is balanced by
strength and freedom, by 'a brave Neglect'. The character of
Homer in the *Temple of Fame* sums up, perhaps in the year in
which the *Essay on Criticism* was published, the critical theory
and the humane attitude that underlie the *Essay*.

But the twentieth-century reader may feel that he learns
more from these lines about Pope and current views of
Homer than about Homeric poetry. Pope's portrait of Virgil
brings us into much closer contact with the poetic texture
of the *Aeneid*, and we are not surprised that Virgil has left
more of a mark than Homer on Pope's heroic style:

> Finish'd the whole, and labour'd ev'ry Part,
> With patient Touches of unweary'd Art:
> The *Mantuan* there in sober Triumph sate,
> Compos'd his Posture, and his Look sedate:
> On *Homer* still he fix'd a reverend Eye,
> Great without Pride, in modest Majesty.
> In living Sculpture on the Sides were spread
> The *Latian* Wars, and haughty *Turnus* dead;
> *Eliza* stretch'd upon the fun'ral Pyre,
> *Æneas* bending with his aged Sire:
> *Troy* flam'd in burning Gold, and o'er the Throne
> *Arms and the Man* in Golden Cyphers shone.
>
> (198–209)

By contrast, the impression of Pindar, 'like some furious
Prophet', is a pure period piece, mainly a sign that Pope was
familiar with fashionable notions of 'Pindarick' frenzy. The
'Happy Horace' of the *Odes* is charmingly described in lines
showing by precise allusions how well Pope knew Horace's
lyric verse.

We can appreciate better what these poets will mean to
Pope from the setting and manner of his praise. The heroes
of literature appear in the elaborate description of '*Fame's*
high Temple' where Pope again displays his remarkable gift

for communicating the most active experience of works of art. In Pope's poetry life is often rendered as art, but here literature is rendered through art that comes alive in description:

> Heroes in animated Marble frown . . .
>
> (73)

Even without Pope's reference to the Farnese Hercules and without external evidence such as his acquaintance with Jervas' collection of casts and engravings, we should see well enough that Pope was trying to make us feel the drama and movement of late Greek sculpture. The lines on Pindar, though not adequate as literary criticism, set us surely in the presence of Hellenistic statues and reliefs:

> The figur'd Games of *Greece* the Column grace,
> *Neptune* and *Jove* survey the rapid Race:
> The Youths hang o'er their Chariots as they run;
> The fiery Steeds seem starting from the Stone;
> The Champions in distorted Postures threat,
> And all appear'd Irregularly great.
>
> (216–21)

Pope's taste is decidedly baroque, and in one unhappy couplet he seems to be imitating Bernini's attempts to get beyond the limits of the sculptor's medium:

> A-cross the Harp a careless Hand he flings
> And boldly sinks into the sounding Strings.
>
> (214–15)

The art of sinking in poetry was never more aptly illustrated —a fine specimen for Pope's treatise.

In *The Temple of Fame* Pope was being seriously descriptive in part simply because he was doing an 'Imitation' of Chaucer. For the *House of Fame* must have seemed to Pope and his contemporaries a most 'descriptive' poem. Pope had another Chaucerian model in the temple scenes of *The Knight's Tale*, which are very similar to Pope's 'living Sculptures', since Chaucer too is describing works of art as both 'artificial' and alive. But in writing the *House of Fame* Chaucer does not seem to have been much interested in this kind of effect. He is satisfied with labelling a statue or a pillar as 'yren' or 'copper', and as always in his poetry description is subordinated to story and allegory. But' in *The Temple of Fame*, as Tillotson says, 'For Chaucer's cinematographic speed and lightness there is Pope's Handelian tempo and harmony, for Chaucer's narrative, Pope's scene.'[1] 'Scene-painting' is common almost everywhere except in the closing section. The visionary landscape at the beginning of the poem shows the great difference between Pope's and Chaucer's manner of describing. Chaucer lists items in a hit-and-miss fashion without giving us any impression of how they look, while Pope composes pictures and creates visual effects that remind us of familiar types of Claudian landscape:

> In Air self-ballanc'd hung the Globe below,
> Where Mountains rise, and circling Oceans flow;
> Here naked Rocks, and empty Wastes were seen,
> There Tow'ry Cities, and the Forests green:
> Here sailing Ships delight the wand'ring Eyes;
> There Trees, and intermingl'd Temples rise:
> Now a clear Sun the shining Scene displays,
> The transient Landscape now in Clouds decays.
>
> (13–20)

The descriptive style, as we have seen earlier, was for Pope 'pompous' and richly allusive, and the descriptive and the heroic were often scarcely distinguishable in his poetry.[2] The Claudian 'prospect' opens with an allusion to *Paradise Lost*:

> In Air self-ballanc'd hung the Globe below . . .

'Tow'ry' ('There Tow'ry Cities') had appeared in the salute to the New Jerusalem in the most Miltonic of Pope's early poems, the *Messiah*. 'Shining' ('the shining Scene') appears in heroic contexts of the *Rape of the Lock* and the *Iliad*, and in heroic and descriptive passages of *Windsor Forest*. Pope's description includes also an echo of Ovid and of Dryden's translation of the *Metamorphoses* and an allusion to the *Aeneid* in Dryden's version. A glance through the notes to the *Temple of Fame* will show how often references to these same writers and works occur, a fair indication that Pope was forming his allusive heroic manner as early as 1710 or 1711.

More surely prophetic of Pope's maturity is the central

conception of Fame and the gradual opening up of the implicit irony through the drama and style of the poem. Pope's Fame, while admittedly less capricious than Chaucer's, is related to the *Fama* of Virgil, who is at once Rumour and noble Fame or *Gloria*. Both aspects of the conception are illustrated in the fourth book of the *Aeneid*, the first in the famous personification, *magnas it Fama per urbes*; the second, in Dido's tragic lament for her lost reputation, *qua sola sidera adibam/fama prior*. The ambiguous character of Pope's goddess becomes clear enough when like Chaucer's goddess she gives glory with malicious kindness to the 'modest' good who do not want it (366–77), or when, after granting it to the band of 'the Good and Just' (318), she denies it to another similar group:

> This Band dismiss'd, behold another Crowd
> Prefer'd the same Request, and lowly bow'd,
> The constant Tenour of whose well-spent Days
> No less deserv'd a just Return of Praise.
> But strait the direful Trump of Slander sounds,
> Thro' the big Dome the doubling Thunder bounds:
> Loud as the Burst of Cannon rends the Skies,
> The dire Report thro' ev'ry Region flies:
> In ev'ry Ear incessant Rumours rung,
> And gath'ring Scandals grew on ev'ry Tongue.
> From the black Trumpet's rusty Concave broke
> Sulphureous Flames, and Clouds of rolling Smoke:
> The pois'nous Vapor blots the purple Skies,
> And withers all before it as it flies.
>
> (328–41)

It is not surprising that 'the black Trumpet' of Fame becomes in the *Epilogue to the Satires* the 'black Trumpet' of Glory-Vice celebrating the triumph of corruption. But the irony of Fame's blessings can be felt long before it comes out in any open gestures. The descriptive and epic grandeur of the first view of the temple suggests the capriciousness and deceptiveness of the goddess:

> O'er the wide Prospect as I gaz'd around,
> Sudden I heard a wild promiscuous Sound,
> Like broken Thunders that at distance roar,
> Or Billows murm'ring on the hollow Shoar:

Then gazing up, a glorious Pile beheld,
Whose tow'ring Summit ambient Clouds conceal'd.
                                        (21–26)

'A wild promiscuous Sound' by itself gives a sufficient hint of
what is to come, and the connotations of the parallel passage
in Ovid, with its stress on credulity, suspicion, and rumour,
add to our awareness that the splendours of the scene are not
altogether substantial. We are far from the Homeric world
where glory, *kleos*, was the sure reward for heroic action and
death. Before Pope's Fame assigns her prizes, we are specifically warned of her fickleness (294–5), and her praise often
sounds double-edged because of the rhetorical exaggeration
with which she speaks. There are varying degrees of irony in
her speeches, from the sweetness of her words of unwanted
kindness to the open sarcasm of her address to 'ambitious
Fools' who pursued fame by military conquest.

In the lines characterizing Fame's suppliants and in their
speeches asking for her favour, we hear more and more the
accents of Pope's mature satirical mode. The address of the
military heroes has the declamatory grandeur of many later
ironic portraits,

> For thee (they cry'd) amidst Alarms and Strife,
> We sail'd in Tempests down the Stream of Life;
> For thee whole Nations fill'd with Flames and Blood,
> And swam to Empire thro' the purple Flood.
>
>   (344–7)

In the chatter of the young men about town, we hear the
malicious gossiping tone of the *Rape of the Lock* and of the
Epistle to a Lady:

> Of unknown Dutchesses leud Tales we tell,
> Yet would the World believe us, all were well.
> The Joy let others have, and we the Name,
> And what we want in Pleasure, grant in Fame.
>   The Queen assents, the Trumpet rends the Skies,
> And at each Blast a Lady's Honour dies.   (388–93)

The portrait of the politician-statesmen is a shrewd and witty
definition of character of a type common in the *Moral Essays*
and *Satires*:

> Calm, thinking Villains, whom no Faith cou'd fix,
> Of crooked Counsels and dark Politicks;

Of these a gloomy Tribe surround the Throne,
And beg to make th' immortal Treasons known.

(410–13)

There can really be little surprise that the scene shifts to the palace of Rumour or that it is described in a style anticipating Pope's satirical 'refrains':[1]

There various News I heard, of Love and Strife,
Of Peace and War, Health, Sickness, Death, and Life;
Of Loss and Gain, of Famine and of Store,
Of Storms at Sea, and Travels on the Shore,
Of Prodigies, and Portents seen in Air,
Of Fires and Plagues, and Stars with blazing Hair,
Of Turns of Fortune, Changes in the State,
The Falls of Fav'rites, Projects of the Great,
Of old Mismanagements, Taxations new—
All neither wholly false, nor wholly true.

(448–57)

So we are not altogether unprepared when we hear the Horatian poet speak out much as he does in the *Imitations* and the *Epilogue to the Satires*, protesting a little self-consciously that his muse is independent, that the quiet life with virtue is preferable to fame at the price of flattery:

How vain that second Life in others' Breath.
Th' Estate which Wits inherit after Death!
Ease, Health, and Life, for this they must resign,
(Unsure the Tenure, but how vast the Fine!)
The Great Man's Curse without the Gains endure,
Be envy'd, wretched, and be flatter'd, poor;
All luckless Wits their Enemies profest,
And all successful, jealous Friends at best.
Nor Fame I slight, nor for her Favours call;
She comes unlook'd for, if she comes at all:
But if the Purchase costs so dear a Price,
As soothing Folly, or exalting Vice:
Oh! if the Muse must flatter lawless Sway,
And follow still where Fortune leads the way;
Or if no Basis bear my rising Name,
But the fall'n Ruins of Another's Fame:

---

[1] Pope is of course following the Chaucerian text in this ironic iteration. It may be that his later use of this type of satirical attack owes something to Chaucer's example.

Then teach me, Heaven! to scorn the guilty Bays;
Drive from my Breast that wretched Lust of Praise;
Unblemish'd let me live, or die unknown,
Oh grant an honest Fame, or grant me none!

(505–24)

If we recognize the Horatian satirist in this epilogue and in the ironic portraits of Fame's suppliants, we can see quite clearly the poet of the *Dunciad* in the ambiguous epic-descriptive scenes, in the speeches and actions of the majestic but frivolous goddess, and in the 'promiscuous' throngs that hover about her. The heroic and the satirical qualities of the poem and of Pope's genius are firmly united by a central consciousness that embraces a youthful Miltonic love of fame, reverence for the heroes of the Greco-Roman literary tradition, and a growing awareness of the illusions and temptations of literary success. *The Temple of Fame*—we may say without too much exaggeration—is Pope's *Lycidas*, the *Lycidas* of a future Horace. The poetic child is father of the mature poet, and the integrity, not to say identity of character, is striking. Pope's sense of his true poetic role, first surely revealed in the *Rape of the Lock* and the 'Atticus' portrait, is all but evident in the conception and style of the *Temple of Fame*. Language and style point clearly if indirectly to what Pope will do later and how he will do it. He lets us see the folly of fame and worldly ambition, just as he will later show up the follies of literature and of public and private life, by using a style that keeps alluding to values expressed and enshrined in poetry of the Greco-Roman tradition. For Pope at the start of his career, as at the end, the imitation of life is also the imitation of literature.

INDEX

PRINTED IN GREAT BRITAIN
AT THE UNIVERSITY PRESS, OXFORD
BY VIVIAN RIDLER
PRINTER TO THE UNIVERSITY